THE BEGINNINGS OF A COMMERCIAL
SPORTING CULTURE IN BRITAIN, 1793–1850

For my family

The Beginnings of a Commercial Sporting Culture in Britain, 1793–1850

ADRIAN HARVEY

ASHGATE

Published by
Ashgate Publishing Limited
Gower House
Croft Road
Aldershot
Hants GU11 3HR
England

Ashgate Publishing Company
Suite 420
101 Cherry Street
Burlington, VT 05401-4405
USA

Ashgate website: http://www.ashgate.com

British Library Cataloguing in Publication Data
Harvey, Adrian
   The beginnings of a commercial sporting culture in Britain,
   1793–1850
   1. Sports – Great Britain – History – 18th century 2. Sports
   – Great Britain – History – 19th century 3. Sports – Social
   aspects – Great Britain
   I. Title
   306.4'83'0941'09033

Library of Congress Cataloging-in-Publication Data
Harvey, Adrian.
   The beginnings of a commercial sporting culture in Britain, 1793–1850 / Adrian Harvey.
     p. cm.
   Includes bibliographical references and index.
   ISBN 0-7546-3643-7 (alk. paper)
    1. Sports–Great Britain–History–18th century. 2. Sports–Great Britain–History–19th century. I. Title.

   GV605.H39 2003
   796'.0941'09034–dc21

2003043679

ISBN 0 7546 3643 7

Typeset in Times New Roman by IML Typographers, Birkenhead, Merseyside
Printed in Great Britain by MPG Books Ltd, Bodmin, Cornwall

Contents

List of Figures and Tables   *vii*

Acknowledgements   *ix*

List of Abbreviations   *xi*

1   Prologue   1

2   Genesis: A National Sporting Culture is Born   7

3   Sex, Sport and Sales: The Sporting Press   31

4   No Time for Idleness? The Law and Sport, 1793–1815   63

5   You Can All Join In: The Law and Sport, 1816–50   83

6   How Many Rats Can You Eat in a Minute? The Rules of Sport   115

7   Big Crowds, Big Money: Mass Entertainment Comes to Britain   151

8   Better Than Working for a Living: Professional Sportsmen … and
    Women   189

Epilogue   *225*

Appendix: Sources   *227*

Bibliography   *231*

Index   *253*

List of Figures and Tables

Figures

2.1 Sporting events and expenditure, 1793–1815   12
2.2 Sporting events and expenditure in Manchester, 1816–50   21
2.3 Sporting events and expenditure in Oxfordshire, 1816–50   22

Tables

2.1 The amount of events and stakes, 1793–1815 (1821/5 prices, guineas)   11
2.2 Sporting events during the French Wars   11
2.3 Sporting expenditure during the French Wars (1821/5 prices, guineas)   12
2.4 Composition of regions   14
2.5 Distribution of sports throughout the regions, 1793–1815   14
2.6 The amount of sporting activity per region, 1793–1815   15
2.7 The existence of a playing season for four sports   16
2.8 The favourite days for sporting events   16
2.9 Annual and weekly sport in each region, 1793–1815   18
2.10 Chronologies for various sports, from *Bell's Life in London*   19
2.11 A comparison between two periods of the average number of events for five sports   20
2.12 Events and expenditure in Manchester, 1816–50 (1821/5 prices)   21
2.13 Events and expenditure in Oxfordshire, 1816–50 (1821/5 prices)   22
2.14 The number of horse-race meetings per year, 1816–50   23
2.15 Total prize money for four years of horse-race meetings (1821/5 prices, guineas)   23
2.16 The distribution of sporting activity in Manchester and Oxfordshire, 1793–1850   24
2.17 The variety and volume of sporting activity in Lancashire/Manchester and Oxfordshire, 1793–1850   25
2.18 A comparison of the amounts of annual and weekly sporting activity for 1793–1815 and 1816–50, in Oxfordshire and Lancashire   26
7.1 Largest stakes on single sporting events, 1816–50   164
7.2 Receipts from sporting events   170
7.3 Crowds exceeding 1,000, 1840–50   175

7.4 Largest crowd and cheapest admission charge for several sports, 1816–50   176
8.1 Distribution of occupations among seven key sports, 1793–1815   193
8.2 Most popular occupations for sportsmen, 1793–1815   193
8.3 Career length for four sports in Manchester, 1816–50   213

Acknowledgements

The person to whom I am most indebted in relation to this work is Professor Roy Foster, then of Birkbeck College, London University, who encouraged me to undertake a full-time Ph.D. I owe Roy and my two other teachers at Birkbeck, Professors Andrew Sanders and Michael Slater, an immense amount and I would like to record my gratitude to them. I undertook my D.Phil. at Nuffield College, Oxford University and owe many people at this institution a debt of thanks. Among them are Glynis Baleham, John Darwin, Gary Magee and Mary Rusher. Naturally, my most substantial debt is to my chief academic advisers, John Stevenson, John Goldthorpe and Brian Harrison. I owe many people thanks for the information that they have provided and would like to record my gratitude to: Caroline Buttle, Selina Chen, Chris Clifford, Anna Gambles, Elaine Herman, Dr J. Horder, Dr J. Innes, Dr N. Johnson, Richard Layte, Tim Leunig, R. Logan, Professor P. O'Brien, Joan Senior, Andy Thompson and Professor E.A. Wrigley. Additionally, I would like to record my thanks to my examiners, Professor Charles Feinstein and Professor Wray Vamplew. With regard to the publication of my D.Phil., I would like to thank the copy-editor Jill Birch and Carolyn Court, Heidi May and Kristen Thorner of Ashgate for fielding all the questions with which I bombarded them by e-mail and the staff at three libraries, Grahame Park, Kingsbury and Mollison Way, for the help they rendered me in using that particular piece of technology. While I am grateful to the staff of various libraries for the provision of books I would like to offer my particular thanks to Grant Miles of the British Newspaper Library for obtaining an excellent photocopy of the cartoon from an 1835 edition of *Bell's Life in London*.

The efforts of all these people would have counted for nothing were it not for the intervention of the staff at the Dryden Ward of Northwick Park Hospital. In March of 2002 I was admitted there and soon diagnosed as suffering from multiple sclerosis. At the time I was unable to walk and was largely oblivious to what was going on around me. Within a little over two weeks I was discharged, having substantially recovered, a result that both delighted and surprised my doctors. I have no doubt at all that this near miracle was due in no small measure to the kindness and consideration of the staff in Dryden Ward and tender my thanks accordingly. The other great component in my recovery was my family, who behaved magnificently. I am very lucky to come from such a background. Collectively, I owe both my family and the medical profession an immense amount and while I still have some problems am very grateful for being as well as I am.

Adrian Harvey
Spring 2003

List of Abbreviations

Annals	*Annals of the Sporting and Fancy Gazette*
Bell's	*Bell's Life in London*
BL. Add. Mss	British Library Additional Manuscripts
Britannica	*Encyclopaedia Britannica*
BWD	*Bell's Weekly Dispatch*
BWM	*Bell's Weekly Messenger*
CSH	*Cambridge Social History of Britain 1750–1950*
EcHR	*Economic History Review*
ER	*Edinburgh Review*
FCR	Sheffield Football Club Records
Gaming	*Select Committee on Gaming*
HO	Home Office
IJHS	*International Journal of the History of Sport*
ILN	*Illustrated London News*
Jackson's	*Jackson's Oxford Journal*
JCMB	*Jockey Club Minutes Book*
JJC	*John Johnson Collection*
JSH	*Journal of Social History*
LCRO	Lancashire County Record Office
LPL	Lancaster Public Library
M&S	*Manchester and Salford Advertiser*
M.Ex	*Manchester Examiner and Times*
MH	*Manchester Herald*
MM	*Manchester Mercury*
MRL	Manchester Reference Library
Newspapers	*Select Committee on Newspapers*
NSM	*New Sporting Magazine*
OCRO	Oxfordshire County Record Office
PP	*Parliamentary Papers*
PRO	Public Record Office
SM	*Sporting Magazine*
VCH	*Victoria County History*
WD	*Weekly Dispatch*
WMC	*Wheeler's Manchester Chronicle*
WR	*Westminster Review*

The indices used to transform financial information into 1821/5 prices were those calculated by A.D. Gayer, W.W. Rostow and A.J. Schwartz, *The Growth and Fluctuations of the British Economy 1790–1850*, Oxford: Oxford University Press, 1953, as found in B.R. Mitchell, *British Economic Statistics*, Cambridge: Cambridge University Press, 1988, p. 721.

Estimates of the population in various regions of Britain during the French wars were produced in 1801 and 1811. Assessments of the income tax paid by various regions stemmed from averaging the government records for 1801, 1803, 1805, 1806, 1808, 1810 and 1812.

Chapter 1

Prologue

SPORT. diversions; game; frolick and tumultuous merriment.

Such was Doctor Johnson's definition of sport in his dictionary of 1755. The focus of this study is much narrower, concentrating on organized competitive sport, though many of its promoters would have been pleased at arousing 'frolick and tumultuous merriment' among their audience, for such qualities would have generated profit, and provided a momentum for them to mount similar spectacles, until eventually they became a regular fixture in the entertainment calendar. It is the contention of this book that between 1793 and 1850 a substantial, essentially homogeneous, commercial sporting culture grew up in Britain, servicing a mass-public. The interests of this audience were stimulated by a sporting press that disseminated information nationally. Throughout the period sporting events were based upon particular skills and regulated by strict rules. Sport, itself, was a highly sophisticated business, employing professional players and utilizing specially created stadia. However, in the decades following 1850 the growth of this culture was to be impeded by factors which, as we shall see, had begun to manifest themselves in the years accommodated by the time-frame of this study.

The chronology of the book is divided into two parts, 1793 to 1815 and 1816 to 1850. Given the scale and the nature of the conflict with France it seemed sensible to distinguish the years between 1793 and 1815 from those that followed. Additionally, it can be argued that the war limited foreign contact and created special, particular conditions for domestic leisure. While, inevitably, alternative periodizations were possible – particular issues within the study inviting alternative chronologies – such divisions were often far from clear. For example, a study of the sporting press could advance a plausible case for dividing the period at 1816 (when substantial newspaper coverage first appeared), 1831 (the emergence of a less tolerant view of the activities that constituted sport), or 1840 (the introduction of the penny post). Such arguments could be replicated for every chapter within the study. Certainly, by 1815 Britain had become far more culturally homogeneous, a newspaper editorial noting that:

the rapid intercourse that exists between every part of Great Britain and the capital must have struck every person who has travelled through the country. We meet with no marked distinctions in the dress or manners of the different provinces. The fashions in the most remote parts of the country are quite the same as London. The rapid intercourse began during the Seven Years War, when Britain first became a great commercial country, and has been increasing ever since.[1]

The later period, the years from 1816 to 1850, witnessed a substantial change in the economic and social structure, especially by comparison with the French wars, due to increased urban and industrial development. It is hoped to highlight the stages of the evolution of British sporting culture by comparing these two eras.

The established view of sporting activity during this period owes a great deal to assumptions derived from the pioneering work of Malcolmson. His thesis was that in pre-industrial England there was an extensive recreational culture organized round the many traditional holidays and conducted on abundant open space. Events were actively patronized by the local gentry and other groups, notably publicans and the church. However, with the onset of the market economy, and particularly of industrialization, and the imposition of longer, more disciplined, working hours in both factory and farm, this culture was undermined. The rapid spread of enclosures and the expansion of urban areas deprived the population of space in which to play. Additionally, mercantile groups used legislation to limit popular recreational practices which they perceived as being disruptive to commerce. The gentry, under pressure from a new 'polite' culture that was strongly influenced by the prevailing evangelical tone, ceased to sponsor recreation. Lacking this help and protection, the former agricultural workers, many of whom were marooned in squalid urban areas by the 1830s and 1840s, found themselves largely deprived of their old culture and effectively in a recreational 'vacuum', dependent upon alcohol for relaxation.[2] The destruction of the traditional sports by industrial society was accompanied by the appearance of an alliance of various middle-class groups and 'respectable' elements of the working class, who actively sought to foster 'civilized' behaviour among the urban population by providing an alternative culture of 'rational recreation'. This was opposed by many in the upper class, who defended the 'old morality', typified by various 'cruel sports'. While the reformers did manage to curb many of these, they had little in the way of recreation to replace them with. However, 'the problem of leisure in an industrial society was solved through codifying sporting rules, which saved both time and space: and through catering for spectator sports, which facilitated vicarious athleticism'.[3] In essence, a large-scale recreational industry, based upon the newly codified sports that had been created in the public schools, was used to entertain the general population.[4] The effect of all this – the imposition of factory discipline on work and play, the development of cheap consumer goods and the monitoring of an active bureaucratic state – was to 'tame' society.[5]

The most recent, comprehensive, study of the sporting activity of the period, by Holt, amends the picture somewhat:

> There was no leisure vacuum in early Victorian Britain. Rather there had been a subtle unravelling of what had once been a more integrated pattern of recreation. First, the

withdrawal of the gentry and later their large tenants from rural life coincided with growing interference from an increasingly powerful middle-class. Second, the combined forces of civilized distaste gradually had an effect on the working-class elite whilst the actual times and spaces for the old sports in town and country were ever more restricted. By no means all the old sports were abandoned, but they were more or less confined to the margins of community life or the remoter parts of the nation ... The enthusiasm of the common people for the old sports was weakened to such an extent that there was a genuine receptiveness on the part of the mass of the population to the revised forms of play nurtured amongst the privileged in the mid-Victorian public schools.[6]

This thesis also accords with the theories advanced by sociologists such as Elias and his followers, who maintain that 'the control of violence in sport was part of a civilizing process', emanating from the public schools, which rationalized popular recreations. The principal example of this is football, a game that was transformed from a wild 'free for all' into a skilful modern sport.[7]

While scholars are agreed that 'the characteristic recreations of the second half of the nineteenth century were radically different from their predecessors', and that 'from the perspective of 1880, 1780 seemed a totally different and distant world', the factors which they identify as causing this are often vague and possess limited explanatory value.[8] Generally, they can be divided into two kinds. The first are a series of social forces, such as economic and social changes, government legislation, reduction in working hours and such like, the convergence of which produces the opportunity for change, often by undermining the 'old sports'. The second crucial group are far less abstract. They are social groups who create and promote sophisticated, codified sport, and are variously referred to by historians as 'reformers', 'opinion formers' and 'missionaries'. Yet, though they may appear more concrete, they are still elusive. Even Bailey, who claimed that the new sports were created by 'middle-class activists who sought to shape working-class choice by providing an alternative world of reformed recreations', based upon 'a play discipline to complement the work discipline', was forced to dilute the role of these middle-class reformers and concede that 'the popular expansion of the new sports' owed a great deal to working men.[9] Cunningham has gone still further, believing that there is little evidence that middle-class missionaries were either particularly active or significant in promoting the new games codes among the masses.[10] Golby and Purdue emphasize the continuity of the culture, particularly 'the fact that sports of one sort or another, especially horse-racing, pedestrianism and cricket, had throughout the century a popular following and played an important part in the leisure activities of many men'.[11] Yet, while acknowledging the role of popular culture, Golby and Purdue have failed to provide a convincing analysis of the size, scope and structure of the sporting world which they have identified. Thus, this culture remained as shadowy and abstract as the middle-class reformers, and it is therefore difficult to envisage how such an attenuated culture could produce the modern sporting world that appeared in the 1880s. Presumably recognizing this, scholars attributed the major emphasis in the creation of the modern sporting culture to external forces, principally those stemming from an expanding economy.[12] Essentially, although historians acknowledge developments within popular culture, such as an increasing provision of sporting facilities by entrepreneurs, the crucial elements are regarded as stemming from the agents of innovation.[13]

Research has failed to delineate clearly how the new sporting world came into being in the second half of the nineteenth century.[14] In essence, all we have are a range of hypotheses, lacking supporting evidence, a strange anomaly given the copious information available for the period. The theories do, however, suffer from a still more serious problem. Essentially, they contend that the creation of the modern sporting world was the product of the intervention of dramatic new forces. Yet the evidence does not accord with this. By the 1880s there was a substantial culture catering for mass-commercial sport, consisting of large stadia, professional players and organized tournaments. The extent of this culture indicates that the skills upon which it was based were well established. Likewise, the dominance of the socially elite over the new sports, in terms of both administration and codification, was short lived. For example, the laws created by the Football Association in 1863 were subject to substantial changes by 1870, many of which stemmed from the initiatives of those without public school backgrounds. In fact, it was the intervention of these same forces which allowed the Football Association (FA), a body that was almost extinct by 1867, to survive and prosper.[15] Similarly, in 1885 the FA was forced to allow football to become still more of a business by permitting professionalism, despite great opposition from many of the game's elite administrators. Analogous processes occurred in athletics and rowing, for example, where social and economic restrictions were dramatically undermined.[16] Cumulatively, they suggest that an experienced commercial and administrative sector, and a set of lower-class participants, long expert in a variety of skilful activities, were seizing control of sport. This surely suggests a culture that was already well established, rather than of recent emergence.

This book aims at revealing the extent of the size and sophistication of commercial sport in Britain between 1793 and 1850. Such an exposition should assist our understanding of the rapid expansion enjoyed by organized sport in the period after 1860. Previous scholars, as we have shown, have been largely unable to account for the dramatic growth that organized sport enjoyed and the rapid changes that occurred in both its structure and organization in the last quarter of the nineteenth century. By contrast, this book, by comparing two periods – the French wars (1793–1815) and the succeeding era (1816–50) – endeavours to identify the evolution of a modern British sporting culture. Such a study suggests two elements that have a considerable potential for explaining the changes occurring after 1860. These are: first, the existence of a sophisticated sporting culture employing professional players and catering for a mass commercial audience. Second, a large number of sports that were governed by strict rules which gave a primacy to skill, involving individuals possessing a wide range of expertise. From this it is contended that by 1850 the bulk of the ingredients required for the emergence of the nationally organized sporting culture that appeared in the 1880s was present. In fact, the major discontinuity was the brief interlude of dominance by an 'amateur' elite during the 1860s and 1870s, a period which impeded the evolution of the commercial sporting culture.

Notes

1   *BWM*, 26 Nov 1815.
2   R. Malcolmson (1973) *Popular Recreations in English Society 1700–1850*, Cambridge: Cambridge University Press, pp. 57, 59, 67, 73–4, 84–5, 88, 100–101, 107, 113, 168.
3   B. Harrison (1971) *Drink and the Victorians*, London: Faber and Faber, p. 331.
4   P. Bailey (1978) *Leisure and Class in Victorian England*, London: Routledge, pp. 14, 27, 40, 169, 175, 181. D. Brailsford (1991) *Sport, Time and Society: The British at Play,* London: Routledge, pp. 44, 77. H. Cunningham (1980) *Leisure in the Industrial Revolution 1780–1880,* London: Croom Helm, p. 91. Harrison, *Drink*, p. 331. Malcolmson, *Popular Recreations*, pp. 89, 170–71. J. Walvin (1976) *Leisure and Society 1830–1950*, London: Longmans, p. 10.
5   Bailey, *Leisure and Class*, p. 174. J. Golby and A. Purdue (1984) *The Civilization of the Crowd: Popular Culture in England 1750–1900.* London: Batsford, p. 63. B. Harrison (1967) 'Religion and recreation in nineteenth century England', *Past and Present*, 38: 116.
6   R. Holt (1989) *Sport and the British: A Modern History*, Oxford: Clarendon, p. 349.
7   E. Dunning and K. Sheard (1979) *Barbarians, Gentlemen and Players*, London: Martin Robertson, pp. 30, 33–4.
8   Bailey, *Leisure and Class*, p. 4.
9   Ibid., pp. 5–6, 139, 145.
10 Cunningham, *Industrial Revolution*, pp. 127–8.
11 Golby and Purdue, *Civilization*, p. 165.
12 Cunningham, *Industrial Revolution*, pp. 128, 177–8.
13 Ibid., pp. 140–41. Holt, *Sport and the British*, p. 349.
14 The archives of the various public schools provide little evidence of either organized or codified sport previous to 1850, see this volume, p. 228.
15 A. Fabian and G. Green (1960) *Association Football*, i, London: Caxton, pp. 151, 153. *FA Minute Books 1863–74*, 24 Feb, 13 March 1866, 12 Feb 1867. R. Graham (1899) 'The early history of The F.A.', *Badminton Magazine*, 8: 79, 82. It is instructive that a close observer such as Cartwright bemoaned the decline of football as a national game in 1864; J.D.C. (1864) 'Football at Rugby, Eton and Harrow', *London Society*, 5: 247.
16 Holt, *Sport and the British*, pp. 106, 108–109.

Chapter 2

Genesis: A National Sporting Culture is Born

Much of the rural past had to be set aside, and most of the migrants discovered that the expanding urban centres had, as yet, only an extremely restricted recreational culture to put in its place ... The reshaping of popular leisure was largely a phenomenon of the period after 1850.[1]

The above view, which posits a recreational 'vacuum' in the period between 1793 and 1850, has a number of advocates. In this chapter we shall consider an alternative vision, which suggests that during this period there was a vigorous commercial sporting culture in Britain. Our examination involves considering three components. In the first place, by employing quantitative data, we will assess both the volume of sporting activity and the total expenditure focused upon it. Second, such data will be used to assess the extent of the homogeneity of British sporting culture. Third, by examining the extent to which individual sports were dependent upon the traditional recreational calendar, it will be possible to discern the existence of a commercial sporting culture at both national and regional levels. Taken together, these elements provide us with sufficient data to determine the size and structure of the sporting culture, and to assess whether it was expanding or declining.

Between 1700 and 1850 the population in urban areas increased at double that of the rate of population increase as a whole.[2] However, until the 1830s, London was effectively 'town life', though cities such as Manchester and Newcastle, soon came to reach metropolitan proportions.[3] In fact, it is easy to overestimate the amount of urban and industrial development that was occurring within the period. Much of industry was small-scale, effectively uninfluenced by labour discipline.[4] Far from being dominated by a few industries, places such as Manchester became increasingly economically diverse, especially in the 1840s.[5] There was also a strong rural presence, reflecting the fact that even in 1851 agriculture remained the largest British industry.[6]

Despite the above evidence, which indicates that there was considerable continuity with the past, a number of those writing about the sporting culture of Britain between 1793 and 1850, claim that commercial developments, particularly relating to urban and industrial growth, had a very deleterious effect on leisure activity.[7] Proponents of the view blame this on four factors. First, enclosures, by removing areas of land from the public into the private domain, deprived the general population of space in which to play.[8] Second, the new labour discipline, in both country and town, ate in to free time, and meant that, whereas previously 'work and recreation were so closely related that they were indistinguishable', the two became completely divorced.[9] Third, lack of adequate nourishment meant that there was insufficient energy for activity.[10] Finally, the newly urbanized population lost their rural culture and identity as manifested in their recreations.

There is little unanimity among historians on any of these issues. For instance, while examples certainly exist of urban and industrial expansion eroding playing areas, such as at Hitchin School, where by 1819 the land that was once used for football was built upon, such cases were exceptional.[11] Likewise, many historians believe that the working hours of urban and agricultural workers were similar.[12] According to one recent study, during the nineteenth century in Scotland it was relative economic deprivation that undermined sporting activity, the process of industrialization expanding recreational choice.[13] The core issue of this debate relates to the standard of living during the early industrial period. Opinions on this subject vary widely for two reasons. First, regional differences are so pronounced as to render national trends of limited applicability.[14] More profoundly, inform-ation is often slight and contradictory, resulting in opinions that are based upon 'controlled conjectures rather than firm evidence'.[15] Economic historians are therefore catholic in their employment of sources, one study using the literary evidence gleaned from novels of the period to criticize the statistics produced by scholars who were attempting to show that living standards were rising between 1820 and 1850.[16]

This chapter rejects assumptions based upon the economy, restricting its attention to data relating to sporting activity, most of which is quantifiable. The chapter is divided into two periods, 1793 to 1815 and 1816 to 1850. The first half of the work focuses upon three issues. First, it considers the volume of activity, in terms of events and expenditure on stakes, throughout the French wars. Then, by using these data, it examines the relative experiences of the various sports in the first, as compared to the second half of the wars. The second issue is to assess the homogeneity of the sporting culture within Britain. Third, by establishing criteria which enable us to determine the extent to which a sport was dependent upon annual holidays, and coordinating such information with data relating to income tax and population, the sporting activity of the various regions within Britain is examined.

1793–1815

The Volume of Activity

For all sports   The belief that the growth and spread of industrial and commercial society in the period after 1750 was accompanied by a decline in the amount of sporting activity, is axiomatic for a number of scholars. Brailsford alleged:

> capital was the implacable enemy of leisure, and so of its major obvious components, sport and recreation. The greater the scale of sporting activity, and particularly the greater its frequency, the louder would be the opposition from the masters of trade and industry.[17]

An alternative view stresses the enormous growth of consumer society within the period. While this was principally a middle-class phenomenon, it embraced many in the lower orders as well. Within this context, leisure is portrayed as a big commercial industry whose growth, typified by horse racing, preceded the Napoleonic war. Plumb states that:

> in the early eighteenth century, culture and sport slowly ceased to be elitist and private and became increasingly public. The more public cultural and sporting activity becomes, the more it provokes emulation ... And social emulation usually leads to increasing consumption and expenditure. And it encourages the entrepreneur to exploit and extend the market.[18]

However, both views are open to doubt because the evidence upon which they are based is often of a questionable nature and too unsystematic to provide an accurate insight into the volume of sporting activity during the period.[19] Such a goal only becomes feasible from 1792, when *The Sporting Magazine* began to appear. It was the first periodical to devote itself to every type of sport, thus providing the historian with a reasonably comprehensive source. This part of the chapter attempts to establish as accurate a record as possible of the amount and type of activity during the French wars. This was accomplished by subjecting *The Sporting Magazine* (1792–1815) and other periodicals and newspapers to a detailed examination. Despite being published in London, *The Sporting Magazine* was able to offer extensive coverage of events nationally due to the fact that its editor, Wheble, had established a wide ranging network of informants. *The Racing Calendar* (1793–1815) provided a definitive annual record of every horse racing meeting, including the financial stakes involved. In addition, complete runs of the following newspapers between 1793 and 1815 were examined for their sporting coverage: the London based, *Bell's Weekly Messenger, The Times* and *The Weekly Dispatch*, and two provincial sources, *Jackson's Oxford Journal* and *The Manchester Mercury*. The latter pair carried adverts and sporting events for the surrounding areas and collectively the English sources appear to have provided a good national coverage. Scotland, by contrast, received little attention in them. However, judging by a number of compilations, there was comparatively little organized sporting activity occurring in the area, and the substantial attention paid to Scottish events in *The Sporting Magazine* and *The Racing Calendar* may well provide an accurate representation of what there was.[20] In addition, relevant secondary sources were referred to, most notably all the compilations by Buckley on cricket. He examined contemporary local newspapers, uncovering hundreds of references that were relevant to this study, issuing them in four volumes.

The above sources yield evidence of 6,736 organized sporting events in Britain throughout the 23-year period, 1793–1815. The term 'organized' sporting event signifies activity that was both pre-planned and governed by rules that were, theoretically at least, accepted by the competitors. Usually their commitment was embodied by a stake of either money or goods, which either the competitors or their backers would surrender to a third, neutral party – generally the referee. At the end of the contest the third party would give up all the stakes to the victor.[21]

We must now explain the meanings of some of the sporting terminology employed in the study. Contemporaries used 'pedestrianism' as an umbrella term referring to any athletic sport, often incorporating a range of tasks. One match consisted of the following: 'to walk 20 miles, run a mile, walk a mile forwards and then backwards, trundle a hoop a mile, wheel a barrow a mile, and pick up 40 stones a yard apart with the mouth'.[22] In this study, however, pedestrianism is only applied to events that involved accomplishing a task, generally travelling a certain distance within a stipulated period of time. Foot-races were any direct contests between individuals, whether they involved walking or running. Athletics is used as a general term denoting any gymnastic feat, such as weightlifting and leaping. The term horse-race meeting incorporates any number of races occurring as part of a prearranged event at a horse racing venue that was recognized in *The Racing Calendar*, a journal closely linked to the supervisory body of horse racing, the Jockey Club. Thus, whether the programme lasted for one day or 14, it still only counted as one event. Horse-race meetings are distinguished from horse races, because the latter were private arrangements between people and not part of a prearranged programme, though they were sometimes held at established venues. The term horse feats is an invention of the author intended to describe those events that were the equestrian equivalent of pedestrianism, the aim being to accomplish a stated distance within a period of time, not race another animal. Aquatics incorporates rowing, sailing and swimming. Shooting generally means pigeon-shooting but includes any competitive event involving guns. There are three additional categories which are used to incorporate less common activities, namely: animal – baiting sports, dog and pony racing; skill – fencing, quoits and tennis; strength – butting, singlestick and wrestling.

Throughout the period there was a general increase in the amount of recorded organized sporting events, though this was by no means uniform and subject to considerable fluctuations. However, as Table 2.2 shows, the general increase in the latter as compared to the former half of the war is clear, amounting to 17.5 per cent. There was also, as Table 2.3 shows, a substantial increase in the total amount of stakes, allowing for inflation. A chronological representation of this information can be found in Figure 2.1 and Table 2.1. To an extent they mirror political and economic events. The only full year of peace, 1802, witnessed a dramatic rise in

Table 2.1 The amount of events and stakes, 1793–1815 (1821/5 prices, guineas)

Year	Events	Stakes	Year	Events	Stakes
1793	268	97,207	1805	284	124,020
1794	255	74,211	1806	296	152,713
1795	220	79,677	1807	333	152,770
1796	253	104,288	1808	328	174,323
1797	209	67,252	1809	323	191,572
1798	232	62,295	1810	310	172,033
1799	211	85,427	1811	381	178,785
1800	248	126,326	1812	382	237,770
1801	282	140,855	1813	393	227,360
1802	334	85,874	1814	327	209,302
1803	235	83,353	1815	339	178,906
1804	293	94,511			

Table 2.2 Sporting events during the French wars

Sport	1793–1804	1805–15	Relation (%)	Total
Aquatics	100	65	−35.0	165
Archery	62	25	−49.5	87
Athletics	25	41	+39.0	66
Cock-fighting	150	210	+28.5	360
Coursing	84	131	+35.5	215
Cricket	780	598	−23.0	1,378
Football	135	138	+2.0	273
Foot race	83	130	+36.0	213
Horse feat	112	124	+9.5	236
Meeting	1,017	1,094	+7.0	2,111
Horse race	138	123	−10.5	261
Pedestrianism	142	357	+60.0	499
Pugilism	126	359	+64.5	485
Shooting	40	123	+67.0	163
Others	46	178	+59.0	224
Total	**3,040**	**3,696**	**+17.5**	**6,736**

Table 2.3   Sporting expenditure during the French wars (1821/5 prices, guineas)

Sport	1793–1804	1805–15	Relation (%)	Total
Athletics	496	423	–14.7	919
Cock-fighting	17,986	30,687	+41.3	48,673
Cricket	106,546	32,898	–69.1	139,444
Foot racing	4,872	12,251	+60.2	17,123
Horse feats	14,475	19,797	+26.8	34,272
Horse races	18,134	16,558	–8.6	34,692
Pedestrianism	28,469	33,910	+27.8	62,379
Pugilism	2,540	17,739	+85.6	20,279
Race meetings	903,567	1,815,326	+50.2	2,718,893
Others	6,191	19,140	+67.6	25,331
Total	**1,103,276**	**1,998,729**	**+44.8**	**3,102,005**

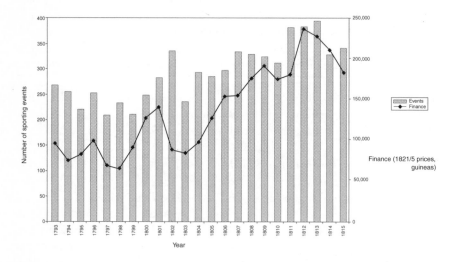

Figure 2.1   Sporting events and expenditure, 1793–1815

the number of sporting events, surpassing anything before 1811. However, far from there being an accompanying increase in the amount of expenditure on stakes, these actually fell drastically. This appears surprising because the Peace of Amiens had a very beneficial economic effect on quite large areas of the country, for instance Lancashire.[23] In many ways it may be futile to attempt to infer too much concerning sporting expenditure from the general economic situation of the country throughout the war. Living standards fluctuated violently but whether this had much of an impact on the type of people that were sponsoring and participating in organized sporting activity is debatable.[24] It is certainly by no means clear whether the war itself necessarily had an inhibiting effect on economic growth.[25] Interestingly enough, the data do reflect the economic downturn which followed the end of the war, though even then the expenditure on stakes remained above any level previous to 1809.

Individual sports   The experiences of the various sports varied dramatically throughout the period, as Tables 2.2 and 2.3 demonstrate. Most enjoyed a significant increase in the volume of events, though this was rarely matched by commensurate expansion in stake money. Generally, there was a substantial decline in the amount of stake money per event for sports other than horse racing. In the earlier period, 1793–1804, 199,709 g. (guineas) was devoted to 2,023 events that were not horse-race meetings, an average of 98 g. an event. In the later period, 1805–15, 183,403 g. were focused upon 2,602 of such events, an average of 70 g. This is a fall of over 25 per cent and suggests that a new group of smaller-scale promoters was becoming involved. By contrast, the expenditure on horse-race meetings escalated substantially, from an average of 888 g. in the earlier period to 1,659 g. in the later, a near doubling. It is clear, therefore, that finance was being increasingly devoted to the most advanced sector of the competitive sporting world. Horse-race meetings grew in sophistication, staging more events over longer periods, attracting greater stake money. During the period 1793–1804, horse-race meetings made up 82 per cent of all sporting stakes. In the later period this went up to 90.8 per cent, a rise of nearly 9 per cent. The percentage staked on all other sports halved, declining from 18 per cent to 9.2 per cent.

The Geographical Distribution of Sporting Activity

Table 2.4 outlines the composition of Britain's geographic regions. By 1815, as Table 2.5 shows, although Britain's organized sporting culture displayed some homogeneity, many activities were either rare or absent in certain regions (occurring on under ten occasions throughout the period). It is clear, however, that London and the Home Counties had more varieties of sport. Additionally, as Table 2.6 demonstrates, these regions also enjoyed more sporting activity per head of the population.

The Sporting Calendar

The time available for sporting activity, both for participants and spectators, has been of particular interest to those historians endeavouring to assess the effect that increased urban and industrial growth was having on leisure. Attention is often

Table 2.4   Composition of regions

Home Counties: Essex, Hampshire, Hertfordshire, Kent, Surrey, Sussex.
London: London and Middlesex.
Eastern: Cambridgeshire, Huntingdonshire, Lincolnshire, Norfolk, Rutland, Suffolk.
Upper Home Counties: Bedfordshire, Berkshire, Buckinghamshire, Gloucestershire, Oxfordshire.
Midlands: Derbyshire, Leicestershire, Northamptonshire, Nottinghamshire, Warwickshire, Worcestershire.
Yorkshire: County of Yorkshire.
Scotland: Country of Scotland.
West of England: Cornwall, Devon, Dorset, Somerset, Wiltshire.
North East: Cumberland, Durham, Northumberland, Westmorland.
North West: Cheshire, Lancashire.
Western: Herefordshire, Monmouthshire, Shropshire, Staffordshire, Wales.

Table 2.5   Distribution of sports throughout the regions, 1793–1815

Region	HR	Cr	Ped	Pug	Cock	FB	H	HF	Cou	FR
Home Counties	273	642	96	147	15	46	76	55	45	53
London	13	355	178	182	25	8	25	50	0	64
Eastern	297	152	22	23	39	2	35	33	73	12
Upper Home Counties	200	84	34	59	74	0	16	15	19	9
Yorkshire	236	51	37	5	27	16	18	8	45	15
Midlands	197	71	12	9	15	46	17	9	6	3
North West	181	2	16	4	115	0	13	14	6	22
Western	310	1	9	4	8	0	3	4	1	10
North East	139	1	6	1	31	83	15	10	0	6
West of England	127	16	29	32	3	0	13	15	10	7
Scotland	138	0	18	4	7	72	9	5	7	4
Unknown	0	3	42	15	1	0	21	18	3	8
Total	**2,111**	**1,378**	**499**	**485**	**360**	**273**	**261**	**236**	**215**	**213**

Region	Aq	Sho	Str	Arch	Ski	Ath	Anim	Total	Under 10	Over 10
Home Counties	25	49	25	14	12	15	4	1,590	1	16
London	115	46	11	10	18	14	13	1,127	1	16
Eastern	5	3	5	0	21	9	2	733	6	11
Upper Home Counties	5	29	9	1	10	7	1	572	7	10
Yorkshire	0	4	1	6	4	5	0	478	9	8
Midlands	0	4	0	23	1	6	3	422	10	7
North West	0	2	1	15	0	3	2	396	10	7
Western	4	0	0	1	1	0	0	356	15	2
North East	2	4	29	0	1	3	0	331	11	6
West Of England	6	5	37	1	3	3	1	308	9	8
Scotland	1	7	0	16	7	1	1	297	13	4
Unknown	2	10	1	0	0	2	0	126		
Total	**165**	**163**	**119**	**87**	**78**	**68**	**27**	**6,736**		

Key: Total volume of events for the particular sport in brackets. HR – Horse-race meetings (2,111); Cr – Cricket (1,378); Ped – Pedestrianism (499); Pug – Pugilism (485); Cock – Cock-fighting (360); FB – Football (273); H – Horse races (261); HF – Horse feats (236); Cou – Coursing (215); FR – Foot race (213); Aq – Aquatics (165); Sho – Shooting (163); Str – Strength (119); Arch – Archery (87); Ski – Skill (78); Ath – Athletics (66); Anim – Animals (27).

Table 2.6   The amount of sporting activity per region, 1793–1815

Region	Events	Population	Income Tax	Event per head	Tax per head
London	1,127	885,702	1,657,466	12.70	1.87
Home Counties	1,590	1,387,941	1,004,708	11.40	0.72
Upper Home Counties	572	675,392	448,104	08.47	0.66
Eastern	733	879,513	626,944	08.33	0.71
North East	331	502,880	337,003	06.50	0.67
Yorkshire	478	916,002	537,270	05.20	0.58
Western	356	688.858	580,213	05.16	0.84
Midlands	422	970,145	615,570	04.35	0.63
North West	396	959,911	491,257	04.12	0.51
West of England	308	1,163,560	672,545	02.64	0.57
Scotland	297	1,702,378	649,868	01.74	0.38

Note: Income tax is £, and both tax and events is per 10,000 of population.

focused upon the declining number of established, traditional, holidays, which is presumed to manifest itself in an increasingly restricted programme of available sport. Other scholars are more keen to emphasize the emergence of a 'leisure industry', with entrepreneurs creating and marketing entertainment as a commercial concern. In this section of the chapter, we will seek to establish the extent to which the sporting culture was dependent upon traditional holidays, by classifying the various sports according to the calendar.

The sporting calendar can be divided into two fundamental parts, those events occurring during annual holiday periods – 'annual' – and those that are independent of this, usually held during a normal working week – 'weekly'. Despite the fact that by 1804 Christmas and New Year's Day were regarded as the only nationally observed holidays, there were an array of annual holidays that were adhered to, often in particular localities.[26] Some, such as those celebrating the birthdays of royalty, were not well established, but most stemmed from religious festivals or local customs.[27] However, with the important exception of Shrove Tuesday, during which football was held, there was little real link between these holidays and particular sports. Principally, annual holiday sport occurred on a regional basis during the few consecutive days that had become established as holidays in that particular area. By the time of the French wars these annual holiday periods had become the fixed times during which the local horse-race meetings occurred. At Manchester, for instance, a conscious decision was made in 1775 by the administrators of the local races to transfer the meeting to the established holiday period from that time forth.[28] While horse-race meetings were not necessarily the product of local holidays, they seem to have become heavily dependent upon them. This observation is supported by the fact that out of 2,100 horse-race meetings that occurred between 1793 and 1815, at only 13 out of 159 venues did the meeting occur over two months from its usual time on more than two occasions.[29] We can therefore treat the bulk of horse-race meetings as being dependent upon annual holidays.[30] An important exception to this were the events at Newmarket. This was the centre of horse racing, conducting seven meetings every year. In no sense were these the product of a local holiday calendar. Cock-fights were often held during horse-race meetings and these can be treated as annual events. Such criteria must be applied discerningly because a number of cock-fights were unrelated to horse-race meetings. Overall, three sports – horse-race meetings, cock-fights and Shrove-football – can be treated as annual, holiday events.

Of the other eleven sports, the events of four of them – archery, aquatics, coursing and cricket – were distributed throughout a certain set period, a strong indication that there was an established season for each particular activity (see Table 2.7). In addition, except for archery, which appears to have been a week-long event, the four sports show a pronounced inclination to occur on certain days, as can be shown by comparing the principal day on which they were held with the second favourite (Table 2.8). By contrast, the comparative differences between the favourite and second favourite days of the three annual sports were quite different. Cock-fighting was essentially a week-long activity, thus tending to render

Table 2.7   The existence of a playing season for four sports

Sport	Total events	Season	Events within season
Aquatics	165	June–September	144 (87%)
Archery	87	July–September	67 (77%)
Coursing	215	November–March	196 (91%)
Cricket	1,180	June–September	1,086 (89%)

Table 2.8   The favourite days for sporting events

Sport	Favourite day	Percentage compared to second favourite
Aquatics	Monday	32 (27)
Coursing	Tuesday	26 (20)
Cricket	Monday	32 (27)
Foot racing	Monday	30 (18)
Horse feats	Monday	26 (20)
Pugilism	Monday	27 (21)
Shooting	Monday	30 (18)

differences between favourite and second favourite days largely insignificant. Similarly, the majority of Wednesdays, the favourite day for horse-race meetings, over Thursdays, the second most popular – 1,679 (27 per cent) to 1,587 (26 per cent) – is almost meaningless. At the other extreme, 266 out of 273 games of football occurred on Tuesdays, the type of majority that emphasizes the established annual nature of the activity. Collectively, about 80 per cent of events for aquatics, archery, coursing and cricket fell within their respective favourite months, a strong indication that they had each established their own individual seasons that were quite independent of an external holiday calendar. Seven other sports – athletics, foot racing, horse feats, horse races, pedestrianism, pugilism and shooting – lacked such clear definition, and although they each occur more often in a particular month, their distribution throughout the year is so even that in no sense do any of them appear to have had an established season. However, in four of them – foot racing, horse feats, pugilism and shooting – a particular day, Monday, was established as by far the favourite playing day (Table 2.8).[31] Thus, although these sports do not appear to have had an established season, the prominent distribution of Mondays indicates that the days for play were not selected according to the criterion of established annual holidays, but were, rather, related to weekly work patterns in which Monday was a well recognized day of rest. It is notable that in his study of recreational events during the early part of the nineteenth century, Mark Harrison reached similar conclusions. He, too, regarded Monday as leisure time, and discovered that the majority of recreational events occurred outside what would usually be regarded as work time.[32] It is clear, therefore, that although there was still no established calendar of regularly occurring commercialized sporting activity, the appearance of which still lay in the future, events were occurring during a leisure time that was independent of established, traditional patterns.

Having established strong criteria for identifying whether a sport can be regarded as annual or weekly, it is time to apply this insight to the various regions in order to assess the degree to which an area's sporting activity was based upon an established holiday calendar. The relative distribution of annual and weekly sport breaks down, essentially, into a north–south divide, the counties around London enjoying a particularly vigorous weekly sporting culture (see Table 2.9).

Summary

An examination of the evidence reveals that during the French wars the volume of both sporting events and expenditure upon them increased, and that an increasing proportion of this expenditure was concentrated on the most advanced sector, horse-race meetings. To an extent this was a national sporting culture, though it is clear that the southern regions enjoyed both a greater variety and volume of organized sporting events. Additionally, a profound regional difference existed between the south and the north, in terms of their dependence on the traditional, annual, recreational timetable. The south was largely independent of this, the north

Table 2.9   Annual and weekly sport in each region, 1793–1815

Region	Annual	Weekly	Total events	% Annual
Western	318	38	356	89.8
North East	276	55	331	83.3
North West	293	103	396	73.9
Scotland	214	83	297	72.0
Midlands	254	168	422	60.1
Yorkshire	279	199	478	58.3
West of England	130	178	308	42.2
Upper Home Counties	223	349	572	38.9
Eastern	158	575	733	21.5
Home Counties	281	1,309	1,590	17.6
London	18	1,109	1,127	1.5
Unknown	0	107	107	0
Total	**2,444**	**4,273**	**6,717**	**36.3**

was not. In essence, the commercial sporting culture was significantly more advanced in the south.

1816–1850

The second half of the chapter utilizes information on sporting activity to demonstrate that the developments identified in the earlier period, 1793 to 1815, continued between 1816 and 1850. This manifested itself in three ways. In the first place, the volume of activity and the finance expended upon it, increased, in relative terms, between 1816 and 1850, as compared to during the French wars. Second, the sports practised nationally displayed a greater homogeneity. Third, whereas during the French wars a profound difference existed between the north and the south in terms of their dependence upon the traditional recreational timetable, by the later period this had evaporated, the various regions adhering to a similar 'weekly' sporting calendar.

The Volume of Events and Expenditure on Stakes

A number of writers have claimed that during certain decades within the first half of the nineteenth century there was very little sporting activity, particularly for the 'lower orders'.[33] However, some scholars contend that there is no evidence of a decline in sport.[34] Crucially, there has been very little attempt to quantify systematically the available data. Four scholars have attempted to examine particular sports in a more systematic fashion, and we must now examine their research.

Bale endeavoured to establish the geographical distribution of cricket activity between 1800 and 1835 by utilizing, principally, the compendious researches of Buckley. From this evidence he suggested that British sporting culture was only integrated to a limited geographical extent.[35] However, a great deal of Buckley's research remained unconsulted by Bale because, having never been published, it was available only in archives.[36] Examination of these reveals a tremendous amount of new information, which could, potentially, transform substantially the conclusions that Bale made. These sources were utilized by Bowen in order to assess the volume of cricket activity between 1750 and 1850. From this data he concluded that after Waterloo the game expanded.[37]

Halladay used data collected by Iota concerning rowing, and concluded from it that: 'there was little organized activity either on the Thames or elsewhere until the mid-1840s and even then developments were to remain hesitant for some years to come'.[38] However, Iota's figures only commence in 1835 and, as his preface makes clear, entirely exclude a whole variety of very popular events.[39] In fact, as the information derived from *Bell's* in Table 2.10 makes clear, there was a significant amount of organized aquatic activity from at least 1829.

Tranter attempted to utilize the *Statistical Account Of Scotland* from 1791–99 and 1845 to assess the relative geographical distribution of sport, concluding that there was no indication of decline. Given the fact that neither survey was interested

Table 2.10   Chronologies for various sports, from *Bell's Life in London*

	1826	1827	1828	1829	1832	1833	1834	1835	1836
Aquatics	–	–	62	45	–	–	–	–	–
Pugilism	46	84	56	74	19	47	31	23	37

	1837	1838	1839	1840	1841	1842	1843	1844	1845
Aquatics	–	90	156	86	145	120	173	144	158
Coursing	–	–	–	–	474	493	587	–	–
Pedestrianism	–	49	121	206	319*	198*	309*	300*	383*
Pigeon	–	70	–	169	267	–	–	–	–
Pugilism	39	38	54	149	165	114	140	149	150
Trotting	–	46	–	50	60	–	49	38	46
Wrestling	–	15	–	32	33	–	–	–	–

	1846	1847	1848	1849	1850
Aquatics	179	183	158	145	–
Pedestrianism	686*	409*	492*	236*	152*
Pugilism	143	126	121	98	86
Trotting	64	52	–	–	–

Notes: Where a box is left empty there was no information given. * = Numbers of runners that had won at least one race that year.

in sport, and that, consequently, all such information was gathered incidently, it can scarcely be regarded as particularly reliable.[40]

By employing a variety of sources we can establish that the volume of sporting activity and the amount of money (in 1821/5, g.) staked was larger, on average, in the years after Waterloo to 1850, compared with those of the French wars, and that organized sporting activity in the 1830s was far more prevalent than many scholars suppose. Our evidence for this stems from four sources, in addition to the earlier mentioned work by Bowen on cricket. First, *Bell's* provided annual chronologies for a range of sports: pugilism, aquatics, pedestrianism (this includes foot racing), trotting, coursing, pigeon-shooting and wrestling (see Table 2.10). An examination of these reveals that the totals for the various years almost always surpass their Napoleonic predecessors (see Table 2.11).[41] Not only that, on a number of occasions we are specifically informed that there has been an immense increase in the amount of activity in a particular sport, even to the point that the paper states that its coverage has been selective. This occurs for coursing, cricket, foot racing, pedestrianism, pugilism, rowing, sailing and steeplechasing.[42]

Table 2.11   A comparison between two periods of the average number of events for five sports

Sport	1793–1815	1816–50	Relation
Aquatics	7	131	–124
Coursing	9	518	–509
Pedestrianism	31	296	–265
Pugilism	21	86	–65
Trotting	10	50	–40

Our second key evidence was derived by systematically gathering data from a number of sources, though principally *Bell's*, relating to sporting activity in the Manchester conurbation for the whole post-Napoleonic period (see Table 2.12 and Figure 2.2).[43] Such quantification revealed a total of 3,087 events (an average of 88.0 events every year), upon which 159,809 guineas was expended (an average of 4,565 g. a year). By contrast, in the earlier period, there were just 203 events in the whole of Lancashire (an average of 8.8 a year), upon which 62,677 g. were expended (average 2,725 g. a year). In essence, despite the fact that between 1816 and 1850 we are dealing only with Manchester, there has almost been a tenfold increase in events and over 25 per cent in expenditure. Third, the same process was undertaken for Oxfordshire (see Table 2.13 and Figure 2.3). During the Napoleonic period there were 135 events (average 5.8 per year) and 22,778 g. in expenditure (average 990 g.), compared with 585 (average 16.7) and 36,324 g. (average 1,037 g. per year) in the latter period. Thus, there was an increase in terms of annual

Table 2.12　Events and expenditure in Manchester, 1816–50 (1821/5 prices)

Year	Events	Guineas	Year	Events	Guineas
1816	4	607	1834	28	5,441
1817	5	1,188	1835	26	5,199
1818	1	966	1836	71	6,462
1819	4	2,430	1837	41	5,232
1820	7	4,131	1838	60	8,235
1821	4	1,654	1839	82	4,013
1822	12	1,523	1840	101	3,954
1823	8	1,928	1841	139	3,659
1824	7	2,544	1842	150	3,392
1825	12	3,651	1843	136	3,209
1826	15	3,445	1844	160	3,325
1827	34	4,327	1845	217	3,923
1828	55	5,410	1846	302	5,922
1829	40	6,166	1847	307	8,608
1830	24	6,709	1848	328	9,667
1831	56	6,637	1849	294	7,602
1832	36	4,637	1850	267	9,061
1833	54	4,952			

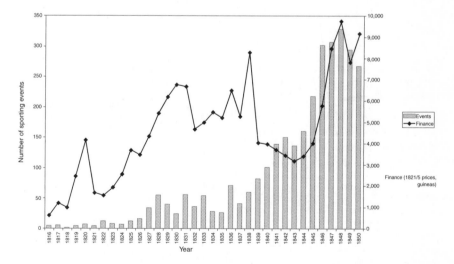

Figure 2.2　Sporting events and expenditure in Manchester, 1816–50

Table 2.13   Events and expenditure in Oxfordshire, 1816–50 (1821/5 prices)

Year	Events	Guineas	Year	Events	Guineas
1816	4	514	1834	11	1,402
1817	4	411	1835	9	699
1818	5	1,023	1836	13	393
1819	7	1,151	1837	21	1,351
1820	2	401	1838	20	985
1821	8	1,603	1839	21	1,307
1822	10	636	1840	24	894
1823	6	988	1841	27	1,837
1824	13	1,359	1842	33	643
1825	10	2,384	1843	48	550
1826	15	2,119	1844	28	528
1827	9	1,517	1845	35	531
1828	18	1,460	1846	26	647
1829	7	1,584	1847	37	53
1830	6	2,123	1848	28	356
1831	7	1,805	1849	39	563
1832	9	1,483	1850	34	34
1833	7	990			

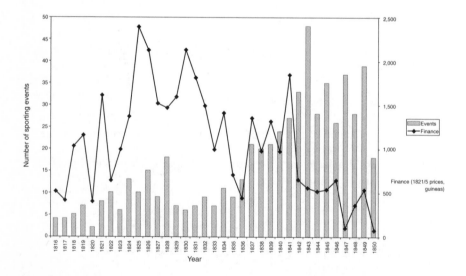

Figure 2.3   Sporting events and expenditure in Oxfordshire, 1816–50

Table 2.14 The number of horse-race meetings per year, 1816–50

Year	Events	Year	Events	Year	Events
1816	97	1828	139	1840	163
1817	91	1829	138	1841	168
1818	92	1830	137	1842	152
1819	93	1831	131	1843	152
1820	100	1832	125	1844	136
1821	108	1833	127	1845	145
1822	111	1834	136	1846	144
1823	111	1835	138	1847	140
1824	112	1836	144	1848	130
1825	119	1837	150	1849	121
1826	125	1838	165	1850	124
1827	133	1839	163		

volume of events and expenditure on stakes in both Oxfordshire and Lancashire during the latter as compared with the earlier period. Fourth, a systematic examination of *The Racing Calendar* between 1816 and 1850, reveals that the sport that was by far the largest in terms of the number of events and the amount of expenditure during the Napoleonic period, horse-race meetings, expanded after Waterloo. Between 1793 and 1815 there were a total of 2,111 events (average 91.78 per year), compared with 4,560 in the latter period (average 104.57) (see Table 2.14). The average for the total expenditure on horse-race meetings for the four benchmark years in the latter period, as set out in Table 2.15, was 195,664 g., compared with like data from the Napoleonic period, namely 118,230 g., an increase of 65 per cent. It is therefore clear that the volume of expenditure on sport was increasing.[44]

The Expansion of a National Sporting Culture

The second component of this part of our study involves considering the factors

Table 2.15 Total prize money for four years of horse-race meetings (1821/5 prices, guineas)

Year	Amount
1820	164,430
1830	209,965
1840	202,137
1850	206,127

Table 2.16   The distribution of sporting activity in Manchester and Oxfordshire, 1793–1850

	HR	Cr	Ped	Pug	Cock	FB
Lancashire	62	2	12	2	63	0
Manchester	83	339	36	207	156	0
Oxfordshire*	33	21	7	19	30	17
Oxfordshire†	59	232	26	21	3	0
	H	HF	Cou	FR	Aq	Sho
Lancashire	11	13	6	12	0	2
Manchester	47	8	210	1,123	52	275
Oxfordshire*	6	4	1	4	0	9
Oxfordshire†	34	9	0	20	51	49
	Str	Arch	Ski	Ath	Anim	
Lancashire	1	14	0	1	2	
Manchester	85	18	279	27	124	
Oxfordshire*	0	0	1	0	0	
Oxfordshire†	3	0	18	1	19	

Notes: The figure for Lancashire is for the period 1793–1815. The figure for Oxfordshire* is for 1793–1815. The figure for Manchester is for 1816–50 and the figure for Oxfordshire† is for 1816–50. See Table 2.5 for key to sports.

that were creating a unified sporting culture in Britain and some of the ramifications of this. As we showed earlier, by 1815 the sporting culture of Britain displayed some homogeneity. Between 1816 and 1850, this increased significantly, as can be seen from the evidence relating to our two case studies, Manchester and Oxfordshire (Tables 2.16 and 2.17). Much of this was due to improvements in communications, particularly the reduction of tolls, and the creation of an enormously efficient network of coaches.[45] During the French wars organized sport in the north had been heavily dependent upon the traditional recreational culture. However, as the following case studies show, this ceased to be so between 1816 and 1850.

The Sporting Calendar

After 1815, Sunday play, which in the earlier period had been rare, effectively vanished, principally because of religious influence. While we know comparatively little about working hours, it is clear that for a large portion of the period Mondays and Tuesdays, particularly the former, were well established as rest days in many varieties of work. A mixture of government legislation, such as the Ten Hours Bill, and discipline emanating from employers, diluted these

Table 2.17 The variety and volume of sporting activity in Lancashire/ Manchester and Oxfordshire, 1793–1850

Region	Population	Sport per 10,000	Varieties of sport	
			Under 10	Over 10
Lancashire	750,520	2.7	10	7
Manchester	778,867	39.5	1	16
Oxfordshire*	114,405	11.8	13	4
Oxfordshire†	155,643	37.6	7	10

Notes: The figures for Lancashire are for the period 1793–1815 and the figures for Oxfordshire* are for 1793–1815. The figures for Manchester are for 1816–50 and the figures for Oxfordshire† 1816–50. The figure for the amount of sport per 10,000 of the population is derived by dividing the population by the amount of sporting activity. The varieties of sport represents the number of different activities (as listed in Table 2.16) recorded per region. Where under 10 events of a particular activity are recorded it is placed in the right-hand column.

holidays, and in the process helped to establish common leisure time.[46] In Manchester, for instance, until 1845, when the half-day Saturday was established for a significant portion of the conurbation's workforce, Saturday was the busiest day of the week.[47] Even after 1845, Monday remained a well established rest day, and for the bulk of the year events at the main sports venue, Belle Vue, were held on Mondays and Saturdays every week.[48] It would be mistaken to imagine that working days necessarily prevented people competing and spectating in sports events. These would sometimes be held early in the morning, or during lunch time, and many workers simply skipped their jobs.[49] Established holiday periods also survived, though there does not appear to have been much uniformity: in Bolton Christmas Day was not a holiday.[50] Wakes were vital and though they were ostensibly based around agricultural rhythms, inhabitants of urban areas, for instance Manchester, adhered to those of the surrounding villages.[51] Much of the sporting activity in certain places, such as Banbury and Lancaster, was seasonal.[52] It also seems likely that sponsorship of sporting events was substantially influenced by the 'London Season', with many patrons basing themselves in the capital from January to May, before returning home in July.

We can, however, provide a very specific insight into the sporting calendar of two diverse regions, Manchester and Oxfordshire, by utilizing systematically compiled data for the period 1816–50. During the Napoleonic war we established that almost two-thirds of sporting activity was 'weekly' rather than 'annual' (Table 2.9). In geographical terms this essentially split into a north–south divide, with the sporting culture of the latter tending to be 'weekly', while annual sport was concentrated in the northern areas. However, during the period between 1816 and

Table 2.18   A comparison of the amounts of annual and weekly sporting activity for 1793–1815 and 1816–50, in Oxfordshire and Lancashire

	Oxfordshire			Lancashire		
Years	Annual	Weekly	Total	Annual	Weekly	Total
1793–1815	63	72	135	125	78	203
	46.6%	53.3%	99.99%	61.5%	38.4%	99.99%
1816–50	62	523	585	161	2,926	3,087
	10.6%	89.4%	99.99%	5.2%	94.7%	99.99%

Note: The figure for 1816–50 under Lancashire relates entirely to the Manchester conurbation.

1850, judging by Manchester and Oxfordshire, an enormous change occurred, as Table 2.18 shows. Annual sport declined dramatically in relation to weekly. Further, the area in which weekly sport became most dominant was urban, industrial, Manchester. While it would obviously be incorrect to claim that the more industrialized an area became the less its sporting culture depended upon annual holidays, because a substantial change in this direction occurred, also, in the more rural Oxfordshire, it is clear that historians who associate industrial and urban expansion with a decline in the time available for participating and spectating at sporting events, do so in contradiction to the available evidence. On the contrary, sporting activity in industrial Manchester blossomed, as Table 2.17 shows. Sport in Manchester increased fifteenfold during the latter period, that in Oxfordshire just over threefold. Judging by the evidence in our two case studies, the amount of sporting activity per ratio of the population, and the percentage of events that were 'weekly', was effectively the same in predominantly rural and urban areas. Such facts suggest general trends that were occurring throughout the country, comparatively uninfluenced by either rural or urban environments.

Conclusions

The evidence adduced in this chapter supports the contention that between 1793 and 1850 a nationally based commercial sporting culture emerged and expanded.[53] This is in sharp contradiction to many accounts of the period, which still emphasize the destructive impact of industrial and urban development on sporting activity between 1750 and 1850.[54] There were three ways in which this culture manifested itself. First, it displayed a commercial dynamism. This can be seen by a systematic analysis of the evidence, which reveals that throughout the period, though there were many fluctuations, there was a general rise in both the volume of events and the expenditure on stakes (see Figures 2.1, 2.2 and 2.3). Also, as early as the French wars, sport was being treated as a commercial business, with the major activity, horse-race meetings, attracting an increasing proportion of expenditure on sport. Second, by 1850, the organised sporting culture, which had displayed some homogeneity by 1815, had attained an almost national uniformity. Third, there was an increasing independence from the traditional recreational timetable. During the French wars, a 'weekly' culture took root in the south, though remaining patchy in the north. In the later period, judging by our two case studies, this 'weekly' culture was pervasive throughout the country, the traditional recreational calendar having shrunk in importance. A significant factor in the growth of this culture were communications, particularly the sporting press, the subject of the next chapter.

Notes

1 Malcolmson, *Popular Recreation*, pp. 117, 171.
2 F.M.L. Thompson (1990) 'The town and city', in F.M.L. Thompson (ed.) *CSH*, i, Cambridge: Cambridge University Press, p. 8.
3 D.J. Rowe (1990) 'North East', pp. 419–20. Thompson, 'The town and city', pp. 15–17. J. Walton, 'North West', p. 364. All three articles in Thompson, *CSH*, i.
4 P. Joyce, 'Work', in Thompson, *CSH*, ii, p. 148.
5 Walton, 'North West', in Thompson, *CSH*, i, p. 362.
6 J.F.C. Harrison (1971) *The Early Victorians 1832–1851*, London: Weidenfeld, p. 10.
7 Bailey, *Leisure and Class*, pp. 1–5, 11–12. W. Baker (1979) 'The making of a working class football culture in Victorian England', *JSH*, 13:2, 242. Holt, *Sport and the British*, p. 49. Malcolmson, *Popular Recreations*, pp. 209, 220–21. R. Malcolmson (1984) 'Sports in society: A historical perspective', *IJHS*, 1:1, 66. R. Storch (1982a) 'Persistence and change in nineteenth century popular culture', in R. Storch (ed.), *Popular Culture and Customs in Nineteenth Century England*, London: Croom Helm, p. 5.
8 Bailey, *Leisure and Class*, p. 14. Malcolmson, *Popular Recreations*, pp. 107–108, 224–5. D. Reid (1988) 'Folk football, the aristocracy and cultural change', *IJHS*, 5:2, 229. J. Walvin (1975) *The People's Game*, London: Allen Lane, pp. 26–7.
9 J. Clapham and M. Clapham (1934) 'Life in the new towns', in G. Young (ed.), *Early Victorian England*, Oxford: Oxford University Press, i, pp. 230–31. Malcolmson, *Popular Recreations*, pp. 98–9. Malcolmson, 'Sport in society', 62. M. Brooke Smith (1970) 'The Growth and Development of Popular Entertainments and Pastimes in Lancashire Cotton Towns 1830–1870', M. Litt, Lancaster, p. 38. W. Vamplew (1988a) *Pay up and Play the Game: Professional Sport in Britain 1875–1914*, Cambridge: Cambridge University Press, p. 7. J. Walton and R. Poole (1982) 'The Lancashire Wakes in the nineteenth century', in Storch, *Culture and Custom*, pp. 100–102. J. Walvin, *Leisure and Society*, pp. 2–4.
10 Cunningham, *Industrial Revolution*, pp. 59–61. M. Judd (1983) 'Popular culture and the London Fairs', in J. Walton and J. Walvin, *Leisure in Britain*, Manchester: Manchester University Press, pp. 12–13. D. Oddy (1990), 'Food, drink and nutrition', in Thompson, *CSH*, ii, p. 256. Reid, 'Folk football', p. 230. E.P. Thompson (1970) *The*

Making of the English Working Class, London: Victor Gollancz, p. 451.

11   Golby and Purdue, *Civilization*, pp. 102, 267. R. Hine (1929) *The History of Hitchin*, London: Allen and Unwin, p. 266.

12   E. Hopkins (1982) 'Working hours and conditions during the Industrial Revolution: a reappraisal', *EcHR*, 35:1, 65–6. D.A. Reid (1976) 'The decline of Saint Monday 1766–1876', *Past and Present*, 71, 82.

13   Golby and Purdue, *Civilization*, p. 90. N. Tranter (1987a) 'Popular sports and the industrial revolution in Scotland: the evidence of the Statistical Accounts', *IJHS*, 4:1, 21–3, 33.

14   F. Botham and E. Hunt (1987) 'Wages in the Industrial Revolution', *EcHR*, 40, 398.

15   N. Crafts (1983) 'British economic growth, 1700–1831: A review of the evidence', *EcHR*, 36:2, 198.

16   Botham and Hunt, 'Wages in the Industrial Revolution', 383. P. Lindert and J. Williamson (1983) 'English workers living standards during the Industrial revolution: A new look', *EcHR*, 36:1, 24.

17   Brailsford, *Sport, Time*, p. 47.

18   N. McKendrick, J. Brewer and J.H. Plumb (1982) *The Birth of a Consumer Society: The Commercialization of Eighteenth Century England*, London: Hutchinson, p. 284.

19   While there is considerable evidence of commercial sporting activity in the period before 1790 the data are too unsystematic to be usefully quantified. There are two exceptions to this. Research on cricket suggests that while the game generally expanded throughout the eighteenth century, it suffered a decline during the Napoleonic wars. R. Bowen (1970) *Cricket: A History of its Growth and Development Throughout the World*, London: Eyre and Spottiswode, pp. 79–80. There are detailed records for horse racing which show that it expanded during the eighteenth century. P. Borsay (1989) *The English Urban Renaissance,* Oxford: Clarendon, pp. 173–95. The following contain some insight into organized sporting activity in the years before 1793: C.B. Andrews (1934) *The Torrington Diaries,* London: Methuen, i, pp. 16, 100, 128, 208, 350; ii, pp. 35, 45, 164; iii, pp. 86, 116, 150, 329; iv, pp. 65, 122–3. *JJC* Sports. Box 2. Box 3. Box 7. M. Richardson (1841–46) *Local Historian's Table Book.* London. Van Muyden (ed.) (1902) *A Foreign View Of England in the Reign of George I and George II*, London: John Murray, pp. 217–18.

20   There are also some excellent indexes of Scottish newspapers from the period: *A Local Index of the Dumfries and Galloway Standard and Advertiser and its predecessors over 200 years* (1980), Dumfries. *The Stirling Journal and Advertiser: A Local Index* (1979), Stirling: University of Stirling. It is instructive that they add relatively little information that is not found in the various London-based sources that were used in this study.

21   Malcolmson offers a similar definition of sporting activity: 'The importance of more intimate kinds of leisure should not be forgotten, but the sources themselves necessitate an account of recreations which highlight the holiday calendar and the more organised and visible forms of sport and pastimes', *Popular Recreations*, p. 16. However, he makes no attempt to quantify the amount of activity, and maintains that the volume of such events suffered a steady decline from 1750 until 1850.

22   *Bell's*, 9 May 1841.

23   C. Aspin (1969) *Lancashire: The First Industrial Society*, Preston: Helmshaw, pp. 35–6.

24   C. Emsley (1979) *British Society and the French Wars 1793–1815*, London: Macmillan, pp. 29, 120–21, 149–52. J. Stevenson (1993) 'Social aspects of the Industrial Revolution', in P. O'Brien and R. Quinault (eds), *The Industrial Revolution*

and British Society, Cambridge: Cambridge University Press, p. 241.

25 P. O'Brien (1993) 'Political preconditions for the industrial revolution', in P. O'Brien and R. Quinault (eds), *The Industrial Revolution and British Society*, Cambridge: Cambridge University Press, pp. 150–51.

26 *SM* May 1804, 80; Dec 1807, 113.

27 *SM* Sept 1793, 367; Aug 1794, 260–61, 282; April 1795, 54–5; May 1795, 94; July 1795, 223; Jan 1798, 176; Aug 1803, 303, 305; May 1806, 99; July 1809, 196; Aug 1810, 229; Jan 1811, 141–2; May 1811, 99, 115; May 1814, 94. J. Brand (1810) *Observations on Popular Antiquities*, Newcastle: J. Johnson, pp. vi, ix, criticized Catholicism for crowding the calendar with holidays, 'nominally consecrated by saints', but actually derived from 'heathen' origins.

28 *Exchange Herald*, 12 June 1821.

29 The author decided that two such deviations per meeting between 1793 and 1815 were justified given the exigencies of factors such as weather.

30 W. Vamplew (1979) 'The sport of kings and commoners: the commercialisation of British horse racing in the nineteenth century', in R. Cashman and M McKernan (eds) *Sport in History*, Queensland, New South Wales, pp. 307–308.

31 Somewhat different conclusions were reached by Brailsford. However, his periodization was different in two significant ways. First, he split up the Napoleonic wars. Second, he included years outside the period. D. Brailsford (1982) 'Sporting days in eighteenth century England', *IJHS*, 9:3, 44, 47. *Sport, Time*, p. 82.

32 M. Harrison (1988) *Crowds And History: Mass Phenomena in English Towns, 1790–1835*, Cambridge: Cambridge University Press, pp. 44, 111, 127, 134.

33 See this volume, pp. 7–8.

34 Cunningham, *Industrial Revolution*, p. 196. Golby and Purdue, *Civilization*, p. 166.

35 J. Bale (1981) 'Cricket in Pre-Victorian England and Wales', *Area*, 13:2, 122.

36 Ibid., p. 119.

37 Bowen, *Cricket*, p. 87.

38 E. Halladay (1990) *Rowing in England: A Social History*, Manchester: Manchester University Press, p. 55.

39 Iota (1858) *The Boat Racing Calendar 1835–1852*, London. *Bell's Life*, pref v. See also Amateur (1852) *The Aquatic Oracle*, London: Simpkin, Marshall & Co., pp. iii.–iv.

40 Tranter, 'Popular Sports', p. 23.

41 They can be found as follows:
Aquatics: 3 Jan 1830, 8 Dec 1833, 14 Dec 1834, 20 Dec 1835, 25 Dec 1836, 2 Dec 1838, 8 Dec 1839, 22 Nov 1840, 28 Nov 1841, 25 Dec 1842, 7 Jan 1844, 5 Jan, 28 Dec 1845, 18 Jan, 27 Dec 1846, 16, 23 Jan 1848, 21, 28 Jan, 16, 23 Dec 1849.
Pedestrianism: 30 Dec 1838, 12 Jan, 27 Dec 1840, 2 Jan, 25 Dec 1842, 8 Jan 1843, 7 Jan 1844, 5 Jan 1845, 11 Jan 1846, 3, 10, 17 Jan 1847, 9 Jan, 31 Dec 1848, 7 Jan, 30 Dec 1849, 12 Jan 1851.
Pugilism: 1 Jan 1826, 30 Dec 1827, 4 Jan, 27 Dec 1829, 3 Jan 1830, 6 Jan, 29 Dec 1833, 28 Dec 1834, 31 Dec 1837, 16 Dec 1838, 29 Dec 1839, 27 Dec 1840, 2 Jan, 25 Dec 1842, 7 Jan 1844, 5 Jan 1845, 4 Jan 1846, 3 Jan 1847, 2 Jan, 31 Dec 1848, 6 Jan 1850, 5 Jan 1851.
Shooting: 30 Dec 1838, 12 Jan 1840, 3 Jan 1841.
Steeplechasing: 17 May 1840, 7 Jan 1844, 5 Jan 1845, 18 Jan 1846, 17 Jan 1847, 2 Jan 1848, 4 Feb 1849.
Trotting: 30 Dec 1838, 12 Jan 1840, 10 Jan 1841, 7 Jan 1844, 5 Jan 1845, 25 Jan 1846,

3 Jan 1847, 2 Jan 1848.

Wrestling: 30 Dec 1838, 5 Jan 1840, 10 Jan 1841.

42 *Annals*, June 1822, 118; Oct 1824, 249; Oct 1827, 212; *Bell's*, 22 Aug 1824, 28 June 1829, 15 April 1840, 1 Oct 1843, 16 Feb 1845, 29 April 1849, 14 April, 5 May 1850. *Sporting Magazine*, June 1817, 142; Aug 1835, 356; Jan 1817, 273.

43 For list of sources see this volume, p. 228.

44 *SM*, April 1822, 14; detailed the expansion of horse racing in 1820 compared with 1779.

45 E. Bovill (1962) *English Country Life 1780–1830*, Oxford: Oxford University Press, pp. 50, 62. E. Bovill (1959) *The England of Nimrod and Surtees 1815–1854*, Oxford: Oxford University Press, p. 11.

46 *M.Ex*, 29 Aug 1849.

47 *Bell's*, 6 April 1828.

48 *Bell's*, 28 March 1847. Holt, *Sport and the British*, pp. 61–2. Reid, 'Saint Monday', 82.

49 Bailey, *Leisure and Class*, pp. 12–13. *Bell's*, 27 Sept 1840, 20 Nov 1842, 11 June 1843.

50 *WMC*, 28 Dec 1833.

51 Walton and Poole, 'Lancashire Wakes', 120.

52 B. Harrison and B. Trinder (1969) *Drink and Sobriety in an Early Victorian Country Town: Banbury 1830–1860*, London: EHR, p. 7. M. Speak (1988) 'Social stratification and participation in sport', in J. Mangan (ed.) *Pleasure, Profit and Proselytism: British Culture and Sport at Home and Abroad 1700–1914*, London: Frank Cass, p. 46.

53 It might be objected that as we are only dealing with the amount of stakes placed upon an event it is misleading to refer to it as a 'commercial sporting culture'. However, it is clear that stakes were simply the most overt manifestation of this culture, for sponsors would devote resources to obtaining the best protagonist available, man or animal, in the pursuit of victory. Also, as we shall show in Chapter 7, there is substantial evidence of promoters staging events in order to glean revenue from spectators.

54 For instance, C. Grafton and P. Taylor (1991) *Government and the Economics of Sport*, London: Macmillan, pp. 2, 4–5.

Chapter 3

Sex, Sport and Sales: The Sporting Press

when he reads the stupid drivelling prints that degrade the English press;– when he considers who are the conductors of the prints, when he reflects on a Topham who commands The World, detailing as a matter of vast importance the vapid amusements and trivial actions of those who are really most contemptible.[1]

As the above demonstrates, by no means everyone approved of the news coverage presented by 'fashionable' papers such as Topham's *The World*, which included such ingredients as theatre, society gossip and sport. Despite this, the public appear to have had a substantial appetite for such 'drivel', especially sport. In fact, after 1792 sporting coverage effectively underwent a revolution and the creation of the national sporting culture that we identified in the previous chapter owed a great deal to such improvements in communications.

While, as we shall see, it would be mistaken to imagine that before 1793 the press did not notice sport, coverage was, by comparison with that of the Napoleonic wars, slight. Between 1793 and 1815 the press transformed the sporting culture, effectively rendering it national. In the years following Waterloo, especially from the 1830s, this was amplified still further with 'weeklies' helping to organize commercial sport. While this magnified the amount of activity, the lack of organizations to supervise events led to a vast increase in corruption, particularly in working-class sports. By ventilating this corruption, the press eroded the image of sport. The 'monthlies' went still further, refusing to acknowledge many of such activities as sport, thus destroying the unity that the culture had possessed in the earlier period. The effect of this was to nourish the idea among the social elite that sport should be conducted without the possibility of financial gain. Thus, a new 'amateur' ethos gained ascendency, compartmentalizing sport along ostensibly moral lines. The effect of this was to deprive commercial sport of considerable finance and expertise, thus impeding its development.

This chapter consists of three principal parts, based upon chronology. The first considers the period before 1793, whereas the second is devoted to the French wars (1793–1815), and the third the years between 1816 and 1850.

The Period before 1793

The eighteenth century witnessed an enormous expansion in the volume and variety of published material owing to increases in literacy and the availability of literature. It has been estimated that by the end of the century some 65 per cent of adult males were literate.[2] It was somewhat ironic that much of this expansion stemmed from the establishment of Sunday schools by the Evangelical movement. Former pupils were often not content with the vast stocks of 'improving' literature that were produced, preferring instead some of the myriad of alternative sources of published entertainment.[3] While a large number of 'chap-books' – small, cheap works sold by hawkers – had long been available, during the century this expanded considerably, with a plethora of small publishers appearing, producing anything which they regarded as having commercial potential, and retailing them through a comprehensive infrastructure which effectively embraced the whole country.[4] Additionally, more expensive material, such as newspapers, which would have usually been beyond the financial reach of most working men, was made available in pubs, coffee houses and reading rooms.[5] The potential of sporting material was soon recognized by astute entrepreneurs and newspapers began to include reports of events.[6] The lack of a copyright law meant that authors were continually confronted by the problem of piracy, a difficulty that afflicted one of the earliest sporting writers, Godfrey.[7] In 1729 *An Historical Record of all Horse-matches Run*, a periodical devoted to the most popular sport, horse racing, made its appearance, attaining an initial subscription list worth £83, its agents having acquired orders in coffee houses and taverns.[8] It was succeeded by *The Sporting Kalendar* (1751) and *The Racing Calendar* (1769), both of which adopted its format. They all sold very well and were able to provide the latest information because they appeared every fortnight.[9] Eighteenth-century newspapers concentrated on providing information, which was often solicited from both readers and advertisers, the latter using the medium to excite consumption.[10] Their readership had a voracious desire for instant intelligence and even weekly provincial newspapers sought to supply the very latest London news by 'express'. London papers serving a 'fashionable' audience, such as *The World,* prided themselves on the immediacy of their sports coverage, boasting in 1787 that they had given the result of a prize-fight a mere six hours after its completion. Unfortunately, they had recorded the wrong fighter as winning.[11]

As the century progressed the range of newspapers covering sport increased. In fact, the MP William Windham criticized the amount of attention the subject received in the press, believing that the space would be better served dealing with politics. Despite his public protestations, the Windham archive reveals that he, like many in the population, was an avid collector of newspaper columns on sport.[12] This need was identified by John Wheble, an experienced publisher and proprietor who had run a number of newspapers, and in October 1792 the first number of his shilling monthly, *The Sporting Magazine,* made its appearance. The periodical was reasonably catholic in its choice of material, an approach resembling that of many contemporaries, such as *The Gentleman's Magazine.*[13] Principally, however, it focused upon sport, though its definition of the subject incorporated everything from comparatively esoteric discussions on art through to vivid accounts of salacious gossip. To an extent, this simply reflected a desire to present material which its readers would find of interest to them. However, the editor clearly had a notion of the material that constituted 'sport' and in 1797 declared that this included agriculture, a 'business' 'analogous' 'to that of sporting'.[14] Moral criteria did not exert any influence on the sporting activities that were contained within the columns; everything from bull-baiting through to pugilism gaining inclusion, the editor deprecating 'whatever tends to the suppression of sporting, reduces the number of articles suitable for our miscellany'.[15] He was rather more guarded concerning literary material, though his moral stance was inconsistent, with articles such as 'Bullock in a brothel' clearly contradicting his declaration that the periodical was 'for all the family'.[16]

Much of the information in *The Sporting Magazine* stemmed from the readers themselves, who were urged to contribute material.[17] The editor insisted that information should be accurate, rejecting contributions where he had 'doubts'.[18] Readers would also respond to one another's letters and sharp debates often occurred within the magazine's columns, acting as an additional check on the accuracy of material.[19] The editor refused to settle disputes but was very conscientious in supplying the best information available to him.[20] Cumulatively, this provided an immense amount of detail. As we have seen, interest in published information on sport long preceded *The Sporting Magazine*. However, the journal transformed the subject by providing a treatment that was both deeper and more wide reaching in scope. Unlike its predecessors, it embraced everything that was regarded as 'sport' and aimed at presenting an accurate, accessible record. By doing so, it mapped the subject out, presenting a thematic framework which others were to develop. A range of issues that were to become associated with established sporting literature first became accessible to a wider audience via its columns. A consideration of the ways this was accomplished forms the subject of the second part of this chapter.

The French Wars

The principal contributions which *The Sporting Magazine* in particular, and the sporting press in general, made can be broadly divided into four categories.[21] First, the sporting press ventilated a great deal of opinion of a political, social and moral nature, relating to sporting activity. Second, it generated a large number of facts. These included verbatim copies of the rules governing particular sports, accurate calendars of forthcoming sporting activity, detailed reports of events and results, as well as tips on developing and improving skill. A third category, stemming in part from the other two, consisted of writing of an historical and biographical character, and richly detailed reports and illustrations, through which it was endeavoured to construct an image of sporting activity. The fourth category concerns the production of popular material, thus transforming sport into a commercially lucrative industry.

Our first category, the dissemination of opinions of a political, social and moral nature concerning sport, found its most strident expression in a series of pamphlets beginning in 1792, mainly by Pigott, entitled *The Jockey Club*, which used sporting themes to make explicit criticisms of leading social and political figures.[22] Such literature had much in common with contemporary productions which pandered to the public taste for scandal. While the pamphlet sold well, both the publisher and bookseller were imprisoned and in the years that followed the government's legislation against seditious literature did much to curb such expression.[23] Wheble, himself, was no stranger to these problems. During the period when he had edited *The English Chronicle* he had been a good friend of Wilkes and even faced imprisonment for the paper's radical contents.[24] However, by the time he came to edit *The Sporting Magazine,* he had rejected such overt personal attacks, even insisting that he would 'avoid politics'.[25] Yet on occasions the veil was lifted, particularly in a series of biographies, 'The Sporting Gallery', where criticisms were unleashed on virtually every important person except the King.[26] Although such personalized attacks were rare, the sporting press was far from placidly acquiescent to the status quo, occasionally making acid comparisons between the money expended on keeping horses and the miserable pay of labourers.[27] While criticism of government policy, such as a piece in *The Sporting Magazine* of 1795 denouncing the war with France, was extremely isolated, there was a willingness to attack influential groups, such as the Society for the Suppression of Vice.[28] These were often denounced for their 'hypocrisy'. Direct intervention in contemporary legal cases concerning sport was only really possible in newspapers, especially dailies. This only occurred on one occasion, when the athlete Wilson was arrested on orders stemming from the Blackheath justices. In that particular instance press reports played an important part in the whole dispute. The initial arrest of Wilson, on charges of creating a breach of the peace, may well have stemmed from reports in *The Times*, which stated that the pedestrian's daily performances were creating anarchy in the area.[29] After his arrest, the press, interacting with influential local people who were sympathetic to him, agitated on his behalf, transforming him into a nationally popular figure.[30]

Throughout the entire period a large portion of the press appear to have regarded themselves as having a duty to reform abuses and encouraged their readers to submit details of such cases.[31] This manifested itself in attacks on the inequalities stemming from the legal framework governing sport, especially the Game Laws. Inevitably the issues raised by the Game Laws resulted in criticism of particular statutes and demands for their reform. While such sentiments posed an implicit challenge to the relevant inequalities within the social system, in no sense was the overall structure criticized. The Game Laws affected readers in a very practical manner and much of their interest probably reflected this.

Of an altogether different nature was the developing concern for the protection and welfare of animals, which was caused by abstract, moral, impulses. *The Sporting Magazine* took animal cruelty seriously from the very first, often discussing the issues involved and publishing articles representing a wide spectrum of views. Its denunciation of pigeon shooting and horse feats anticipated that of other papers dealing with sport, such as *The Times* and *The Weekly Dispatch*.[32] Such issues transcended sporting literature and by the early nineteenth century many provincial newspapers, especially those in areas where local festivities included bull-baits and such like, paid increasing attention to these moral concerns.[33] However, as with the Game Laws, the issues raised by notions relating to animal cruelty, had profound political overtones. Attempts were made, especially by socially privileged groups, such as the Society for the Suppression of Vice, to legislate against particular lower class sports because of their cruelty, while leaving similar activities, against which the same accusations could be levelled, untouched because their exponents were wealthy. *The Times* opposed legislation of any sort against cruel sports for pragmatic reasons, because it believed that such pursuits kept the lower orders from indulging in political subversion.[34] Most other relevant publications adopted a moral stand, tempered by ideals of rational justice. This tended to mean that they saw little moral difference between the cruel sports indulged in by the lower orders and those of their social betters. The coverage these issues received was often extensive, occasionally interacting with debates in parliament. Cumulatively, this fostered a great awareness and helped to mould public sensitivity. In fact, in 1813, *The Sporting Magazine* stimulated an attack on the moral behaviour of the aristocracy by exposing the cruelty practised by members of the Royal Stag Hounds. It was revealed that they had a deliberate policy of cutting the legs of the deer they were about to chase in order to prevent it running too fast.[35] Such revelations created a storm of criticism, demonstrating that the practices of the established political order were being judged by new moral concerns which projected far greater attention to the welfare of animals. This attitude was extended to include humans, and attention was focused on both the amount and type of violence that was regarded as legitimate within society. Essentially this involved a debate on the validity of pugilism and duelling as modes of resolving disputes and fostering honour and courage.[36] Given the fact that one of the principal justifications for sport was that it was regarded as creating military and social discipline necessary for a nation at war, sporting writers were generally supportive of these practices. Yet such adherence was not without qualification and reservations were expressed about the deployment of pugilism and duelling in particular circumstances, especially when they resulted in deaths.

By presenting a spectrum of opinions on the way the legislation and the ideas of the wider society affected sport, the sporting press assisted in educating its readership. However, its influence rarely extended beyond this, even on issues on which it appears to have taken a lead, such as animal cruelty. These only gained national prominence when they were adopted by influential groups, whose views were often hopelessly at variance with those of the sporting press. For instance, while the Society for the Suppression of Vice devoted substantial attention to attacks on animal cruelty, its wider programme endeavoured to curb many recreations, and was anathema to the sporting press. Thus, although by providing a forum for its readers' views *The Sporting Magazine* and its contemporaries assisted in creating public opinion on political, social and moral matters, its influence was slight.

In our second category, however, the compilation and exposition of facts, sporting literature exerted far more influence. *The Sporting Magazine* had a very specific aim – the compilation of accurate factual information which would 'enable the reader to avoid betting disadvantageously'. Abstract philosophizing was rejected, 'for we profess ourselves sportsmen not moralists' and gamblers in almost every activity, from cards to cricket, were provided with detailed results and useful background information, such as horse pedigrees.[37] Each month space would be devoted to 'Sporting Intelligence'. Such information was transmitted by readers and evidently rendered verbatim, such as:

> On the 8th instant, William Harris, miller, of Peterborough, undertook for the trifling bet of two guineas, to walk from Peterborough bridge to Wisbech bridge, and back again (42 miles) in seven hours and fifty six minutes; and after resting himself twenty five minutes, he returned to Peterborough, amidst a crowd of spectators.[38]

Those pursuing field sports were given easily understood explanations of the terms used in the Game Laws and an outline of their effects. Tips were offered on numerous sports and these embraced an ability range from the beginner through to the more experienced. Practical matters, such as buying horses and training dogs, were also dealt with. In addition, the codes of the laws for various sports, such as horse racing, cricket, boxing and cock-fighting, were provided, verbatim, and this assisted in disseminating them nationally, creating the possibility of establishing rules that could be adhered to throughout the country. They also introduced readers to new sports, providing a description of steeplechasing as early as 1793, and an outline of curling, a game unknown to English readers.[39]

From January 1793 *The Sporting Magazine* contained an almanac, detailing forthcoming horse races and such like, as well as listing important dates in the calendar, notably the start and finish of the shooting season.[40] This effectively mapped out the sporting year and was a feature emulated by newspapers. However, the more frequent appearance of newspapers enabled them to carry up-to-date details of forthcoming events, as well as adverts. They enjoyed a particular advantage in covering longer events, especially pedestrian matches that were spread over a number of weeks, because they could provide regular bulletins. However, although newspapers were able to provide information far more quickly, they were unable to devote as much space, and even their most copious accounts were likely to be overshadowed by those of *The Sporting Magazine*, which would sometimes provide two or more reports of the same event.[41]

As we have seen, the readership of the sporting press was presented with a well organized structure of accurate, empirical information. Within it, sport had a calendar of events that were conducted according to set rules by competitors that had acquired skills by proper training. The information in the press made this world comprehensible and accessible. Yet, in addition to these facts, writers provided further dimensions by creating an image of sport that transcended the everyday world. It is to this, our third category, that we must now turn. The creation of an attractive, interesting, image for sport was accomplished in three ways. First, journalists and artists would present sporting activity and the sporting world as glamorous and fashionable in itself, by way of prose and art. Second, writers would pay great attention to the characters of sportsmen, which were portrayed as being of interest. Third, histories of sports would be produced, setting contemporary developments in a much wider chronological context.

In 1811 *The Manchester Mercury* provided a description of the meaning of the following pugilistic idioms: 'The fancy, A glutton, A milling, A Doubler, A floorer, The knock-down was clean, Nobbing, A rally, Dibbing'.[42] Throughout the period, the columns of the press helped to disseminate, if not perhaps create, the unique vocabulary which was to be employed in pugilism. 'The Fancy', a widely used slang term for those associated with robust sports in which gambling played an important part, communicated in a type of sub-English, which was full of vigorous phrases. It was a slang that seems to have had strong underworld links and was adopted by the boxing fraternity.[43] All communications from pugilists appeared in its parlance, one from the American, Molineaux, 'To The Military Lifeguards Man' read:

> As my late unsuccessful combat has set the knowing ones afloat to find another big man to mill me, and having just got flash enough to know some of the phrases, by which I understand you are the man I am next to contend with, I hereby challenge you for three hundred guineas, and as much more as your friends think proper any time betwixt this and Christmas.[44]

The origin of this language is rather unclear, though many of the challenges issued in it by near illiterate boxers were clearly the work of journalists.[45] A vital figure in its dissemination and popularization was the author and dramatist, Pierce Egan, who utilized much of the vocabulary in his history of boxing that appeared in 1812. This slang was uniquely tailored for the terms used in pugilism and was thus distinctively British, utterly thwarting French attempts to translate, which were always ridiculed.[46] Contemporaries found it seductive and it successfully conveyed the glamorous, dangerous, image that sport loved to project.

Another vital force in creating the public image of sport as something glamorous and powerful was art. Engravings of sporting subjects had always been part of *The Sporting Magazine*, larger versions of the prints being sold separately. *The Sporting Magazine* prided itself on cultivating a taste for art among its country readership, and provided highly descriptive reviews of exhibitions, focusing particularly on pictures involving animals.[47] Such concern implicitly conferred a social prestige on the subject. Many important artists, such as Gilpin and Moreland, were involved in this enterprise. Both sportsmen and animals tended to be presented in heroic terms, with the emphasis being on the bravery rather than the cruelty within a scene. Generally, the vitality of animals was highly respected and at a bull-bait the artist sought to 'portray the courage and contending passion of the majestic bull'.[48] Such presentations had a robust immediacy that completely circumvented all moral problems. Although the scene that was being presented was potentially very cruel, the viewer's attention was absorbed by the strength and courage of the animal.

The second facet in the creation of an interesting image for sport was its concern for the characters of particular sportsmen, especially biography. The sporting press covered the various quarrels between sportsmen in some detail, particularly that between Mr Flint and Colonel Thornton. They also focused on the low life led by certain individuals, such as the painter, Moreland, who regularly produced commissions while in prison in order to secure release from debt. In this they were simply pandering to contemporary desires for salacious material and 'character assassination'.[49] Yet, predominantly, they were analytic, applying a scientific approach to the composition of biography. Generally speaking, only infamous criminals among the lower orders received personal attention in the press.[50] However, sporting literature often focused on the characters of individuals who had displayed a significant aptitude for particular sports, regarding them as worthy subjects for both biographies and obituaries. Some, such as Wilson, an itinerant vendor, even received a highly detailed biography in *The Times*.[51] While such an occurrence demonstrated that sporting literature focused attention on a wider social spectrum than was customary elsewhere, such accounts tended to be aridly factual.

Alternatively, there were two other approaches to biography. Pierce Egan's *Boxiana* presented pugilists, who were men from a humble social sphere, in dramatic, fictionalized terms, elevating them to immortal status. By contrast, *The Sporting Magazine*, though its reports often represented the activities of individuals as heroic, treated the characters of the protagonists in a more abrasive manner. While it was quite willing to satirize the whole genre of biography, as with 'The history of Pero – a buck hound', generally it adhered to a very exacting criteria which stressed the requirements of balance and honesty.[52] The aim was to provide a scientific analysis of the character of the biography's subject. This was the approach they adopted in every case save that of Lord Derby, where they declared 'that we touch on no part of the characters of Noblemen and Gentlemen whose portraits we give, except that which relates to their sporting transactions. Little pitiful biography of living character is beneath the dignity of literature'.[53] Aside from this, its biographies were ruthlessly honest, while endeavouring to be fair.[54] This could sometimes lead to a number of contradictory accounts of an individual appearing in the same journal, as with Lord Barrymore.[55] Often, obituaries were hard-hitting, such as that of the cock-feeder, Bromley, who 'considered it a degradation to hear their opinions or receive their instructions; although they were ostensible and pecuniary principals of the match, their ideas and admonitions were almost invariably held in the utmost contempt'.[56] Bromley was from the lower-orders, but many aristocrats, notably Lord Camelford, suffered stinging attacks. Thus, despite a certain good-humour, typified by entitling its obituary column 'Sportsmen under the turf', *The Sporting Magazine* was merciless in its treatment of characters, and many of them, both aristocrats and commoners, were revealed as being thoroughly unsavoury; Tattersall was greedy, Elwes mean, O'Kelly dishonest.[57] While the effect of the rest of *The Sporting Magazine* was to foster sport, such biographies must surely have detracted from this, portraying the sporting world as the domain of the dishonest.

The third facet in creating an interesting image for sport was the production of works of history. While the editor of *The Sporting Magazine* recognized that the assembling and organization of a mass of information was a very useful way of dealing with contemporary material, he was aware that a more analytic approach was necessary in accounts relating to the history of a sport. Previous to this books on subjects such as boxing had been concerned with giving instruction concerning its skills, providing only the briefest of histories.[58] By contrast, *The Sporting Magazine* provided the model for many later histories of boxing, firmly setting the contemporary sport within an historical context.[59] The editor's approach was revealed in his forthright condemnation of his (unnamed) predecessors who presented 'a jumble of facts and falsities, without order and connection'.[60] Instead, he rendered a careful delineation of changes in style, and endeavoured to explain the reasons for this.

Cumulatively, the sporting press's presentation of sport portrayed an interesting world, set firmly in history, that was peopled by characters. This exciting, attractive, factually based, up-to-the-minute, sporting literature, enjoying a national circulation, transformed sport into an industry; the subject of our fourth concern.

The national circulation of sporting literature meant that the events they recorded reached a very wide geographical area. Likewise, the regularity of the appearance of sporting information, especially the columns in weekly papers, increased the excitement the reports created. These reports, which were often highly detailed, were the life blood of sporting literature, serving to attract and develop the readers' interest. The product of all this publicity was that many sporting figures attained national fame, the exploits of the pedestrian, Wilson, for example, attracting four books.[61] When the boxer, Molineaux, visited Brighton he was regularly mobbed.[62] Another boxer, the Game Chicken, was so famous that fraudsters made a good living from impersonating him.[63] Similarly, a madman claimed he was the boxer Tom Cribb.[64] During the pedestrian exploits of both Captain Barclay in 1808 and Wilson in 1815, the surrounding area was filled with spectators, many from far off, drawn by media reports. Barclay's exploit, which involved walking 1,000 miles in 1,000 hours, stimulated many similar attempts, the most bizarre of which involved a clergyman attempting to read six chapters from the Bible every hour for six weeks: an exploit that was terminated when the protagonist fell into a coma.[65] Most famously of all, the equestrian, Mrs Thornton, was imitated throughout the country, especially in theatres.[66]

The press did not simply reflect sporting culture – in pursuit of their commercial interest they transformed it. Columns often contained challenges from competitors and they also ventilated the numerous disputes that arose.[67] In one case, that relating to the pedestrian, Eaton, in 1815, there is strong evidence that interested commercial parties utilized the press to instigate a smear campaign against him.[68] Reports of the latest gossip on sporting figures served to whet the public's appetite for information and this desire was exploited, though rarely by the protagonists themselves, with the production of books aimed at cashing in on exploits such as Captain Barclay's match. The most adroit manipulation of this public craving for truth was by the jockey, Chiffney. In 1791, while riding a horse belonging to the Prince of Wales, he had been involved in a very dubious, and highly publicized race, and in 1803 exploited the public's immense appetite for such gossip by issuing a small biography, at the high price of five guineas to subscribers.[69] Similarly, the commercial success enjoyed by *The Sporting Magazine* showed that there was a ready market for a range of works introducing and explaining particular sporting skills. These gradually appeared, as in boxing (1807), pedestrianism (1812) and cock-fighting (1815).[70] Treatises were also produced on practical problems related to sport, such as veterinary science. One of these was translated into French.[71] There was also a market for books uniting sport and tourism, notably the imaginative, and highly unreliable, record by Thornton of his excursion in Scotland, where he claimed to have used dogs to hunt fish.[72]

Cumulatively, the emergence of sporting literature, transformed the commercial viability of almost every sport, by generating increased public attention. The growth was mutual, sport and sporting literature interacting with one another. *The Sporting Magazine* was a sound commercial proposition from the very first and by 1795 it was selling 3,000 copies a month, to a readership that appears to have belonged to the middle and upper income groups.[73] This generated a minimum of £1,800 a year which was quite good, though obviously dwarfed by the revenue of most London papers, that were estimated to be selling an average of 42,000 copies each every month, about £8,400 a year.[74] Newspapers featuring sport, such as *Bell's Weekly Messenger*, also did well, despite some difficulties at its commencement in 1796. By 1805 it was achieving sales of 11,500 every week, which probably meant that it was reaching some 60,000 people.[75] Sport was becoming recognized as a vital ingredient in generating circulation and received increasing attention from the press.

This growth was reflected in other markets. The number of picture galleries specializing in sporting material increased.[76] By 1800 there were numerous prints of sporting subjects being produced, with books of them selling at around six shillings each.[77] Eight years later, these included pictures of sporting heroes.[78]

Many new books which aimed at imparting particular sports skills appeared on the market. These were rarely published by subscription and were obviously aimed at a mass readership. This was clearly perceived as a substantial audience, Osbaldeston claiming to have paid £500 for the secrets in *The British Sportsman,* his latest book, copies of which cost just a guinea.[79] The profit generated by the sales of books was sufficient to result in a number of court cases over such matters as the rights to draw particular horses, royalties for prose, and related issues.[80]

Although *The Sporting Magazine* dealt with many sport-related issues from the wider society, it exerted little influence. The major contribution that it made was to disseminate, on a regular basis, information on every type of sport, nationally. By doing so, the sporting press identified a commercial market which they did much to expand. Their success, in turn, prompted other elements of the media to intensify their efforts, resulting in further books, prints and newspaper columns, all devoted to sport. *The Sporting Magazine* provided a framework within which sporting knowledge could be organized. On the most fundamental level, information on rules and expertise was made accessible, and the journal's columns utilized for a dialogue between readers.[81] Sport was also given a new structure with the publication of a sporting calendar. From the conceptual point of view, the creation and production of sporting histories and biographies set contemporary developments in a wider context, inevitably affecting the way they were perceived. As we have seen, *The Sporting Magazine* pioneered and developed many ideas that were intrinsic to sporting literature. However, from the point of view of publicizing contemporary events, more immediate elements of the media, especially newspapers, exerted the principal influence.[82] They enjoyed a much wider, and less specialized, readership and also appeared more regularly. This meant that they could stimulate and foster excitement, a crucial element in generating public interest. Throughout the Napoleonic period the sporting press improved the quality of sporting activity and magnified the attention which the public focused upon it, effectively creating what might be termed a 'national culture'.

The Sporting Press after 1815

The years immediately following Waterloo witnessed the appearance of a torrent of diverse printed matter, including many overtly radical productions. Despite government prosecutions, the latter blossomed, but their content was untypical, for the principal aim of most of the material was to entertain. Much of it was cheaply produced ephemera, typified by the chap-book, though the techniques that were employed, such as woodblock illustrations, soon manifested themselves in Sunday newspapers; a medium that was regarded as innately subversive by virtue of appearing on the Sabbath.[83]

Until at least 1830 a great deal of information on sporting activity was derived from ephemera, such as free or cheap handbills, or transmitted orally, by bellmen and other officials.[84] Yet such sources were increasingly superseded by the regular appearance of detailed coverage within the sporting press, both newspapers and specialist periodicals. As we saw earlier, *The Sporting Magazine*, despite covering every sport, included regular columns on art, drama and such like. Similarly, newspapers were extremely catholic in their contents, focusing upon any subject which might entertain its readers, including politics, scandal, crime and sport.[85] Given that sport was just a facet of a newspaper's content, the scale of their coverage was dwarfed by that of the specialist sporting press, but they shared the same definition of what constituted sport and this embraced everything from bull-baiting to pugilism. By 1850 this consensus was replaced by an antagonistic diversity concerning the activities that were regarded as 'sport'. Similarly, the attention which the press devoted to the corruption in various sports meant that the image of such activities became degraded. In this part of the chapter, the reasons for these changes are explored. This examination consists of three sections. The first, examines the way changes in the wider society expanded the press. In the second, the interactions between various developments that were internal to the press is considered. The final piece assesses the impact that such changes had on the image of sport. It is to the first, the impact that changes in the wider society had on the press, that we now turn.

By the 1820s Britain was spanned by a network of coaching stations, enabling the rapid dissemination of information. This included sports results, the early communication of which was of such commercial value that bets were taken on the speed of their delivery.[86] While this yielded impressive achievements, it taking just three and a half hours for the result of Doncaster's St Leger to arrive at Manchester, the onset of the railway and telegraph in the 1840s transformed everything.[87] Previously, detailed news from London had taken 13 hours to reach Manchester, whereas the telegraph transmitted it almost instantly.[88] More profoundly, the introduction of the penny post in 1840 meant that information from a whole stratum of the population appeared in the press. Before this, postage had been expensive and as it was payable by the recipient, the press had discouraged such communications.[89] An important expansion also occurred in the literacy rates of the population, Schofield suggesting that by 1840 as many as 75 per cent of the working class may have possessed a rudimentary reading knowledge.[90] In 1836 changes in government regulations concerning the stamp duty enabled the prices of newspapers to fall and their size to increase, improvements amplified by developments in steam printing machinery.[91] Generally, with the exception of short-lived legislation in 1850 that prevented the delivery of newspapers on Sunday, parliament assisted the dissemination of literature.[92] Cumulatively, this expanded the market enormously, transforming the potential profitability. While the costs of newspapers and periodicals generally precluded their purchase by the lower orders, they were available in pubs and coffee houses.[93] 'Improving' institutions, such as Mechanics' Institutes, rarely stocked such matter, because their administrators considered sport irreligious and deprecated newspapers for fostering political discussion.[94] As we can see, a variety of occurrences in the wider society, related to a general expansion within the economy, were transforming the potential of the press. In our second section we will examine how such factors interacted with internal developments within the press.

In the period following the Napoleonic wars there was a large expansion in betting facilities, enabling an increasingly socially diverse participation, thus magnifying interest in sport. This revolutionized the commercial potential of the sporting press and led to increased competition to secure this expanding market. While the biggest selling newspaper of the period, *The Times,* contained just 24 sporting items in 1816, *Bell's Weekly Messenger* pioneered a more extensive treatment, devoting space to the subject every Sunday.[95] However, its bitter rival, *The Weekly Dispatch,* transformed coverage, allowing its expert journalist, Pierce Egan, a full page each week to deal with a variety of sports.[96] His reports, which incorporated London slang, were self-confident celebrations of English life in general and 'national' sport in particular. The following account of a Russian prince's visit is typical:

> The Grand Duke Nicholas honoured the milling circle with his presence, accompanied by Lord Yarmouth and several amateurs of the highest order; it being presumed that the Grand Duke's knowledge of the English nation would be incomplete, and his tour not finished, if he had returned home without witnessing the old English sport of boxing. The grand caterer of the day, to make it all right, and as a sort of wind-up to the scene, ordered the game bull to be exhibited, and a let-go match by the dogs, for a silver collar. The Grand Duke took his place in a covered wagon at an early period, when a flag was flying to signalize the royal stand.

A report of the boxing match followed, won by Fisher:

> Fisher, upon getting on his clothes, was introduced to stand, *sans cérémonie*, to the notice of the Grand Duke, by Richmond. The Duke, in return for his mark of attention, not only took off his hat to the conqueror, but shook him heartily by the hand, with all the cordiality of an Englishman. He seemed very attentive to the battle and made several remarks to the gentlemen of his suite.

A bull-bait then occurred, and Nicholas:

> appeared much surprised at the gameness displayed by the English bull-dogs, in their determination to pin the bull. These dogs were of the first order, and afforded not only much amusement and laughter to his Imperial Highness, but also to the plebeian multitude. The bull, at length, broke loose from the stake; and, to describe the consternation, scampering, laughing and shouting, that took place, would require the pencil of a Hogarth.

Egan concluded with a celebration of popular culture:

> every thing was conducted with the utmost regularity, and his Imperial Highness had a

good opportunity of witnessing the independence and humour of the English people, in the enjoyment of their sports.[97]

Such reports meant that sport was second only to the Queen Caroline scandal in generating circulation.[98] There was also an established market for horse-racing intelligence, provincial papers, such as *The Manchester Mercury*, carrying a regular weekly column from 1819.[99] The popularity of sport was such that newspapers whose 'Methodist' editors opposed its inclusion faced financial disaster, a writer noting: 'a well circulated provincial paper, formerly much distinguished for its turf intelligence, has become nearly rejected for the puritanical cant of its editor'. Also, 'the present *Times*, after having sillily endeavoured to abuse as barbarous the science of pugilism, is at length obliged to retrace its steps and give an account of a battle, driven to this by its loss of customers'.[100]

Despite the fact that by the early 1820s there were a large number of newspapers and periodicals competing for the sporting market, their contents were similar, reflecting a consensus in the perceived requirements of their readership. Thus, they provided copies of sporting rules and relevant government legislation, with explanations where necessary, as well as helpful advice on the cultivation of a particular skill and warnings of possible problems.[101] They also sold goods from their offices. Additionally, by publishing challenges from readers and letters on suggested rules, they allowed wider participation in the sporting culture.[102] Significantly, they were reluctant to become involved in arbitrating betting disputes, and their most important contributions were the detailed lists of results and forthcoming events, especially information on betting.[103] The public was becoming increasingly adept at utilizing the sporting press to publicize events, often slipping them in as unpaid advertisements by masquerading as bulletins on a pedestrian's progress.[104] The principal difference between the sporting coverage offered by newspapers stemmed from the personalities of those writing the columns. After 1815 sporting journalists ceased to be shadowy figures, with papers boasting about employing particular writers, using them to boost circulation. Two of the principal ones were Egan and Kent, both of whom were renowned for the descriptive style of their reports, and knowledge of the inner workings of the betting ring.[105] Journalists were often regarded as 'insiders', possessing great insight into the chances of various competitors. This sometimes led to attempts being made to bribe them.[106] Some editors were defiantly independent, notably Dowling, editor of *Bell's*, who, in 1824, declared:

> we are not identified with any party amongst the Sporting Men – and that, though continuing mixing (for our editorial purposes) in that class of society, denominated in the slang of the day 'the fancy', we are personally unknown to every individual of the fraternity.[107]

At the beginning of the period *The Sporting Magazine* was the fourth best selling monthly periodical in London.[108] While it was still badly organized, information on varying topics simply being heaped together, and occasionally prone to copy articles from newspapers, the coverage it offered was excellent, embodied by the detailed calendar of forthcoming events that appeared every month. Yet such supremacy soon ended. Improvements in communications generated rapid information dissemination, and this inevitably favoured the daily and weekly press, rather than the monthly, especially those that began devoting serious coverage to sport.[109] Consequently, sales of *The Sporting Magazine* shrank to just 1,500 by 1822, leading the editor to introduce a new approach to subject matter. From 1819 fox-hunting had been given increasing coverage, with the first comprehensive list of British packs appearing two years later.[110] However, it was the editor's decision to employ Nimrod, at lavish cost, from 1822 to 1827, to furnish beautifully written pieces on fox-hunting, that commenced the transformation of *The Sporting Magazine*. Despite an increase in price, Nimrod's articles doubled sales, inevitably leading the magazine to pay still greater attention to fox-hunting.[111] Nonetheless, contents remained catholic, including, for instance, dog-fighting. Additionally, coverage became more contemporary and the lay-out improved.[112]

By the middle of the 1820s the sporting press was becoming far more accomplished in utilizing the expanded opportunities presented by improvements in communications. Great efforts were made to furnish readers with accurate, up-to-date, information on all sports. Such comprehensiveness resulted in *Bell's* issuing a 'chronology of the ring' in 1826, which included details of all the major prize-fights of that year.[113] The sources for this encyclopaedic venture were readers and journalists. Readers were increasingly encouraged to submit news, though warned that their accounts must be 'verified'.[114] From 1824 *Bell's* began to employ 'expert' writers for particular sports, such as aquatics, and also sent journalists to cover events.[115] Although they were 'gentlemen', reporters had hard lives, there being few facilities for them, and they suffered persistently bad treatment at inns and were occasionally arrested at prize-fights.[116] Yet the reward for this effort was a new level of coverage, typified by the Aaron–Bateman fight of 1828, for which the paper gave four different accounts.[117] Stylistically, *Bell's*, by utilizing and expanding models that had probably been developed by Egan, created wonderfully structured reports of prize-fights. These consisted of a preamble detailing the venue and combatants, followed by a round-by-round description of the fight, concluding with an analysis of the conflict.[118] They also cultivated a sympathetic relationship with the sporting world, effectively giving fixtures free advertising. Editorially, the sporting newspapers adopted a highly combative approach, publishing material that was often bitterly critical of their own views and opening their columns to anyone.[119] By contrast, much of the mainstream press, *The Morning Post* for instance, refused to permit a right to reply.[120]

Although by 1820 vivid accounts of crime and politics, notably Peterloo, had established *The Weekly Dispatch* as a significant paper, much of its audience appeal depended upon a varied and compendious coverage of sport, which had made it the principal sporting organ. The scope of its contents was amplified by the paucity of sporting intelligence in other newspapers, as the minuscule coverage of *The Times*, just 58 items in 1825, demonstrated. In fact, much of the press was hostile towards sport, especially pugilism, though occasionally they would sponsor fights in order to report on the 'outrage'.[121] However, when *Bell's* appeared in 1822 *The Weekly Dispatch* confronted a serious rival and mounted a well orchestrated campaign of subversion, based upon bribing news vendors.[122] At first it worked, *Bell's* sales falling from 5,000 in 1823 to 2,600 by 1824. However, due to the initiatives outlined in the last paragraph, *Bell's* prospered, sales improving from 7,150 in 1826 to 25,000 by 1828, absorbing *Pierce Egan's Life in London* in the process, and exciting a great deal of jealousy.[123] *The Weekly Dispatch* was also enjoying considerable prosperity, sales having improved from 11,000 in 1828 to 20,000 in 1829, reaching 27,000 by 1830.[124] The 'radical explosion' in the press at the end of 1830 transformed the paper's status.[125] While later critics claimed that *The Weekly Dispatch* was 'blasphemous' and 'scurrilous' in its radicalism, contemporary editorials were 'loyal to the king', dismissing Cobbett as 'a firebrand'.[126] Similarly, their advocacy of reform throughout 1831 rarely intruded on sporting material. This persisted, and it is clear that when *The Weekly Dispatch* did decide, in 1834, to replace sport with increased political coverage, their decision was based upon sound commercial principles, their advocacy of 'the cause of the people' having produced weekly sales of 30,000.[127] Essentially, by presenting itself as the organ of radical opinion, a role for which *The Times* denounced it in 1840, *The Weekly Dispatch* obtained far more sales than it could have achieved by competing with *Bell's* to secure the sporting market. In fact, by 1837 the weekly sales of *Bell's* were 16,365, those of *The Weekly Dispatch,* 50,115.[128]

From the late 1820s agitation for political reform excited great popular attention. This was reflected in much of the new press, such as *The Poor Man's Guardian,* who ignored sport and were consequently unaffected by the remarkable growth of *Bell's*. By contrast, the sporting monthlies were quite unable to compete, as the failure of *The Annals of Sporting and Fancy Gazette,* a well run periodical with some 5,000 readers, that embraced every sport, demonstrated, and they were even forced to try and poach one another's subscribers.[129] However, the final factor forcing dramatic change upon *The Sporting Magazine* was the appearance, in May 1831, of a bitter rival, *The New Sporting Magazine*, operating in territory which had previously been effectively its own, namely field sports. *The New Sporting Magazine* aggressively defined its subject matter, specifically excluding lower-class activities such as pugilism because they were not 'respectable', and implicitly denouncing its older rival as a second-rate work.[130] Such charges were given an added bite because they were endorsed by Nimrod, the star writer who had left *The Sporting Magazine* after a bitter quarrel in 1827, and used the new periodical to denounce the plebeian behaviour of his erstwhile employer. These attacks had their effects. Conceding that it could no longer compete with the weeklies in lower-class sports, and fearing that its less elite diet might not appeal to a readership keen on field sports, *The Sporting Magazine* abandoned pugilism after August 1831, ostensibly because of its corruption, though continuing to report the still more fraudulent world of horse racing.[131] Two years later, in an effort to broaden its appeal it began again to cover pugilism, but soon found that this was not feasible.[132]

There was nothing unusual in the sporting press debating the morality of various activities. In their time, bull-baiting, cock-fighting, fox-hunting, sport on the Sabbath and such like, had attracted a variety of attention. From early on, the press recognized their role in curbing cruel practices, such as horse-feats, female pugilism and 'up and down fighting' (in which everything was allowed), by publicizing them, though on occasions even organs opposing cruel sports denounced the hypocrisy of those trying to interfere.[133] By the 1830s pugilism excited the most moral attention, though attacks upon it had a long history, *Bell's Weekly Messenger* initiating them in 1816.[134] Papers such as *The Times* denounced the practice because of 'national morals' and were echoed in this by rip-roaring exposés in minor journals, including some of the newer monthlies.[135] Defenders were decidedly fewer, though they did represent the political spectrum, including both the Liberal *Bell's* and the Tory *Blackwoods*, and were often critical of boxers' sins.[136] Yet all the participants in this debate, whether pro or anti, shared a common aim – the generation of circulation. By completely ignoring pugilism, and ceasing to define it as a sport, the established monthlies were severing the previously unified culture in two.

The primary aim of the commercial press was to increase circulation in order to attract advertising, 'the real sinews of the newspaper press'.[137] While a variety of subterfuges could be employed to boost sales figures, ultimately success depended upon pleasing the reader.[138] The monthlies were aimed at a much smaller, and wealthier, audience and therefore able to make a virtue of excluding many popular sports. By contrast, newspapers, no matter how 'respectable', were forced to solicit as widely as possible. Sport proved to be an increasingly marketable commodity and as the period wore on commanded ever greater space in newspapers. These incorporated a very broad spectrum, from the 1½d *Sporting Times*, through to *The Times*. There was a connection between legally dubious sports like boxing and 'scandalous' papers, such as *The Town*, whose editor was even given a benefit by pugilists in gratitude for his support.[139] Similarly, an influential journalist within the circle, Swift, wrote a book on boxing.[140] Yet many of boxing's firmest journalistic supporters, notably *Bell's*, were highly respectable. Despite 30 years of covering all sports, the paper was rarely sued and unlike several other papers they obeyed the government's ban on advertising sweepstakes.[141] Thus, although many of the papers favouring sport, such as *The Era* and *The Manchester and Salford Advertiser*, were owned by publicans, and thus regarded as morally and socially subversive by some, collectively, they were far from representing a radical counterculture.[142] Their primary aim was commercial success and to this end they embraced a number of contradictory strains, embodied by the journalist Pierce Egan. He was fiercely patriotic, especially to George IV, who he often praised for his British love of sport, but capable of unleashing violent social criticism.[143]

Ultimately, the inclusion of a particular sport was principally determined by financial factors, as the example of pugilism demonstrates. While certain fights, for instance the championship of 1841, excited little attention, and reports critical of particular boxers, such as Bendigo in 1845, resulted in *Bell's* being blacked in Nottingham, the profits from covering pugilism could be substantial, the fight between Bungaree and Broome boosted *Bell's* weekly circulation by over 12,000 copies.[144] Those papers that tried to reject pugilism tended to lose out. For instance, at its commencement in 1838 *The Era* declared that it would not cater for the 'depraved appetite' and include pugilism. Two years later, with their circulation falling, they commenced a regular column, increasing their sales by almost a third.[145] In fact, the paper came to depend upon sport and carefully nurtured this audience, aping *Bell's* prize-fight reports, and providing special pull-out news-sheets.[146] *The Era* had no monopoly on a willingness to sacrifice principle for profit. From 1845 *Bell's* had often denounced pugilism as 'corrupt' and when, in 1850, its editor, Dowling, was beaten up having refereed a championship fight, one might have expected the paper's patronage to end. Yet despite denouncing the corruption and bullying that had come to dominate pugilism, *Bell's* continued covering it: such reports were just too commercially profitable to do otherwise.[147]

The attitude of the mainstream press displayed similar financial motives. Despite its high moral tone, *The Morning Chronicle* spent lavishly to ensure the earliest possible intelligence of a prize-fight's result.[148] Sporting coverage in Sunday papers increased steadily, and certain journalists, such as 'Ruff', produced racing intelligence for many of the leading papers.[149] *The Sunday Times* carried no sport in 1830, but a whole page by 1840. Likewise, in the mid-1840s the volume of sport in *The News Of The World* experienced a big growth, though the paper's reputation still owed much to its capacity to be 'more freely offensive'.[150] Sport was less prominent in the daily press but by 1850 *The Times* contained 266 items, an elevenfold increase over 1816. It was also prominent in many provincial organs, though their capacity to publicise forthcoming events was impeded by legislation which treated such material as advertising.[151]

From the late 1830s the role of the sporting newspaper attained a new significance. Communications from readers multiplied, and by the mid-1840s *Bell's* was receiving 1,500 letters a week.[152] The infusion of so much information and the desire to retain and cultivate this readership, led the press into areas undreamt of by Wheble, the original editor of *The Sporting Magazine*. *Bell's* prided itself on transforming the popularity of various sports, and with a circulation of over 20,000 a week, was the ideal medium for reaching fans and therefore able to attract substantial advertising, as well as utilizing the offer of free publicity to entice cooperation from sportsmen.[153] Lacking plausible rivals, *The Era* never attaining a weekly circulation above 5,000, the editorial power possessed by *Bell's* was considerable.

As with sporting news from previous periods, much of the intelligence in *Bell's* stemmed from readers, often free-lancers. While they did occasionally dupe the editor, he appears to have managed to sift out most nonsense, dismissing claims concerning 'four and a half minute miles' as 'unlikely'.[154] Increasingly, sporting papers hired local men as correspondents, who would submit news of events in their vicinity. Additionally, there was more use of the journalistic assignment, with reporters sent off to Lancaster Regatta and such like.[155] The editor made significant efforts to obtain accurate information, checking results with referees and monitoring discrepancies.[156] This resulted in an extensive, factually correct, record, embodied by the end of year chronologies which *Bell's* produced for most sports between 1841 and 1849. Such information surpassed that of other sources in numerous fields. For instance, their coverage exceeded even the most diligent local paper, such as *The Manchester and Salford Advertiser*, which recorded 45 foot races in Manchester throughout the 1840s, *Bell's* noticing 884.[157]

While much of Dowling's role involved checking the accuracy of the information he received, he was far from being a passive observer. On the contrary, he often solicited specific types of information, such as inviting readers to comment upon particular rules.[158] The decision on the publication of material depended entirely upon his editorial stance. Thus, in an endeavour to end the practice of using 'bag foxes' (captured foxes that were released and hunted) in fox-hunting, the paper refused to publish reports of such events.[159] Its attitude towards a petition calling for 'Peace, order and fair play', started by some boxers, was altogether different; they publicized it and rendered the project every assistance because they believed it would help supply boxing with respectability.[160] *Bell's* was especially keen on exposing corruption in sport and would also warn its readers about the sharp practices found in particular adverts; even some in its own columns.[161]

There were, however, some limitations on *Bell's* capacity to obtain information. As the period progressed their contacts began to utilize *Bell's* desire to meet the public's craving for knowledge, and manipulated the provision of such a commodity. Cricketers such as Lilywhite, having obtained a monopoly on news from Lords, only provided intelligence to subscribers.[162] Access to information was also used to curb press criticism, sometimes directly, as when the Jockey Club framed rules to prevent the press cross-questioning riders after a race, or subtly, by restricting information to favoured journalists.[163] Even having obtained this raw data, a number of factors inhibited its publication. At the practical level, information had to be toned down or censored because it was likely to lead to libel action. Similarly, the press was also forced to restrict some news because its contents were of interest to the authorities. As cock-fights, dog-fights and steeplechases often contravened the law, journalists avoided providing details in order to protect the protagonists.[164] In 1843 reports from *Bell's* were used by the police to prosecute a boxer and from then on sensitive information was occasionally kept from the paper.[165] Nonetheless, the paper was regarded as the medium of sporting intelligence and when the Jockey Club declared a case involving Lord Cardoss outside their jurisdiction he appealed to *Bell's* to 'receive any evidence that can be brought forward to support the actual charge of my having bet against my own horse'.[166] While the spectacle of the most powerful body administering sport effectively handing a case over to the press for decision, might appear to represent the extent of the fourth estates power, it can be more accurately regarded as a blatant example of the weakness of the authorities that purported to regulate horse racing. By 1850 *Bell's* had made sustained efforts to regulate sporting activity but had signally failed to do so, as we shall now see.

The practice of publishing challenges in sporting publications was an old one. Whereas originally this had been restricted to letters from top personalities, especially pugilists, gradually the ability range catered for had been expanded, until, with the onset of the penny post, newspapers such as *Bell's* and *The Era,* contained a flood of communications incorporating every level of skill.[167] A typical example read 'Samuel Stokehouse of Leeds is open to run Richard Turner, on all fours, for from £25–50, or any other man in England. His money is ready at The Horse And Groom, Quarry Hill, Leeds'.[168] The editors of sporting columns were increasingly drawn in to the supervision of sport. Initially, they acted as stakeholders. *Bell's* commenced this role in 1828 and by the 1840s the involvement of newspapers was extensive.[169] This transformed commercial sport by dramatically increasing the volume of events. Every year, hundreds of competitors would submit postal orders to the offices of weekly papers.[170] This embraced every sport, including activities that had become illegal, for instance a cock-fight in 1850. By the 1830s *Bell's* editor, Dowling, was resolving large numbers of sporting disputes every week. The following was typical:

TO CORRESPONDENTS
ANSWERS

We have received a question from Birmingham respecting a dog-fight, which is not clearly put. The rule of the pit is, if a dog is let go before time is called he looses, but if there were neither umpires nor referee, it is a draw, as there is no person to decide disputes.[171]

The extent and complexity of this involvement grew, and though initially expressing a clear reluctance, by the 1840s Dowling was undertaking the task in almost clockwork fashion.[172] Such was his immersion in events that it was common for *Bell's* offices to be filled with competitors disputing the result of an event.[173] Inevitably, the cumulative roles performed by Dowling – publishing challenges, acting as stakeholder and deciding disputes – resulted in his organizing events. This was too much for *The Era*, who condemned Dowling and insisted that he 'should assume an impartial and independent position'.[174] Although this was doubtless prompted by jealousy, they had a point, as Dowling was losing his neutrality.

For many years Dowling had been an extremely public figure in London sporting circles, suffering threats and abuse 'while in the execution of our duties'.[175] Yet he believed himself immune from trouble, and when his watch was stolen while refereeing a prize-fight, declared:

> there is a freemasonry among the frequenters of the Ring, the value of which we have on more occasions than one experienced; and we are quite sure the gentleman that favoured us with his 'polite attention' must have made a mistake which, when discovered will be quickly rectified.[176]

The following week he learned that this was not to be and wrote:

> For the future we shall, and we advise all persons who regard their own safety to refuse the office of umpire, for they may be assured their personals and persons are not safe.[177]

This revelation had come too late for Dowling, for he had already become so heavily involved in the supervision of sport that the 1850 bout between Paddock and Bendigo could not occur without him being referee.[178] As it was, despite rendering an impartial decision, he was beaten up. So badly was he frightened by this, that, though as stakeholder he should have presented the victor with his winnings at a ceremony, he stayed away, the responsibility being discharged by a friend.[179] Dowling ceased attending fights.[180]

By then, it had become clear that the press, no matter how influential it regarded itself, could not supervise sport. In many ways, it always had been powerless. A trivial incident in 1847, perhaps one of many, summed up its impotence. There had been a dispute at the Lancaster Regatta and the authorities had written to Dowling for his verdict. His reply did not accord with their wishes so they ignored it.[181] Unusually for the period, no criminal activity was involved, the letters to *Bell's* were not full of lies, but the result was the same, effectively anarchy. Thus, by 1850, the limitations of the weekly sporting press were clear.

The position of the monthlies was far worse, the sales of both weeklies and books had marginalized their impact on the general public. By providing rapid intelligence and a more intimate relationship with their readers, weekly papers had completely outsold monthlies. Additionally, there was a substantial market for increasingly diverse and accessibly priced books, sometimes sold by hawkers. With print runs of 20,000 they attracted both lucrative advertising and top writers, such as North, yielding fees of £1,000.[182] Much of this material, imparting skills and detailing rules, would have previously been ideal for the monthlies. Their response to this twin threat was almost inevitable. They abandoned a whole range of sports, ostensibly because they were not 'respectable' and concentrated on a select market. Most monthlies did not even recognise the existence of pugilism and other lower-class activities, dismissing them as 'those sports which have a tendency to demoralise will be altogether avoided'.[183] While such a response probably extended their life, their general impact dissolved. For instance, in 1836 *The New Sporting Magazine* had an annual turnover of about £2,000, *Bell's* had at least ten times that.[184] Despite Prince Albert patronizing the various monthlies dealing with field sports in 1841, both *The Sportsman* and *The Sporting Review* were absorbed by *The New Sporting Magazine* in 1845, and all three were consumed by *The Sporting Magazine* the following year.[185] By then, that periodical had long occupied a nostalgic world of field sports, represented by a detailed country diary and fictional works set in a previous age.[186] The journal continued to reach, and represent, many of the socially elite, especially in an older, rural, England, but ignored the mass audience. In fact, as the failure of *The Field* in 1853 demonstrated, a weekly devoted exclusively to field sports was a poor commercial venture, simply underlining how split the sporting world had become.[187]

Judging by the views of The Select Committee on Newspaper Stamps, which met in 1851, the respectability of both the press and its readers was improving. While conceding that many in the working-class could not understand *The Times*, they believed that there was an increasing convergence within the general press, with the worst elements disappearing.[188] By contrast, during the post-Napoleonic period a great divergence occurred within the sporting press. This stemmed from two factors which undermined the image of sport. First, the corruption present in competitive sport was scrutinized by both the sporting and national press and formed the subject of a number of didactic novels.[189] Second, a variety of activities ceased to be included within the monthlies' definition of 'sport' on account of their lack of respectability. During the Napoleonic war sport was portrayed as a glamorous, heroic activity. By the time of the Great Exhibition, such sentiments were restricted to a very few sports. The distinction between 'respectable' and 'unrespectable' sport stemmed basically from the social profile of their supporters. 'Respectable' sport consisted of field sports, horse racing and cricket. 'Unrespectable' activities were most other competitive sports for money.[190] The press undermined the image of commercial sport by exposing the corruption within it, thus fostering the idea of 'amateur' activities, that were pursued without the possibility of financial gain. It is this subject, the impact of the media's presentation on the image of sport, that we next consider.

Advances in technology had transformed mass production, thus stimulating the market for sporting ephemera, including statuettes, songs and pictures.[191] Artists were often present at sporting events, even prize-fights, and both Marshall and Ackermann made fortunes from painting and producing prints of horses.[192] It was a lucrative business, and disputes sometimes resulted in legal actions. The most prosperous sport was fox-hunting, the embodiment of 'respectability'. A combination of Nimrod's prose and cheap mass-produced pictures, cultivated a mythic world of daring jumps and breathless riding, a fantasy milked to the full by Ainsworth in his epic account of Dick Turpin's ride to York, in *Rockwood*.[193] 'Ringwood' observed the reality: 'Don't let the uninitiated suppose that the crowd would charge these fences abreast, as they could sheep-hurdles. No such thing: they diverge right and left, and get through corners or gates'. As for the elite world of Melton Mowbray, 'these exclusive notions have in great measure evaporated'.[194] Modernity, typified by the railway and urban life, was rejected and the most successful sporting prose of the period – Nimrod's hunting tours and

Mill's evocations of old England – were pure escapism.[195] By contrast, Surtees enjoyed little critical or commercial success. His novels presented the reality of the hunting field, a place where fences were rarely jumped and hunts consisted of small tradesmen dependent on 'bag foxes' to avoid blank days.[196]

The growing division of sports into respectable and unrespectable increasingly determined their treatment by both the press and outside observers. The spectre of corruption tainted public perceptions of many competitors. Consequently, pugilism, the sport which had enjoyed the most attractive image of all during the Napoleonic wars, declined in public estimation. Many writers, regarded the growing expertise in the sport as being completely overshadowed by its corruption:

> [T]o the present school the merit of having perfected the Science, let us also recollect that they have brought an almost indelible disgrace upon it, by their immoral and unprincipled conduct.[197]

After 1830 the robust slang that had animated boxers into heroes was often replaced by a cynical and sarcastic eye. This was embodied by the great classic of pugilism, *Boxiana,* the first three volumes of which had been written by Egan, who, while noting his subjects' faults, revealed a sport that was full of heroism. By contrast, the fourth and final volume was written by Bee, an embittered outsider who focused on the most disreputable aspects of the sport, especially corruption.[198] Public perceptions of boxers had changed, and it was appropriate that the nearest approximation to a contemporary national hero, Tom Spring, had his name improperly used for both a sweepstake and a newspaper: in essence he was treated as a commodity.[199]

Far from impeding the demise of the hero, the art of biography accentuated it. Although there was a profound need for credible figures who could reconstruct sport's image, writers proved to be either unwilling or unable to present them. Biographers were quite clear about the genre's aim: *The Sporting Magazine* was typical when it declared that:

> Every life contains some useful precept, and every human circumstance has its moral. The biography which publishes the fair truth, still loses its full purpose if it not be attended with a comment that may prove serviceable to others.[200]

The resulting biographies displayed a robust frankness concerning their subject. The world which they revealed was a very harsh one, as was made clear in, for example, the obituary of Richmond.[201] They were not, however, sensationalist, even drawing a polite veil over the disreputable activities of Beardsworth, a sporting promoter who indulged in every kind of fraud and deception, dismissing them with the curt declaration that much matter was 'better left in oblivion'.[202] They also showed a desire to limit the scope of their inquiry, restricting their considerations of aristocrats to their sporting deeds, rather than their activity, or lack of, in politics.[203] Cumulatively, the only insight they provided readers with concerning the correct image of sport, was that the days of sport's nobility were long dead. The obituary of the boxer Jackson was characteristic:

> the loss of such a man at such a season is a matter of serious import, as with him may seem to have passed away the last link of the chain by which the sympathies of the great were attached to the destinies of British boxing.[204]

That of Cribb was a eulogy to the past, contrasting it sadly with contemporary corruption:

> Now, alas!, all such concert is at an end, and although a few may be disposed to cling together as the enemies of disorder, still the great majority keep aloof, and therefore pickpockets and ruffians put all control at defiance.[205]

This attitude was pervasive. In 1838, though displaying an affectionate sympathy for medieval times, when 'men were ignorant of all other cares', Howitt had extolled the progress of the modern age. Twelve years later, he regarded modernity as empty, declaring that England was 'rich but joyless'.[206] While the pessimism concerning the future that was expressed by sporting writers anticipated an aesthetic genre from slightly later in the period, the stance simply reflected the popular appetite for nostalgia, embodied by the Young England movement.[207] This was a tone that was untypical of most popular literature, which tended to stress the resolution of difficulties and regarded the future with considerable optimism.[208] It was typified by the popular scientific work of 1844, *The Vestiges of the Natural History of Creation*, that was premised upon the notion that 'as civilization advances, reason acquires a greater ascendency'.[209]

In stark contrast to this, the historical writing of the period reflected the bitter divisions within sport; *The Sporting Magazine*, for instance, failing to even note the deaths of Jackson or Cribb, having long since ceased to recognize boxing as a sport (aside from a report on a charity event).[210] Whereas during the French wars writers had effectively created the whole genre of the sporting history, between 1816 and 1850, despite the vast amount of literature that was produced, there were surprisingly few good histories. Much of the literature was simply compilations of facts, such as *Fistiana*, which basically owed more to the betting public's mania for data as found in the annual collections produced relating to coursing, horse racing and steeple chasing, rather than creative historical writing. Other works were often shoddy, as with the indifferently assembled secondary material issued by Whyte in his history of horse racing. Aside from Blaine's colossal compilation from 1840, there were few attempts to try and reintegrate the sporting culture.[211]

By contrast with this, during the French wars the slang term 'the fancy' represented sport, simply indicating 'those who "fancy" a particular amusement or pursuit'.[212] It was an inclusive term. By 1850 sport was split into two camps. However, many regarded the distinction between 'respectable' activities and the rest as a sham, for they disapproved of both hunting and betting, and wanted sport to be reconstructed along moral lines.[213] Yet circumstances precluded such a solution. The top sporting journalists, Egan, Kent and Nimrod, had each died in poverty; a fate Surtees avoided because of his large inheritance. Yet his cynical eye could not conjure an image sufficiently seductive to reintegrate sport. A new myth was required and it was not until 1857 that *Tom Brown's Schooldays*, a work that was to have enormous transatlantic sales, began to restructure the notion of the sporting hero.[214] Press coverage of sport during the Napoleonic wars presented a unified culture in which actions, and often individuals, were heroic. Between 1816 and 1850 this culture fragmented into warring factions and the image of sport shrank.

Conclusions

There was a great irony in the impact which the sporting press had on commercial sport. In many senses, they almost created it. Unquestionably, the press deliberately fostered activity, becoming intimately involved in every aspect. However, it lacked the capacity to administer the resulting culture and prevent significant inroads by corrupt elements. This aspect of commercial sport commanded increased attention, eroding public sympathy and respect. Additionally, those elements of the sporting press that were unable to participate in the coverage of competitive sport, and focused instead upon more expensive, exclusive sports, such as fox-hunting, used the corruption in competitive sport as a moral justification for their stance. Cumulatively, these twin developments, the increased attention on the corruption of competitive sport, and the moral justification of alternative, 'gentlemanly', activities, provided the environment for an increased deprecation of commercial sport and the espousal of new ideas of 'amateurism', in which competitive events for stakes were deemed morally indefensible. These notions were to hold sway for the quarter of the century following 1850 and were to seriously impede the expansion of commercial sport. The reason why the press detailed so much corruption within sport was due to the failure of both Parliament, and the bodies administering sport, to prevent illegality; in the next chapter we consider the behaviour of the first of these, Parliament.

Notes

1   C. Pigott (1792a) *The Jockey Club*, iii, London, p. 209.
2   L. Stone (1969) 'Literacy and education in England 1640–1900', *Past and Present*, 22, p. 120.
3   Some religious tracts did target sport; see *The Cock-fighter. A True History* (1795).
4   V. Neuberg (1971) *Popular Education in Eighteenth Century England*, London:

Fontana, pp. 115–25. 140, 151. P. Rogers (1974) *The Augustan Vision*, London: Weidenfeld, pp. 78, 85. M. Spufford (1981) *Small Books and Pleasant Histories*, London: Methuen, p. 45.

5   J. Black (1987) *The English Press in the Eighteenth Century*, London: Croom Helm, pp. 107, 302.

6   For the careers of some see P. Egan (1832) *Pierce Egan's Book of Sports*, London, pp. 181–4.

7   Capt J. Godfrey (1747) *A Treatise on the Useful Science of Self Defence*, London, introduction.

8   J. Cheny in *An Historical List of all Horse-Matches Run* (1729), London, pp. 168–70.

9   Black, *English Press*, p. 82.

10 Ibid., pp. 97, 283, 294. McKendrick et al., *Consumer Society*, pp. 41, 43, 54.

11 19 Jan 1787.

12 BL. Add. MSS 37931, *Windham Papers*, lxxxviii, p. 418. *SM*, March 1795, 283–4; Nov 1804, 85.

13 *SM*, Oct 1792, 20.

14 *SM*, Aug 1797, 252; Sept 1797, 324; Oct 1797, 15–19; Nov 1807, 62; April 1811, 16–20; May 1813, 88.

15 *SM*, Nov 1810, 72.

16 *SM*, July 1806, 105; Sept 1809, 293.

17 *SM*, July 1795, 222.

18 *SM*, Nov 1798, 60.

19 *SM*, Dec 1799, 118.

20 *SM*, July 1795, 174; July 1806, 243.

21 The very first issue detailed its aims: *SM*, Oct 1792, iv–vi.

22 Pigott, *The Jockey Club*, Parts 1, 2, 3. Also related are the following anonymous pamphlets: *An Answer to Three Scurrilous Pamphlets Entitled The Jockey Club* (1792), *Animadversions On A Late Publication Entitled The Jockey Club* (1792), *The Female Jockey Club* (1792), *The Minor Jockey Club, or, A Sketch of the Manners of The Greeks* (1792). It appears to have given birth to a genre: *The Whig Club, or a Sketch of the Manners of the Age* (1794).

23 Emsley, *British Society and the French Wars*, p. 48. C. Pigott (1793) *Persecution: The Case of Charles Pigott Contained in the Defence He had Prepared*, *SM*, Oct 1793, p. 37.

24 F. Lawley (1892) *Index of the Engravings of The Sporting Magazine 1792–1870*, London, p. 7.

25 *SM*, Sept 1793, 324.

26 *SM*, March 1794, 399; June 1796, 119–21.

27 *SM*, Aug 1795, 279.

28 *SM*, Jan 1795, 219.

29 *Times*, 20 Sept 1815.

30 *MM*, 17 Oct 1815.

31 O. Napea (1816), *Letters from London: Observations of a Russian During a Residence in England*, London: Hughes, p. 233. Napea was a pseudonym of J. Badcock.

32 *SM*, Feb 1793, 253–4; July 1794, 199. *Times*, 5 Aug 1799. *WD*, 29 May 1803.

33 Black, *English Press*, p. 259. *SM*, Dec 1801, 132–4.

34 *Times*, 4 Feb 1804.

35 *SM*, Dec 1813, 102.

36 Black, *English Press*, pp. 262–3. *WD*, 10 Jan 1802.
37 *SM*, Oct 1792, iii, v.
38 *SM*, March 1793, 370.
39 *SM*, April 1793, 57; May 1812, 51–4.
40 *SM*, Dec 1792, 113.
41 *SM*, Dec 1810, 97–102.
42 *SM*, 22 Oct 1811.
43 *BWM*, 2 Feb 1812. M. Clapson (1992) *Popular Gambling and English Society 1823–1961*, Manchester: Manchester University Press, pp. 17–18.
44 *BWM*, 27 Oct 1811.
45 J. Ford (1971) *Prize-fighting*, Newton Abbot: David and Charles, p. 57.
46 *SM*, Sept 1802, 331.
47 *SM*, May 1793, 108; Nov 1807, 62.
48 *SM*, Feb 1803, 273.
49 *SM*, Oct 1796, 4.
50 *SM*, April 1793, 48; Aug 1804, 271.
51 *Times*, 25 Sept 1815.
52 *SM*, Feb 1795, 204. March 1813, 282–4.
53 *SM*, March 1808, 215.
54 *SM*, April 1793, 5–6; Jan 1800, 170–71; Feb 1800, 236–7.
55 *SM*, April 1793, 8.
56 *SM*, Feb 1800, 262.
57 *SM*, May 1793, 112; Sept 1793, 335; Sept 1795, 335; Dec 1808, 119.
58 Ford, *Prize-fighting*, pp. 169–70.
59 See P. Egan (1812), *Boxiana*, ii, London: Smeaton, pp. 16–24.
60 *SM*, Oct 1792, 16.
61 See *British Museum Catalogue* entry for George Wilson, pedestrian.
62 *BWM*, 21 April 1811.
63 *SM*, June 1806, 146.
64 *SM*, Nov 1808, 91; Jan 1809, 203.
65 *SM*, July 1809, 199.
66 *Times*, 24 Aug, 28 Aug, 1 Sept, 11 Sept 1804.
67 *SM*, Feb 1806, 222–3.
68 *SM*, Nov 1815, 91–2.
69 *Bell's*, 4 July 1830. *NSM*, Oct 1840, 286.
70 See, for instance, W. Thom (1813) *Pedestrianism*, Aberdeen. A work Barclay revised. *SM*, Dec 1812, 110.
71 *SM*, Aug 1804, 232.
72 M. Brander (1961) *Soho for the Colonel*, London: Geoffrey Bles, pp. 17–18.
73 *SM*, Oct 1795, 2.
74 Black, *English Press*, p. 105.
75 *BWM*, 17 Nov 1805.
76 *SM*, Nov 1807, 60–62.
77 *SM*, March 1800, 297.
78 *SM*, Feb 1808, 265.
79 *Jackson's*, 16 Aug 1800.
80 *SM*, May 1798, 105–107; June 1799, 145–6; Dec 1802, 112.
81 *SM*, Sept 1809, 258–9.
82 *BWM*, 7 Aug 1813.

83   R. Williams (1992) *The Long Revolution*, London: Longman, p. 192.

84   *Annals*, July 1827, 41. *Bell's*, 28 July 1850. *WD*, 6 Dec 1818.

85   G. Cranfield (1978) *The Press and Society,* London: Longman. pp. 119, 223. S. Koss (1981) *The Rise and Fall of The Provincial Press in Britain*, London: Hamilton, i, pp. 51–2. I. McCalman (1988) *Radical Underworld*, Cambridge: Cambridge University Press, pp. 210, 220. An example of the catholic nature can be gleaned from the shortlived *Bell's Penny Dispatch Sporting and Police Gazette, and Newspaper of Romance and Penny Sunday Chronicle*. It began its seven-month life by presenting salacious material – 'Daring Conspiracy and Attempted Violation', complete with engravings of masked figures in a ladies room. Later this was replaced by radical politics, weekly articles describing 'The Wholesale Murder Of The Working-Class'.

86   *WD*, 8 April 1821.

87   *Bell's*, 27 Sept 1835.

88   *Bell's*, 19 Sept 1847; 24 Feb 1850. *WMC*, 26 March 1831.

89   Bovill, *English Country Life*, p. 71.

90   R. Schofield (1973) 'Dimensions of illiteracy in England 1750–1850', *Explorations in Economic History*, 10, 435.

91   *Bell's*, 18 May 1845. *WMC*, 17 Sept 1836.

92   *Bell's*, 23 June 1850.

93   *Bell's*, 27 Nov 1827. *Newspaper Stamps*, 1036. *SM*, Oct 1822, 15.

94   *Bell's*, 16 Jan 1848. *NSM*, June 1831, 143–4. *Newspaper Stamps*, 260.

95   *BWM*, 6 April 1816.

96   *BWD*, 30 July 1820.

97   *WD*, 16 Feb 1817.

98   J. Stevenson (1977b) 'The Queen Caroline Affair', in J. Stevenson (ed.) *London in the Age of Reform*, Oxford: Oxford University Press, pp. 117–48.

99   See 12 Jan onwards.

100 *SM*, Oct 1817, 2.

101 *Bell's*, 17 May 1835. *SM*, July 1826, 194–6; Feb 1828, 298; Sept 1831, 351; Nov 1831, 27.

102 *BWM*, 1 April 1821. *SM*, March 1821, 283; July 1825, 195–6.

103 *BWM*, 7 April 1816. *WD*, 5 Jan 1817.

104 *BWM*, 27 Oct 1816.

105 Egan, *Book Of Sports*, p. 68.

106 *Annals*, Jan 1823, 54; Feb 1825, 113; Aug 1827, 102.

107 *Bell's*, 13 June 1824.

108 *SM*, Feb 1819, 251.

109 Given its small sales, *Annals'* claims (Nov 1827, 251–2) that it was their appearance which caused the *SM* to change are untenable.

110 *SM*, Oct 1819, 25; Dec 1821, 141. Contra, curiously, May 1845, 293.

111 *NSM*, March 1832, 360; April 1832, 391–4.

112 *SM*, Oct 1823, 38–47; Jan 1825, 308; May 1825, 60.

113 *Bell's*, 1 Jan 1826.

114 *Annals*, Jan 1822, 53.

115 *Bell's*, 22 Aug 1824.

116 *Bell's*, 14 Oct 1827; 12 April 1829. A. Mason (1994) *Sport in Britain*, London: Faber and Faber, p. 47.

117 *Bell's*, 13 July 1828.

118 According to one 'insider', such reports were cultivated to deceive the public by

presenting fixed fights as being honest; Deale (1828) *Life in the West; Or, The Curtain Drawn, by a Flat Enlightened*, London: Saunders and Otley, ii, pp. 54–5.

119 *Bell's*, 29 Aug 1824. *WD*, 23 Sept 1821.

120 *Bell's*, 1 Nov 1829.

121 *Bell's*, 9 Jan 1825. *SM*, Dec 1824, 223.

122 *Bell's*, 9 Nov 1823.

123 *Bell's*, 23 Dec 1827, 24 Feb 1828, 9 March 1828.

124 *WD*, 3 Jan 1830, 2 Jan 1831.

125 Cranfield, *Press*, pp. 126–7.

126 *Newspaper Stamps*, 1225. *WD*, 14 Nov 1830.

127 *WD*, 4 Jan 1835.

128 F. Bourne (1887) *English Newspapers*, London: Chatto and Windus, ii, pp. 102–103.

129 *Annals*, Jan 1823, 72; Feb 1828, pp. 93–4.

130 *NSM*, May 1831, 3.

131 D. Brailsford (1988) *Bareknuckles*, Cambridge: Lutterworth, p. 86.

132 *SM*, July 1833, 277.

133 *Annals*, Sept 1827, 163–4. *SM*, May 1821, 88; Sept 1825, 359–60.

134 *SM*, 14 Jan 1816.

135 *Bell's*, 9 Jan 1825, 23 Sept 1827, 12 Jan 1834.

136 *Bell's*, 4 Aug 1833, 7 Dec 1834, 25 Dec 1842.

137 Cranfield, *Press*, pp. 154, 200. *WMC*, 4 Jan 1834.

138 J. Wiener (1978) 'Circulation and the stamp tax', in J. Dan Vann and R.T. Van Arsdell (eds) *Victorian Periodicals: A Guide to Research*, New York: Heffer and Sons, pp. 160–62.

139 For an analysis of *The Town* see D.J. Gray (1982) 'Early Victorian Scandalous Journalism: Renton Nicholson's *The Town 1837–1842*', in J. Shattock and M. Wolff (eds) *The Victorian Periodical Press: Samplings and Soundings*, Leicester: Leicester University Press.

140 *Bell's*, 16 June 1839. H.D. Miles (1906) *Pugilistica*, Edinburgh: Weldon and Co., i, pp. xi–xii.

141 *Bell's*, 12 Aug 1827, 7 Feb 1836, 17 Jan 1847. PRO *HO* 45, 2339.

142 Harrison, *Drink*, p. 60.

143 J.C. Reid (1971) *Bucks and Bruisers: Pierce Egan and Regency England*, London: Routledge, p. 30.

144 *Bell's*, 25 April 1841, 8 May 1842, 21 Sept 1845.

145 *Era*, 1 Sept 1838, 20 Dec 1840.

146 *Era*, 14 Feb 1841, 13 June 1841.

147 *Bell's*, 14 Sept 1845, 30 April 1848.

148 *Bell's*, 17 July 1831.

149 'Doncaster: Its sports and saturnalia', *Bentley's Miscellany*, xx (1846), 290.

150 Bourne, *Newspapers*, ii, pp. 122–3.

151 *M.Ex*, 13 July 1850.

152 C. Chinn (1991) *Better Betting with a Decent Feller*, London: Harvester Wheatsheaf, p. 69.

153 *Bell's*, 24 Sept 1834, 14 Feb 1841, 3 June 1849.

154 *Bell's*, 4 Jan 1835, 24 Dec 1848, 27 May 1849.

155 *Bell's*, 1 Aug 1830, 12 Sept 1847.

156 *Bell's*, 18 Jan 1846, 22 March 1846.

157 A. Harvey (1990) Leisure in the Bleak Age, MA, London University, p. 10.

158   *Bell's*, 15 July 1838.
159   *Bell's*, 26 Dec 1841.
160   *Bell's*, 11 Dec 1842.
161   *Bell's*, 13 Dec 1846, 30 Jan 1848.
162   *Bell's*, 2 July 1848.
163   *Bell's*, 8 March 1846, 21 May 1848.
164   *Bell's*, 30 May 1841, 14 June 1846.
165   *Bell's*, 15 Jan 1843, 21 March 1847.
166   *Bell's*, 20 Oct 1850.
167   A rare example previous to this was *SM*, July 1796, 177.
168   *Bell's*, 24 May 1840. Though many were hoaxes; 15 Jan 1837.
169   *Bell's*, 1 June 1828.
170   *Bell's*, 23 Aug 1840, 1 Jan 1843, 17 Nov 1850.
171   *Bell's*, 1 Jan 1837.
172   *Bell's*, 6 Jan 1839, 26 April 1840.
173   *Bell's*, 31 Dec 1848.
174   *Era*, 9 Dec 1849.
175   *Bell's*, 28 June 1835.
176   *Bell's*, 30 April 1848.
177   *Bell's*, 7 May 1848.
178   *Bell's*, 10 Feb 1850, 16 June 1850.
179   *Era*, 23 June 1850.
180   *Bell's*, 28 June 1835, 26 Dec 1847, 23 June 1850.
181   *Lancaster Rowing Club Minute Books*, Jan 1847 (in *LPL*).
182   *Bell's*, 15 July 1838, 24 July 1842, 14 Jan 1849.
183   *The Sportsman and Veterinary Journal*, July 1837, preface.
184   *Bell's*, 20 Nov 1836.
185   *Bell's*, 28 March 1841.
186   *SM*, July 1846, 1; Jan 1848, 135–7.
187   J. Welcome (1982) *The Sporting World of Surtees*, Oxford: Oxford University Press, pp. 159, 163.
188   *Newspapers*, pp. 587–90, 1002, 3196.
189   *Bell's*, 13 Feb 1831, 26 Sept 1847. *SM*, Oct 1817, 22–5.
190   *SM*, March 1837, 395.
191   *Bell's*, 1 Sept 1844, 7 Sept 1845. *JJC. Harding Collection*, II–III. *JJC* Sports; Box 15.
192   *Bell's*, 14 June 1835, 16 May 1841. J. Ford (1988) *Ackermann*, London: Ackermann, p. 109. W. Sparrow (1931) 'The origin of racing journalism', *Chambers Journal*, 21, 340.
193   *SM*, July 1834, 280.
194   R. Carr (1976) *English Fox-hunting*, London: Weidenfeld, pp. 65–7, 76–7. *SM*, July 1832, 190–94.
195   *Bell's*, 20 June 1847.
196   Welcome, *Surtees*, pp. 108, 139, 187.
197   *Bell's*, 9 Oct 1831.
198   *Boxiana*, iv (1824), pp. 108, 121, 189, 492, 496, 501, 553, 568, 607.
199   *Bell's*, 14 June 1840, 18 Feb 1849.
200   *SM*, Aug 1817, 206–10.
201   *Annals*, Aug 1823, 120. *Bell's*, 3 Jan 1830.
202   *SM*, Dec 1835, 203.

203 *Bell's*, 2 Nov 1834. *Exchange Herald*, 17 April 1821.
204 *Bell's*, 12 Oct 1845.
205 *Bell's*, 12 Oct 1845, 14 May 1848, 21 May 1848.
206 W. Howitt (1850) *The Country Year Book*, New York, pp. 37, 39, 42, 68. W. Howitt (1838) *Rural Life of England*, London, ii, 262.
207 M. Girouard (1981) *The Return to Camelot: Chivalry and the English Gentleman*, London: New Haven, pp. 146, 184.
208 S. Smith (1980) *The Other Nation*, Oxford: Oxford University Press, pp. 263–5.
209 (1969 edition), p. 373.
210 *SM*, June 1848, 442.
211 D. Blaine (1840) *An Encyclopaedia of Rural Sports*, London: Longman, p. vii.
212 *Oxford English Dictionary*.
213 *ILN*, 27 Sept 1845, 27 Dec 1845.
214 R. Park (1987) 'Sport, gender and society – a transatlantic Victorian perspective', in J. Mangan and R. Park (eds) *From 'Fair Sex' to Feminism*, London: Frank Cass, p. 60. K. Sandiford (1983a) 'Cricket and Victorian society', *JSH*, 17:2, 305.

Chapter 4

No Time for Idleness?
The Law and Sport, 1793–1815

When we follow them into their retirements, where no disguise is necessary, we are most likely to see them in their true state and may best judge of their natural disposition.[1]

Leisure is, without doubt, highly valuable to man, but taking man as he is, the probability seems to be that in the greater number of instances it will produce evil rather than good.[2]

These differing views of recreation were reflected in the ambiguous outlook of official society, which was a mixture of tolerance and intervention. Until at least the 1830s, the supervision of recreation was essentially a matter for the local authorities: Parliament rarely taking a direct lead. This attitude was crystallized by pugilism, a practice that was not formally proscribed by either statute or proclamation, its suppression being left to local discretion.[3] Generally, while on occasions innocent looking pastimes were subject to prosecution, official society tolerated recreations.[4] In fact, the law declared that those 'assembling at wakes, or other festival times, or meetings for exercise of common sports or diversions, as bull-baiting, wrestling, and such like, are not riotous'.[5]

Between 1793 and 1850, both local and national government were supportive of commercial sport. During the French wars, officials and legislators protected sport by preventing groups that were endeavouring to create a change in moral attitudes from interfering with recreational activities. After 1830, parliamentary involvement in sport broadened, including both repression and provision. While both were often patchy in their effect, historians have been inclined to overrate the impact of repression and underestimate the influence of provision. However, as the following chapters will show, those aspects of local and national government which fostered and strengthened the commercial sporting culture proved to be of far more significance than those tending towards its limitation.

This chapter, which relates to the period between 1793 and 1815, is the first of two that deals with the role of the government in supervising sport. It consists of two parts, the first of which considers the attitudes of those making the laws, principally Parliament, while the second focuses upon those supervising the laws, both the local courts and authorities.

Sport and Parliament

The Evangelical revival that occurred in the last quarter of the eighteenth century implicitly attacked many of the recreational practices of the landowning elite. Yet it was the war with France, which commenced in 1793, that gave such criticism an added bite. The threat of Jacobinism posed an acute ideological challenge, leading many to scrutinize both the role and behaviour of the English aristocracy and gentry. Some believed that the conduct of the aristocracy had grown worse not better, an exasperated writer declaring 'the example of the Gallic nobles, so far from checking the brutal intemperance of our heredity legislators, seemed to stimulate them to a more than ordinary excess'.[6] Whereas in the past the sports of the gentry had not been subjected to intense scrutiny, they now confronted criticism from two divergent movements, one religious and conservative, notably the Evangelicals, and the other secular and radical, espoused by various Jacobin and rationalist groups. Defenders of the established social order had, therefore, to confront attacks from two different directions and their justifications of the traditional structure often involved identifying the useful roles that sport performed, invariably associating it with the qualities required of a gentleman. In essence, the gentry's sports became a political and social issue.

Religious critics stressed the need for landowners to present a correct moral example. While the most extreme Evangelical view, envisaged a pious, non-sporting, landed elite, in practice, though many Evangelicals regarded sport as a very dubious form of recreation for the leaders of society to indulge in, they were careful not to challenge the existing social structure.[7] Instead, they focused their attention on the morals of the lower orders.

Debates concerning the social behaviour of the landowning elite were essentially restricted to secular thinkers. Commentators were united in denouncing the pleasure-loving gentry for vacating the responsibilities of government, declaring 'cards and dice are at present the chief sports of our quality of both sexes', and urging them to 'revive the ancient, manly and innocent sports of their country, which will tend to make their tenants and dependants brave and good subjects'.[8] Beyond this, there was little agreement on the moral and political posture which the gentry should adopt.[9] One vision of the ideal squire was of an essentially unintellectual person, who ruled by projecting the correct moral outlook and upholding traditional relationships, which included supporting established sports.[10] They praised the 'frugal, manly, open countenance of the traditional squire who was both easy of access and philanthropic'.[11] Reformers regarded the model of the traditional squire as hopelessly inadequate, condemning it as producing nothing but Squire Westerns, as in Fielding's *Tom Jones*, and believed that it was necessary to take a far more active role in governance, typified by 'improving landlords'.[12] They were also harshly critical of the way the aristocracy and gentry sponsored 'cruel sports'.[13] This criticism was somewhat paradoxical, given their specific concern with easing the tensions between the ranks, because contemporary writers were agreed that such sports provided substantial rapport between the classes.[14] Their vision was of the lower orders being morally and intellectually improved by the enlightened paternalism of the ruling class. To many adhering to the views concerning the French revolution expressed by Edmund Burke, who regarded criticism of the established order as a crucial factor in undermining its stability, this must have seemed a dangerous contention. This may explain why the reforms for which they provided the intellectual background, notably those attempted concerning the Game Laws, failed.

Scholars such as Malcolmson maintain that the period witnessed a significant intrusion by government, often at the prompting of both religious and commercial interests, into the recreational lives of the common people.[15] However, as we shall see, Parliament did not generally interfere in the lives of the population, and sport was largely unmolested, a fact which Malcolmson himself acknowledged: 'There was no systematic and sustained campaign which was intent upon undermining the essential fabric of the traditional holiday calendar'. Even when pressure was applied it had little effect: 'although fairs continued to be attacked and sometimes prohibited in particular localities during the first half of the century, it seems that their numbers did not significantly decline until later in the century'. The controversial sport of bull-baiting was not the victim of legislation: 'the reasons for [bull-baiting's] decline are not at all clear'.[16] It is instructive that the only major Act restricting popular sport, that of 1740 (13 George II, Cap 19) stipulating that the minimum prize money must be 50 guineas, which eliminated many minor race meetings, occurred outside the period.[17] After that, there was little effort made to curb popular entertainments; the laws of 1780 banning commercially organized sport on Sundays having little impact because such events had always been rare.[18]

As we shall see, throughout the war, the British government recognized that sport had a role to play in maintaining the social structure and Parliament acted to ensure the supply of recreation appropriate to the particular social classes. On the one hand this involved defending the Game Laws, because they were perceived as enabling landowners to entertain themselves on their estates, thus encouraging them to fulfil local administrative functions. Likewise, Parliament, by rejecting movements that tried to legislate against sports, especially those that were deemed cruel, that were regarded as forming an important component in the poorer classes' access to recreation, ensured that the lower orders were provided with entertainment. Their motives for this were mixed; including a benign protection of the pleasures of the poor and also a basic pragmatism, namely the fear that the curtailment of recreation would lead to the spread of internal subversion. There was no attempt by Parliament to innovate in terms of the legislation it passed, the aim was simply to preserve the status quo. The only positive legislation introduced during this period concerning recreation aimed at utilizing certain sport-related skills to repel an external enemy, rather than combat internal subversion. The organization of such attempts to apply sport-derived skills to military matters was left to the relevant local authorities.[19]

The following examination of Parliament's behaviour towards sport focuses on three areas. First, it considers the Game Laws, a piece of deliberate socially divisive legislation, explaining the rationale behind them and assessing their consequences for social stability. The second area examines Parliament's refusal to legislate against cruel sports, despite the influential nature of the groups that were calling for reform, and discusses both the reasons for and consequences of, this. The third area assesses both Parliament and the King's attempts at deriving concrete military benefits from sport.

The Game Laws

The Game Laws were one of the pillars of landed society, embodying social privilege and status by restricting access to choice foods. The various laws were often revised. They stipulated that game could only be killed legitimately by those owning game certificates, documents that were only available to substantial property owners (possessing land to the value of £100 in 1792; 31 George III, Cap 21), and that it was illegal to trade in such meats.[20] This restricted the legitimate consumption of a whole range of food to a small group of landowners. While such restrictions was bound to create animosity, two developments, one political and one related to sport, considerably accentuated the problems.[21] The fear of Jacobin revolution made landowners regard the preservation of the existing hierarchy as important. Consequently, in 1796 they rejected legislation that aimed at abolishing many of the most contentious provisions of the laws, by granting those renting land more access to the game upon it.[22] A change had also occurred in sporting fashion with the replacement of the old form of shooting by the battue. This was a highly organized activity, depending upon an immense number of birds. These could only be supplied by being specifically bred, resulting in the emergence of large game preserves on many estates. This, inevitably, drew attention to the immense disparity in the access to this food, as well as providing considerable temptation for those outside the privileged minority.

The specific intention of the Game Laws was to be socially exclusive and its defenders had difficulty justifying such divisive regulations because they lacked any traditional precedent.[23] Thus, their practicality was always stressed. In 1794 'Laureat', in his influential treatise *Essays on Sporting,* articulated the widely held rationale for them.[24] It was felt that by providing sport for the gentry their presence on their estates could be ensured, enabling them to fulfil crucial administrative, social and economic functions instead of gravitating to London.[25] Additionally, the laws 'prevent the man, whose family depends entirely upon his labour for support, from quitting his flail, his plough, or his spade, to range the woods'.[26] Despite this, most contemporaries appear to have regarded the Game Laws as creating far more problems than they solved, undermining social relations at every turn. At the most fundamental level, the relationship between landlord and tenant, damage was regularly inflicted. Farmers renting land were powerless to prevent the depredations of hares and birds, who could eat their crops at will.[27] Also, landowners were impeded from taking their tenants hunting, a social act which assisted the cementing of relationships, because such behaviour had become legally dubious, occasionally resulting in prosecutions initiated by paid informers.[28] The laws were no more successful in promoting harmony between the privileged possessors of game certificates. It was fairly common for groups of such sportsmen, though complete strangers to an area, to raid local coverts, which the landowner had set aside for the breeding of game, slaughtering much of his investment.[29] There were also a number of incidents in which landowners squabbled over the rights of shooting in particular areas.[30] In addition to this, it was inevitable that tension existed between landowners that cultivated the different sports of fox-hunting and shooting, the preservation of foxes being generally inimical to those who created coverts in which to breed game. All these difficulties were considerably worsened by the power invested in one of the landowners' servants, the gamekeeper. Although in some regions careful attempts were made to ensure that gamekeepers were both civil and honest, by rewarding such behaviour, all too often these employees proved to be arrogant and overbearing, stirring up trouble by shooting local dogs that had accidentally strayed onto their estates.[31] Also, the employment of man traps and spring guns, devices that sometimes injured the innocent as well as the guilty, poisoned local relations.

More disruptive still, were the numerous convictions stemming from the laws themselves. Contemporaries regarded the penalties as harsh, especially as those punished sometimes included old women and small children.[32] On occasions juries refused to convict offenders, poaching being considered a legitimate activity, thus undermining respect for the law.[33] Fundamentally, the whole aim of the Game Laws was absurd. Game was a popular food and comparatively easy to obtain. By restricting access, its value was inevitably increased, making poaching a lucrative activity. Thus, poaching increased, becoming a highly organized commercial enterprise. Evidence from *The Black Book* of 1831 asserted that the aristocrats themselves were responsible for providing much of the illegal supply of game, doing so for their own profit on a regular basis.[34] Given the scope and the extent of poaching it may well be that this was the case in the Napoleonic period, with aristocrats explicitly orchestrating a process that involved the systematic breaking of the law. While many landowners and gamekeepers broke the Game Laws without fear, numerous poor people suffered imprisonment for comparatively petty offences.[35] The commercial rewards of poaching were such that gangs of hard core criminals grew up and steadily perfected their skills. In fact, it was freely conceded that many villains commenced their careers as poachers.[36] The Game Laws, like prohibition in America, had created a thriving underworld activity that undermined the social fabric.

The Moral Assessment of Recreation

While attempts to increase the social access to gentry sports failed, a movement was emerging that intended reevaluating recreation, by examining it according to religious criteria. Despite the fact that arguments against cruelty to animals had been well developed for some three hundred years, for the bulk of the eighteenth century even the clergy, whom one might have expected to subject sport to a sustained moral analysis, seem to have viewed the topic in a complacent manner.[37] At the local level, the church sometimes displayed a sympathy towards bull-baiting.[38] Certain clergymen conformed to the well established caricature of simply being 'squires in orders', for they participated in activities, such as pugilism, horse racing, shooting, fox-hunting and duelling, that were common to the gentlemanly elite from which they were drawn. [39]

The onset of the Evangelical movement, especially socially elite groups such as The Proclamation Society, prompted a change in attitudes. They projected a more censorious morality, which denounced all sporting activity by the clergy. Whereas in the past, traditional country sports were considered morally justified, the state of such activities became at best, problematic, and more usually 'sinful'. It was typified by an article, 'Three Dialogues on Hunting, Shooting and Fishing' by the Dean of Saint Paul's, which systematically demonstrated that all three sports were unsuitable for the clergy.[40] Not only that, exponents of this morality sought to impose their views on the wider society, dictating the type of sporting activity that was permissible on Sundays.[41] This was particularly so for the Methodists, who, from 1807, held camp meetings in opposition to popular sporting events.[42]

During the Napoleonic war it was the press rather than the clergy that first articulated sentiments concerning the rights and welfare of animals, though a good deal of such feeling was present in polite society.[43] *The Sporting Magazine*, followed by other papers, denounced certain activities, such as pigeon-shooting, cock-fighting and horse feats, as cruel, and encouraged action against them.[44] Animals were portrayed in a soft, empathetic way, with the emphasis on their intelligence and affection.[45] Their slaughter had become a moral problem and distinctions were made between those killed for food and those for sport.[46] The public's pity was aroused by a variety of cases and even the use of live bait by fishermen was criticized.[47] Petitions were started against the caging of a young deer and the Jockey Club were encouraged by Astley's to inspect their displays and confirm that they were not hurting their ponies.[48]

In 1802 the Society for the Suppression of Vice was created, consisting, principally, of members of the professional classes and the lesser gentry. By funding spies and prosecutions they secured the conviction of those practising recreations which the Society, with its strong Evangelical views, deemed immoral. Potentially, this was socially subversive. However, in practice, they avoided offending the powerful.[49] Thus, while few people would criticize the Society for failing to adhere to the vegetarianism advocated by some writers, the fact that their attention was concentrated almost exclusively on the misdeeds of the lower orders detracted from their credibility.[50] Many of the objections which the Evangelicals had to cruel sports were derived largely from concern that these leisure activities were interfering with the work routines of the poor.[51] More seriously still, a crucial distinction was regularly made between the sports of the upper and lower classes. This was most eloquently argued for by Lawrence, who distinguished fox-hunting from bull-baiting, because in the former case the animal was free whereas in the latter it was tethered.[52] Fox-hunting was never denounced by the Society, despite the fact that it resulted in many horses being ridden to death.[53] This silence was probably due to the fact that key supporters of the Society were not unsympathetic to the sport. It was only in 1809 that the Society began to criticize horse feats seriously, their denunciation having been anticipated in *The Sporting Magazine* by some 15 years.[54]

The actual achievements of reformers are debatable. In the long run they may have raised the public's consciousness of the issues in a significant manner, though many bull-baits, such as those at Engton and Kirkham, the former of which was replaced by an oratorio, vanished of their own accord.[55] In the short term their failure resulted in still worse abuses.[56] Much of their effort had a theatrical quality because legislation preventing many of the abuses, such as bull-baiting, had long been available to the local authorities, should they determine to use it.[57] As it was, for all the petitions, pamphlets, debates and sermons, bull-baiting persisted in certain areas throughout the whole period, enjoying substantial support.[58] Not only that, whereas in 1793 a Jockey Club investigation had declared that Astley's performing ponies were well treated, by 1815 evidence demonstrated that many stage animals suffered abuse.[59] Most strikingly of all, in 1814 it was revealed that the King's Royal Stag Hounds regularly broke the leg of the deer they were about to chase to ensure that he did not run too fast.[60] During the period there were some inroads made against cruel sports, notably the revoking of the Royal Cockpit's licence by the trustees of Christ's Hospital, but generally speaking there seems to have been very little change.[61] This lack of success appears to have extended to all the efforts of the Society for the Suppression of Vice to influence leisure activities.[62]

Given the highly influential make-up of the reform societies, and the fact that they had, in part at least, a reasonably good moral and intellectual case, it is worth examining the arguments offered by their opponents that successfully defeated them in 1800, 1802 and 1810, for these provide a key insight into the way sport was viewed by an influential group within Parliament.

The chief spokesman opposing legislation against bull-baiting was the arch-Tory, Windham, the secretary for war, though a number of others, including Canning, Grosvenor, Gasgoine, Frankland and Ellenborough, also contributed. Windham stated that the bill was a scheme by Methodists and Jacobins who 'wished to destroy the Old English character', and that such an unnecessary intrusion of puritanism was 'part of a plan for reforming the manners of the people'.[63] The debate on the abolition of bull-baiting in 1800 saw both sets of protagonists adopt political postures that were inconsistent with their general stance. Thus, the more liberal sought to curb a popular recreation 'out of humanity to the common people', while arch-Tories, as Sheridan wryly observed, sought to defend bull-baiting because 'there should be no sort of distinction between the different orders of the state', sentiments which would have usually meant that 'the speaker would be denounced as a Jacobin'.[64] While Sheridan was correct in highlighting the absurdity of Windham, a ferocious opponent of measures intended to dilute social inequalities, speaking up on behalf of the rights of the common people, the Tory's adoption of many popular, radical, notions, throughout the period, was amazingly successful.

In the years before the war, radicals had criticized the existing social structure along two principal lines. First, they condemned the government for eroding the traditional liberties of the English people, whose rights, so they claimed, had originally been established in Saxon times.[65] Second, they contended that these values had been replaced by the rule of a corrupt, francophile upper class.[66] The upper class, having suddenly been made aware of their isolation from popular culture by the French revolution, appropriated national traditions, and used them as a means for bonding the diverse social ranks together.[67] Much was made of tradition, character and strength, with the government's supporters presenting the king as the defender of British liberty against the French invaders. By thus utilizing the strong distaste which many in the lower orders felt for foreigners to bolster the established social order, the loyalists were able to completely undermine the radicals' position.[68] Thus, the vision of the Englishman as a hapless victim of a corrupt government, was replaced by the self laudatory proverb that he was more than a match for three Frenchmen.[69] This transformation was reflected in the cartoon-figure of John Bull. The image of John Bull had been used in many early cartoons that were overtly critical of the social order. Yet, during the war this aspect became sublimated.[70] In fact, images of a downtrodden, overtaxed, John Bull were replaced by a much starker contrast; that between the happy, well fed Englishman, a bluff, honest, stocky beef eater, who loved his way of life and was fiercely proud of his freedom and independence, believed by some scholars to embody the urban bourgeoisie, and the ragged, barefooted, half-starved French, who were the cruel tools of all-powerful despots. Such a portrait was virulently xenophobic and provided strong emotional reasons for uniting the nation and preserving the existing social order. This patriotism did much to absorb political tensions, helping to promote a more relaxed attitude towards class and social position.[71] Ultimately, the myth was that all Britons, high and low, were united by this vision and had a common interest in battling for its preservation. Such imagery was pervasive in 1803, when efforts were made to mobilise the general population in support of the militia that Windham was endeavouring to create.[72]

As we have already demonstrated, the various reform societies were often guilty of hypocrisy.[73] This was best summed up by Sidney Smith who claimed that they were only interested in prosecuting those with an income of under £500 a year.[74] His sentiments were echoed by many, who spoke up for 'the much grudged pleasures' of working people, and urged that they be allowed their joys.[75] Critics also contrasted the great concern for animals with their near indifference to the sufferings of ordinary people.[76] They were also aware of the selective nature of the legislation, which was usually careful to avoid offending the powerful. Smith's views were intellectual and his motives philanthropic. He did not approve of the cruel sports of either the rich or the poor, but he did not make distinctions between them based on social rank. Windham, by contrast, denounced the hypocrisy of reforming groups, but far from condemning 'cruel sports', regarded them as having many virtues. At the most pragmatic level, he considered the provision of such entertainment as a vital way of preventing the population turning to Jacobinism and other fanaticisms, typified by religious tracts and political pamphlets.[77] In essence, sport would keep the population politically and socially docile. Additionally, many critics recognized that animal sports, especially fox-hunting, were thrilling, supplying something vital to existence.[78] Windham, however, went beyond this, even regarding 'cruel sports' as uniquely British, crucial components in maintaining the national character. He declared that 'bull dogs give character to the country', and praised all sporting animals, hunting dogs, fighting cocks, bull dogs or race horses.[79] They symbolized the instinctual strengths of the British tradition and defied effete modern fads.

Windham seems to have embraced an unchanging rural tradition that he regarded as being under threat from modern, urban, and essentially foreign, concepts.[80] However, he was fully aware that it was dying out. In fact, one of his chief arguments against legislation relating to 'cruel sports' was that they were already in decline. He regarded the intended legislation as 'frivolous', believing that men were not made moral by laws.[81] This sums up much of the official attitude to sport throughout the Napoleonic wars. With the important exception of the Game Laws, there were few attempts to legislate, the population being left to their own devices. If anything, Parliament regarded its role as preventing intrusion into the everyday lives of the people.[82]

Sport and the Military

The Game Laws were the only systematic attempt by the government to use sport as a way of bolstering the social structure. Although sport's military value was recognized by the establishment, in only one instance – the provision of funds to prevent the Veterinary College going bankrupt – did this belief manifest itself in a financial commitment.[83] Generally, Parliament did not foster sport. Indeed, aside from Windham's legislation conscripting a militia, with a special role for game-keepers – as sharpshooters – the government failed to avail itself of pre-existing sporting expertise.[84] A variety of initiatives were taken at the local level to try and use sport to cultivate military abilities, such as shooting competitions, but these were not successful.[85] On the contrary, they served to create animosity within, and between, regiments.[86] Similarly, the illegal shooting expeditions undertaken by officers, during which they slaughtered the game of local landowners, simply antagonized local feelings towards the army.[87]

While fox-hunting did create some excellent riders, meetings often resulted in large numbers of top quality horses being ridden to death.[88] The military value of horse racing, though the sport had long been promoted by royalty for this very reason, was similarly dubious.[89] Throughout the French wars a variety of reasons were advanced in support of horse racing, but as a commentator declared in 1811, the sport was largely irrelevant to the production of a good bloodstock.[90] Financial pressures in the sport often led to horses being prematurely raced, thus impeding their development.[91] Similarly, handicap races penalized good horses.[92]

Sporting activity produced little of military value for the British war effort. In fact, it is evident that various sporting groups used their professed military value as a justification of their own peacetime activity. Parliament did try and provide a framework within which sport could be usefully applied to fighting the war, but the practical application of this was left to individual volition. Consequently, the response was patchy.

The Local Supervision of Sport

The second part of our consideration of the regulation of sport during the French wars concentrates on the local administration. This consists of two components. First, we identify the very diverse responses made by the local authorities to events occurring in their areas, which were based upon two criteria; the preservation of law and order and the commercial benefits that could be derived from sport. Second, the attitudes of the courts are considered.

Local Government

Sport may not have made a tangible contribution to the British war effort in terms of practical achievements, but it certainly did a good deal for preserving peace in England by providing the population with accessible entertainment. During the French wars Parliament made no real attempt to interfere with the everyday conduct of sport, leaving such supervision to the local authorities.[93] Much of their activity was probably quite straightforward, involving the enforcement of established local laws, such as the prosecution of boys playing football in the street or those conducting games on Sundays.[94] Yet, they were also confronted with a whole range of problems where their response was dictated by a variety of local factors. Primacy was usually given to the maintenance of law and order but in certain circumstances the local desire for the commerce generated by sport could supersede this. The degree of supervision employed varied widely. For some activities, legal power was simply used to control and limit the facilities accompanying an event, such as the presence of gaming tables and alcohol booths.[95]

The power available to the local authorities varied considerably, with certain areas having access to well disciplined forces of constables to enforce the law.[96]

While the process of prosecution was essentially a private initiative, in Oxfordshire, for instance, the County was willing to provide funds in cases that were of public concern.[97] Magistrates had curious limitations upon their authority. They could, for instance, act against boxing displays in theatres, but had no power to prosecute the Fives Court.[98] The most draconian response to activity was to either ban or disperse it. This need not have involved much force, and was probably often accomplished by threats, such as those used against Nottingham's innkeepers, who were confronted with the loss of their licences if they permitted cock-fights.[99] The military were rarely used, and in only one instance – the employment of a cavalry charge to disperse a prize-fight – was there any real indication of trouble.[100] The authorities usually enforced their will and it is noticeable that the crowd, though often full of petty criminals, posed little threat to the established order, even policing themselves by punishing those caught cheating at gambling.[101] On only three occasions were there pronounced criminal threats. The worst of these occurred in 1799, when a gang of bandits ran amok at Ascot, killing several stewards, their depredations only being ended by the arrival of the local military. Large gangs of villains armed with bludgeons, numbering forty or so, carried out robberies in 1802, at a cricket match, and 1813, at a prize-fight, but caused no casualties.[102] Aside from these, the only other hint of menace occurred in 1801, when a prize-fight had been thwarted leaving a huge, tense, disappointed crowd. Although the local people felt some fear and hired vigilantes to protect them, there was no trouble.[103]

Certain sports, particularly bull-baiting and prize-fighting, were the subjects of concern by local authorities because they tended to attract criminals.[104] However, pugilism rarely suffered from official intervention probably because of the high esteem in which the sport was held by a large section of influential opinion. Despite its increasing size and sophistication, urban British society adhered to many old, rurally based values, notably an appreciation of physical strength and courage.[105] These had key roles in regulating town life and were embodied by two activities, duelling and pugilism. Each of these had been employed as a way of resolving disputes from at least the early eighteenth century. Patriotic writers often extolled the manly sports of the British, claiming that they reflected a courageous, robust, individualism, in which the nation could take pride.[106] Pugilism was regarded as humane and fair and its practice was presented in chivalrous terms.[107] It was also a symbol of national courage, embodying the worth which Englishmen placed upon their own individual honour.[108] The French, it was argued, did not like pugilism because they were not a free people and relied on the authorities to resolve their disputes. By contrast, the British dealt with their own problems in a straightforward manner, according to established rules of fair play.[109]

Such an ethic owed much to the status of the duel. Conflicts between gentlemen were sometimes resolved by weapons, such as swords and pistols, the use of which reflected the protagonists' social position; though these weapons were occasionally employed by tradesmen and even schoolboys in the years after the French revolution, when the habit spread socially.[110] Predominantly, duels were considered to be the legitimate means with which gentlemen could defend their honour and thus 'preserve civilization'.[111] Duelling gave value to social life and helped to sanction the privileges which the upper class possessed, because, in the very last analysis, they were willing to sacrifice their lives for the defence of their honour.[112] The principal quality that it fostered was courage and it was regarded as 'dishonourable' to practise shooting.[113] Duelling was pervasive among the upper class and even politicians, such as Canning and Castlereagh, resorted to it.[114] So common was duelling that *The Sporting Magazine* had a regular monthly column, 'Affairs of Honour', devoted to them, and noted that some of the military 'hate one another far worse than Buonaparte'.[115] Many, however, regarded this concern over the preservation of honour as being a jealous imperative that removed scope for social manoeuvre, resulting in unnecessary deaths.[116] They adhered to the same notions of honour, bitterly opposing recourse to the law, but believed it could be better served by either pugilism or wrestling.[117] Increasingly, therefore, pugilism was regarded as a better way of resolving disputes between gentlemen and aspirants actually began taking lessons from renowned pugilists.[118] Although, of course, this was far from common, it was indicative of the high respect in which the sport was held by the social elite. This was acknowledged by everyone, and at a trial a magistrate stated 'he was sorry to say that some of the higher orders of this country countenanced this abominable practice'.[119]

Given such a social background, it is understandable that few people appear to have regarded pugilism as illegal. As we have seen, pugilism was not formally proscribed, and despite determined pronouncements from the King's Bench, and high profile prosecutions, such as that of Burke, the sport persisted.[120] Everything depended on the attitude of the local magistrates. Those in areas such as Buckinghamshire attacked the activity vigorously, while elsewhere it often remained untouched.[121] An indication of exactly how little impact official society had on pugilism can be gleaned from the following statistics. Between 1793 and 1804 a total of 134 prize-fights were arranged. Of these, just eight were prevented. Far from the application of the law becoming stricter, the latter half of the war, 1805–15, witnessed 366 prize-fights, of which only seven were prevented. In total, only 15 out of 600 prize-fights were either prevented or terminated by officialdom; just 2.5 per cent. This prompted commentators who wished to curb the practice to advocate alternatives. Lawrence advocated the creation of a cheaply priced theatre where youths could witness sparring because he believed that 'such a plan were to reduce the number of battles, by withdrawing the public taste from serious boxing to bloodless sparring, to which also the practice of betting might attach'.[122]

Paradoxically, while pugilism often went unpunished, other, more innocuous looking sports, were often prevented.[123] In essence, the perceived threat of a sport was influential, but not decisive, in the response of the authorities. Protests by significant local people, such as the law suit instigated against Plaistow sports and the actions against the fair at Fairlop, could result in their being banned.[124] Both were lower-class entertainments, but attacks were also initiated against sports which enjoyed the patronage of a more select audience, as with the sparring exhibitions given by boxers at theatres in Cambridge and London.[125] Generally, the authorities appear to have tolerated sports and adopted a flexible policy similar to that which they used in response to other social conflicts. In fact, on many occasions they actually assisted sporting events by providing the protection of constables, even though there was no discernible financial reason for doing so.[126] Of a different order altogether were the attempts by corporations to host certain sporting activities. In those particular cases, the most dramatic example being the Cribb–Molineaux fight of 1811, the local authorities actively solicited events, the expected financial benefits to the community outweighing concerns over the preservation of the law.[127]

As we have seen, there was no unified response by the local authorities towards events. Nor did support or opposition for various sports break down along class-based lines: both opponents and defenders represented a wide social spectrum. One incident crystallises this. In 1815 a Justice at Blackheath, Williams, had the pedestrian, Wilson, arrested for breach of the peace. However, his action was vigorously opposed by neighbouring magistrates. Not only was Wilson released, but his friends had Williams placed before the King's Bench to answer for his conduct.[128] Overall, it would be misleading to regard there being a significant dispute between sportsmen and the authorities. Practitioners of sport were rarely arrested and on at least one occasion when they were, the authorities had legitimate reasons for being concerned.[129] A marshal in the police had formerly been a prize-fighter, and it was not unknown for boxers to resort to the law to resolve disputes.[130] In fact, sportsmen were sometimes held as being above the law: the winner of the prestigious rowing boat race, Doggett's Coat and Badge, was also granted exemption from being pressed.[131] Essentially, despite isolated incidents, sport had quite an easy relationship with officialdom, and sporting crowds appear to have been remarkably passive. Likewise, there was a considerable logic in the general acceptance of the heroic ethic, as manifested in duelling and pugilism. Both activities were believed to foster discipline and courage, qualities vital in fighting a Napoleonic battle.[132] There, two massed armies stood firing volleys at one another from a short distance. Casualties were enormous, exceeding, proportionately, those suffered in the First World War.[133] Thus, *Bell's Weekly Messenger*, having enumerated the numbers killed in duelling and prize-fights declared that such casualties were 'as nothing, compared to the keeping up of the courage of the country'.[134]

Use of the Courts

Although the local authorities dealt with many of the problems arising from recreations, many sporting disputes had to be resolved in court. Such cases were a direct result of the failure, or non-existence, of the various societies that endeavoured to supervise sport. Generally, bodies such as the Jockey Club, were reluctant to involve themselves in deciding disputes and mediation was often dependent upon the existence of a third party whose opinion was respected by both protagonists. Given the often curious rules that governed events, it is unsurprising that the courts were often called upon to decide matters. One of the most intriguing cases had profound social implications, for it depended upon whether a farmer could win a horse race that was restricted to gentlemen. A packed court listened as the arguments attempted to discover whether the contemporary definition of gentleman included farmers.[135] The commonest sporting cases resulted from the attempts by gamblers to recover their stakes.[136] Almost everyone in the legal system, especially jurors, regarded this as an abuse of the court's time and in an effort to discourage gambling refused to intervene on behalf of the plaintiff unless there was irrefutable evidence of fraud.[137] Occasionally cases were uncovered that were so corrupt that action was taken by the court.[138]

Enclosures, generally speaking, do not appear to have had much of an impact on sports, judging by the number of cases that appeared in court. Chiefly, it was golfers who seemed to have felt threatened by the process, endeavouring to either defend land or their access to it.[139] By contrast, the issue of trespass generated numerous disputes in fox-hunting, some of which finished up in court. Their motivating factors can, essentially, be divided into four groups. The first, was principally related to sport. Disputes over territory between various hunts could be especially bitter, such as that occurring in Yorkshire in 1809.[140] Another flash point was the contentious practice of digging out foxes on someone else's land. Foxes were much sought after and such squabbles had an alarming capacity to mushroom: in 1815 two aristocrats, Moberley and Joliffe, fought a duel over just this issue.[141] A second cause of animosity related to political rivalries. In 1810, Sir William Manners and the Duke of Rutland clashed over the incursions of the Belvoir hunt, and one of the major complaints against the pack was that its master 'always opposes Lord Grantham at the election'.[142] A third type of clash was simply related to the problems which intruding packs caused, especially those whose members lacked local roots because they were based upon subscription and therefore eligible to outsiders. Disputes of this type commenced when magistrates began to reject a ruling made in 1786 by Lord Mansfield that had assured packs of immunity from prosecution for trespass.[143] Throughout the whole period a number of different areas forbade hunting and in 1810 an association of noblemen and gentlemen was created to prevent hunting on their land.[144] Lastly, by far the bitterest cases were produced when fox-hunting was used as a vehicle to express deep personal antipathy. The most vociferous case erupted in 1809, involving Capel's Old Berkely Hounds fox-hunting pack, and land belonging to Lord Essex.[145] The protagonists were not only aristocrats related to one another, but also men bonded by intense mutual antipathy. Lord Essex forbade Capel's pack from hunting on his land and sought to enforce this both by employing informers and compelling his tenants to prosecute the hunt.[146] Between 1810 and 1812 there were a whole spate of court cases which only stopped when the Berkely hunt ceased making incursions on Essex's land.[147] The precedent Essex established persuaded some fox-hunting packs to disband.[148]

On the face of it, by 1811 fox-hunting seemed to be in a very precarious position with a number of magistrates declaring that there was no rational justification for it.[149] As it was, the trouble passed. Fox-hunting packs quickly readjusted their territory, withdrawing behind new, somewhat contracted, boundaries. By the end of the war they appear to have been quite secure, an indication that fox-hunting was rooted firmly in a series of relationships within many communities, and that this effectively negated the relevance of legal decisions.[150]

It is clear that like Parliament, the local powers, generally avoided interfering with sport, thus allowing its commercial exploitation to expand. In the next chapter we will examine this process in the years after 1815.

Notes

1   J. Strutt (1801) *The Sports and Pastimes of the People of England*, London: William Reeves, p. xv.

2   T. Malthus (1798) *First Essay On Population*, London, ch xviii, p. 370.

3   See *Statutes at Large From the 9th year of King George II to the 25th year of King George II* or *Bibliotheca Lindesiana. Handlist of Proclamations issued by royal and other constitutional authorities* (London, 1893–1901). It is instructive to examine various editions of Burn, *Justice of the Peace*. Prize-fighting is not referred to as an illegal act until the 1869 edition (v, 145), where the earliest case cited is from 1831.

4   In Berkshire, for instance, a group of boys were fined three shillings each for playing cricket on a village green outside their parish one Sunday evening; see *Bell's*, 20 Aug 1843. Fishing and quoits also suffered; *Letter dated 17 Aug 1840 prohibiting quoits at a pub in Preston*. LCRO. DDPR 130/21. *WMC*, 2 Nov 1833.

5   R. Burn (1762) *Justice of the Peace*, London: H. Miller, iii, p. 213, and later editions (1797) iii, p. 112, (1820) v, p. 16, (1825), v, p. 19, (1830), v, p. 20.

6   *SM*, April 1795, 248.

7   *SM*, Aug 1795, 248–50.

8   *SM*, April 1813, 30.

9   *SM*, Sept 1807, 284–6, June 1813, 106.

10 *Jackson's*, 26 Oct 1793. *SM*, Jan 1808, 94–5; Dec 1808, 135; April 1813, 29–30; Nov 1815, 71.

11 *SM*, Nov 1797, 151–2; April 1802, 4; May 1802, 69; June 1802, 138, 163–4; July 1802, 179–80; Aug 1802, 236–7. W. Taplin (1803) *Sporting Dictionary*, London, ii, pp. 336–7.

12 *SM*, Jan 1800, 185. Thom, *Pedestrianism*, pp. 206–207.

13 *SM*, Aug 1803, 273; April 1813, 30.

14 *SM*, Jan 1794, 168.

15 Malcolmson, *Popular Recreations*, pp. 89–94, 100–104.

16 Ibid., pp. 122–3, 146, 149.

17 P. Langford (1989) *A Polite And Commercial People: England 1727–1783*, Oxford: Oxford University Press, pp. 296–7.

18   Brailsford, 'Sporting days', 174–5, 177–8. Walvin, *Leisure and Society*, p. 9.
19   See this volume, pp. 71–2.
20   *SM*, Oct 1792, 6.
21   *SM*, March 1796, 330–31.
22   P. Munsche (1981) *Gentlemen and Poachers: The English Game Laws 1671–1831*, Cambridge: Cambridge University Press, pp. 127–8.
23   Ibid., pp. 130, 166.
24   *SM*, April 1793, 15.
25   *SM*, April 1794, 15; Sept 1797, 313–14.
26   *SM*, April 1794, 15.
27   *SM*, Feb 1812, 194–6; July 1812, 157–8.
28   *BWM*, 7 Jan 1810. *WD*, 10 April 1803.
29   *BWM*, 24 Oct 1813. *SM*, Jan 1803, 225.
30   *SM*, Feb 1803, 291–2; Dec 1808, 102–103.
31   *SM*, June 1793, 136; July 1793, 255; Dec 1811, 134; June 1815, 105.
32   Munsche defends the Game Laws in *Gentlemen and Poachers*, pp. 159–68. However, there is substantial evidence refuting his contentions; see for example *SM*, March 1793, 366; Sept 1794, 343.
33   Munsche, *Gentlemen and Poachers*, pp. 102–103. Though magistrates were by no means always hostile to defendants, pp. 95–6, 161.
34   Bovill, *English Country Life*, p. 194. Munsche, *Gentlemen and Poachers*, p. 152. J. Wade (1835) *The Black Book, Or Corruption Unmasked*, London: Effingham Wilton, p. 271.
35   *SM*, Oct 1793, 50.
36   *SM*, Dec 1793, 156; Sept 1809, 291. *WMC*, 19 Sept 1812.
37   K. Thomas (1983) *Man and the Natural World*, London: Allen Lane, pp. 152–3.
38   *BWM*, 30 May 1802. *SM*, Dec 1808, 120.
39   C. Moritz (1797) *Travels Chiefly on Foot, Through Several Parts of England in 1782*, London, p. 91. *SM*, April 1793, 59; Nov 1793, 93; June 1794, 151–4; May 1799, 88; Nov 1801, 59; Aug 1803, 273; Nov 1803, 87; Sept 1804, 296–80; Dec 1804, 132–4; Dec 1808, 145–6; July 1813, 155–6.
40   *SM*, Jan 1797, 254–8; Dec 1797, 161–2; March 1802, 340; July 1803, 243–4.
41   *SM*, Sept 1815, 245.
42   S. Kendall Phillips (1980) 'Primitive Methodist confrontation with popular sports', in R. Cashman and M. McKernan (eds) *Sport, Money, Morality and the Media*, Queensland: New South Wales, p. 295. *SM*, Oct 1801, 51.
43   Black, *English Press*, p. 257. Langford, *Polite and Commercial*, pp. 503–505. *Times*, 4 Feb 1804.
44   *BWM*, 21 Aug 1808. *SM*, Feb 1793, 253; May 1802, 101–102; March 1803, 306–307; Sept 1803, 328; Oct 1803, 48; Nov 1803, 62; Jan 1808, 195. Strutt, *Sports and Pastimes*, pp. lii, 205, 224. Taplin, *Sporting Dictionary*, i, p. 93.
45   *SM*, Oct 1794, 87–9; Dec 1794, 140. *WD*, 2 Sept 1804.
46   *SM*, Oct 1795, 40–42.
47   *SM*, Aug 1793, 285. *MM*, 7 Nov 1809.
48   *SM*, Nov 1794, 59–61; Oct 1795, 17–19. *Times*, 11 Aug 1795.
49   J. Innes (1990) 'Politics and morals', in F. Hellmuth (ed.) *The Transformation of Political Culture*, Oxford: Oxford University Press, pp. 75, 87, 112.
50   *SM*, March 1803, 342–4. Vegetarianism was intimately associated with political and social radicalism. See Thomas, *Natural World*, p. 296.

51 *BWM*, 20 April 1800. *SM*, Feb 1807, 241.

52 *SM*, Nov 1802, 90–96.

53 *SM*, Nov 1794, 106; Jan 1799, 195–9; Feb 1799, 254–5.

54 *SM*, Oct 1794, 40–41.

55 H. Fishwick (1874) *The History of the Parish of Kirkham in the County Of Lancaster*, Lancaster: Cheetham Soc., p. 274. *SM*, April 1793, 57.

56 *SM*, May 1800, 80.

57 *SM*, Jan 1802, 197–8. Thomas, *Natural World*, p. 158.

58 *BWD*, 2 May 1802, 9 May 1802. *SM*, March 1802, 340; April 1802, 36–7; Dec 1808, 120; Aug 1813, 243; Oct 1814, 29.

59 *SM*, April 1815, 18–20; May 1815, 67–70; June 1815, 109; Aug 1815, 215–16.

60 *SM*, Dec 1813, 102.

61 *SM*, Oct 1810, 43.

62 Cunningham, *Industrial Revolution*, pp. 42–4.

63 *BWD*, 30 May 1802. *BWM*, 20 April 1800, 30 May 1802, 21 May 1809, 13 May 1810. *Cobbett's Annual Register* (1802), i, p. 626. W. Cobbett (1819) *Parliamentary History of England From the Earliest Period to the Year 1803*, xxv, 1800–1802, London: Longman, p. 213. *SM*, April 1800, 34–40; June 1809, 118–22.

64 Cobbett, *Parliamentary History*, xxxv, pp. 202–203, 211.

65 G. Newman (1987) *The Rise of English Nationalism: A Cultural History 1740–1830*, London: Weidenfeld, pp. 46, 63, 118, 183–4.

66 Ibid., p. 135.

67 P. Burke (1978) *Popular Culture in Early Modern Europe*, London: Temple Smith, p. 283. Newman, *English Nationalism*, p. 144.

68 L. Colley (1992) *Britons: Forging the Nation 1707–1837*, London: New Haven, pp. 5–6, 367–8. Newman, *Rise*, pp. 228–30.

69 W. Litt (1823) *Wrestliana*, Whitehaven: R. Gibson, p. 56.

70 J. Surel (1989) 'John Bull', in R. Samuel (ed.) *Patriotism: The Making and Unmaking of British National Identity*, London: Routledge, iii, pp. 10, 16, 21.

71 Colley, *Britons*, p. 322.

72 S. Cottrell (1989) 'The devil on two sticks: Francophobia in 1803', in Samuel, *Patriotism*, i, pp. 259–60.

73 *SM*, Feb 1805, 272.

74 *ER*, xiii (1808–9), 335, 338, 342.

75 *BWD*, 30 May 1802. *BWM*, 20 April 1800, 5 Jan 1812. The attacks had a significant impact on Cobbett's attitude; I. Dyck (1992) *William Cobbett and Rural Popular Culture*, Cambridge: Cambridge University Press, pp. 22, 29, 46. *SM*, Oct 1806, 8.

76 *SM*, Jan 1806, 198–9.

77 *BWD*, 30 May 1802. *Times*, 4 Feb 1804.

78 *SM*, Feb 1805, 272–4.

79 *BWM*, 20 April 1800. *SM*, July 1793, 236; Sept 1793, 362; Nov 1793, 77; Dec 1802, 150–51; Feb 1803, 273; Nov 1803, 92.

80 *SM*, Aug 1803, 306. Windham, himself, was sincere in his promotion of British sports, possessing considerable expertise in pugilism, hence being nicknamed 'boxing Windham'. R. White (1963) *Life in Regency England*, London: Putnam, pp. 109–10.

81 BL Add. Mss. *Windham Papers*, xc 58. *BWM*, 20 May 1810.

82 Langford, *Polite and Commercial*, pp. 296–7.

83 *SM*, April 1795, 7; June 1795, 124. *Sportsman*, Jan 1835, 10.

84 Emsley, *British Society and the French Wars*, pp. 53–4, 101, 128. *MM*, 15 May 1798.
    SM, Dec 1796, 159; March 1798, 55; March 1805, 314; Aug 1809, 228; July 1810,
    183–4. Thom, *Pedestrianism*, pp. iii–iv, 37.

85 *BWM*, 16 Aug 1801. *SM*, Aug 1801, 259; Sept 1801, 320; Aug 1803, 276; Jan 1804,
    218.

86 *BWM*, 25 Oct 1801. *SM*, June 1796, 167; Sept 1811, 270.

87 *BWM*, 24 Oct 1813. *SM*, March 1808, 278–9; Sept 1810, 256.

88 *Bell's*, 5 Oct 1834. *SM*, March 1793, 367; Nov 1793, 83–4.

89 *SM*, Sept 1806, 251.

90 *SM*, June 1802, 163–4; March 1804, 337; June 1811, 105–106; Nov 1815, 72.

91 *SM*, June 1797, 129–31; April 1803, 19.

92 *BWM*, 23 Sept 1804.

93 *MM*, 1 Jan 1793.

94 *MM*, 11 Nov 1800.

95 *Jackson's*, 17 Aug 1793, 17 March 1810.

96 J. Stevenson (1977a) 'Social control and the prevention of riots in England
    1789–1829', in A. Donajgrodzki (ed.) *Social Control in Nineteenth Century Britain*,
    London: Croom Helm, pp. 40, 46–7.

97 D. Eastwood (1985) Governing Rural England: Authority and Social Order in
    Oxfordshire 1780–1840, D.Phil. Oxford, pp. 189, 195.

98 Brailsford, *Bareknuckles*, p. 48.

99 *SM*, Feb 1804, 287.

100 *BWM*, 14 Aug 1796. *SM*, Jan 1794, 222; June 1799, 129; Sept 1801, 326; Oct 1801,
    43; June 1806, 135–6.

101 *SM*, May 1799, 107.

102 J. Ford (1972) *Cricket: A Social History 1700–1835*, Newton Abbot: David and
    Charles, pp. 129–30. *SM*, Oct 1813, 24. *Times*, 3 June 1799.

103 *SM*, Oct 1801, 45. Fear of possible disorder led to the Derby and Oaks horse races
    being held at Newmarket. D. Birley (1993) *Sport and the Making of Britain*,
    Manchester: Manchester University Press, p. 155.

104 *WMC*, 29 Oct 1814.

105 G. Borrow (1851) *Lavengro*, London: John Murray, i, pp. 327–8. Carr, *Fox-hunting*,
    p. 219.

106 Dyck, *William Cobbett*, pp. 20–21.

107 *BWM*, 30 Sept 1804. *SM*, Oct 1792, 16; Sept 1806, 261, 264–5; Nov 1808, 63–6; April
    1811, 38. *Times*, 10 Oct 1811.

108 *BWM*, 10 Jan 1808.

109 *SM*, May 1814, 91; July 1815, 147; Dec 1815, 142; contra the French, Jan 1808, 195.

110 G.B. Buckley (1937) *Fresh Light on Pre-Victorian Cricket 1709–1837*, Birmingham:
    Cotterell, p. 53. V. Kiernan (1988) *The Duel in European History*, Oxford: Oxford
    University Press, pp. 187–9. *SM*, April 1798, 34–6; June 1798, 151–2; May 1799, 92;
    Nov 1803, 63; March 1804, 297–8; Aug 1804, 272. Van Muyden, *Foreign View of
    England*, p. 212.

111 *SM*, May 1803, 69.

112 Kiernan, *Duel*, pp. 6, 15, 152–3.

113 *SM*, May 1803, 70.

114 *SM*, Sept 1809, 257.

115 *SM*, May 1808, 57–9; Sept 1808, 250; Oct 1810, 1–3.

116 *SM*, March 1804, 300; Oct 1814, 29–30.

117   *BWM*, 23 Aug 1807. T. Parkyns (1727) *The Inn-Play or Cornish-hugg Wrestling*, London, p. v.
118   *BWM*, 23 Aug 1807.
119   *SM*, Jan 1805, 171–2. *WD*, 15 May 1803.
120   *SM*, Jan 1805, 171.
121   *SM*, Feb 1808, 265; March 1808, 322; May 1808, 73–4, 96–7; Aug 1811, 242.
122   *SM*, May 1811, 80.
123   *SM*, Aug 1800, 235.
124   *SM*, Jan 1794, 167–8; July 1810, 166.
125   *BWM*, 11 Aug 1805. *SM*, Oct 1802, 17; Dec 1807, 148.
126   *BWM*, 10 May 1812, 22 Oct 1815.
127   *SM*, Oct 1811, 20.
128   *SM*, Oct 1815, 44.
129   *BWM*, 20 May 1798.
130   *SM*, Aug 1809, 214–15; Oct 1811, 44.
131   *SM*, Aug 1801, 231.
132   *SM*, Feb 1809, 239.
133   Emsley, *British Society and the French Wars*, p. 169.
134   *Bell's*, 10 Jan 1808.
135   *SM*, Aug 1803, 267.
136   *SM*, Sept 1806, 276–7; Feb 1808, 266.
137   *SM*, Dec 1792, 172; April 1794, 116; Dec 1794, 144.
138   *SM*, Sept 1809, 292; Oct 1809, 25.
139   *SM*, Dec 1813, 143–4; Oct 1815, 42–3.
140   *SM*, Feb 1809, 249.
141   *SM*, Oct 1815, 1–4.
142   *SM*, Nov 1810, 70–71.
143   Thomas, *Natural World*, pp. 164–5.
144   *SM*, Dec 1795, 120; Oct 1810, 29; Aug 1812, 280.
145   *BWM*, 15 Oct 1809. Bovill, *Nimrod and Surtees*, p. 103. *SM*, July 1809, 157–9.
146   *SM*, Nov 1810, 71; Aug 1811, 222–3.
147   *SM*, May 1810, 83; Sept 1810, 269; Nov 1810, 72; Nov 1812, 57–8.
148   *SM*, May 1810, 83.
149   *BWM*, 11 Aug 1811.
150   *SM*, Aug 1811, 222–3.

Chapter 5

You Can All Join In:
The Law and Sport, 1816–50

This, the second half of our consideration of the role of government in the supervision of sport, considers the years between 1816 and 1850. It consists of two parts, the first of which concentrates on the impact of national influences – Parliament, monarch and the military; the second part assesses the behaviour of the principal facets of local administration, both government and courts.

National Influences on Sport

Parliament and Sport

As we have seen, during the French wars there were few attempts to legislate against sport. From the early 1830s increasing attention was paid to new, primarily urban, concerns, especially the dislocation resulting from industrialization. This was often referred to as the 'condition of England question', a pervasive perspective, that found expression in literature, particularly novels, parliamentary enquiries, and the speeches of politicians. It was typified by Carlyle's declaration that there were no green fields in Manchester.[1] The concerns excited by such perspectives transformed the way sport, and recreation generally, were perceived, with many groups acknowledging it to have an important role in society, thus necessitating some form of intervention. The groups' reasons for involvement can be broadly divided into six categories, the discussion of which follows.

Organized religion, especially the Evangelical branches of Protestantism, provided a strong incentive for intervention. They can be broadly divided into two types. The Sabbatarians were principally concerned with curbing the number of activities on Sunday. By contrast, both the Methodists and the Temperance Movement offered alternative entertainments and were often heavily involved in secular affairs.[2] A second group were the industrialists. While they had a variety of intentions, these were usually related to economic self interest, and often involved the replacement of more disruptive forms of recreation with subdued varieties, in order to increase labour discipline.[3] A third group consisted of educated elements of the working class, especially those who are sometimes referred to as the 'labour aristocracy'.[4] They regarded recreation as having a vital social and economic significance, which could assist the political emergence of the lower orders.

Consequently, they supported the suppression of many vices and their replacement by 'respectable' activities, particularly 'rational recreations', such as chess and cricket. Additionally, they pressed for shorter working hours and the increased provision of parks. Much of this programme, though shorn of its more radical political elements, was shared by a fourth group, middle and upper class liberals. The fifth group were conservatives, typically the Young England movement, who blamed modern developments for eroding and undermining society. They were highly supportive of recreation, opposing legislation that was designed to limit its variety, and urging the introduction of shorter working hours and an increased provision of parks. As we saw earlier, from the beginning of the nineteenth century a number of bodies, motivated by 'humane' issues, had sought to introduce laws protecting animals from cruelty, they are our sixth group.

With the exception of the last group, whose attention was focused upon animals, the various divergent bodies shared an underlying assumption: the belief that the appropriate type of recreation would create social harmony.[5] Naturally, their precise vision of this harmony varied considerably and this was reflected in the programmes that they devised to accomplish their goals.

The Sabbatarians were the most uncompromising of the religiously motivated groups, concentrating their efforts on increasing legal restrictions. However, after the failure of their bill in the Parliament of 1834, such pressure receded; Agnew, its sponsor, losing his seat in 1837.[6] The Sabbatarians were basically hostile to most recreations, and their leisure activities were entirely home-based. Most other religiously orientated groups sought to provide alternative entertainments, particularly when they were attacking 'cruel sports'.[7] Typical were the Temperance Movement and the Methodists, who presented a significant alternative recreational culture. This consisted of numerous counter attractions, notably railway excursions – from which Thomas Cook derived the inspiration for his travel agency – and 'love feasts', a mixture of picnics, hymns and games.[8]

Industrialists, the educated working-class and liberals, were united in their support of Mechanics' Institutes, Athenaeums and Lyceums. Yet their response to the various elements of the programmes that were available in these institutions varied considerably. 'Rational recreations', such as music, were seen as helping to 'improve' their practitioners, and attracted considerable support.[9] By contrast, sport was often regarded as unsettling the discipline of workers, and therefore disapproved of by those favouring business and industry. However, many educated workers and liberals, though often regarding 'rustic' entertainments as 'stupid', favoured certain sports.[10] Chief among these was cricket, a game that was fostered by some of the more liberal clergy.[11] Cricket's wide-ranging supporters saw it as creating working-men who were 'independent of being and civil without being servile. It is this mingling of the different classes in manly and friendly strife that constitutes the chief charm and national good of cricket'.[12] Ultimately, no matter what the volitions of the various groups who tried to structure the programmes of the 'improving' institutions, people wanted entertainment.[13] Lacking significant financial support, it was this fact which forced the various institutions to dilute their intellectual diet in order to expand their audience.[14] This they did by including sparring, cricket, and billiards – a game that was usually linked to gambling and regarded as morally unsavoury.[15]

The clearest diagnosis of the problems of modern society stemmed from conservatives, such as 'A country gentlemen', who deprecated the increase in education, writing: 'All states and empires have had their periods of declension, and that declension has generally been traced to an over indulgence in the fine arts'.[16] Traditionalists were especially critical of the 'baleful consequences amongst the lower orders, produced in general by the march of intellect', perceiving it as creating 'the sickly mechanic', who was too dry and educated, his spirit having evaporated, leaving a 'shrivelled penman'. The lives of these hapless workers required the excitement of the sports that were 'the gift of our fore-fathers'.[17] Defenders of the traditional attitudes towards sport linked the attacks posed against them by modern critics with similar criticism of the social order. Thus, those attacking boxing and fox-hunting were often condemned as radicals advocating 'chartism and the knife', who instead of resolving quarrels as traditional Britons, in an open, manly, fashion, resorted to the weapons of covert assassination.[18] Such a fusion of sporting and social values was thoroughgoing, the destruction of established sport being a manifestation of the decline in social values, typified by political demonstrations forcing the cancellation of athletic fixtures.[19] For traditionalists, the discouragement of pugilism had created these 'dismal and murderous times'.[20] They expressed great nostalgia for the past, especially its heroic boxers, and suspicion of modern attitudes, which they regarded as creating effeminacy. The link was clear; the suppression of sport led to a decline in the national character, particularly that of the working class. This was a long established mode of argument, and the Pugilistic Club's declaration in 1816 that their aim was to 'keep up the national character' was continually being refashioned by conservatives.[21]

At the most elementary level was the belief that were 'British sports' to vanish:

> Secret societies and debating clubs will be begun; demagogues and radicals will tell them, and make them believe, that they are slaves and oppressed, and that the rich are taking all pleasures to themselves.[22]

It was a theme echoed by many, Chief Justice Best criticizing Evangelical reformers for 'stirring up a more troubled sea'.[23] Papers and periodicals were full of letters and editorials urging the upper class to provide sport for the lower orders.[24] Some regarded the lack of appropriate recreations as having a drastic effect, a correspondent stating:

> the ring has degenerated and many other kindred sports have either degenerated with it or wholly disappeared. In the meantime every unmanly vice fearfully increases. Crimes, which I will not pollute your pages by describing, originally of foreign growth, once

confined to large cities and effeminate occupations, appear even in agricultural districts.[25]

Conservatives, particularly the Young England movement, perceived sport as a way of recreating the traditional structure of society, based upon ranks of patronage. This was to be accomplished by fostering recreations that were considered to be older, usually 'rustic sports', in which all could participate.[26] The element of shared enjoyment between the various ranks was crucial, some commentators even praising 'cruel sports' because they were seen as creating this unity.[27] A number of conservatives were supportive of acts designed to increase the time and space available for recreation, as well as the creation of institutions to foster 'national sports'. They also proved to be fierce opponents of our sixth group, those advocating legislation against 'cruel sports', the subject to which we now turn.

During the French wars campaigns against particular recreational practices had failed to attract wide-ranging support. In the years after Waterloo, groups composed of widely varying elements – religion, commerce and trade unions – became more active, attacking particular targets. The most notable example of this was alcohol, which suffered sustained attack from both the religious Temperance Movement and atheistic radicals such as Engels.[28] Accompanying this broadening of the range of social interests represented by pressure groups, were changes within Parliament that heightened their impact. First, while one must be wary of overstating the extent of middle-class as opposed to aristocratic power within Parliament after 1830, it did result in an increased presence of MPs sympathetic to reforming ideas.[29] More importantly, the Whig administration sought to impose a more pervasive form of government, by initiating and directing action, embodied by the Poor Law of 1834, which many regard as a significant piece of centralizing legislation. This contrasted sharply with the early post-Waterloo years, where much of the creative legislation stemmed from an interaction between pressure groups and backbenchers.[30] Consequently, the impact of any resulting legislation was magnified, especially by comparison with that of the French wars. Thus, after 1830, ideas concerning sport and recreation advanced by the various pressure groups had far more potential impact than those of their predecessors.

Despite their earlier failures during the French wars, pressure groups advocating the introduction of legislation against animal cruelty were increasingly successful in the later period. From the 1820s a number of new groups, including the Animals' Friend Society and the Royal Society for the Protection of Animals (RSPCA), two bitter rivals whose mutual animosity sometimes resulted in court cases, appeared.[31] At first their interventions were haphazard, most notably in failing to prevent the sadism of a lion bait in 1825, having earlier intervened successfully to prevent the College of Surgeons' experiments on living animals.[32] This was a confusion typical of the inconsistent legislation introduced concerning animal cruelty during that period.[33] The chief sponsor of such issues was the MP, Martin, who was a renowned duellist and debtor who favoured flogging in the army: facts which made it easy for the press to ridicule him.[34] Likewise, some of the research undertaken by parliamentary committees, notably a visit to a rat pit to determine the amount of cruelty there, invited derision from critics.[35] However, by the following decade, the RSPCA, though quite small, and with operations effectively restricted to London, was a very effective organization that mounted a well coordinated campaign, involving spies, constables and carefully briefed officials, as well as adroit propaganda, which employed artists such as Cruikshank.[36] The resulting legislation concerning 'cruel sports' that they promoted illustrated the extent to which Parliament had changed by comparison with the period of the French wars.

The laws which the Society and their parliamentary supporters introduced, particularly those of 1835 and 1849, were regarded by the MP, Sir M. Ridley, as displaying pronounced class bias. Upper-class sports, such as fox-hunting, despite their obvious cruelty, remained untouched, while the activities of the lower orders were proscribed.[37] This was despite the fact that the label 'Cruel sport' was applied to six activities by the 1830s: bull-baiting, cock-fighting, steeple-chasing, fox-hunting, battues and pigeon-shooting. Bull-baiting had been slowly losing support since the eighteenth century, despite the espousal of patriots such as Cobbett, who spoke up for the courage it fostered.[38]

By the 1830s, bull-baiting's following stemmed, essentially, from the lower orders. Each of the other sports were chiefly practised by the upper and middle ranks, and had influential followers, who would defend them as being 'humane', or for only inflicting a 'necessary degree of suffering', distinguishing them completely from the 'cruel' baiting sports.[39] The indignant response of the aristocrat, Grantley Berkeley, to the RSPCA's criticism of his favourite sport, cock-fighting, sums up such feelings: 'let the society confine its endeavours to the protection of domestic animals and to the suppression of cruelty disgustingly practiced in the open streets and markets upon maimed and worn out horses'.[40] In fact, cock-fighting was the only one of the sports to enjoy substantial support from both the upper and lower orders. It also had intellectual credibility: scientists, especially phrenologists, declaring it 'natural'.[41]

Harrison rejects accusations that the campaign against 'cruel sports' was guilty of class bias because this 'ignores the pan-class nature of so much brutal sport at the time'. He also justifies the failure of the RSPCA to criticise many upper-class sports as being due to the fact that they could 'only move as fast as public opinion, which naturally extended its sympathies first to tame animals', sentiments echoed by Golby and Purdue, who contend that 'only the most purely cruel sports were prosecuted'.[42] Harrison stated that: 'The Christian attack on traditional recreation in the nineteenth century is perhaps better understood in terms of culture-conflict than of class-conflict'. He then goes on to outline the diverse nature of the social class from which both sides drew their support.[43] It is certainly true that attitudes towards 'cruel sports' did not break down along class lines. Defenders of such activities included: MPs such as Sibthorpe; aristocrats such as Berkeley; middle-class intellectuals such as Blaine; and working men.[44] Similarly, attackers stemmed from diverse origins, including both the Chartists and concerned aristocrats.[45] However, the actual enforcement of the laws can be demonstrated to show immense class bias, as we shall now see.

Cock-fighting was the only upper-class sport during the period to be made illegal, in 1849, but still persisted to the point of being noticed in the press.[46] Almost all of the action taken against cruel sports in the period up to 1850, for instance in 158 out of the 159 cases between 1838 and 1841 for which it was possible to trace the offender's occupation, involved the prosecution of working-class individuals.[47] A police raid on a dog-fighting den in 1846 typifies the class bias in the law's application; while all the nobles and gents were discharged, despite the fact that some of them owned the competing animals, certain members of the lower orders were arrested.[48] In large measure the RSPCA appears to have been an essentially upper- and middle-class organization, whose victims were, almost entirely, from the lower ranks.[49] It seems more accurate to regard the RSPCA as intervening largely against working-class, rather than upper- and middle-class activities. It is misleading to suggest that this reflected public opinion. The destruction of overridden horses in fox-hunting and steeplechasing and the mass slaughter of pigeons, had long attracted odium.[50] However, their practitioners were very influential and it was this, rather than any discerning sensibility, that was crucial.[51] This, essentially, is the point. While the social origins and attitudes of both sides in the conflict relating to 'cruel sports' varied, it was invariably members from the lower orders who were prosecuted. In this, the most practical sense, the RSPCA reflected the bias of a social system in which pugilists were indicted for fighting while Wellington went unpunished for duelling.[52]

While the legislation against 'cruel sports' was the most overt example of the influence exerted by the concerted action of pressure groups and MPs, it was by no means the only one. Agitation by the various political commentators and pressure groups led to a greater awareness of social problems and the belief that these could be eased by acceptable forms of recreation, which would unite the various classes.[53] Such attitudes led to periodic suggestions by conservatives that funds should be provided for the establishment of academies in which the nation's sports could be fostered.[54] One such was the following:

> several of the leading members of both branches of the British legislature ... to erect an institution in which every species of athletic exercise and game which tend to develop manly courage and human vigour.[55]

There was also a concern that the lack of a mutual appreciation of sport by the various classes removed an important component in ensuring society's unity. Thus, there were increasing demands for the creation of sporting events in which the various classes could mix, as either competitors or spectators. This formed the intellectual rationale for the promotion of sports such as horse racing, cricket and rowing.[56] A number of parliamentary committees were created to examine such possibilities, and it is to one of these that we must now turn.

In 1833 the Select Committee On Public Walks set out to consider the state of recreation in Britain's cities. An examination of its deliberations shows that it was not particularly interested in an objective assessment of existing working-class recreation, but simply in its inability, in their eyes, to confer a 'civilized' moral tone.[57] The sports of the lower orders were perceived as a problem and little effort was made to understand them. Far from being a body brought together for an objective and informed examination of the evidence the committee was essentially just a group of London-based MPs pontificating about the state of the nation. London had eight witnesses giving evidence concerning its recreations, none of whom was an MP. In stark contrast, of the remaining 17 witnesses, who were dealing with the provinces, only five were not MPs.[58] Some of the informants were patently inadequate for the task. The MP for Sheffield, Parker, responded to the leading questions which were designed to condemn the city's lack of facilities by declaring: 'not residing in the town; and not being there much in the evening, I am scarcely competent'.[59] Unsurprisingly, the committee found that greater public provision of walks would 'help wean the working class from dog-fights, box-ing ...' and create careful people who would promenade and mix with other classes thus 'promoting civilization and encouraging industry'.[60] Among the key pieces of evidence submitted to the committee was that of Dr Kay, in which he stated that Manchester's working-class had only the theatre for recreation.[61] An examination of the local newspapers, with their array of notices of cheap entertainments, shows this to be incorrect.[62]

Unlike the deliberations of the committee on public walks, which did not result in significant changes to the law, the findings of the Select Committee On Gaming, a body that met in 1844, had a profound impact on sport. The committee was created in response to the enormous amount of corruption and litigation that was manifesting itself in gambling, especially horse racing, a fact that was of particular interest to the committee's members, most of whom were key figures in the sport. A complex web of statutes governed gambling, effectively restricting the amount of money that could change hands to £10, by rewarding those informing on anyone who betted more than this (so called Qui Tam actions). These laws were being utilized for purposes that were essentially blackmail. The Jockey Club felt especially threatened by this, and were so grateful that the committee used its authority to abolish the 'many obsolete statutes that threatened destruction of the best interests of the turf', that they made Palmerston, who had been the leader of the committee in the Commons, an honorary member of the Club.[63] Aside from a desire to please the Jockey Club, it is hard to understand the logic of the Committee's recommendation that the law should cease to regulate horse racing, a conclusion that completely contradicted their two principal contentions. These were that horse racing was of vital importance to the nation, and that the sport was riddled with corruption; claims which surely supported increased legislative supervision, not its complete removal. Instead, they insisted that horse racing was entirely a private matter, with the various horse owners having no responsibility to the public.[64] Thus, paradoxically, at a time when governmental involvement was generally expanding, the legislature withdrew entirely, leaving 'gentlemen' to resolve disputes among themselves.[65] By contrast, the law's attitude towards high-class gaming houses, such as Crockford's, was becoming more aggressive, endeavouring to reform their proceedings.[66]

As the above evidence indicates, much of the positive legislation designed to foster sport and mix the classes, tended to serve the purposes of members of the committee, such as Palmerston on Gaming, rather than the public. Responses to some sporting legislation were equally interested, typified by various members of the Lords whose reaction towards provisions concerning game was often determined by how profitable their own trade in it was.[67] Most infamously of all, the scrapping of the law permitting Qui Tam actions in 1844 was prompted by the fact that Lord Bentinck was confronting a case worth half a million pounds under it.[68] Motives were sometimes personal rather than financial, as with Redesdale's opposition to a railway in order to protect his fox-hunting territory.[69]

Occasionally, legislation relating to sport stemmed from obvious concerns. By 1831 the Whig government was quite unable to ignore the issues raised by the Game Laws, because one-sixth of the entire prison population stemmed from their transgression.[70] They were described as 'the most divisive issue in the kingdom' and it was acknowledged that only military intervention could uproot the highly organized poaching networks that had developed.[71] The government sought to undermine this by new legislation (1831 1 & 2 William IV Cap 32), which put an end to the laws that had previously prevented those renting land from having access to the game upon it, and had banned the sale of game. While initially subject to considerable criticism, the new laws eventually managed to eradicate many of the difficulties.[72]

Some of the most important legislation in terms of its impact on the creation of a commercial sporting culture stemmed from Acts concerning other issues. Between 1830 and 1850 three pieces of the legislation produced by Parliament had a pronounced effect on sporting activity: these were the Beer Act of 1830, the Act of 1846 on Inclosures and the Factory Act of 1847.

In 1830 the Beer Act lifted the restrictions on the creation of beerhouses, especially their supervision by middle-class magistrates, enabling the lower orders to utilize them as a focus for their recreational activities.[73] While this significantly improved the access of the working class to recreation, the 1846 Act (8 & 9 Vict Cap 118) on enclosure, which was part of a long running battle, reduced the population's access to open space.[74] However, the Factory Acts of 1833 and 1847, provided time in which to take recreation, particularly with the introduction of the half-day Saturday.[75]

Ultimately, it is important not to exaggerate the extent of Parliament's desire and ability to intervene in sporting matters. As noted earlier concerning cruel sports, the government had problems evolving the correct machinery to administer particular issues, a difficulty characterized by the following example.[76] In 1848 the attorney general tried to prevent the sale of sweepstake tickets from shops because it had become a big business that was attracting a great deal of fraud. However, because the ban which the government introduced was not accompanied by any effective means for ensuring their suppression, the legislation only succeeded in removing the legitimate, law-abiding, operators, thus leaving the fraudulent with a complete monopoly of the field.[77]

The Military Uses of Sport

The application of the military value of sport stemmed from a mixture of official and private initiatives and was focused upon three areas: medicine, physical training and sailing. As we observed during the French wars, medicine received the most overt assistance from Parliament. Between 1793 and 1828 the Veterinary College was provided with £3,000 a year to foster the science of horse medicine.[78] The government's desire to encourage animal medicine was based upon sound pragmatic reasons but carried out in an Alice-in-Wonderland fashion, culminating in students undergoing 'the farce of being examined as to their veterinary acquirements by a board of Medical Examiners … ignorant as to Veterinary matters'.[79] While many people observed that this meant that the nation lagged behind its continental rivals, little was done to amend this, though gradually the animals which they studied came to include sheep and cattle.[80] By contrast with such lavish endowments, there was little recognition of the military benefits of physical training which sport might offer the army. This was hardly surprising, for sport within the army often appears to have been morally corrosive, fostering cruelty, gambling and violence. Aside from Manchester, where there was some contact on the sporting field, the rare occasions when the military and civilians met usually resulted in violence.[81] Gradually, Parliament began to devote attention to the potential benefits of sport, and from 1841 every barracks was provided with a cricket ground.[82]

The navy was a different matter, and from the first attention was devoted to sailing, though most of the resources stemmed from private coffers. William IV was a patron of The Royal Yacht Club, a society whose professed aim was to foster the navy by developing well designed craft and supporting boat-builders.[83] However, as commentators observed, resources were not deployed sensibly. Little, for instance, was done to help watermen and sailors, despite their obvious military value. Such support was left to others, and when these failed to generate sufficient funds, even events such as the Thames Regatta, described by many as the 'nursery of the navy', were allowed to die.[84] No less serious was the opposition to technological innovations. Both the paddle-wheel steam-launch of 1827 and the 'Mosquito' of 1848 were either banned or stifled.[85] The admiralty seem to have been especially good at the latter. In 1833 the government boat *Pantaloon* was easily beaten in a race by the superior design of the *Waterwitch*. However, Parliament were not informed of this and persisted in funding boats that were of an inferior design. By 1851 this meant that British craft were generally inferior to American vessels.[86] Thus, although occasionally there were valuable ancillaries introduced, such as a library of nautical charts, the navy failed to derive much advantage from sporting activity.[87] This characterizes Parliament's general experience of the military dimension of sporting activity.

The second component of the establishment, the royal family, displayed little interest in the social values of sport, but their patronage of horse racing was regarded as having profound military value by providing excellent cavalry mounts. While this involvement varied considerably depending upon the individual, certain members owning particular horses, generally it focused upon two areas. First, the Royal Stud at Hampton Court produced a range of thoroughbreds. Second, annual plates were supplied as prizes at a number of meetings. With Victoria's accession in 1837 the Hampton Court stud was disbanded. This excited a great deal of comment, particularly from those who feared the perceived decline of British horses in relation to those of the continent. Occasionally, advocates of this expressed extreme views, effectively denouncing those dealers that sold horses to the French as near traitors.[88] Unquestionably, Victoria's action convinced many that she was opposed to horse racing, and in the early 1840s both she and Albert had to undertake a number of initiatives, such as attending Ascot, patronizing field journals and such like, to dispel this image.[89] This failed, and in 1850 the Hampton Court stud was reopened.[90] As to royalty's second major contribution to the sport, the provision of plates, much of this was a sham. Many of the plates were derived from a bequest made by a turf lover.[91] The rules controlling the races for the plates meant that they were unlikely to improve the breed of horses. Entry was socially exclusive, thus precluding many good horses.[92] The age of entry was too low, resulting in horses being entered that were too young, thus impeding their development.[93] Likewise, the distances raced were too short to be of military relevance.[94] Also, it was not uncommon for the plates to be awarded without a competition, and in 1832 the rules were changed to require at least three runners for the race to be held.[95] Most seriously of all, royalty did not always set a correct moral example, the King's horse becoming tainted with corruption in 1829.[96]

Cumulatively, it is clear that government involvement in regulating both the social and military implications of sport was sporadic, and largely subordinate to private initiatives. Interventions were invariably prompted by influential lobbyists, and funds only provided when alternative sources did not exist, as with the Veterinary College. Retrospectively, this was very sensible, for while advocates of sports often portrayed them as having military value, fox-hunters and steeple-chasers arguing regularly over which was the more useful, in practice comparatively little benefit appears to have been derived.[97] They were of rather more economic significance, employing large numbers of people and encouraging the breeding of useful horses.[98]

During the years after Waterloo, the impact that Parliament's legislation had on sport varied, reflecting a much broader range of opinions that were current throughout society. The attack on 'cruel sports', clearly damaged a commercial culture. On the other hand, the increased provision of land and leisure hours, especially the latter's standardization, assisted the growth of a commercial sporting culture. Also, the abolition of various laws that had impeded competitive sport created a framework in which supervisory bodies could develop. By contrast with these developments, the official promotion of sport was of far more limited importance, exerting little impact on the commercial sporting culture.

The Local Supervision of Sport

The second part of this chapter examines the response of the local powers, and consists of two elements, local government and the courts.

Local Government

Despite the fear of revolution which haunted the government in the early years after Waterloo, the authorities displayed a very relaxed attitude towards sporting crowds. Prize-fights, unlike demonstrations, were not required to obtain the prior permission of the judiciary before being staged.[99] Given the fact that fears of a standing army meant that there was no unified police force, such a response was doubtless a pragmatic calculation, and a correct assessment of the political docility of sporting crowds.[100] Such passivity on the administration's part was slow in changing, despite efforts to centralize power after 1834, and predominantly the supervision of sport was principally a matter for the local authorities.

The effectiveness of local constables varied substantially, many showing significant tolerance towards recreational practices.[101] Interventions were usually restricted to proclamations, such as those relating to the observation of the Sabbath, or the enforcement of minor laws.[102] Yet in certain cities disciplined forces of constables, equipped with substantial local power, had long been functioning. Although they were not a professional force, they were often very effective at regulating local life.[103] In Oxfordshire, the local police and proctors ensured that there was little illegal sport, despite the presence of University students, many of whom fostered such activities, sometimes most unusually:

> eight to ten members of the University have been rusticated ... for having amused themselves with cock-fighting in a very peculiar locality. Some of them ... were awaiting ordination.[104]

Despite the proctors recording numerous informal fights, especially between the

Gown and the Town, there were only 61 prize-fights between 1816 and 1850.[105] Until the 1830s pugilism received little attention in official legal records.[106] After this, far more action was undertaken, with local boxers, such as Perkins, being imprisoned and £68 being spent in 1847 prosecuting Gill, an event that confirmed the determination of the authorities to curb the sport.[107] Some bull-baits and dog-fights did occur, but infrequently.[108] Thus, although a County Police Force was not established there until 1857, Oxfordshire had little illegal sport.

While the establishment of the Metropolitan Police in 1829 provided a model for other local forces, as late as 1839 its effect was still only 'patchy', many provincial areas failing to introduce them.[109] Often their role was principally one of surveillance but in Lancashire they were deployed in a very aggressive fashion, exciting so much antagonism that special efforts were made to recruit working-class policemen.[110]

The existence of an efficient police force provided the means for enforcing the laws relating to recreation, yet their successful deployment depended upon the cooperation of local people, especially magistrates.[111] Many of these were motivated to support such legislation by a variety of reasons – religious, economic and administrative. Additionally, pressure groups would urge the prevention and suppression of local activities, via petitions and meetings.[112] Often, this stemmed from religious reasons, and a wide variety of sports were attacked, including hurling, rowing and wrestling.[113] The disruption of labour discipline caused by some activities also made them a subject for concern, a prize-fight near Ensham was condemned because it would 'induce servants and labourers to neglect and desert the business of their neighbours and employers'.[114] Storch considered the efforts of the police against working-class recreations as a 'direct complement to the attempts of urban middle-class elites to mould a labouring class amenable to the new disciplines of work and leisure'.[115] While in certain instances this was doubtless true, one must be wary of linking struggles involving popular recreations with local economic conflicts between employers and labourers. For instance, Delves portrays the opposition to the suppression of Shrove-football in Derby as being related to the anger felt by the local framework-knitters, and the working class generally, for their declining economic position.[116] However, many working-class people signed petitions against the football; likewise, some of those charged with suppressing the football were sympathetic to the game.[117] The footballers were not workers but simply 'grown-up youths', precisely the same category of player that we find at the Kingston-Upon-Thames game in 1867.[118] Finally, if the protests were a manifestation of working-class anger at economic conditions, it is curious that the Chartist newspaper, *The Northern Star*, supported the suppression of the football.[119]

Opposition to sport was sometimes motivated by politics, as with a meeting against pugilism at Worksop in 1847.[120] Generally, attacks on sport were related to fears concerning law and order, which were intensified by contemporary political and social tensions. More profoundly, there had been a substantial change in public attitudes towards certain sports, particularly pugilism.

As we have seen, during the war the dominant ethic in urban society was based on the concept of 'honour', embodied by duelling and pugilism.[121] With Napoleon's defeat duelling soon fell into decline and was made illegal in 1819. The number in the elite who regarded such practices as 'chivalrous', believing that they strengthened values and order in society, declined steadily.[122] Thus, while the public's residual respect for the duel ensured that juries would not convict those that were guilty of its practice, there was an increasing tendency for alternatives to be advocated in its place.[123] These would often be based upon models drawn from sporting activities. Boxing was often regarded as a sublimated form of duelling and the handbills of pugilists sometimes promoted the sport this way.[124] Similarly, some gentlemen began to use whips rather than guns. Duellists were often represented as bullies and shooting galleries promised to develop expertise, thus enabling customers to avoid being intimidated by threats from card cheats and such like. By 1835, writers were advocating the creation of a Jockey Club to arbitrate disputes between gentlemen, and therefore render the duel obsolete.[125] In essence, the duel had lost its moral and social legitimacy, and by 1843 even the military, that bastion of tradition, made it 'a grave offence'.[126]

What then of pugilism? In the early postwar years boxing was often credited with creating 'the saucy independence which distinguishes the mob', a quality that greatly impressed the Russian, Duke Nicholas, when he visited in 1817.[127] It had varied, and influential supporters, including a Benthamite society in London, and George IV, the latter employing boxers as ushers at his coronation.[128] Journalists declared that pugilism prevented Britons being 'servile', for, unlike the French, the population was 'independent from monarch, government and religion'.[129] Pugilism encouraged 'fair play' and was based upon the strict observance of humane rules, with competitors 'shaking hands at the end'.[130] This diluted barbarity, by presenting an alternative to the cruel methods of combat that were found in Lancashire and Scotland, where there were no restrictions on either the type of violence used, or unequal sides. It also prevented continental methods of fighting, which employed knives, from becoming popular. [131] Skill in pugilism was regarded as enabling the population to control ruffians and bullies and thus acted as an important component in the self-regulation of society.[132] Thus, far from urging pugilism's suppression, many, including a number of magistrates, advocated that it be made fully legal, describing prize-fights as a 'Methodist meeting' by comparison with an election.[133] In fact, in 1830, a magistrate issued a pamphlet denouncing the hypocrisy of those in the upper class who prosecuted the boxer, Byrne, for fighting, while permitting Wellington, who had just fought a well publicized duel, to go free.[134] Many influential people advocated the promotion of pugilism and were bitterly critical of those in the upper class who failed to support the 'old sports', and accused them of sapping the martial valour of the lower orders.[135] They went on to specifically contrast the virtues of the working class with the 'decadence' and 'French effeminacy' of many in the social elite, an MP declaring 'the lower orders are seldom wrong in the bulk of their judgement'.[136]

Yet, the erosion of the heroic military ethic, as encapsulated by duelling, was to undermine pugilism. Steadily, the justifications for it evaporated. For instance, after 1818, the use of boxing to settle arguments between different ranks, ceased.[137] The press was filled with stories of the corruption and cruelty in the sport, which magnified the public's response to the deaths which sometimes occurred at prize-fights. There had also been a significant change in the attitude of both competitors and spectators compared to the pre-Waterloo period. By the 1830s, in marked contrast to previous eras, boxers had ceased to obey the law when ordered to disperse.[138] Likewise, the crowds attracted were far more prone to disorder, violence and plunder.[139] One commentator observed: 'the frequent repetition of these lawless scenes ought to warn those who take interest in such sights at least to avoid mixing in a circle where it is impossible to avoid similar attacks'.[140] Inevitably this undermined the sport, despite the efforts of propagandists, who, in 1840, promoted regular sparring displays on Monday evenings, a time selected to enable the working class to attend, the group whose conduct, it was believed, would benefit most substantially from the virtues that the sport would inculculate.[141] Such efforts failed, as did the calls for the cultivation of pugilism as part of a series of measures for national defence, by maverick voices, such as Wellington, in one of his periodic warnings of an imminent invasion by the French.[142]

The difficulties stemming from the interference of criminals experienced by pugilism was typical of the problems confronting most sports throughout the period. Gangs of well organized thugs persistently intruded into sporting events, intimidating stakeholders, competitors and referees, preventing contests from being fairly conducted in some areas.[143] By the 1840s the extent of criminal activity and intimidation was so great that certain legally dubious sports, such as pugilism, were almost destroyed. Many legal sports, for instance foot racing, suffered similar problems. Often, the crowd was left to supervise itself, administering rough justice against suspected pickpockets.[144] However, from the authorities' point of view, given the large number of disturbances that were motivated by political and social protest in the years between 1830 and 1850, sporting events must have appeared remarkably innocuous, for these problems were entirely absent.[145]

The army was rarely ever deployed to deal with sport-related events.[146] This was due to the essentially apolitical nature of the crowds that were attracted and the fact that the only organized groups were the criminals, whose aim was theft not social disruption. Additionally, the police possessed a range of options for enforcing their will. Many of these long preceded the introduction of the rural police, but the new force was able to impose itself more effectively, as a study of its effect at Banbury has shown.[147] As the period wore on, a combination of paid and unpaid spies, the electric telegraph, and even a perusal of the sporting papers, provided the police force with much greater information.[148] Their application of this intelligence varied considerably. At its most rudimentary, police action might simply involve posting placards forbidding particular activities, such as naked running, or stationing themselves at Regattas to prevent minor crime.[149] Action would be taken against venues, pubs being threatened with the loss of their licence if they permitted various activities, such as pugilism, rabbit-coursing and betting.[150] They would also be instructed to either close or bar their premises to those associated with pugilism.[151] Similar pressure discouraged the owners of railways and steamships from permitting the organizers of prize-fights hiring their machines.[152] More constructively, however, the authorities would often try and replace an illegal sport with an acceptable substitute.[153] Horse racing and rustic sports were commonly provided in replacement for blood sports. On occasions, quite remarkable transformations could occur. At Windsor, the local festival was a renowned bull-bait but this was completely sanitized until it became one of the most popular annual rustic festivals in the country.[154]

It is easy to overrate the impact that events such as the introduction of the rural police had. During the preceding period deliberate official suppression had significantly reduced 'cruel' sports, such as bull- and badger-baiting.[155] The experience of other sports was less predictable, magistrates sometimes treating offenders leniently and even chastizing their persecutors.[156] Pugilism, for instance, depended upon the attitude of local magistrates.[157] A prize-fight in Yorkshire witnessed 'a jolly looking beak put in his appearance, but seeing everything quiet and as it ought to be, made no objection to the sport, and took as great an interest in the contest as anyone present'.[158] The behaviour of juries varied. In Oxfordshire they were often hostile to the Game Laws.[159] Other, local, influences, particularly religious, could intervene, as with those preventing the introduction of horse races at Wormwood Scrubs.[160] Generally, most sports were unaffected. There is little evidence of this changing throughout the bulk of the period up to 1850. For instance, cock-fighting remained enormously popular in certain areas and was a part of many race meetings.[161] The death of its great patron, Lord Derby, did not impair this, and as late as 1846, despite it contravening local laws, a magistrate declared that it was quite legal in private.[162] In fact, it was still being advertised in the press in 1849.[163] Ratting, though occasionally prosecuted, expanded dramatically in the 1840s and was even declared legal by the High Court in 1850.[164] Dog-fighting, though never attaining the same commercial heights, remained very popular right into the 1850s. Most significant of all, Shrove-football, the game whose decline is supposed to typify the suppression of popular recreations during the period, was hardly effected by official action: in only seven out of 46 places were they either suppressed or moved.[165] Horse racing expanded, the legal harassment suffered by some new courses, such as the Hippodrome, being extremely unusual.[166] Similarly, as we saw earlier in regard to pugilism, many magistrates and influential local people were sympathetic to sport, speaking up for manly activities.[167] A notable example of this was the bull-run at Stamford, an event that was only curtailed by pressure emanating from rate-payers, who were tired of meeting the substantial sums involved in its attempted suppression.[168] At Oldham, Radicals controlled the council and protected cruel sports from intervention.[169]

Examples certainly exist that demonstrate that the law was administered in a manner that was biased against the lower orders. For instance, in 1830, at a trial of some pugilists, despite Justice Littledale declaring that 'in such cases rank made no distinction in the character of the offence, and it would be the duty of the Grand Jury to find their bills according to the evidence before them'. There was no attempt to prosecute 'the highly respectable individuals hinted at'.[170] However, it must be emphasized that attempts to suppress popular sports can rarely be adequately understood as manifestations of class conflict. Generally, both supporters and critics stemmed from diverse social origins. It is a situation typified by an event from Derby in 1846, when a special constable stood bail for one of those that he had arrested for playing football: the offender was his son.[171]

In certain areas the introduction of the rural police did result in increased interference, with those pubs that staged sporting events, such as wrestling and cock-fights, experiencing prosecution more commonly than in the past.[172] Yet many illegal activities occurred; a horse race was even conducted through Wigan's main street in 1844.[173] The law was often evaded, for example in 1840 a fight was held in Manchester early in the morning, watched by a crowd of over eight thousand.[174] On at least five occasions in Lancashire during the period the police were routed when attempting to intervene against sporting events, and arrested men were sometimes rescued. A journalist recorded a policeman's remarks at one trial in Manchester: 'it was stated to be common practice in that part of the town when the police interfered to put down a disturbance for the mob to attack, and, if possible, drive them away'.[175] An attempted interference at Bury led to 'a complete rout of the police' and those regularly, and overtly, enjoying various illegal sports on Sunday in Rochdale were perfectly safe because 'the rural police never so much as attempt to put a stop to such disgraceful and irreligious practices'.[176] At Ashton, in 1844, the police complained about being 'regularly assaulted' when attempting to intervene at prize-fights, and clearly sought to avoid confrontation.[177] Numerous ruses were employed to stage illegal sports and various modes of transport were used, such as trains and steamboats, as well as the electric telegraph for communication.[178] Cumulatively, a large amount of illegal sport continued to occur throughout Britain despite the increased police presence. In fact, at Hyde, an animal belonging to a special constable was involved in a dog-fight.[179]

The strength of the forces attacking popular recreation is often overrated. On at least two occasions, at Liverpool and Doncaster, religiously motivated attempts to prevent the introduction of horse-race meetings failed.[180] Sport was a substantial commercial industry, upon which many jobs depended, and in both Oxfordshire and Surrey the police and government declined to interfere with the financial benefits anticipated by the local community, although the sporting activity was illegal.[181] In fact, the police often performed an important role in fostering sport by keeping order. The most famous example was the prize-fight between Langan and Spring at Warwick in 1824, but throughout the period there were many similar instances in a range of sports.[182] By the 1840s, a police presence was the only way of successfully ensuring that many sporting events remained immune from the interventions of criminal gangs, who endeavoured to fix results. A foot race in Manchester was typical: 'The rural police, in great numbers, were in attendance, and the racing community are indebted to them for their willing services in preserving order and affording fair play.'[183] A comparison of two race meetings demonstrates the role of the police in transforming the commercial potential of sport. At Epsom in 1827 the police permitted the crowd to swamp the track because the chief constable had not been given the £25 that he expected to receive from the race organizers.[184] By 1850 the coordination of improvements in transportation and policing meant that there was almost no crime during the Doncaster races.[185]

Local Courts

The sporting culture that blossomed in the years after 1815 rapidly outgrew many of the structures that had administered it, resulting in a wide variety of disputes being referred to the court. These represented, essentially, two categories of problems. The first stemmed from disputes over ownership, the second, rules.

The bitterest disputes relating to ownership, stemmed from fox-hunting. This was surprising, because, unlike the Napoleonic wars, where fox-hunting packs had been far more vulnerable to prosecutions, hunts after the Game Act of 1831 were protected from 'frivolous acts of trespass'.[186] The growing commercialism of sport also led to disputes, notably when the owner of Epsom race course, Briscoe, the local MP, tried to enlarge his share of the profits, behaviour which made his electorate threaten to withdraw their support.[187] More usually, sporting business of this type was of slight economic value, such as claims for unpaid wages and disputes over fishing rights.[188]

The second type of problem – disputes concerning rules – was far more common. Difficulties relating to rules rarely stemmed from weaknesses in the codes themselves, but rather from the lack of an authority to administer events. This resulted in many disputes in a range of sports being handed over to the courts to decide the winner, a practice that had long been occurring in gambling, much to the disgust of jurors.[189] From the 1820s it became an increasing part of sport, to the extent that by the 1840s it was quite common in many of the larger events, such as the Caunt–Bendigo fight of 1845, and even some of the smaller ones, because of the inability of the competitors to agree upon a referee.[190] While the courts did endeavour to bring some order to the sporting world, a second development completely undermined this. Beginning in 1829, losing competitors began utilizing the courts to claim back their stakes by suing the stakeholder. It was an ominous development because much of sport depended on a neutral stakeholder surrendering the loser's money to the competitor whom the referee had declared to be the winner. Thus, a stakeholder, carrying out his legitimate role within the sporting world, could find himself culpable for the money. By the 1840s it had became so common that losers would often have a preprepared written notice that they would thrust upon the stakeholder as soon as the event finished, warning him that if he surrendered the stake he would face legal action.[191] No stakeholder was safe from this threat, making sport ungovernable.

In 1845 Parliament abolished the complex variety of laws that had previously governed gambling disputes, thus rendering bets non-recoverable. This helped to ease such sporting disputes by removing them from the public world of the court and into the domain of the private agreement, where they had, predominantly, always been.[192] This was, essentially, the key to the whole ethos of upper-class sport. It was based upon individual character rather than bureaucratic adminis-tration. To an extent it depended upon a personal relationship, but the crucial element was the concept of the 'gentleman'.[193] This ensured that there would be no disputes. Such institutions as they possessed would be private, not public, bodies, such as the Jockey Club. Ultimately, everything depended upon a man's 'honour'. The court shared this view and often expressed its deference to the Jockey Club in sporting disputes, urging plaintiffs to submit their cases to them.[194] As an informal association they were regarded as the correct structure for regulating disputes between gentlemen, and many regretted that similar bodies did not exist to resolve other problems, such as quarrels that resulted in duels and land disputes at fox-hunting.[195] In fact, individuals intent upon defending their 'honour', often turned to the Jockey Club rather than the law courts.[196] A quote from *Bell's* sums up this attitude: 'Men who bet ought to be governed by strict principles of honesty; and where they are found wanting in these, exposure is a better remedy than legal redress'.[197]

During the French wars sport, with the important exception of horse racing, had been surprisingly free of disputes given the comparative lack of supervisory structures. After Waterloo, however, the private agreements that ensured obedience of sporting rules by all levels of society, broke down. This stemmed from two factors. Principally, the amount of sporting activity and the money involved in it expanded dramatically. Secondly, the patterns of social deference, which had ensured that agreements between 'gentlemen' would be obeyed and emulated throughout society, lost their significance. Whereas in the past, sponsors were often patrons that knew one another, and referees figures of social importance, after 1815 such relationships became increasingly rare. One of the few remaining vestiges of such a world, the Jockey Club, restricted its activities, and after 1842, prompted by the courts' refusal to acknowledge that they had any special power, ceased considering cases relating to betting.[198] The demise of a structure based upon individual personality and social position left a vacuum, which required the creation of an objective, bureaucratic administration. The nearest approximation to this was the legal system. Ironically, however, the code of laws that it represented completely contradicted those agreements upon which sporting activity was based, hence helping to undermine these still further. The committee that met in 1844 appreciated this and decided against expanding and rationalizing the objective power of the law. Instead, they advocated a return to the closed, elite, world, urging that bets should only be made with 'gentlemen'; a structure based upon 'honour' rather than law.

It is easy to overestimate the influence exerted by the local authorities in the supervision of sport. Throughout the period between 1816 and 1850 a great deal of illegal commercial sport occurred, sometimes with comparative official connivance. The police became an increasingly important element in the presentation of commercial sport, by preventing criminal interventions. In the main, the courts complicated commercial sport, by imposing a set of external regulations upon it, which led to a very unsatisfactory situation. To an extent this was solved by their withdrawal from such matters, though it would be some time before the voluntary associations that were required to administer sport would appear.

Conclusions: A Moral Change?

During the French wars both Parliament and the local authorities appear to have regarded there as being two types of sport; those relating to the Game Laws were not commercial, access to them was dependent, almost entirely, upon social rank, whereas other sports were potentially commercial, accessible to anyone with sufficient money. Both types of sport fulfilled certain social roles. Those emanating from the Game Laws related to the social structure and were about entertaining those who were administering power. Commercially accessible sport was largely concerned with entertaining those who were being administered. Throughout the period Parliament resisted all attempts to limit either category. This attitude was echoed at the local level, though the discretionary powers available to officials meant that there were some regional variants, especially in attitudes towards sporting crowds. Cumulatively, the authorities appear to have endeavoured to balance the maintenance of a strictly defined social order with the demands of a thriving commercial sector.

Between 1816 and 1850 far more people appear to have expressed opinions concerning the nature and value of recreation. Whereas during the French wars interested pressure groups had been principally motivated by religious reasons, and usually focused upon the suppression of particular activities, their successors were far more diverse, often giving an additional emphasis to the fostering of recreations. Accompanying, and interacting with the growth of such pressure groups, was the emergence of a more interventionist government at both local and national levels. However, in many ways such a development was still embryonic and an analysis of governmental involvement indicates that the state was still far from being a cohesive centralized unit. Most initiatives were piecemeal and often motivated by a variety of incidental factors, rather than indicating the imposition of a blueprint. Significantly, in the nation's major sport, horse racing, the government renounced its supervisory powers, thus demonstrating its willingness to deliberately limit its authority.

While a variety of repressive statutes were introduced throughout the period, and greater efforts made by both local and central authorities to enforce them, it is clear that they were less effective than some scholars have envisaged.[199] While it is true that the working class proved largely incapable of presenting an organized defence of popular culture, in practice, they diluted and evaded restrictions.[200] Attacks on 'cruel sports' were often unsuccessful, animal sports proving particularly tenacious in Lancashire, where in 1850 concerned people advocated the formation of a local branch of the RSPCA to combat dog-fighting.[201] The authorities dealt only with the most visible offences and by employing a degree of guile, such as staging prize-fights on the borders of several counties, illegal sports survived for much of the period.[202] Pugilism lasting until at least 1860.

A major innovation in the attitude of both local and national authorities in the years between 1816 and 1850 were initiatives designed to increase and regularize the provision of recreational opportunities, by providing time, space and facilities. Once again, this must not be over emphasized, for their imposition was often sporadic and patchy. It is clear, for instance, that much of the concern in areas such as London, Manchester and Coventry, with the lack of land available to the general population for casual recreation, was often exaggerated. However, on occasions, a fusion of local and national government with private initiatives created some new parks, notably those in Manchester that were developed in 1846.[203] While the amount and type of sport which they permitted was soon restricted, such facilities were going some way towards restructuring the local recreational environment in a manner that would have seemed extraordinary in 1793 or 1815.[204]

Many of the developments which most assisted the expansion of a commercial sporting culture were the incidental by-product of Acts relating to other issues, notably half-day Saturdays. Similarly, the creation of an efficient national police offered sporting events much greater protection than in the past, enabling its activities to expand, despite an increasingly well organized criminal fraternity. Sports such as pugilism, that by virtue of being legally dubious were deprived of this protection, were steadily eroded by the combined pressure of harassment by both the magistracy and criminal gangs.[205] Similarly, the fact that 'the police had in great measure put a stop to foot-racing on a turnpike road' meant that commercial sports' grounds developed.[206] Retrospectively, among the most important pieces of legislation to be introduced concerning sporting culture was the Act passed in 1845 (8 & 9 Vic Cap 109), which meant that bets relating to sport ceased to become legally recoverable, thus closing a loophole which losing protagonists had often used to regain their stakes.[207] Given that Parliament was unable, or unwilling, to provide active, intelligent, legal supervision, the removal of divisive and obstructive legislation enabled commercial sport to begin to regulate itself.

While during the Napoleonic war both local and national government had essentially left sport generally, and commercial sport particularly, unmolested, between 1816 and 1850 a shift in stance occurred. Cumulatively, this created an environment in which the commercial sporting culture could flourish. This was accomplished by helping to remove various impediments and fostering particular conditions in which the opportunities for mass-spectating increased. Once again, it must be emphasized that this process was often far from deliberate, and generally stemmed from an assumption that society should largely regulate itself.

What was the moral impact of this growth in the regulation and commercialization of sport? Before addressing such a question we must bear in mind that there was no agreed definition of 'cruel sport'. A piece by 'ZB' is typical of this moral ambiguity. Having declared that 'excepting bull-baiting, and the game laws, we have been progressively improving in our various diversions, and strenuous in our exertions to ameliorate the conditions of the brute creatures', he goes on to praise coursing and fox-hunting.[208]

The growth of commercial sport had a varied impact on activities that were sometimes defined as 'cruel'. While bloodless sparring had long been staged in respectable arenas, and was regarded as an agreeable spectacle for both sexes in 'genteel' society, there was a general growth in such displays, the taste for which was somewhat replacing bloodthirsty bareknuckle fights.[209] On the other hand, 'there are in the Metropolis, from half a dozen to a dozen places, where miserable animals are kept for the purpose of being baited'.[210] Similarly, fox-hunting, a sport that seemed to be facing extinction around 1810, expanded significantly by the end of the war, resulting in the deaths of more foxes than ever.[211] The sport's growth was due largely to commercial factors, embodied by packs formed by individual subscription. Thus, the number of fox-hunts, grew from 72 packs in 1821 to 84 by 1850.[212]

Of altogether more significance than commercial factors were changes emanating from legislation. After Waterloo, a series of laws and campaigns by reformers sought to change the sporting culture of Britain. In the main, though it was repression, rather than education, that eroded the support for 'cruel sports', a change did take place in public tastes within this period, though by no means as drastic as the 'mighty revolution' claimed by Howitt in 1838.[213] This manifested itself at all levels.

Throughout the 1820s, individual members of the upper class proved indifferent to criticism posed against them, whether for their gambling, cheating at cards, or neglect of their estates.[214] In fact, in 1825, some 40 aristocrats created The Society For The Encouragement Of Vice, principally to fight one another's paternity suits.[215] On the rare occasions when they showed themselves sensitive, their tendency was to attack their presumed critic, as with the cowardly assault using a whip by Grantley Berkeley and his brother against the editor of *Fraser's*.[216] Yet gradually, their collective conduct was toned down in certain areas, and by the end of our period the aristocratic involvement in prize-fighting and 'cruel sports' was effectively non-existent.

The lower orders, too, displayed improvement. In 1822 a vicar and policeman in Derby had provided the population with a bull for the annual bait.[217] While by 1850 such an occurrence had long been inconceivable, bull-baiting was slow to die, examples existing from Chowbent (1840), Lavenham (1842) and Lydgate (1849).[218] In many areas, the sports and recreations, especially during holiday times, had been considerably toned down.[219] A correspondent at Manchester in 1847 noted:

> the remarkable change that has taken place in the habits and manners of the masses in Lancashire, where a few years ago the sports – at a race-course, wakes, or other merry meetings were too frequently marred by the disgusting exhibitions of up-and down fights, now abandoned as a barbarism of a bygone age, and given place to ardent encouragement of more manly sports.[220]

However, three years later, the local youths were still conducting illegal sports, by playing cricket and pitch and toss in one of the city's busiest roads. They may well have been discouraged from playing cricket in the new parks by the restrictions which the council had recently introduced. These were intended to make the parks prettier but simply drove many potential users away.[221] This summed up the popular response to many of the attempts by groups to 'improve' them. Most scholars would agree with Perkin's remark that 'Between 1780 and 1850 the English ceased to be one of the most aggressive nations of the world and became one of the most inhibited'.[222] Scholars have attributed a variety of reasons, ranging from religion through to gas lamps, for this taming of society.[223] However, if one examines the period from 1793 to 1850 through the lens of the sporting culture, it is less clear whether a major change had occurred.

Popular sport in the period after Waterloo was probably less cruel than its predecessor, but almost certainly more corrupt. This manifested itself as early as 1819, when, during a prize-fight:

> such confusion occurred as was never before beheld. The immense multitudes closed in upon the inner ring in one mass, aided by plunderers ... Such disorder has never been seen at a fight, and it is hoped never will again, or measures must be taken of a different kind.[224]

By 1850 such events were common place. In 1805 a magistrate, the Rev. Dr Yate was informed that the Perkins–Ballinger prize-fight was occurring at Staunton:

> he instantly proceeded alone to the spot, there not being time to collect peace officers; he could not reach it before the battle had begun; but he rushed into the field, and with great personal risk, took Perkins out of the ring to his own house and bound him over to keep the peace.

All this, in the midst of a crowd of 2,000.[225] By 1848 'an inspector and two police' confronted by a crowd of 'nearly three hundred', declared 'of course they should not attempt to stop the fight as it would be madness in them to attempt to do so in the face of such a numerous party'.[226] Many of the structures that had once administered sport had vanished. Thus, despite there being an abundance of activity, there was little in the way of supervision. Whereas, generally, with the important exception of horse racing, during the Napoleonic period competitors from every social rank appear to have obeyed the rules that had been agreed upon, and referees and stakeholders experienced little difficulty enforcing their decisions, in the post-Waterloo world this was not the case. The increasing amounts of money in sport in particular, and society in general, created a level of corruption and criminal activity unimaginable in 1793. It is ironic to observe that while there is no evidence that horse racing helped to break down class barriers by mixing the population together in a love of sport, there is ample proof that frauds relating to gambling had a capacity to level all, ensnaring aristocrats and paupers alike.[227]

In 1835 the Pontefract electorate subscribed a plate to their MP, the former pugilist, Gully, for his 'personal principle and private character'. A year earlier, he had been fined £500 for striking Redesdale for spreading a story that he had refused to pay a gambling debt.[228] By 1850, Gully's robust defence of his honour would have seemed as curious as the heralding of the new champion boxer, Caunt. It occurred in a room full of pickpockets, and culminated in a parody of a crowning, Caunt's waist proving too wide for the champion's belt.[229] By then, the supremacy that commercial values had obtained in boxing was both clearly established and recognized, having completely superseded the moral justifications for such activity. Similarly, shooting galleries had long ceased to promote themselves as preventing intimidation by duellists. Instead, they promised prospective customers an increased ability to prevent burglars.[230] Thus, defence of the abstract notion of honour was replaced by protection of concrete valuables. Two years later, the last ever duel occurred in England. It was a farcical affair and both combatants were uninjured. The heroic ethic was largely discredited and obsolete, compromised by both corruption and absurdity. In time, the term 'gentleman' was to be redefined, with the hereditary component being replaced by an emphasis on conduct.[231] But this had yet to occur, a fact which meant that although the value structure that had been represented by sport during the Napoleonic wars was gone, there was nothing to replace it with. This was to have a profound impact on the supervision and administration of sporting events by referees and officials, the subject to which we turn in the next chapter.

Notes

1   T. Carlyle (1843) *Past and Present*, London: Chapman Hall, p. 255.

2   Harrison, *Drink*, pp. 330–31. M. Quinlan (1941) *Victorian Prelude: A History of English Manners 1700–1830*, Columbia: Columbia University Press, p. 103.

3   Brailsford, *Sport, Time*, p. 48. Harrison, *Drink*, p. 331. A. Howkins (1981) 'The taming of Whitsun', in E. Yeo and S. Yeo (eds) *Popular Culture and Class Conflict 1790–1914*, London: Harvester, p. 187. Malcolmson, *Popular Recreations*, pp. 90–94. D.A. Reid (1990) 'Beasts and brutes: popular blood sports', in R. Holt (ed.) *Sport and the Working Class in Britain,* Manchester: Manchester University Press, p. 131. *SM*, July 1824, 214.

4   Bailey, *Leisure and Class*, p. 175. Holt, *Sport and the British*, pp. 42–3. D. Reid (1982) 'Interpreting the festival calendar: wakes and fairs as carnivals', in Storch, *Popular Culture*, pp. 132, 146. Joyce (1990) 'Work' discusses the 'labour aristocracy' question in Thompson, *CSH*, ii, pp. 174–5.

5   Cunningham, *Industrial Revolution*, p. 76.

6   *Annals*, Sept 1822, 202; Oct 1822, 250. *Bell's*, 20 July 1834, 10 Sept 1834, 29 May 1842, 16 July 1843, 4 Feb 1844, 24 March 1844. *SM*, Jan 1819, 187.

7   Cunningham, *Industrial Revolution*, p. 88. *SM*, March 1817, p. 295. Walton and Poole, 'Lancashire Wakes', p. 106. *WMC*, 3 Sept 1831, 24 Aug 1833.

8   Harrison, *Drink*, p. 330. Kendall Phillips, 'Primitive Methodist Confrontation', pp. 299–300.

9   Bailey, *Leisure and Class*, pp. 35–6, 51, 55, 100. Cunningham, *Industrial Revolution*, p. 91. *SM*, Dec 1833, 112.

10 *M&S*, 4 Sept 1841.

11 *Bell's*, 9 May 1841, 6 Aug 1843, 18 Aug 1844, 25 June 1848. Howitt, *Rural Life*, ii, 278, 311. Sandiford, 'Cricket and Victorian Society', p. 303.

12 *Bell's*, 22 July 1849.

13 J. Lowerson (1984) 'Sport and the Victorian Sunday: the beginnings of middle-class apostasy', *IJHS*, 1:2. D. Vincent (1981) *Bread, Knowledge and Freedom: A Study of Nineteenth Century Working Class Autobiography*, London: Methuen, pp. 183–4.

14 Cunningham, *Industrial Revolution*, p. 100.

15 *Bell's*, 28 Jan 1844. *M&S*, 30 Jan 1841, 15 March 1845. *M.Ex*, 5 Jan, 1850, 12 Jan 1850. *WMC*, 1 Nov 1828, 26 Feb 1829.

16 *SM*, Sept 1822, 299.

17 *Annals*, Dec 1825, 376. *Bell',s* 16 Oct 1825; 30 Oct 1825; 19 July 1835; 18 Oct 1841. *SM*, April 1829, 393; Aug 1832, 323–5; Sept 1832, 357–9.

18 *Bell's*, 19 Jan 1840. *NSM*, May 1840, 311. Radicals were opposed to hunting. Thomas, *Natural World*, p. 184.

19 *Bell's*, 30 Sept 1838.

20 *SM*, Dec 1817, 136.

21 *Bell's*, 2 April 1837. *SM*, Nov 1816, 83.

22 *SM*, July 1825, 201

23 *SM*, Dec 1829, 95–6.

24 *Bell's*, 17 Oct 1830; 1 Jan 1843. *SM*, March 1831, 300; Dec 1833, 112.

25 *Bell's*, 2 April 1837.

26 Cunningham, *Industrial Revolution*, p. 51. B. Disraeli (1844) *Coningsby*, London: Allen and Co., p. 111.

27 *SM*, April 1828, 400, 403.

28 Bailey, *Leisure and Class*, pp. 47–8. F. Engels (1844) *The Condition of the Working Class in England*, 1958 edition, London: Blackwell, pp. 318–19. Harrison, *Drink*, pp. 330–31.

29 F.M.L. Thompson (1963) *English Landed Society in the Nineteenth Century*, London: Routledge, pp. 45, 47, 63. W. Vamplew, *Pay up*, p. 10.

30 D. Eastwood (1985) *Governing Rural England*, D.Phil., Oxford, p. 331. D. Eastwood (1994) 'Men, morals and the machinery of Parliamentary legislation, 1790–1840', *Parliamentary History*, 13:2, 93–6.

31 *Bell's*, 3 July 1825; 5 Nov 1843; 14 Jan 1844. *SM*, March 1821, 33–5; Aug 1825, 288. Malcolmson, *Popular Recreations*, p. 173.

32 *Bell's*, 26 June 1823; 24 July 1825.

33 See the preamble to 1 & 2 Vict Cap 79.

34 *Annals*, June 1822, 396–7; Oct 1822, 240–41. *Bell's*, 25 May 1823, 15 Feb 1824, 22 Feb 1824, 29 Feb 1824, 14 March 1824, 4 April 1824, 11 April 1824, 11 Sept 1825, 9 July 1826, 17 June 1827. *BWM*, 24 June 1821. *SM*, March 1823, 298; May 1823, 66; June 1823, 137; Sept 1823, 295; Sept 1825, 337.

35 *Bell's*, 13 March 1825.

36 *Bell's*, 6 May 1832, 22 Nov 1832, 13 Dec 1832, 24 May 1840, 25 April 1841. *SM*, March 1839, 426; May 1839, 379.

37 *Bell's*, 6 May 1832, 30 March 1834, 19 July 1835, 11 Oct 1835, 16 July 1837, 9 Feb 1840, 12 Aug 1849. *Hansard*, 14 July 1835, pp. 537–8; 13 June 1849, p. 126. Harrison, 'Religion and recreation', 116.

38 *SM*, March 1816, 290.

39 *Annals*, Sept 1824, 188; Oct 1824, 237–8, 379. *Bell's*, 27 Nov 1825, 9 June 1839, 23 June 1839, 18 Oct 1841. Howitt, *Rural Life*, ii, p. 270. *NSM*, March 1840, 206–208. *SM*, March 1816, 290; Dec 1817, 135–6; Sept 1822, 293; June 1823, 137; May 1839, 379. It is unclear why pigeon-shooting did not appear in the various parliamentary debates on cruel sports. M. Kellet (1994) claims in 'The power of princely patronage: pigeon shooting in Victorian Britain', *IJHS*, 11:1, 66–8, that it was because pigeon-shooting did not attain the status of a major popular sport until after 1860. In fact, it had long been extensively practised, there were over two hundred events in 1840; *Bell's*, 3 Jan 1841.

40 *Bell's*, 23 June 1839.

41 *Bell's*, 12 June 1825. K. Allan (1947) Recreations and Amusements of the Industrial Working Class in the Second Quarter Of the Nineteenth Century, Manchester University MA, p. 88. *Statistical Account of Scotland (*1845), vi, p. 211.

42 Golby and Purdue, *Civilization*, p. 55. B. Harrison (1973) 'Animals and the state in nineteenth century England', *English Historical Review*, 88, 789. Harrison, 'Religion and recreation', 117–18.

43 Harrison, 'Religion and recreation', 121–2.

44 Blaine, *Encyclopaedia*, pp. 150–51. Cunningham, *Industrial Revolution*, pp. 20, 72–3. Egan, *Book of Sports*, pp. 135, 258. Egan, *Boxiana*, iii, pp. 577–97. J. Hammond and B. Hammond (1930) *The Age of the Chartists 1832–1854*, London: Longman, p. 133.

45 Cunningham, *Industrial Revolution*, p. 46. *Derby Mercury*, 18 March 1846. Holt, *Sport and the British*, p. 43. D. Thompson (1971) *The Early Chartists*, London: Routledge, p. 58. B. Delves (1981) 'Popular recreation and social conflict in Derby 1800–1850', in Yeo and Yeo, *Popular Culture*, London: Harvester, pp. 104–105.

46 *Bell's*, 14 June 1846, 24 Nov 1850. Reid, 'Beasts and brutes: popular blood sports', in Holt, *Sport and the Working Class*, p. 18.

47 Harrison, 'Religion and recreation', 116.

48 *Bell's*, 22 April 1838, 13 May 1838, 20 May 1838, 16 Sept 1838, 26 May 1839, 2 June 1839, 23 June 1839, 5 April 1846. *M&S*, 22 May 1841. *NSM*, May 1839, 434–5.

49 Harrison, 'Religion and recreation', 116.
50 Concern for the suffering of foxes did not begin until 1869. Thomas, *Natural World*, p. 164.
51 *Annals*, March 1822, 197–8, 202; April 1822, 273; May 1822, 302–303; June 1822, 417; Sept 1824, 188. *Bell's*, 18 Jan 1824, 19 Oct 1828, 16 May 1830, 9 Jan 1842. Carr, *Fox-hunting*, p. 198. Harrison, 'Animals', 819–20.
52 *Bell's*, 13 Sept 1829.
53 Bailey, *Leisure and Class*, p. 169. Cunningham, *Industrial Revolution*, p. 47. Golby and Purdue, *Civilization*, p. 84.
54 *Bell's*, 3 Sept 1843. *SM*, June 1828, 161–2.
55 *Bell's*, 13 Aug 1843.
56 *Bell's*, 30 Jan 1831, 23 Jan 1842, 5 July 1846, 17 March 1850, 14 April 1850. *SM*, June 1826, 136.
57 F. Mort (1987) *Dangerous Sexualities: Medico-Moral Politics in England since 1830*, London: Routledge, p. 21.
58 *Public Walks*, p. 348.
59 Ibid., p. 404.
60 Ibid., pp. 344–5.
61 Ibid., p. 340 n, 402.
62 *WMC*, 7 Jan 1832, 28 Jan 1832, 31 Aug 1833, 26 Oct 1833. It must be remarked that this was not a criticism made by contemporaries in their reviews. *WMC*, 14 April 1832.
63 *JCMB*, 2 Oct 1845, pp. 144–5.
64 'English Gaming Houses', xi, *WR* (1829), 318, 320. *Gaming*, 1517–18, 1566, 1617, 3107–9. W. Vamplew (1976) *The Turf: A Social and Economic History of Horse Racing*, London: Allen Lane, p. 203.
65 *Gaming*, v.
66 Ibid., vi–vii.
67 *Bell's*, 6 Nov 1831. *SM*, Jan 1834, 250–51; March 1848, 218. *WD*, 17 Sept 1817.
68 Vamplew, *Turf*, pp. 200–201.
69 Carr, *Fox-hunting*, p.109n.
70 *Annals*, Aug 1822, p. 80. Bovill, *English Country Life*, p. 196. Munsche, *Gentlemen and Poachers*, pp. 135, 139. *Sporting Rights to Grassyard Hall Estate*, LCRO. (DDGA 30/9).
71 *Annals*, Aug 1822, 79–80; March 1822, 186–7; Sept 1822, 157; Dec 1824, 325; Oct 1827, 182. *SM*, Feb 1818, 205.
72 *Bell's*, 10 Nov 1844, 12 Jan 1845, 19 Jan 1845, 23 Feb 1845. *NSM*, June 1834, 112–13. *SM*, Feb 1834, 281; April 1834, 483–4; June 1834, 143–4; Aug 1834, 337–42; Dec 1834, 156–9; Feb 1841, 361–5; March 1841, 441; Feb 1845, 139.
73 Harrison, *Drink*, pp. 85, 183.
74 Cunningham, *Industrial Revolution*, pp. 93–6.
75 Brailsford, *Sport, Time*, pp. 51–2. H. Cunningham, 'Leisure and culture', in Thompson, *CSH*, ii, p. 285. M.B. Smith, 'The growth and development of popular entertainments and pastimes', p. 186.
76 See this volume, pp. 177–82.
77 *Bell's*, 19 Nov 1848, 3 Dec 1848, 10 Dec 1848, 24 Dec 1848; 28 Jan 1849. PRO HO 45 2506, 2339.
78 *Annals*, Feb 1828, 115.
79 *Annals*, July 1823, 8–16. *Bell's*, 12 April 1840.
80 *Bell's*, 2 March 1834. *Encyclopaedia Britannica* (1910–11), xvi, p. 4.

81   *Annals*, June 1825, 367. *Bell's*, 16 April 1843. *SM*, Dec 1816, 145.

82   *Bell's*, 4 Aug 1833, 28 March 1841.

83   *Bell's*, 4 Sept 1831, 2 Oct 1831, 9 Oct 1831, 22 Dec 1844, 26 July 1846. *SM*, July 1837, 145.

84   *Bell's*, 25 April 1830, 10 Nov 1833, 11 Jan 1846, 5 Sept 1849.

85   *Britannica*, xxxviii, p. 890.

86   *SM*, June 1833, 104–105; Aug 1833, 289; Sept 1833, 365, 406–407; Oct 1833, 467; Aug 1835, 308–309; Aug 1836, 290–91.

87   *Bell's*, 16 Jan 1848. *SM*, Sept 1834, 397–400.

88   *Bell's*, 5 June 1831, 12 June 1831, 6 Aug 1837, 10 Sept 1837, 24 Sept 1837, 1 Oct 1837, 22 Oct 1837, 31 Dec 1837, 14 Jan 1838, 21 Jan 1838, 25 Oct 1840, 17 Jan 1841. *SM*, July 1837, 144, 235–6; Sept 1837, 359; Oct 1837, 425–32. *Gaming*, 1517–18, 1566, 1617.

89   *Bell's*, 31 May 1840, 7 June 1840. *SM*, May 1840, 1–5.

90   *Bell's*, 7 July 1850.

91   *Bell's*, 4 July 1830.

92   *Bell's*, 14 March 1830, 6 March 1831, 24 June 1832.

93   *Bell's*, 26 Dec 1830.

94   *Bell's*, 25 April 1837. *SM*, Jan 1837, 213; Aug 1837, 339.

95   *Bell's*, 15 April 1832.

96   *Bell's* 1 Nov 1829, 15 Nov 1829, 20 Dec 1829. *SM*, Sept 1832, 375–7; Oct 1832, 439.

97   *SM*, July 1831, 150; Sept 1832, 375–7; Oct 1832, 439; July 1833, 189; Nov 1839, 48.

98   *Bell's*, 11 March 1832, 9 Aug 1835.

99   *SM*, Dec 1819, 124–7.

100 R. Storch (1975), 'A plague of blue locusts', *JSH*, 20, 69.

101 Eastwood (1985) Governing Rural England, D.Phil., Oxford, p. 247.

102 *MH*, 16 May 1820, 14 June 1824, 11 Sept 1824. *Orders of JP's to constables and overseers concerning playing at leaping, football and quoits on the sabbath*, LCRO, DDNW 9/12 (1840).

103 C. Emsley (1987*) Crime and Society in England 1750–1900,* London: Longman, p. 180. A. Redford (1940) *History of Local Government in Manchester*, London: Longman, i, p. 43.

104 *Bell's*, 24 Nov 1844. See also: 2 Nov 1828, 30 May 1830, 27 July 1845, 15 March 1846.

105 *Police Report* (5/6 Nov 1844). *SM*, June 1827, 72 records actions taken by proctors in 1816/17.

106 *Bell's*, 25 July 1830. Eastwood (1985) Governing Rural England, D.Phil., Oxford, pp. 55–7. *Oxfordshire Quarter Sessions Rolls 1687–1830, V* Easter 1817, p. 313, 19 Oct 1828. The magistrates bound Perkins over for £40; see *Prize-fighting*, 'Pitched battle at Botley 1828', *OCRO* (MOR LX/4). The proceedings from the county records against prize-fighters were republished in *Jackson's*, 22 May 1830.

107 *Bell's*, 6 March 1831, 31 Oct 1847.

108 *Bell's*, 27 Nov 1825. *Oxfordshire Quarter Sessions Rolls*, ix, 19 Oct 1828.

109 Emsley, *Crime*, pp. 171, 181.

110 *M.Ex*, 14 Oct 1843. Storch, 'Locusts', 68.

111 Eastwood, *Governing Rural England*, pp. 2, 83. R. Storch (1976) 'The policeman as domestic missionary: urban discipline and popular culture in northern England 1850–1880', *JSH*, 9:4, 483.

112 *SM*, May 1821, 103.

113 *Bell's*, 29 May 1842, 16 July 1843. J. Rule (1982) 'Methodism, popular beliefs and village culture in Cornwall 1800–1850', in Storch, *Popular Culture*, p. 55.

114 *Jackson's*, 28 July 1827.

115 Storch, 'Missionary', 481.

116 Delves, 'Popular recreation', pp. 93–4.

117 *Derby and Chesterfield Reporter* 24 Jan 1845, 7 Feb 1845. *Derby Mercury* 18 March 1846. HO 45/05 2923.

118 *Derby and Chesterfield Reporter*, 27 Feb 1846. *Surrey Comet*, 29 Feb 1868.

119 *Northern Star*, 28 Feb 1846.

120 *Annals*, July 1827, 23. *Bell's*, 17 July 1831, 22 Aug 1847.

121 Kiernan, *Duel*, p. 190.

122 *Bell's*, 19 Sept 1824.

123 Kiernan, *Duel*, p. 204.

124 *SM*, Feb 1802, 267–8.

125 *Annals*, June 1823, 394. *JJC*, Sports, Box 10. *SM*, Sept 1835, 365. *WD*, 2 Nov 1817, 6 Dec 1818.

126 Kiernan, *Duel*, p. 217.

127 See this volume, p. 74.

128 Brailsford, *Bareknuckles*, p. 79. *WD*, 7 May 1820.

129 *Bell's*, 5 Sept 1824. Egan, *Book of Sports*, p. 59. *WD*, 16 Feb 1817, 23 Feb 1817.

130 *Bell's*, 24 Nov 1822.

131 *Annals*, Feb 1823, 130–31; March 1823, 180. *Bell's*, 28 Nov 1830, 28 Aug 1831. *SM*, Oct 1817, 203; Jan 1824, 210; Feb 1824, 249.

132 *Annals*, April 1823, 285–6.

133 *Bell's*, 11 July 1830, 25 July 1830, 17 July 1842, 1 Jan 1843, 8 Jan 1843, 13 Aug 1843. *SM*, Dec 1829, 95–9. The attitudes held by magistrates towards pugilism varied substantially; a regional analysis of this can be found in Brailsford, *Bareknuckles*, p. 40.

134 *Bell's*, 20 June 1830, 11 July 1830, 25 July 1830. *SM*, Aug 1830, 272–4.

135 *Bell's*, 28 Nov 1824, 22 April 1827, 27 Feb 1831, 11 Oct 1840. *SM*, March 1831, 301; March 1837, 395.

136 *SM*, Sept 1822, 298.

137 Napea, *Letters From London*, pp. 77–9. *WD*, 6 Sept 1818, 27 Sept 1818.

138 *Bell's*, 26 Oct 1828, 19 Nov 1848.

139 *Bell's*, 2 May 1824, 10 Oct 1824, 29 July 1825, 5 Aug 1827, 11 Dec 1842. *SM*, Oct 1819, 5–8.

140 *SM*, Sept 1821, 267.

141 *Bell's*, 13 Dec 1840.

142 *Bell's*, 5 Dec 1847.

143 *Bell's*, 6 Oct 1844, 27 Oct 1844, 15 Dec 1844, 9 March 1845, 5 Oct 1845, 20 Dec 1846, 12 Nov 1848. *MH*, 18 May 1826.

144 *Bell's*, 15 Aug 1830, 13 Aug 1843. *WD*, 8 July 1821.

145 *Bell's*, 30 Sept 1838. *M&S*, 22 June 1839. Stevenson, 'Prevention of riots', in Donajgrodzki, *Social Control*, pp. 30, 39.

146 *M&S*, 1 Feb 1840, appears to have been the only case in Manchester.

147 Harrison and Trinder, *Banbury*, pp. 13, 47.

148 *Bell's*, 15 Jan 1843, 20 Aug 1843, 21 March 1847, 14 April 1850.

149 *M&S*, 22 July 1843, 19 Aug 1843.

150 *Bell's*, 2 Aug 1846, 28 Nov 1847, 3 March 1850, 24 March 1850. *SM*, Sept 1820, 292.

151 *Bell's*, 6 March 1831, 12 March 1837.

152 *Bell's*, 4 Feb 1844, 5 Jan 1851.

153 Cunningham, *Industrial Revolution*, p. 88. Delves, 'Popular recreations', p. 110. *M&S*, 3 Oct 1840. *SM*, Oct 1818, 40.

154 *Bell's*, 2 Aug 1842.

155 *Annals*, July 1826, 57. *BWM*, 5 Aug 1821.

156 *M&S*, 12 Nov 1842. PRO HO 45. 1800.

157 Brailsford, *Sport, Time*, p. 38.

158 *Bell's*, 9 March 1845.

159 Eastwood (1985), Governing Rural England, D.Phil.: Oxford, p 177. According to Munsche, *Gentlemen and Poachers*, p. 103, this was not typical of the bulk of the country.

160 *SM*, Aug 1817, 242.

161 *Annals*, June 1827, 347. *Bell's*, 11 March 1832.

162 *Bell's*, 20 March 1836. *SM*, June 1835, 153. *M&S*, 28 March 1846.

163 *Bell's*, 4 Feb 1849.

164 *Bell's*, 18 Jan 1829, 24 Dec 1848.

165 It is odd that Magoun contends that the decline of Shrove-football was due in large measure to official suppression; F. Magoun (1938) *History of Football*, Bochum-Langendreer, p. 144. Judging by the evidence set forth on pp. 101–102 of his work it is clear that such interventions had little impact.

166 *Bell's*, 14 May 1837, 29 Oct 1837.

167 See *Annals*, April 1822, 271; Sept 1827, 165. *Bell's*, 11 Jan 1824, 1 May 1825, 12 March 1837, 31 March 1839, 7 April 1839, 16 Aug 1840, 7 Feb 1841, 11 Feb 1841, 25 July 1841, 17 July 1842, 6 Oct 1844, 9 March 1845. *BWM*, 21 July 1816. *WD*, 23 March 1817, 13 May 1818, 12 July 1818. *WMC*, 14 Aug 1830.

168 Malcolmson, *Popular Recreations*, p. 133. PRO HO 52, 47: 40.

169 R. Poole (1983) 'Oldham Wakes', in J. Walton and J. Walvin (eds) *Leisure in Britain*, Manchester: Manchester University Press, p. 84.

170 *SM*, July 1830, 255; Aug 1830, 274.

171 *Derby Mercury*, 25 March 1846.

172 *Bell's*, 9 June 1837, 23 June 1837, 17 March 1850, 21 April 1850. *M&S*, 29 June 1839, 13 March 1841. *NSM*, May 1839, 434. *WMC*, 13 April 1838.

173 *M&S*, 8 April 1843, 6 July 1844. *WMC*, 30 June 1838.

174 *Bell's*, 19 April 1840. *M&S*, 20 July 1839.

175 *M&S*, 25 April 1840.

176 *M&S*, 3 Oct 1840, 31 Oct 1840.

177 *Bell's*, 11 Jan 1829, 13 Aug 1843, 6 July 1845. *M&S*, 3 Oct 1840, 20 April 1844. *WMC*, 10 June 1837, 30 Sept 1837.

178 *Bell's*, 18 May 1828, 28 Sept 1828, 21 July 1833, 4 July 1841, 11 Feb 1844, 19 April 1846, 20 Dec 1846, 30 Jan 1848, 11 June 1848, 21 Jan 1849, 5 May 1850, 29 Dec 1850.

179 *M.Ex*, 15 June 1850.

180 *Annals*, March 1828, 123, 164. *Bell's*, 17 Oct 1830, 18 Sept 1836, 4 Dec 1836, 27 Aug 1837, 8 Sept 1850.

181 *Bell's*, 25 May 1823, 30 May 1830. PRO HO 45, 05696.

182 *Annals*, July 1822, 35; Dec 1826, 365. *Bell's*, 28 Nov 1824, 22 Jan 1832, 6 May 1832, 1 Dec 1839, 2 April 1843, 11 June 1843, 4 Feb 1847, 9 May 1847.

183 *Bell's*, 11 June 1843.

184 *Annals*, July 1827, 8. *Bell's*, 3 June 1827.
185 *Bell's*, 3 Nov 1850
186 *Bell's*, 8 April 1832.
187 *Bell's*, 12 April 1835.
188 *Annals*, April 1822, 225–6. *Bell's*, 28 Dec 1828, 5 April 1829, 14 Aug 1831. *BWM*, 11 Oct 1818. *NSM*, May 1839, 435.
189 *Bell's*, 19 Sept 1830, 18 July 1841.
190 *Bell's*, 3 July 1831, 11 Jan 1846.
191 *Bell's*, 18 Oct 1829, 24 March 1844, 1 June 1845.
192 C. Boyle (1889), 'Gambling', *QR*, 168, 151.
193 *Bell's*, 16 Nov 1828.
194 *Bell's*, 13 Nov 1831, 22 April 1832, 24 June 1832, 11 Nov 1832.
195 *SM*, May 1834, 36–40; Sept 1835, 365; Nov 1837, 66.
196 *SM*, Dec 1837, 66.
197 *Bell's*, 16 Nov 1828.
198 *JCMB*, 12 Oct 1842, p. 102.
199 See, for instance, Cunningham, *Industrial Revolution*, p. 44; Walton and Poole, 'Lancashire Wakes', p. 115; Storch, 'Missionary', 292–3.
200 Bailey, *Leisure and Class*, p. 27. Storch, *Popular Culture*, p. 13.
201 *Bell's*, 5 Jan 1845. Holt, *Sport in Britain*, p. 64. *M.Ex*, 10 April 1850, 25 May 1850, 1 June 1850, 15 June 1850. *SM*, April 1836, 436.
202 *Bell's*, 15 May 1836. Walton and Poole, 'Lancashire Wakes', pp. 115–16. Storch, 'Missionary', 489–90.
203 *Bell's*, 8 April 1850. *M&S*, 24 April 1841. Hammond, *Chartists*, p. 115. Redford, *History of Local Government*, ii, pp. 213, 219.
204 *M&S*, 1 May 1847.
205 *Bell's*, 13 Feb 1825, 7 July 1847, 12 Nov 1848. Brailsford, *Sport, Time*, p. 64.
206 *Bell's*, 14 April 1850.
207 The impact of this legislation was gradual. The Chief Justice at the Court Of Common Pleas refused to acknowledge its relevance in 1846, and in the following year stakeholders were still uncertain of their legal position. *Bell's*, 27 Dec 1846, 21 March 1847, 28 March 1847.
208 *SM*, Feb 1802, 266–7; Dec 1802, 131; May 1815, 71.
209 *SM*, April 1796, 46–7; Oct 1814, 42.
210 *SM*, April 1822, 39.
211 *SM*, May 1810, 83; Aug 1810, 243; March 1815, 299.
212 *Bell's*, 10 Nov 1850. *SM*, Dec 1821, 141–2, 196–7.
213 Cunningham, *Industrial Revolution*, p. 24. Howitt, *Rural Life*, pp. 275–6.
214 *Annals*, July 1822, 23–5. *Bell's*, 12 Feb 1837. *SM*, March 1837, 397–9. *WR*, xi (1829), 316, 319, 325.
215 *Pierce Egan's Life in London*, 2 Jan 1825.
216 *Bell's*, 7 Aug 1837, 4 Dec 1837. 'Trial of Fraser v Berkeley and another, Dec 3, 1836', *Fraser's Magazine*, 15 (1837), 100–142.
217 *Bell's*, 22 Sept 1822.
218 *Bell's*, 20 Nov 1842. *M&S*, 3 Oct 1840. Walton and Poole. 'Lancashire Wakes', p. 122n.
219 *BWM*, 5 June 1820. Howkins, 'Taming of Whitsun', pp. 200, 204.
220 *Bell's*, 10 Jan 1847.
221 *M.Ex*, 14 Sept 1850, 13 Nov 1850.

222　H. Perkin (1969) *The Origins of Modern English Society*, London: Routledge, pp. 280–81.

223　Bailey, *Leisure and Class*, p. 174. Cunningham, *Industrial Revolution*, p. 24. Golby and Purdue, *Civilization*, p. 185. Harrison, *Drink*, p. 336. Malcolmson, *Popular Recreations*, pp. 161, 163.

224　*SM*, Oct 1819, 8.

225　*SM*, Oct 1805, 39.

226　*Bell's*, 19 Nov 1848.

227　Deale, *Life in the West*, ii, p. 117. Vamplew, *Turf*, pp. 130–31.

228　*Bell's*, 24 May 1835, 9 Aug 1835.

229　*Bell's*, 10 Feb 1850.

230　*Bell's*, 8 Dec 1850.

231　Bailey, *Leisure and Class*, p. 74.

Chapter 6

How Many Rats Can You Eat in a Minute? The Rules of Sport

A man has been matched for a stake of £25, to worry twenty five rats with his teeth in ten minutes, his hands being tied behind his back. Also, to draw the badger with his teeth in one minute.[1]

For many scholars, such an event would typify much of the sporting activity previous to 1850, which Bailey, for example, describes as being 'formless and convulsive', and often full of 'violence and excess'.[2] Such brutal displays of energy were embodied by Shrove-football, a game that was 'rough and wild, closer to "real" fighting than modern sport'.[3] The supervision of such activity would appear to depend upon the laws enacted by Parliament and their enforcement by the local magistrates and courts. It is generally maintained that traditional recreations were very rudimentary, possessing few rules, and involving a substantial amount of violence. The economic and social changes stemming from industrialization, especially in the Victorian era, meant that such activities were largely wiped out and replaced by civilized, codified sports, which were derived from the public schools. Walvin's remarks are typical:

[T]he new urban society required new games for a new type of people, just as it needed new attitudes to work. It was no accident that the recreations spawned by industrial society were to be disciplined, controlled and orderly, regimented by rules and timing.[4]

The classic example of this process was football, scholars identifying 15 characteristics which distinguished the original 'folk-game' from the 'modern sport'.[5]

Holt rejected the idea that traditional games were 'childish or primitive', acknowledging that 'without seeking to devalue the impact of either the public school system or the progress of industrialists, it is important to see that the major changes were underway before the Victorians'.[6] He does, however, segregate pre-Victorian sport into 'two broad themes':

Firstly, the importance of sports as an element of festive culture that was orally transmitted and had a high customary tolerance for violent behaviour of all kinds, along with gambling, eating and drinking ... This was traditional sport in the sense that the seasons, the 'holy days' of the church, the rites of apprenticeship, the patronage of the landed, and the customs of the locality, were determining factors of play. However, there was a second level too. This was the more organized world of pugilism, rowing, racing and cricket where written rules were well established.[7]

As we shall see, such distinctions probably obscure rather more than they illuminate, because they suggest that the respective sets of rules possessed significantly different levels of sophistication. In fact, the evidence indicates that the most important distinction between sporting rules was unrelated to their being either written or verbal. Rather, the crucial difference was between codes and contracts, two sets of laws that were distinguished by their intended comprehensiveness. A code sought to govern every single event of a particular sport. By contrast, the life of a contract was limited to a single event for which it had been drawn up. The laws found in both codes and contracts incorporated a blend of influences, a fact which often renders distinctions between 'traditional' and 'organized' sport, artificial. Further, during the Napoleonic period at least, rules were generally of secondary importance by comparison with the referees that were administering them.

Fundamentally, the vast bulk of sporting events that were conducted in Britain between 1793 and 1850 were administered by strict rules that prevented cheating. Consequently, it was worth competitors cultivating their skill. The picture that we have of most 'traditional' sporting events, which portrays them as violent and unruly, is unrepresentative. This is characterized by the way football is portrayed as consisting, almost exclusively, of the Shrove game. In fact, Shrove-football was completely untypical of the football that was generally played, in which 'skill and the application of a slight degree of force avails much more at this sport than greater strength unskilfully directed'.[8] Even 'cruel sports', such as bull-baiting, cannot be simply dismissed as bloodthirsty exercises that lacked rules: 'in regular well conducted baiting, a certain spot for the let-loose is marked out, and there stands the bull-ward, with a crock in his hand and a whip'. This meant that dogs had to attack head-on.[9]

Thus, while the legal structure provided a framework within which sporting activity occurred, of more significance for the vast majority of events was the supervision implicit within the activity. This stemmed from two sources, rules and referees. Predominantly, sport was a skilful pursuit, governed by a framework of laws that were administered by referees. Consequently, those who wished to improve their ability could do so by cultivating the particular science. These three elements – rules, referees and science – form the structure of this chapter. This will show that rationalized, rule-based sport, long preceded the introduction of codified games that had been developed at public schools, and that influential notions positing a 'civilizing process', in which popular culture was 'tamed' by external influences, are erroneous. By removing this chimera, the real difficulties confronting sport, and the reason why its progress was impeded in the years immediately following 1850, namely the withdrawal of the socially influential from its supervision, and the extent of criminal intervention, can be focused upon.

The chapter consists of two halves, relating to the periods 1793 to 1815 and 1816 to 1850. The first half consists of three parts: rules, referees, and training.

1793–1815

Rules

Long before 1793, sporting events were being conducted according to mutually agreed rules. While these were not adhered to nationally, there was sufficient continuity, often via a process of negotiation, to provide a basis for understanding. The successful presentation of a sporting event depended upon two elements: rules and supervision. Competitive sport throughout this period was essentially governed by an agreement between the protagonists to adhere to certain rules and accept the supervision of referees, a fact they acknowledged by the mutual provision of agreed stakes. Throughout the French wars sporting events were generally quite organized. They usually occurred on carefully measured areas that were set aside from the surrounding territory, sometimes by ropes and rails.[10] Competitors tended to wear marks which enabled them to be easily distinguished from one another, particularly in horse racing, hurling and football.[11] The objective of an event was clearly stated, such as an advert for a backsword tournament that made it clear that victory was gained by making an opponent's 'blood run one inch', and efforts, usually successful, were made to commence and terminate the match at an exact time.[12] Although contests did sometimes drag on, or the correct breaks cease to be enforced, generally rules were adhered to.[13] However, on occasions the spirit was clearly broken: when a horse dropped dead before completing the stipulated distance in a wager, his backer simply had the corpse loaded onto a fish cart and driven the remaining miles, before pocketing the winnings.[14]

At the very onset of the French wars a number of sports had codes. These were derived from four basic sources. The first group stemmed from royal or aristocratic patronage, as with cock-fighting – the rules for which stemmed from the royal cockpit – and coursing – from the Duke of Norfolk. The former, which by 1793 appears to have had only the most attenuated links with royalty, was tremendously influential – its rules being adhered to almost nationally.[15] By contrast, the latter, though exerting a significant influence, was just one of a number of essentially locally based codes that were competing for attention. A second group of written laws were produced by socially influential clubs, and were an inevitable corollary of wagering.[16] There were many of these in archery and coursing, the Jockey Club was the authority for horse racing, the Cumberland Society for sailing, as well as the Marylebone Cricket Club (MCC), the London Chess Club and the Skittles Association.[17] Many of these clubs had their own distinctive uniform and most of them produced rules that were only intended to regulate the affairs of their own socially exclusive body. Exceptions to this were the MCC and the Jockey Club.[18] The former constituted its rules in 1774 and to a certain extent appear to have intended that they would be adopted elsewhere.[19] However, no real effort was made to promote this, even though cricket was played in a comparatively small geographic area.[20] The Jockey Club were even more reserved and it was only gradually that they were given, and appropriated increased powers.[21] Despite extending their geographic influence, they remained a secretive body, appearing to make no attempt to represent national interests. A third source for written codes were the efforts of individuals: Broughton, pugilism; Parkyns, wrestling; Thornton, hawking.[22] While Broughton's was effectively the only written code for pugilism, its lack of strict definition meant that many competing interpretations, ostensibly based upon it, thrived. Parkyns' treatise was just one of a number of wrestling codes.[23] A fourth group of written rules stemmed from unknown origins, where there appears to have been no clear inventor, such as the wrestling rules used in the north of England.[24]

During the French wars two major changes affected these codes. First, efforts were made to modernise them; second, some sought to make them national. In practice, the two aims tended to interact. In coursing, the process was overt. The sport had numerous codes, the two principal ones each claiming to be derived from its founder, the Duke of Norfolk.[25] While they both modernized the sport, neither was able to proselytize sufficiently to establish themselves nationally.[26] More usually, the creation of a national code was an unintended by-product of modernizing a sport's rules, as pugilism demonstrates. The code established by Broughton was subject to many diverse interpretations, but in 1807 a dispute erupted concerning the alleged unfairness of a blow. Protagonists on both sides cited precedents and a conscious decision was taken to adhere to the more recent interpretation.[27] Intermittent disputes continued to appear, and unsuccessful efforts were made to get the Jockey Club to judge them. By 1812 it was decided that pugilism required a body of its own to decide disputes.[28] In 1814 the Pugilistic Club was constituted, made up of all the wealthy patrons and a number of experts on pugilism.[29] Its members were very organized and able to achieve their twin purposes of financing fights and ensuring that these were conducted strictly according to the rules.[30] Nonetheless, they still attempted to get the Jockey Club to arbitrate disputes, though the latter's refusal meant that the Pugilistic Club had to extend their role by revising the interpretations of boxing's laws still more extensively.[31] This did not mean that other, local styles of fighting vanished, but simply that all the satisfactorily financed contests would be conducted according to the club's rules. In essence, the supervision of rules was fused with financial power, effectively creating a national association. As we have seen, the Jockey Club were a private body who consciously endeavoured to remain so. However, the complexities of the sport that it administered demanded a constant revision of its rules. Essentially this stemmed from the fact that the very large sums of money involved in horse racing attracted a large criminal and semi-criminal involvement, necessitating strict supervision. In order to resolve disputes in a neutral fashion, the club was forced to construct, and update, a detailed code, which it published annually from 1807.[32] In the desire to avoid disputes ending up in the law courts, many courses placed themselves under the club's jurisdiction. This encompassed highly exclusive bodies such as the Bibury club, though even by 1815 the Jockey Club's authority was still not completely acknowledged nationally.[33] Efforts were made by other sports to obtain arbitration by the Jockey Club, but with the possible exception of a coursing dispute in 1804, the club remained aloof.[34] The MCC's authority was very diffuse and though occasional efforts were made to revise its rules, their's remained one of a number of codes.

Throughout the French wars there was little desire to establish national laws. Sport, at its most organized, was based upon clubs, and almost entirely segregated from non-members, typified by the various club uniforms.[35] Far from embracing everyone interested in a sport, membership of a club was restricted, and its events generally inaccessible to outsiders. Such distinctions were pervasive. For instance, many rowing races were only open to those from a certain area or a particular job and explicitly prevented manual workers racing gentlemen.[36] As we have seen, the Pugilistic Club was the closest a society came to exercising authority nationally; a position its members attained because they were made up of all boxing's principal patrons and administered a sport in which the participants belonged to the lower orders. At the most organized levels, there appears to have been no real desire to create national rules.

The most common form of laws governing a sporting event was the contract, the stipulations of which applied only to that particular match.[37] These were usually signed agreements between competitors, often in response to written challenges.[38] A typical example was the Gregson–Gulley fight;

> Conditions of the battle.
> 1. The battle to take place on Tuesday following the First Spring Meeting, between the hours of ten and twelve O'clock.
> 2. To fight in a roped square of forty feet.
> 3. Neither to fall without a knock-down blow, subject to the decision of the umpires.
> 4. These umpires to be chosen upon the ground, vis two, and one as referee.[39]

It was very rare for difficulties to result from this. A less binding form could be found in adverts for competitions, where the relevant stakes, prizes, rules and objectives would be listed. Neither contracts nor adverts were necessarily rivals to a written code, but were often used as a necessary addition to it, that resolved ambiguities.[40] As Holt observes, many sporting events had complicated rules which were simply agreed to verbally.[41] These were very common and often based upon existing practice, or even tradition, as with the Old Hats pigeon-shooting club.[42] Some, however, referred to unique circumstances, agreeing to provide competitors with certain privileges or inflict particular handicaps.[43] An example of this from a trotting match of 1804 was the stipulation that 'if the horse gets into a gallop must stop and turn about'.[44]

Referees

Remarkably enough, few of the sports that were administered by either written or verbal contracts made any effort to establish a written code. This surely indicates that they were organized successfully. Much of the credit for this belongs to referees, who seem to have been regarded as satisfactory. It was this, far more than the existence of a code – written or verbal, which determined whether an event was considered fairly contested. A referee's authority appears to have depended a good deal on his social position, especially the networks of deference that functioned within a community, rather than a minute knowledge of the rules. Thus, a number of events were supervised by aristocrats, gentlemen and even the clergy.[45] However, at the other end of the social spectrum, the crowd themselves would sometimes intervene to establish fair play. This involved heckling away cheats, preventing interested gamblers from disrupting an event, and even insisting that a very bloodthirsty fight be terminated as a draw.[46]

Generally, during the French wars, referees tended to be of more importance than rules in the correct supervision of events. This reflected a social structure that was personal rather than objective and based upon character and local position not intellectual expertise; hence, passing gentlemen would be selected as referees.[47] In most sports, referees were invested with considerable power and able to determine what was deemed admissible.[48] Great trust appears to have been placed in them. For instance, in 1810 a pedestrian, Captain Aiken, managed to run five miles in 30 minutes, thus winning his 50 guinea bet. Despite the fact that he only accomplished his goal by a few seconds, the money was handed over without protest, so great was the respect for the referee.[49] The fact that a particular sport had a written code seems to have been largely irrelevant to preventing disputes. It was not unknown for cricket umpires to cheat and for the starters at horse-race meetings to be intimidated by influential owners.[50] At a more general level, there was a big debate in coursing over whether a gentleman should be permitted to act as a judge in an event in which he had a financial interest.[51]

While overt instances of sportsmanship were very rare, there does not appear to have been any ill-will either, it being very rare, for instance, for opponents to fail to drink together after the event.[52] This seems to have been the case in even the most aggressive sports, such as hurling, and it appears that the level of violence in most activities has been overstated by historians.[53] Generally, the emphasis was on skill.[54] Cheating certainly did occur, afflicting 10 out of 585 pugilistic contests, and the occasional cricket match but was tiny in relation to the large volume of events.[55] The sport with the worst record was rowing. There, competitors would sometimes combine to sabotage the chances of a favourite, as at Vauxhall, where one of the boats deliberately fouled the favourite, thus enabling another vessel to win.[56] Many accepted practices within the sport were inherently contentious and rules sometimes tried to curb them.[57] With the exception of horse racing, there was very little fraud in sport, though occasionally competitors deliberately lost because they had been bribed, or won, having concealed their true identity. The fact that over 87 per cent of all the total finance staked upon sporting events was devoted to horse racing, meant that it was almost inevitable that the sport should attract illegal activity. While the substantial sums involved meant that this had enormous significance, in no sense was the fraud and crime found in horse racing represent-ative of sporting activity as a whole.

The level of supervision expected for almost every type of sporting event was considerable: for instance at a pedestrian match 'there were six umpires, four on foot, and two on horse back'.[58] Those performing any type of event that involved accomplishing a specified task within a period of time were required to furnish independent confirmations from witnesses, often publicans and such like, proving this. For instance, while accomplishing the feat of riding the same mare for 180 miles, from Lincoln to Manchester and back, the competitor, Spicer, was required to obtain the signatures of gentlemen in local inns confirming such facts.[59] Almost every event was carefully monitored by an umpire, who provided a detailed, signed report.[60] In essence, claims were scrutinized with considerable thoroughness. Given this, it is hard to understand why modern scholars doubt the accuracy of the accounts which contemporaries provided, believing that both times and distances were mistaken.[61] In just one instance are their doubts completely justified. This was the claim 'which can any day be proved by affidavit ... James Lidget (aged 63) ran one mile in three minutes and a half'.[62] Obviously, this was impossible. However, the event itself was not attempted for money and the level of supervision was almost certainly far less exacting than was usually the case. Invariably, whenever there were sums at stake the supervision, especially by those financing it, was intense. On occasions, notably in the Barclay match of 1809, upon which £16,000 had been wagered, elaborate precautions were taken to prevent criminal interventions. This indicates that the figures recorded under such circumstances deserve to be treated seriously. Ultimately, should competitors feel aggrieved at the referee there were a number of bodies that they could appeal to.[63] They varied considerably. The Jockey Club's procedures involved a committee, while the Pugilistic Club's decisions came from one man, Jackson, a wealthy ex-champion, esteemed for his social position, sporting knowledge and integrity.[64] Jackson's verdict had immense credibility and he helped to structure a great deal of sporting activity by establishing particular principles, such as the notion that all bets must be paid even if there was strong evidence of fraud.[65] In fact, aside from horse racing, there were very few disputes in most sports.[66] Foot racing was reasonably representative, with only two out of 213 events throughout the period having to be rerun.[67] On the rare occasions when there were sound reasons for doubting that a result had been obtained in an honest manner, very thorough investigations were initiated. For instance, when it was believed that the pedestrian, Wood, had been doped during an event, a doctor provided detailed medical evidence.[68] Collectively, the intense supervision attending most sporting events, coupled with processes established by the various societies' rules, reduced the number of sport-related disputes which finished up in court and provided strong evidence of fair play.

Science

The strict adherence to rules that we identified in the previous section meant that sport could be validly presented as a science in which success could be substantially improved by following the correct advice. The science of sporting activity consisted of three components: physical training, animal breeding and new technology. Physical training focused on two areas: first, the creation of a healthy body; second, the cultivation of expertise.

Training designed to improve a competitor's physique occurred in the countryside or at certain specific locations.[69] This was because there was a long tradition in British intellectual thought that identified city life, especially that of London, as being synonymous with poor health.[70] Programmes designed to improve an athlete's resources were divided into two basic groups. The first, which was intended for jockeys, was devoted solely to assisting them lose weight rapidly, paying little attention to their bodily strength.[71] By contrast, the second – which was relevant to all other athletes – aimed at creating a tough physique. This was accomplished by a threefold technique that involved sweating (which entailed the athlete swathing himself in layers of clothes), exercise and feeding.[72] Such a process was regarded as culminating in one man, Captain Barclay. In 1809 he accomplished his famous 'match', which involved running 1,000 miles in 1,000 hours. For a period of some seven weeks he ran one mile every hour. Such a display of stamina astonished contemporaries and every aspect of both his training and the routine he employed during his ordeal were scrutinized.[73]

Barclay did not invent the techniques used to create such a robust constitution, but his success did a great deal to systematize it. Contemporaries certainly regarded themselves as creating a science and they even contrasted their methods with those of the ancient Greeks, who they regarded as knowing little about gymnastic training.[74] Barclay, himself, had trained his body to perfection and was able to excel in a variety of athletic sports. His aim was to 'establish a regular system of training' and this was regarded as performing a 'patriotic and valuable service' to the nation.[75] His contest against another top athlete, Captain Fairman, was eagerly awaited because a comparison of the strengths displayed by their very different physiques was felt to provide excellent material for the drawing of 'various scientific deductions'.[76] Barclay's wonderful achievement helped to allay the pervasive intellectual fear that civilization caused physical degeneration. On the contrary, Barclay showed that with correct scientific training civilized man could surpass his predecessors and that 'improved social order does not impair our physical powers'.[77] Thus, the sickness that was regarded as the inevitable consequence of the dramatic increase in urbanization could be halted.

At least five people specialized in producing strong, healthy, physiques.[78] This is not to say that there was a strict consensus among them concerning diet. Generally, beef, alcohol and hard work were regarded as the fundamentals.[79] Barclay, during his match, breakfasted on roasted foul and a pint of strong ale at 5 am, lunched at 12 am on large portions of either beef or mutton chops, drinking porter and two or three glasses of red wine. His supper at 11 pm consisted of 5–6 lb (2.5–3 kg) of cold fowl and vegetables.[80] There were, of course, exceptions. Boxers were especially prone to drunkenness and when in serious training would completely abstain from alcohol.[81] By contrast, most pedestrians, despite their very careful daily regime of food and care, which even included especially designed clothes, often depended upon spirits to sustain them during their promethean feats, which involved walking 50 miles a day for 20 successive days and such like.[82] On occasions, some events specifically stipulated that a certain diet had to be adhered to throughout the feat; such as, alcohol only, water only, and one that declared that the protagonist must first eat 400 oysters.[83] While much was always made of the severity of sporting exertion, death and severe injuries were very rare.[84] Similarly, the brutality of sport was often exaggerated. One of the few examples of callousness occurred after a prize-fight, where a badly injured fighter was left for hours without medical attention while his patron sat engrossed in other fights.[85]

The level of instruction available in a variety of sports improved dramatically during the French wars. In 1727 Parkyns provided a treatise that taught wrestling. Despite the fact that he had derived his technique by simply noting down the instructions that an expert had given him, he felt the need to present the material in highly ponderous scientific terms that tended either to obscure the very practical advice he offered, or present inflated explanations of the obvious, such as, 'a greater impetus is required to move a greater weight some space, than to move a less weight the same space'.[86] By contrast, the style of many sporting treatises in the Napoleonic period was reasonably accessible, as with Egan's descriptions in *Boxiana* of the various punches in a boxer's armoury. Although Egan was prone to employ overelaborate medical terminology, his meaning usually remained clear.[87] In addition to accessible treatises there were many sportsmen that set themselves up as tutors, specializing in particular activities.[88] By undertaking regular tours, they distributed their attention throughout the country.[89] A few of the very top pugilists, such as Richmond, opened sparring schools where the wealthy, generally aristocrats, came for training.[90] Expert tuition was available in many sports, such as riding, fencing, swimming and rackets.[91] Yet the contributions of professionals must not be overstressed. In cricket, for instance, they were insignificant in developing the improved batting techniques that emerged in 1804.[92]

By 1815 there was a significant amount of help available for those interested in pursuing a particular sport. The value of training was also acknowledged and athletes often undertook vigorous programmes in preparation for some task.[93] In fact, towards the end of the period, the importance of training was such that contracts would sometimes stipulate that the protagonists must perform without training.[94]

The second aspect of sporting science, the breeding of animals, was highly developed long before the French wars.[95] Fundamental advances, by Meynell and others, had changed fox-hunting. The selective breeding of hounds was taken to ever more involved heights and the fourth Duke of Beaufort was typical of many in the great attention he paid to the lineage of his hounds.[96] Similar developments occurred in coursing, where Colonel Thornton extended the achievements of Lord Orford in producing a dog that could display its superiority over a variety of terrain.[97] Long before 1793 fighting cocks had been extensively bred and throughout the whole period cock-fighting owed a great deal to the assiduous attention of Lord Derby and his assistants.[98]

While fox-hunting, coursing and cock-fighting were developed by private efforts, horse racing was patronised by both royalty and Parliament. However, although from 1791 Parliament expended large sums supporting the Veterinary College in order to foster horse medicine, little progress was made.[99]

In most senses the sporting technology of the French wars was completely overshadowed by some of the developments that had been initiated in an earlier period, notably the application of steel spurs in cock-fighting.[100] In fact, between 1793 and 1815 there were only three innovations in the technology available to sportsmen: the use of aniseed instead of bag foxes in fox-hunting; Shoubridge's gimmicky application of a double-barrelled rifle for shooting; and improvements in boat-building.[101] The last was only really available to the very wealthy.

1816–50

As we have seen, during the French wars sport was generally well supervised and comparatively untroubled by problems relating to corruption and cheating. However, in this, the second half of the chapter, dealing with the years after Waterloo, it appears that criminal interventions did much to undermine many of the advances that were occurring in supervision.[102] Once again, it is divided into three sections – rules, referees and science.

Rules

Between 1816 and 1850, both the amount and sophistication of rules witnessed an extraordinary growth, embodied by the steady increase in the number of written codes. This stemmed from the expansion in both the volume and geographical spread of sporting activity, and a growth in published material.

Evidence suggests that many codes evolved in three stages. Initially, they were verbal agreements between friends, often based upon previously established patterns. These would become steadily more refined, whence they would be transferred to manuscript, a process often accompanying the members' constituting themselves on a more formal basis, as occurred in 1842 at the Manchester and Salford Rowing Club.[103] After a further period of adjustment, it was common for rules to be printed and distributed to members, as with the Wensleydale Coursing Club in 1831.[104] While such a process was usually influenced by the wealth and literacy of the sportsmen, this was not always the case; both the illiterate, lower class, watermen, and the socially elite, Red House Pigeon Club, relied entirely upon oral rules.[105] While it was obviously easier to disseminate written rather than verbal codes, it was often the case that oral tradition exerted a profound influence. For instance, the code governing the wrestling practised in Lancashire dominated that region, despite remaining entirely oral.[106] Similarly, much of the impact of written codes stemmed from their oral adoption and transmission, as with notions such as 'time' and 'enough' in pugilism.[107]

Primarily, codes appeared in two printed sources, books and the sporting press. Generally, the aim of books was to propagate their particular code, especially in a sport such as wrestling, where there were many competing bodies of rules.[108] In such cases, rule books were often of ambiguous benefit. Within the space of a few months, rowing, a sport that had previously been without a printed code, was beset by a number of radically distinct law books.[109] Thus, while potential competitors at Henley were able to familiarize themselves with the rules used there, the advantage they gleaned was strictly limited, for Henley's laws were by no means universal.[110] Such difficulties were compounded by commercial pressures, as increasingly large print runs enabled the production of inexpensive rule books, sometimes costing as little as sixpence.[111] These were within reach of almost everyone, leading to the dissemination of numerous contradictory codes, as societies sought to establish their particular version of a sport by publishing its rules cheaply. Despite this, many old texts, such as one on wrestling from 1727, continued to be used.[112] The role of the press also changed. During the French wars they had been content to simply report events and give readers' letters without adding comment, as well as reproducing codes verbatim, though sometimes appending explanations. After 1815 both the volume and scope of their treatment changed. They provided far more sets of rules, often those that had not previously been printed. More importantly, their reports of events often contained suggested solutions to particular problems and offered improvements to existing laws. Similarly, readers would submit letters full of suggestions. The following is a characteristic example, relating to pugilism:

1. Let future fights be as much as possible for honour.
2. Suffer no man's character to be whispered away as having been engaged in a cross.
3. Let us hear no more of the absurd and mischievous practice of persuading men to fight under their proper athletic weight.
4. It might be as well if the attention of one or more medical men, of known skill and character, were always procured at future fights.
5. By all means encourage big men to contest, in preference to little ones.[113]

This excited far more debate and created a climate of criticism, often undermining the respect in which existing rules were held and encouraging the creation of alternatives.

Despite the large increase in the amount of codes, contracts remained the most pervasive means used to govern sporting contests, incorporating both written and verbal agreements. Their scope could be extensive. Most fundamentally, they could stipulate whether a competitor was permitted to enter. Many events, notably pigeon-shooting, excluded individuals above a certain ability.[114] Others insisted on particular residence requirements. This was common in cricket but its most contentious use was in wrestling, where it was often employed, and occasionally even changed, to exclude talented individuals.[115] Many were appalled at the following innovation that was introduced by the Cumberland and Westmorland Society:

> no person who has not been resident in London for at least six months previous to the day of wrestling, shall be allowed to enter the lists. The motive for this, though not openly acknowledged, is a fear entertained by some candidates, that they will be floored by a lad named Robinson.[116]

If the event involved the use of a particular piece of property, such as a horse or boat, rules would sometimes specify that this must belong to the competitor entering it.[117] Their complexity varied considerably, inevitably so – given that some were simply read aloud to the competitors.[118] At the simplest were statements such as that relating to pigeon-shooting, declaring that the birds would be drawn out of the same bag, through to the enormously detailed specifications concerning sailing.[119] While there was a tendency for articles to resemble one another, often being prepared according to a set formula by the proprietors of sports' grounds, many were unique, designed to incorporate particular types of advantages, such as the 'players' team having larger wickets than the 'gentlemen' at cricket, or establish idiosyncratic criteria, usually relating to the physical age or size of competitors.[120] Often, these reflected the stipulations of an individual, such as Dr Bedale who challenged:

> any man in the world, not exceeding twelve months younger, nor 5lbs heavier than himself, for £100 a side, whom swims at least thirty miles in one tide or goes the farthest in five hours. He is forty five years old and weighs 13st 8lbs.[121]

Rules themselves, as found in both codes and contracts, became increasingly complex, stemming from a number of alternative, often competing, foci. They were also influenced by new criteria, such as morality, which tended to manifest itself in two ways. The most profound change in attitude was the refusal to play for money. As stakes represented one of the key elements in Napoleonic sport, this development effectively created the notion of 'amateur' sport. Second, far more attention was paid to the physical suffering inflicted in sport, with 'humane' rules being advocated. In the case of pugilism, such changes aimed at making the sport more 'respectable', especially in official eyes.[122] However, the new code of 1838 failed to accomplish this, and its overelaborate provisions tended to result in long, boring, fights, thus alienating its supporters.[123] This problem troubled the sport's advocates considerably. A desire to please the public exerted a strong influence on the rules of a number of sports. In cricket, the MCC reduced the time between innings, and fined batsmen who were late, in order to speed the game up.[124] More profoundly, the admission of 'up-hand bowling' (round-arm) in 1828 (formally sanctioned in 1835), ended the dominance of batting, which had meant that 'matches not infrequently lasted three or four days'.[125] Attempts were also made to produce better competitions, with sports such as sailing restricting the sizes of the yachts that were eligible for various races and streamlining the appeals procedure.[126] New laws also assisted the presentation of events. In 1845 the Cumberland and Westmorland Wrestling Society changed its rules in order to prevent spectators having to spend hours 'staring at an empty ring'.[127] Such concern was a comparative novelty. Many rules were simply created in response to specific problems. For instance, when it became apparent that boxers were justifying their absence from fights because of interference by the police, pugilism's authorities sought to define the term 'magisterial interference' more closely. Coursing competitors advocated that the identity of a dog's owner be concealed because:

> it is well known that the judges in these events were generally men in very poor circumstances easily placed under obligation to some members more than others. They procure dogs, and are allowed to decide the courses in which those very dogs that they sold are engaged.[128]

These reflected much older concerns, namely the desire to curb cheating and corruption. The resources provided by the expansion of the sporting press were utilized in this struggle, with crucial information, such as animal pedigrees, and the misdeeds of wrong doers, being circulated.[129] While modern developments did exert an influence, many rules, and their interpretation, were based upon pre-existing precedents, found in books, archives and oral sources. For example, a ratting dispute in 1849 used pictures from the 1820s to establish the practices that were current then, in order to resolve the relevant laws.[130] Often, the lack of a precedent meant that an event was rerun, as with a rowing dispute in 1827.[131] The spread of information, far from leading to standardization, simply fragmented the sporting culture still further, by creating a dynamic for change which the bodies existing to administer sport, clubs, were unable to organize effectively. In the next section we examine the impact that this flood of information on rules had on clubs.

By their very nature, clubs were exclusive, generally along social lines, and implicitly local. Consequently, unless they commanded immense status, in terms of both social and sporting prestige, they were unlikely to provide a nucleus for a national organization. Geography, also, exercised an influence, the laws of certain sports tending to vary regionally. While this was clearly the case in wrestling, each variety of which was heavily related to a particular location, the practice of emigres of establishing a club of their native style in their new location meant that rules were widely disseminated. Thus, for instance, Cumberland and Westmorland Societies were distributed throughout the country.[132] Generally, improved communications meant that it was becoming increasingly common for competitors from different clubs and regions to come into contact.[133] As they each tended to advocate their individual code, it proved difficult to create standardized laws in many major sports, though attempts were occasionally made in sailing and rowing.[134] Coursing enjoyed more success, its clubs organizing national meetings in which a code was assembled.[135] The laws created in 1839 gained the adherence of most of the top clubs, though it was not until 1858 that a credible universal code was established.[136] Such permanent accommodations between clubs were rare. More usually, compromises were temporary, with a lifespan limited to a single event. Likewise, competitors would alternate in one another's codes, as in wrestling.[137] Given that a great deal of the sporting activity in the post-Napoleonic period occurred between comparative strangers, accommodations between codes were crucial. Compromise rules were created by the framing of articles, thus enabling proponents of quite distinct codes to play together. The product could often be very brief, the rules for a wrestling event in Leeds were: 'Play to be hand to collar, fair back falls, light shoes and padding to be worn, if approved by the parties'. This was designed to cater for competitors from many diverse codes, including Yorkshire, Devon, Cornwall, London and Ireland.[138] By contrast, articles for pugilism often had to be very detailed, the Brown–Sampson match falling through because its organizers 'did not seem to understand the necessity of guarding against subsequent objections'.[139]

The increasingly catholic nature of articles undermined the status of individual clubs, by creating a climate in which larger, national, associations, could emerge. This was an almost inevitable product of the expansion, in terms of both volume and geography, of sporting activity. There was an awareness in many sports, particularly coursing, of the need for a unified, national code.[140] During this period such developments remained largely embryonic, though providing the foundation for a far more organized, and widespread, sporting culture.

Generally, national codes exerted less influence on British sport between 1816 and 1850 than in the preceding era, with the major bodies of the French wars, the Jockey Club, the MCC and the Pugilistic Club, suffering a decline in status. This was reflected in terms of the quality of their membership, the supervision they offered and their national authority. In fact, the Pugilistic Club expired in 1824. In terms of the nature of their membership, the Jockey Club was the only one of the three to retain an influential elite. Many of the top people in society were members and its dealings often resembled those of a highly select London club, even to the point of keeping their members' identities secret until 1834.[141] By contrast, the MCC, especially in the 1830s, lost many of its socially important patrons, and had few top cricketers.[142] Until its demise, the Pugilistic Club was a fusion of expertise and social rank. However, the membership of its successors, such as the Fair Play Club, the New Pugilistic Club, the Association For First Rate Professionals and the Amateur Sporting Club, was of a much lower calibre, amounting to little more than rather disorganized trade unions.[143] Such patrons as they had did not enjoy the social prestige of their predecessors and were unable to structure the sport. Thus, the Pugilistic Benefit Association (formed 1852) was beset by squabbles between the boxers and their supporters.[144] During the French wars, both the Jockey and Pugilistic clubs, especially the latter, had provided effective supervision. In the years after Waterloo the Pugilistic Club was amazingly efficient, given the legally dubious nature of the sport, with cases being investigated thoroughly. Yet, ultimately, 'roguery' swamped pugilism, causing the club to collapse.[145] Its successor, the Fair Play Club, did initially try to eradicate fraud, banning those who were most guilty of it, but by 1829 its credibility disappeared when it refused to examine a case of malpractice involving a member of its own committee.[146] After this, they ceased to decide disputes, and enquirers were urged to 'go to Tattersall's and take the opinion of sporting men'.[147] Neither the Jockey Club nor MCC did any better. Despite its socially elite membership, the Jockey Club lacked both the authority and inclination to enforce their will and were therefore quite inadequate for dealing with a sport that involved as much money as horse racing. The sport was rife with dubious practices and many members, including Bentinck, the architect of its reforms, were heavily implicated in these.[148] Thus, its occasional actions, such as the banning of Beardsworth – an owner who often resorted to dubious practices – in 1834, and their refusal to allow the influential loser of the St Leger in 1819 to have it rerun, scarcely amounted to decisive intervention.[149] Nor, despite the immense public interest in the external verification of particular sporting events, notably the dog Billy's ratting feats, which were attributed by some to his use of drugged rats, did the club involve itself in the supervision of other sports.[150] Even influential members, such as Rous, were intimidated by threats of legal action from intervening in a disputed foot race.[151] The MCC periodically discussed rule changes but made no attempt to enforce them nationally. The introduction of reformed laws at Lords was due to a change in the leaseholder, with Dark replacing Ward, rather than an assertive display by the committee.[152] Despite this, there was little uniformity in cricket's rules, one player observing 'In almost every village of the cricketing counties there is a farmer's boy, who throws his ball under the pretence of bowling round, and if you appeal to the umpire, he tells you it is allowed at Lords.'[153]

During its brief life, the Pugilistic Club had exerted national authority, but with its disappearance boxing lacked a credible central authority to restore public confidence in its integrity. A fair idea of the respect in which its successors were held can be gleaned from one boxer describing the committee as 'a set of scarecrows'.[154] Circumstances prodded the Jockey Club into the public eye, forcing it to expand the comprehensiveness of its rules and to publish decisions on various cases in order to guide others. They were not a progressive body, as was shown by their tepid endorsement of the railway connection at Newmarket in 1845.[155] Their principal aims were to retain power and privacy, and the deliberations of the Select Committee on Gaming revealed that it was rather better at preserving its own authority than instigating reform. By contrast, as the period progressed, the MCC gradually began to adjudicate cases, though it was still far from exercising supreme authority within the sport.[156]

Between 1816 and 1850 two significant developments occurred within the rules governing sport. One, was the vast increase in both the sophistication of rules and their availability. The other, related to the clubs and associations who governed particular activities. Without exception, the authority of these bodies declined. The overall effect of this was the multiplication of increasingly detailed codes, each of which had failed to attain national supremacy.

Referees

During the French wars the structures supervising sport were comparatively closed, based either upon the exclusivity of the club, or on local social networks of patronage and deference. Three developments in the post-Waterloo period undermined this. The most significant was the dramatic increase in the volume of events. Flowing from this was a much greater interaction between the various geographical regions, and a significant increase in the social diversity of those promoting and organizing sport. Cumulatively, these factors emasculated the authorities that had previously organized activity, accentuating the complexities resulting from the plethora of competing codes.

Before Waterloo, referees had tended to come from a higher social class than the competitors and much of the latter's obedience stemmed from social deference. Events were also well supervised. This pattern continued until the early 1820s, with the socially respectable, particularly men such as Barclay and Jackson, acting as referees, and certificates and signed reports being presented to show that particular facts were true, such as the stipulated distance had been accomplished.[157] Acknowledging this structure, articles, for example those relating to the Nottingham–England cricket match of 1818, insisted that only gentlemen could act as umpires.[158] In a wider context, this attitude pervaded the judiciary, for until at least the 1830s it was felt that only members of the gentry could act as magistrates.[159] Such notions disappeared much earlier in sport, last occurring in the Spring–Langan fight of 1824, where an official was objected to because 'he was a tradesman and Cribb insisted that none but a gentleman could hold the watch'.[160] While the increase in the volume of activity inevitably meant that groups outside the upper ranks took an increasing part in sporting events, the principal reason for the withdrawal of 'gentlemen' from the supervisory role was the amount of trouble, in terms of lawlessness, disobedience and financial squabbles, they encountered. These rendered the role of referee 'thankless'.[161] Efforts were still made to collect documentation substantiating particular facts, but these were increasingly fraught with forgery and misinformation. Additionally, even the opinion of 'experts' seemed to be contentious, vets sometimes differing over the age of a horse.[162] Many of the difficulties probably emerged because of the increasing amounts of money that were focused upon such activities. In this sense, as other sports began to emulate the finance involved in horse racing, they became afflicted with similar difficulties relating to corruption that had damaged that sport during the French wars.[163] However, the crowd trouble experienced after 1815, especially from gangs of organized brigands, was of a quite different order to the earlier period, and indicated a transformation of criminal activity.[164] Such difficulties meant that after 1830 it was very rare for gentlemen to act as referees, and when they did so it tended to be in more secluded surroundings, notably of legally dubious sports, such as ratting.[165]

The withdrawal of the gentry from the role of referee meant their replacement by those from lower in the social order. On occasions, there were no referees at all. This was usually due to a failure among the competitors to agree upon an official, and often resulted in a dispute that was only settled in the law courts.[166] Sometimes, the crowd were left to ensure fair play, which they did by beating up 'cheats'.[167] Decisions were also made by the competitors themselves, for example many pigeon-shooting disputes were resolved by a show of hands.[168] The proprietors of the expanding number of sports' grounds, such as Belle Vue, rarely employed competent officials, prompting *Bell's* to identify the need for: 'a fit and proper person appointed at Belle Vue to act as referee, who would decide without fear or favour, instead of having, as is often the case, a yokel or publican whose customers may be interested in the race'.[169]

At first, comparatively little attention was paid to the calibre of individual selected as referee. Gradually, however, there were increasing demands in most sports for qualified, independent officials and efforts were made to obtain them. Many judges at coursing events were elected and made increasingly independent of the non-expert committees.[170] Sportsmen, themselves, often acted as referees. Boxing matches were sometimes supervised by pugilists or other athletes, such as the great runner, Seward.[171] On occasions, disputes in cricket were held over and referred at a later date to groups of expert players. Above everything, however, increasing efforts were made in cricket to ensure that umpires were qualified. By the mid-1840s, the MCC stipulated that all the umpires that it employed must have passed a test on the laws.[172] At a similar period, when the All England XI began touring, they insisted on using their own umpires, thus setting a standard that improved the quality nationally.[173] Significantly, even in socially elite events, such as the Henley Regatta, there was a demand to replace important local people as judges with 'some disinterested men, of known integrity and thoroughly conversant with boating matters (and such men, surely, our universities or London, if not our provincial, boat clubs can supply in most places)'.[174]

In most fields, such as coursing, foot racing and pedestrianism, paid, experienced officials were deferred to for their knowledge. Generally, the standard of supervision increased throughout the period, with officials exhibiting a much surer grasp of the rules. This was the case for even the most contentious decision of the period, Paddock's disqualification in the fight with Bendigo in 1850. The resultant uproar greeting that decision was clearly motivated by partisan feeling, all conceding that the verdict was technically correct. Thus, changes in sport shadowed those occurring in the wider society from the 1830s, with 'gentlemen' referees, like their compatriots who had previously acted as unpaid administrators for the government, being replaced by paid officials, who though invariably from lower in the social scale, had a greater knowledge of the rules.

Improvements in the knowledge of officials did not compensate for the astonishing growth of criminal intervention. Aside from horse racing, where the large sums involved inevitably attracted criminals, the first sport to really become afflicted with the problem was, logically, given its dubious legal status, pugilism. The majority of the many associations which the sport set up to try and regulate itself concentrated on trying to prevent intrusions into the ring. Thus, nominated officials, sometimes on horseback, always carrying whips, struggled to keep the ring clear of intruders.[175] In many ways, pugilism created the first professional sporting officials, with a range of individuals from the commissionary, who provided the ropes and stakes, through to the ring-keepers, performing such roles, often on a regular basis, for money. Despite the fact that the sums and perks provided for this increased steadily, the job was rarely done properly, and on occasions it was clear that the ring-keepers were in league with the criminals.[176] As the period wore on, other sports, such as foot racing and pedestrianism, were increasingly afflicted by this, and had to employ officials to try and prevent criminal intrusions. The state gradually began to help. Whereas early on, such interventions were very rare, by the 1840s the police often ensured 'fair play' by preventing criminals intruding.[177] Ultimately, whatever the improvements in the standard of knowledge possessed by referees, and the efforts made to minimize the impact of increasingly organized criminal interventions, the massive increase in the amount and variety of sporting activity, demanded some type of national organization which could provide expert opinion. A letter from Manks, a top runner, urged action:

> an effort should be made to place pedestrianism on a more healthy footing, and endeavour if possible to establish an honest and honourable tribunal, whereby the delinquencies and dishonest practices too frequently occurring might be exposed, and the party, whoever he might be, excluded from all grounds where running is allowed.[178]

Effectively speaking, nothing of the type existed. While sporting clubs did perform a number of roles, particularly in regulating tensions between members and thus keeping disputes in events such as sailing out of the courts, they remained parochial, rarely involving themselves with outsiders.[179] In fact, even the most influential body, the Jockey Club, often tried to avoid becoming involved in horse-racing disputes, despite the appeals of the law courts, who would often urge plaintiffs to submit such cases to them. Clubs gave still less attention to the lower orders, and with the exception of a committee made up of members of prestigious rowing clubs deciding a disputed race between two watermen, upon which there had been heavy betting, it was almost unknown for clubs to supervise such events.[180] This, coupled with the withdrawal of gentlemen from administering much of the sport involving the lower orders, meant that predominantly working-class sports, such as foot racing and pedestrianism, were dependent upon entrepreneurs for their supervision.[181] As these individuals tended to lack the status and social position of the gentry, they were more easily influenced by external, sometimes criminal, involvement. Thus, it was the press, especially *Bell's Life*, which performed such a role, acting as a veritable switchboard for sporting information. *Bell's* acted as: organizer, putting competitors in touch with one another, assisting the framing of articles and solving queries concerning rules; stakeholder, receiving stakes via postal orders and relinquishing them to the winning party upon receiving the referee's signed report; and often referee, disputes being referred to them for decision.[182] The last was not a role they relished, and it is noticeable that they would try to assist the creation of supervisory bodies, such as publishing news of the Fair Play Petition established by some boxers in 1842, and persistently urge that a 'jockey club' be set up in particular sports.[183] Requests from readers forced the press to devote ever more space and energy to resolving disputes. However, journalists avoided becoming absorbed in the minutiae of the various highly contingent rules by adhering to certain abstract assumptions, that had the status of imperatives. The origin of these is unclear, though they appear to have represented some commonly agreed principles, and thus provided a framework for the resolution of disputes. There were five of them. The most fundamental was that the referee's decision must be obeyed.[184] Second, the results of all subsidiary bets were determined by the referee's decision.[185] Third, in the event of the referee deciding that there had been cheating, all bets were cancelled.[186] Fourth, the exact terms of the articles decided any dispute.[187] Finally, events in which a competitor used an alias were void.[188] To an extent the press did manage to limit the effect of corruption, carrying out investigations and consulting with referees on rumours of there having been intimidation. Yet, because, on occasions, they were having to act as both referee and arbitrator, they were sometimes forced to concede that it was impossible to make a decision, especially when they were being bombarded by all types of contradictory information, often stemming from dubious sources, and thus had to leave it to the competitors themselves to sort out.

Bell's was also confronted with a still profounder problem, in that its verdicts on events were not always adhered to by the competitors, even stakeholders refusing to comply with their decisions.[189] Their experience mirrored the problem that increasingly confronted referees, that of having their will obeyed. For instance, in

Manchester during the 1840s disputed verdicts, often resulting in fights, were common in foot racing.[190] This was often the case elsewhere, and a variety of sports were afflicted; in 1845 a 'disinterested' bystander at the request of both competitors in a game of quoits, gave a verdict, only to have the losing party reject his decision.[191]

While such behaviour jeopardized events at a local level, a succession of disputes were destroying the very fundamentals upon which sporting activity was based. As noted earlier, a number of imperatives existed that took precedence over all other factors, thus ensuring a degree of order despite some criminal intervention. However, in 1828, a stakeholder was taken to court by the losing competitor in a dog fight who was seeking to obtain his money back.[192] The stakeholder, who had only been acting according to the articles of the sporting event, stood in contradiction of the nation's law and was 'in a very perilous position'. In the years that followed it became common for losing competitors to sue stakeholders, even *Bell's Life*, a paper that in its capacity as stakeholder rigidly adhered to obedience of the referee's decision no matter what its personal views on the matter, having to hand cases over to its attorney.[193] Thus, one of the fundamentals regulating sporting activity collapsed. The most profound principle of all, that the referee's decision must be obeyed, was also eroded. In 1829 a stakeholder, believing that the decision reached by the referee, who had consulted both Jackson and Egan, concerning a prize-fight was wrong, surrendered the stakes contrary to their verdict. His decision was 'honourable' but 'a very dangerous precedent'.[194] In a highly publicized event in 1845 the understanding finally collapsed completely, when the referee in the Caunt–Bendigo fight awarded victory to the latter because of the violence of Bendigo's supporters, whose 'whips and staves fell within an inch of his caster, while they fell heavily on the nobs of some of his neighbours'.[195] Many of those who lost money on the fight, including the great boxer Spring, refused to pay their bets, rejecting the most fundamental tenet of all, that the referee's decision must be obeyed, effectively putting an end to the imperatives that had regulated sport.

In the hope of shielding referees from the pressures confronted in the fight of 1845, it was declared that boxers whose fans threatened the referee would be disqualified.[196] However, in 1850 the editor of *Bell's Life*, while refereeing a fight, was beaten up by the loser's fans. Effectively, organized pugilism had become little more than anarchy. Surveyed as a whole, the vast increase in the amount of money involved in sporting events between 1816 and 1850 made it inevitable that they were far less 'fair' than in the preceding period. Certain aspects showed no decline. As with earlier years, every type of race, from rabbits to men, usually occurred on properly organized courses, care having been taken in choosing and measuring the ground.[197] Fouling was punished and in cricket and wrestling referees were forbidden to bet on the events they were supervising.[198] While it was not uncommon for officials to be linked to the competitors, occasionally they displayed great objectivity, as a game of football at Rochdale showed:

one of the Bodyguards (being tired) putting another person not connected with the game to kick for him, and their own umpire declaring it foul play according to the rules agreed to by both parties, decided the game.[199]

However, not everyone was so neutral. While the use of two umpires, one from each side, at cricket, was not designed to combat bias, but to allow each to have a periodic rest, some officials displayed outrageous favouritism.[200] One wrote justifying his conduct for giving a member of the opposing team out for using his bat to prevent the ball hitting the wicket by stating 'I certainly did (believing it contrary to the rules of cricket) pronounce Perkins out for persisting in not moving his bat from the blocking hole, although the ball came against it'. [201] In a horse race between Hay and Hill for £40 the former was 'thirty yards ahead' when 'one of the umpires appointed on Mr Hill's part, crossed the road, under the pretext of his horse becoming unmanageable, jostling and disconcerting the rider, and thus allowing Mr Hill's groom time and opportunity to arrive first'.[202]

Lack of sportsmanship was found everywhere, even amongst the elite 'gentlemen' rowing for Oxford University, an observer remarked 'the University gentlemen either forgot or are determined to evade the rules drawn up for the match'.[203] Conduct in the first boat-race of 1829 was even worse; Cambridge's Digby stated that 'all Cambridge men would have been thrown into the river if their boat had won, so incensed were the Oxfordshire people at this venturing to appear on their waters'.[204] The supervision of numerous events in the post-Waterloo period was inadequate. On occasions, pigeon-shooting degenerated into a 'massacre'.[205] In pedestrianism and sailing, umpires often lagged behind the competitors, and occasionally their vehicles almost crushed spectators.[206] The rules of rowing permitted too much latitude, resulting in a great deal of deliberate bumping and blocking. Some sports might just as well have not had rules; one wrestler's tactics, which went unpunished by the referee, involved 'catching his opponent by his ears, and shaking him like a dog'.[207]

Yet the above difficulties were trivial compared with the major problem confronting legitimate sport within the period, the massive extent of criminal involvement. It was at its most intense in horse racing where acts of sabotage, as attempted on 'Old England', the favourite for the Derby, by his trainer, on behalf of a consortium who had betted heavily against it winning, were common. Owners were also guilty of corruption, backing their own horses to lose and ensuring that the jockeys 'pulled up injured, according to orders'.[208] Most infamous of all were the use of bogus pedigrees, enabling the illegal entry of horses for races for which their age excluded them, as with the 'Running Rein' affair, in which the winner of the Derby was ineligible for the race.[209] Other sports were also afflicted. Many foot races and prize-fights were regularly organized frauds, and certain areas of the country, for instance Staffordshire and Nottinghamshire, were dominated by corruption.[210] Cheating, often on a systematic basis, was present in every sport, touching referees, competitors, stakeholders and spectators, whether they were 'gentlemen' or not.[211]

Its variety was breathtaking. The boxer Dutch Sam tried to get his prospective opponent arrested in order to claim the stakes.[212] On the second day of a cricket match, the Mountsorrel players took the field to bat but were horrified to discover that 'although it had been a very fine night, the ground was completely saturated'.[213] Evidently their opponents had soaked the wicket during the night. Still more overt, were attacks by the crowd on either their opponents or the referee. When the referee, Curtis disqualified Britton in his fight with Molyneaux, Britton's fans 'immediately chased Curtis round the ring' and both Curtis and Molyneaux only avoided being beaten up because 'a gentleman took them behind on the back of his horse and galloped away'.[214] Rowing was no different. The boat of the favourite at the Horsleydown Regatta, Miller, was deliberately sunk by his opponent, Hopkins.[215] At the elite, Royal Thames Yacht Club, 'a skiff rowed three times at the bowes of the Alert', preventing her winning.[216] Confronted with such widespread behaviour, the rules administering sport came to seem increasingly irrelevant.

The erosion of the deferential structure that had previously administered sport, embodied by socially elite individuals and clubs, meant that supervision and arbitration was increasingly left to bodies that enjoyed far less prestige, such as the press. This, effectively, meant that most sports had no central authority to administer them, the elite having withdrawn from the public world into their private clubs, the domain of the 'gentleman's' agreement.

Science

While one might have expected the increased corruption to have undermined the development and application of techniques designed to improve competitors, the employment of science in sport had its own momentum, and continued to be recognized. In this section we consider three elements: man, animals and technology.

The years after Waterloo did not witness a dramatic change in the techniques used to develop athletes' physiques. The ingredients of the diet regarded as necessary to create and maintain an athletic constitution remained similar to those popular in the earlier period.[217] Aside from the occasional competitor who espoused the virtues of cabbage and milk, the staples were meat and alcohol.[218] The latter, especially spirits, was regarded as strength-giving, and given the polluted state of most water, was probably safer to drink.[219] Some practices were beginning to be challenged. While techniques for losing weight were well established, the most pervasive, 'sweating', primarily the use of the vapour bath, came to be regarded as dangerous, especially after causing a jockey's death.[220] There appears to have been more use of drugs, the runner, Bradshaw, placing himself under the care of 'a sporting chemist and druggist'.[221] Far more change occurred in the fostering of skill. The introduction of stricter rules, such as the increased attention to size and weight in boxing, led to advances in the cultivation of particular talents.[222] Blaine observed that every sport was coming to depend upon science.[223]

In response to this, large numbers of professional trainers came to the fore. Their techniques were often very costly, training having become a big business. It was alleged that preparing a boxer for a major fight could cost £500.[224] Experts also produced treatises on particular sports, most of which claimed, like *Fistiana*, to significantly improve practitioners.[225] A large number of works on betting systems also appeared and it is clear that sporting and sport-related literature was regarded as a profitable venture.[226] However, the period displayed a general tendency of scepticism towards experts, even Newmarket's horse-racing trainers being dismissed as hopeless for any other course.[227] Such sentiments often manifested themselves in overt anti-professionalism, as with those who blamed the decline in rowing at Oxford University on the employment of watermen and urged that 'only gentlemen can train gentlemen'.[228] Even a sport as tolerant as cricket was not uninfluenced by such calls for gentlemen to cease relying upon the bowling of their social inferiors: the I Zingari team was specifically created for just this purpose.[229]

Throughout the post-Napoleonic period, there was an increased dissemination of the scientific techniques designed to create physical strength and ability. Some skills had a distinctly practical application, with continental techniques of self-defence steadily replacing pugilism. In the past, villains had always been envisaged as confronting their victims head on, enabling the deployment of boxing. However, modern footpads attacked from behind, thus necessitating a type of wrestling.[230] Similarly, there was a growth in firearms training, disseminated by teachers in shooting galleries.[231] The cultivation of such ability was regarded as vital in order to prevent intimidation by 'card cheats', who would threaten their accusers with a duel. Generally, however, regimes promised more abstract rewards. There was a growing acceptance of the equation that an athletic body was healthy, and great attention was devoted to exercise and diet.[232] Sport was also closely linked to hygiene, especially swimming and cleanliness. Servicing, and doubtless stimulating, this market were a number of 'professors', often foreigners, offering training in their gymnasia. Additionally, large numbers of books and articles, some written by aristocrats, catered specifically for this 'middle-class' readership.[233] Many of these works were aimed at women, a group that would have otherwise remained excluded from this culture.[234] Despite the new emphasis on health, it was very rare for writers to advocate an overt display of the muscles during the performance of sport.[235] Such classical notions tended to be submerged by a reluctance to give offence and most sportsmen competed heavily clothed, even with overcoats and umbrellas.[236] It was only the lower class who would row 'in buff, or what is almost as bad, in short knee-breeches or drawers, or in trousers turned up above the calf, with legs bare and the jersey cut away so as to show the breast and armpits, gentlemen row in common trousers and jerseys with sleeves'.[237]

This concern with health and hygiene may have reflected a contemporary concern, namely the decline of 'modern' man by comparison with his predecessors.[238] Many regarded modern habits and manners as causing physical degeneration and the belief in the unhealthiness of the city was such that the rules of the London Cumberland and Westmorland Wrestling Society excluded provincials because 'wrestlers from the country being in the practice of attending the London meeting, and carrying off the principal prizes, the young men of the metropolis, who are pent up six days a week in dark and dreary warehouses having no chance'.[239] To an extent, sport was regarded as both a gauge of this process, efforts being made to compare the relative standards of past and present athletes, and an antidote to degeneration, with scientific techniques being employed to combat harmful environmental effects.[240] This is emphasized by an examination of a popular gymnastic treatise, the contents of which clearly catered for a broad public, including sections on 'field sports' and 'athletics'. Their military intent was also clear, a chapter being devoted to 'the modern system of war'.[241] In 1843 it was suggested by some influential people that a national gymnasium be established in order to foster courage.[242] By the 1860s, the steady refinement of sports was attracting criticism. However, towards the end of the century it became clear to many that the growth of sporting science was leading, inevitably, to ever greater achievements; a belief quite different from the pessimism expressed between 1816 and 1850.[243]

The second facet of scientific training related to animals. While there had long been an awareness of the importance of an animal's pedigree, after 1815 such information was disseminated more widely, large numbers of works discussing techniques on breeding animals and systematizing the relevant data.[244] This practice achieved a remarkable level in both coursing and fox-hunting, with dogs being bred for specific types of country.[245] Interest in selective breeding was especially prominent in 'cruel sports', such as ratting and dog-fighting, where the offspring of champions fetched good prices. Yet the variety of animals being selectively bred was narrowing, reflecting public taste. Bull-dogs began to disappear, replaced by dogs bred especially for the popular sport of 'ratting'.[246] Likewise, as fox-hunting and hare-hunting gave increasing emphasis to speed rather than scent, dogs specializing in the latter skill ceased to be bred.[247] While one might have expected there to be a decline in the amount and quality of horses bred, due to the abolition of the Royal Stud at Windsor in 1839 and the savaging of the Royal Veterinary School's budget, according to observers the overall quality improved.[248] Generally, modernity, in the shape of the steam engine, though often regarded with trepidation by equestrians, did not have a negative impact on horses: Manchester's entry for the St Leger of 1831 was even trained by racing a steam engine.[249] Horses were still loved and regarded as worthy of study, the modern science of phrenology devoting discussions to the qualities of character revealed by the skull of the deceased champion, Eclipse.[250]

The third and final aspect of scientific sport related to technology and experienced a significant growth, reflecting the increased expenditure on sport.

During the period the major achievements in sporting technology were aquatic. A very large number of specialist boat-builders developed, especially in London, producing ever-more refined designs.[251] These were spread nationally via such events as the Thames Regatta and it was not uncommon to find journalists attributing victory in a rowing match to a boat's design.[252] The size of yachts mushroomed, and became so specialized that 'most men are now pretty well convinced that if they wish to win matches they must give up all idea of going to sea in comfort'.[253] Many denounced such changes as 'unsportsmanlike' and it is certainly difficult to regard yachts participating in races after 1830 as being anything other than specialist vessels.[254] A British boat owner rejected a challenge from an American because he feared that his opponent's yacht 'might be a vessel just thrown together for the purpose'.[255]

Sporting technology was becoming a substantial business, with increasingly specialized products. Marketing, rather than invention, was crucial, as the failure of ingenious devices, such as the instant ice-rink, demonstrated.[256] Generally, a much wider market was being sought. In firearms, for instance, this led to severe arguments over patents, and the appearance of a variety of guns, in terms of size and materials, many of which were dangerous to use.[257] Commercial forces introduced refinements in cricket, notably in bats, gloves and pads, and above everything, the catapulta.[258] This bowling machine was used widely, revolutionizing batting skill and undermining the employment of many professional bowlers. Throughout the period most sports witnessed some refinements, such as those occurring in the stopwatch, and particular areas came to specialize in manufacturing equipment, for instance St Andrews and golf balls.[259] By 1850 the production of sporting equipment had become a big business, able to command its place among the exhibits at the Great Exhibition.

Conclusions

The fundamental structure of sport throughout the French wars remained largely unchanged. Almost all organized sporting events occurred without appreciable dispute. The majority used rules based on established written codes. Beneath these were a web of written and verbal agreements that were derived from a variety of sources. These do not appear to have been regarded as inadequate and even in sports such as pedestrianism, which was incredibly popular, there was no suggestion that efforts should be made to establish a common, written, code. Given the large number of events which took place and the significant sums which these involved, it is evident that the lack of machinery governing sport was regarded as satisfactory. Two factors seem to have been responsible for the consensus which prevailed between competing parties concerning obedience to the rules. One, was the use of stakes. Potentially, it might have seemed that such a provision would encourage the losing party to renege on guarantees. In practice, this was rare. In large measure this was produced by the second crucial factor that established a consensus between competing parties, the referee. Referees enjoyed considerable power and appear to have almost always exercised this uncontentiously. Many of them were selected because they were 'gentlemen', occupying a higher social class than those they were supervising. To a certain extent, obedience to the rules of sport could be regarded as a manifestation of social deference.

Two important changes relating to the rules of sport did occur during the French wars. First, an increasing number of authorities appeared to which disputes could be referred. These regulatory bodies were by no means all powerful and ultimate authority lay with the law courts. Second, such sporting bodies steadily established a closely defined series of rules and precedents which structured the sport and enabled disputes to be more easily resolved. Their authority was largely based on social position, though in the case of Jackson his acknowledged expertise in sporting matters meant that he was regarded as the repository of unbiased wisdom.

Between 1816 and 1850 the enormous increase in both the volume of sporting events and the expenditure on sporting activity resulted in a number of changes that had a profound impact on both rules and referees. In the first place, there were far more codes of rules. More importantly, the structures that had previously organized and administered sport were undermined by the huge increase in the involvement of groups from outside the established social order. Whereas previously, much of the supervision of sport had been based upon networks of deference stemming from social relationships, the inclusion of wider groups within this culture undermined its functioning, often resulting in virtual anarchy. Dowling's comments concerning boxing in 1848 had long been applicable to many popular sports: 'matches are now got up by persons in the humbler classes, whose passions and prejudices are above control, and who, in consequence, when the event comes off, are incapable of maintaining that order'.[260] Many of these new patrons had close relations with the criminal world, which exerted an increasing influence on sport. The trouble resulting from this, in terms of corruption and crowd violence drove many of the elite away. Typical was a prize-fight in Berkshire, where swarms of well organized pickpockets almost broke into the ring, whence 'a rebuke from Mr Gully and two or three other gentlemen near him, only produced sneers, and a threat of using the chivey upon him'.[261] When Gully, a former champion boxer, was treated like that what hope was there for anyone? Thus, the supervisory role which the socially elite had once performed was vacated. The impact of such a withdrawal was that in a variety of sports efforts were made to create new supervisory structures, including the recruitment of more expert officials and the creation of codes which were more widely acceptable. However, the impact of these new groups was often diluted because they lacked the prestige of the upper ranks.

As to the elite themselves, changes in the qualities that defined a 'gentleman', accompanied, it appears, by a certain defensiveness concerning their social status, meant that they seem to have restricted their involvement to particular sports and clubs, thus ensuring that interference by outsiders was minimal. They also began employing new criteria to detach themselves, inventing and espousing the ideals of amateurism and using these to segregate sporting participation. This was a significant attempt to compartmentalize sporting activity along implicitly social lines, by portraying the financial element as improper. Thus, competitors from outside the social elite were excluded from intruding into the domain of their superiors for ostensibly moral reasons.

The withdrawal of the socially prestigious from the organization and supervision of sport seriously weakened its administration. Thus, paradoxically, while the quality of rules became increasingly sophisticated, displaying wider creativity, the structures administering sport declined in status and importance. This impaired their ability to establish the primacy of a particular code. It was a problem crystallised by the changing structure of the contract. During the French wars the contract had tended to be a compromise between comparatively amorphous notions concerning the rules used in a sport. By contrast, in the later period, the contract often mediated between two comparatively sophisticated sets of rules. It would require either the establishment of a convincing consensus, or the intervention of the socially influential, to elevate the product of such a compromise into a code encompassing the sport nationally. In 1850 such criteria was absent from many popular sports. The lack of status of the various supervisors of sport had a still more fundamental effect. It meant that they were increasingly unable to enforce their decisions. The inevitable result of this was a substantial increase in the number of disputes that were not satisfactorily resolved. Cumulatively, this seriously weakened the supervision of sport.[262]

Sport, like society, was in the midst of a fundamental change. As we have noted, the elite's supervision of such activities had declined substantially.[263] This was encapsulated by a statement from one of the protagonists in a dispute concerning boxing from 1830. He offered to submit the case to either a barrister or Captain Barclay.[264] The available choices neatly summed up the changes in the administration of sport. Increasingly, 'gentlemen', such as Captain Barclay, were becoming replaced by outside experts, who imposed legalistic concepts rather than moral notions of right and wrong. In this sense, post-Napoleonic sport mirrored many of the wider changes in society, notably the erosion of a social and administrative structure based on deference and its gradual replacement by newer groups that emphasized expertise rather than rank. Similarly, the amateur ideal, with its espousal of the moral qualities possessed by 'gentlemen', could be regarded as an attempt to undermine the power of commerce and expertise, by insisting that such abilities were not relevant to the correct exercise of authority.

The refusal of the privileged to participate in the organization of sport on a national level, advocating instead separate, elite, clubs, was to seriously impair the development of commercial sport. It also contradicted the inclusive potential of such activities, depriving Britain of national sporting organizations.

In 1846 patients and attendants at Hanwell Lunatic Asylum played a cricket match together. While for many years an annual match had been occurring between two teams of Greenwich pensioners, eleven with one arm against eleven with one leg, this was the first recorded occasion of a match involving the mentally ill.[265] Cricket was becoming a national institution, incorporating the whole population. This sentiment was amplified when the game's supporters urged, in 1850, that visitors to the Great Exhibition should not simply be able to appreciate a display of cricket equipment, but also witness a match.[266] Their aim did not achieve fruition, probably because the machinery for organizing such a national sporting event did not exist. This was certainly the reason for the nation's failure to take up the Pasha of Egypt's challenge to race his champion horse against the best thoroughbred in Britain for £10,000. Despite the fact that horse racing was regarded as so important in Britain that Parliament did not sit on Derby day, the Jockey Club lacked the power to nominate a champion and the challenge thus fell through.[267]

This lack of a central organizing authority in most sports persisted and manifested itself in various ways. For instance, despite the immense status enjoyed by cricket, underarm bowling was common in many provincial matches, occurring regularly at Barrow until well into the 1890s.[268] Similarly, despite the fact that tedious aspects of cricket's rules were resulting in the large-scale alienation of the public, attempts to change them failed.[269] The main factor that impeded football's growth was the wide variety of codes; as late as 1873 a breakdown of the rules used by clubs in Britain revealed: Rugby, 114; Association, 68; both, 5; Sheffield, 35; others, 12.[270]

Yet despite the obstruction presented by the elite, with their espousal of amateurism and strict adherence to narrowly defined clubs, and the machinations of organized crime, commercial sport emerged. This stemmed from the interest that its increasingly expert competitors excited amongst the general public, a development that was directly related to the expansion in the dissemination of training.

Between 1793 and 1850, while there were few significant advances made in either animal breeding or sporting technology, a vast expansion occurred in the scope and availability of training in every type of sport. This was made accessible by a large increase in the number of books that were published and 'professionals' who toured nationally. Cumulatively, this multiplied the amount of experts and significantly improved their quality. Thus, skilled protagonists, the raw material for competitive sport, without which a commercial sporting culture could not hope to flourish, came into being. Increasingly, entrepreneurs would cultivate this interest, by creating specialist venues and events: the subject of our next chapter.

Notes

1   *Bell's*, 17 Nov 1833.
2   Bailey, *Leisure and Class*, pp. 2, 8.
3   Dunning and Sheard, *Barbarians*, p. 30.

4   Walvin, *Leisure and Society*, p. 10.

5   Dunning and Sheard, *Barbarians*, pp. 33–4.

6   Holt, *Sport and the British*, pp. 12–13.

7   Ibid., p. 28.

8   'Football', *Chambers Journal*, 1842, 441. This is made abundantly clear in many contemporary texts, see the author's article, 'Uncovering football's missing link: the real story of the evolution of modern football', *European Sports History Review*, 1 (1999). In a letter from the editor of *IJHS*, James Mangan, dated 6 October 1994, this article was accepted for publication in that periodical and was supposed to appear in an issue of *IJHS* some time in 1995. Unfortunately Mangan overlooked this.

9   *Annals*, Feb 1823, 121.

10 *SM*, Aug 1795, 277; Nov 1807, 91–2; March 1811, 307. *Times*, 20 Sept 1815.

11 *SM*, Jan 1793, 206–207; Aug 1795, 276; Sept 1812, 275.

12 *Jackson's*, 26 Oct 1793. *SM*, July 1804, 218; Feb 1807, 251; April 1809, 95.

13 *BWM*, 17 Oct 1813, 31 Dec 1815.

14 *SM*, July 1809, 195.

15 *SM*, Sept 1792, 95–6. Taplin, *Sporting Dictionary*, i, pp. 137–8.

16 Birley, *Sport*, p. 161.

17 *JJC*, Sports in general: Large Folder 2. *SM*, Jan 1794, 206–208; Feb 1794, 239; Oct 1798, 42–3; June 1801, 137–9; June 1802, 154; Dec 1808, 140–41; Oct 1809, 33; Dec 1811, 106–108. *Times*, 28 July 1808.

18 Buckley, *Pre-Victorian Cricket*, pp. 207, 211, 220. HPT (1924), *Old Time Cricket*, Nottingham, pp. 4, 16. *SM*, June 1793, 134–6.

19 Bowen, *History of Cricket*, pp. 54, 65–7.

20 Ibid., p. 71.

21 They are not mentioned in J. Pond, *The Sporting Kalendar* (1751). They are detailed in *SM*, Dec 1792, 145–7; Jan 1793, 188–90. The Jockey Club was formally organized in 1768. *SM*, July 1795, 219.

22 *SM*, Nov 1792, 81–2; Nov 1793, 126–9.

23 Parkyns, *The Inn-Play*, pp. 60–64.

24 *SM*, July 1793, 245–6

25 *SM*, Dec 1792, 139–40; March 1793, 334.

26 *SM*, April 1802, 57; Dec 1808, 140–41; Oct 1809, 33.

27 *SM*, Aug 1807, 224–5, 239.

28 *SM*, Jan 1812, 189.

29 *Bell's*, 12 Oct 1845. *BWM*, 27 June 1813. *SM*, June 1813, 142.

30 *SM*, May 1814, 70.

31 *SM*, Sept 1814, 241.

32 Vamplew, *Turf*, pp. 78, 81–2.

33 *VCH*, *Oxfordshire*, ii, pp. 364–5.

34 *SM*, Jan 1804, 169–70; Feb 1804, 285.

35 *SM*, May 1798, 73.

36 *SM*, Sept 1796, 324; Aug 1803, 267; June 1807, 107; Sept 1809, 260.

37 *BWM*, 16 Sept 1804, 29 Sept 1811. W. Sketchley (1814) *The Cocker*, London, p. 49. *SM*, Jan 1808, 209.

38 *BWM*, 27 Oct 1811.

39 *BWM*, 27 Dec 1807.

40 *Jackson's*, 23 Feb 1793. *Times*, 27 Jan 1797, 28 July 1808.

41 Holt, *Sport and the British*, p. 13.

42   *SM*, Feb 1793, 252–3.
43   *BWM*, 26 April 1807. *Jackson's*, 15 Jan 1803. *SM*, Dec 1793, 129; Oct 1801, 31; Dec 1808, 141; June 1811, 145.
44   *SM*, Feb 1804, 287.
45   *SM*, May 1806, 90; June 1808, 145–6; Dec 1808, 145–6; Sept 1812, 246.
46   *BWM*, 24 Sept 1797, 23 Oct 1803. *SM*, April 1803, 56; Sept 1812, 283.
47   *BWM*, 23 Aug 1801.
48   *SM*, July 1795, 223; Aug 1804, 261–3; Sept 1806, 273; Nov 1808, 55–6; Dec 1809, 97; Oct 1813, 42.
49   *SM*, Nov 1810, 91.
50   Buckley, *Pre-Victorian Cricket*, p. 42. *SM*, Nov 1809, 53.
51   *SM*, Nov 1808, 71.
52   *SM*, Sept 1795, 331; Oct 1800, 35; Sept 1808, 287; Nov 1808, 55–6, 62; Jan 1809, 157–8. A notable exception to this was a dispute at a cricket match at Maldon which resulted in a duel. Buckley, *Pre-Victorian Cricket*, p. 53.
53   Bailey, *Leisure and Class*, pp. 8–9. J. Maguire (1986) 'Images of manliness and competing ways of living in late Victorian and Edwardian Britain', *IJHS*, 3:3, 286.
54   *SM*, March 1802, 348.
55   *BWM*, 12 Aug 1804, 2 Dec 1804, 30 Dec 1804, 26 May 1811, 31 Dec 1815. Buckley, *Pre-Victorian Cricket*, p. 73. *SM*, March 1793, 368; Feb 1797, 283; Aug 1804, 261–3; Aug 1807, 225; Jan 1812, 185.
56   *SM*, Aug 1800, 231–2; July 1804, 210–11; June 1806, 112. *Times*, 19 Sept 1798.
57   *BWM*, 17 June 1804.
58   *SM*, Dec 1803, 150.
59   *BWM*, 20 Feb 1803. *SM*, Feb 1803, 290.
60   *SM*, Nov 1813, 92.
61   Brailsford, *Sport, Time*, p. 28. M. Shearman (1889) *Athletics and Football*, London: Longman, p. xvi. In the later period there were often doubts as to whether events had been correctly timed; *Annals*, Aug 1822, 121. *SM*, Sept 1823, 301–302; Oct 1823, 25–6; Nov 1823, 55–6.
62   *SM*, July 1813, 193.
63   *BWM*, 5 Aug 1798, 2 Dec 1804. *SM*, Dec 1800, 96–7; Jan 1804, 169–70; Feb 1804, 285; Oct 1807, 4–6, 39; April 1808, 46; June 1809, 103.
64   *BWM*, 2 Aug 1807.
65   *SM*, Dec 1814, 160.
66   *BWM*, 2 Sept 1804, 2 Dec 1804.
67   *SM*, May 1806, 90; April 1809, 45.
68   *BWM*, 18 Oct 1807. *SM*, Dec 1807, 103.
69   *BWM*, 7 July 1805, 17 April 1808. *SM*, Jan 1813, 191.
70   J. Sambrook (1986) *The Eighteenth Century: The Intellectual and Cultural Context of English Literature 1700–1789*, London: Longman, pp. 75, 79, 81, 84. *WD*, 12 Feb 1804. W. Speck (1983) *Society and Literature in England 1700–1760*, London: Macmillan, p. 133.
71   *SM*, March 1813, 270.
72   Thom, *Pedestrianism*, p. 236.
73   Ibid., pp. 126, 222–48.
74   *SM*, July 1798, 211–14.
75   *SM*, Nov 1813, 57.
76   *BWM*, 1 Nov 1807.

77   Thom, *Pedestrianism*, p. 252.

78   *BWM*, 25 Oct 1807, 13 May 1813. *SM*, Nov 1801, 94; Oct 1811, 23; March 1812, 299.

79   *BWM*, 30 Dec 1798, 15 Nov 1801, 24 Sept 1815. *SM*, May 1793, 125; Aug 1809, 244; Feb 1813, 210–13; March 1813, 266–70.

80   Thom, *Pedestrianism*, p. 126.

81   *BWM*, 9 Feb 1806.

82   *BWM*, 22 Oct 1815, 26 Nov 1815. *SM*, July 1809, 164; Sept 1815, 245–6. *Times*, 11 Oct 1808, 31 Oct 1811.

83   *SM*, Sept 1810, 281. *Times*, 30 Sept 1811.

84   *BWM*, 7 Feb 1808, 31 Oct 1813. *SM*, July 1803, 224; Oct 1805, 47; Aug 1811, 241.

85   *SM*, Oct 1803, 6–7.

86   Parkyns, *Inn-Play*, pp. 12, 27.

87   Egan, *Boxiana*, ii, pp. 16–24. Ford, *Prize-fighting*, p. 124.

88   *SM*, Jan 1808, 210; June 1813, 143.

89   *SM*, Oct 1805, 46.

90   *Bell's*, 3 Jan 1830. *BWM*, 23 Aug 1807, 8 May 1808, 29 Aug 1813.

91   *BWM*, 12 Sept 1802. Egan, *Book of Sports*, p. 227. *SM*, March 1794, 311; Dec 1808, 104; Sept 1812, 248.

92   *SM*, June 1793, 185; Nov 1796, 92; Jan 1828, 242.

93   *BWM*, 2 June 1805. *SM*, Nov 1810, 91; April 1813, 45.

94   *SM*, Aug 1809, 244; Oct 1812, 39; Dec 1812, 138; April 1813, 46; Dec 1813, 146.

95   McKendrick, Brewer and Plumb, *Consumer Society*, p. 318.

96   Egan, *Book of Sports*, p. 388. G. Hutchinson (1939) *The Heythrop Hunt*, London: John Murray, p. 5.

97   *SM*, Sept 1801, 286; Dec 1801, 113–14; Jan 1803, 174; Sept 1803, 311; Jan 1804, 223; Feb 1804, 285; May 1805, 67.

98   *Bell's*, 2 Nov 1834.

99   *SM*, Nov 1792, 40–41; Jan 1793, 228; July 1793, 225–7; March 1794, 303–305; Jan 1795, 188; Aug 1796, 258, 321; Jan 1803, 224; Jan 1804, 170–71.

100 *SM*, Dec 1802, 132.

101 *BWM*, 27 March 1808. *SM*, Feb 1793, 306; Oct 1814, 40. *Times*, 4 Feb 1804.

102 For the growth of this criminal intrusion in sport see this volume, pp. 133–6.

103 *M.Ex*, 14 Aug 1850. The earliest detailed insight into this process concerns Sheffield FC, who were founded in 1857, having been active since at least 1855. *FCR* 2. *FCR* 10 (Sheffield City Archives).

104 *JJC*, Sports Box 2.

105 *Annals*, June 1822, 393–4. *SM*, Aug 1828, 336.

106 *Bell's*, 11 May 1845.

107 *Annals*, Dec 1824, 355.

108 Litt, *Wrestliana*, pp. 73–7.

109 *Bell's*, 22 April 1849.

110 *Bell's*, 19 May 1850.

111 *Bell's*, 14 June 1850.

112 *Bell's*, 27 April 1727.

113 *Bell's*, 23 April 1837.

114 *Bell's*, 20 Jan 1828.

115 *Bell's*, 19 Oct 1845.

116 *Bell's*, 24 Feb 1828.

117 *Bell's*, 4 March 1842.

118 *Bell's*, 27 April 1834.
119 *Bell's*, 29 July 1832, 7 Oct 1832.
120 *Bell's*, 2 July 1837, 2 April 1848.
121 *Bell's*, 3 June 1832.
122 *Bell's*, 28 April 1839.
123 Brailsford, *Bareknuckles*, pp. 97–8.
124 *Bell's*, 17 May 1840.
125 *Bell's*, 13 July 1834. K. Sandiford (1984) 'Victorian cricket technique and industrial technology', *IJHS*, 1:3, 273. *SM*, July 1827, 119.
126 *Bell's*, 8 July 1838.
127 *Bell's*, 13 April 1845.
128 *Bell's*, 26 June 1842. *SM*, July 1825, 206.
129 *Bell's*, 4 Nov 1832.
130 *Bell's*, 15 July 1849, 22 July 1849.
131 *Bell's*, 7 Oct 1827.
132 See, for instance, *Bell's*, 19 April, 26 April, 31 May, 7 June, 14 June, 21 June 1840.
133 *Thacker's Courser's Annual Remembrancer and Stud Book 1850–1851*, London, 1851, p. 6.
134 *Bell's*, 24 Nov 1850, 1 Dec 1850.
135 *Thacker's Annual Remembrancer and Stud Book 1850–1851*, pp. 1–5.
136 *Bell's*, 12 Feb 1839. *Britannica*, vii, p. 321.
137 *Bell's*, 30 May 1847.
138 *Annals*, April 1828, 230.
139 *Bell's*, 16 May 1830.
140 *Bell's*, 18 April 1841. *SM*, Feb 1827, 241.
141 *Bell's*, 12 Jan 1834.
142 Bowen, *History of Cricket*, p. 101.
143 *Bell's*, 4 Oct 1829, 3 Nov 1833, 12 Jan 1840.
144 Brailsford, *Bareknuckles*, p. 132.
145 *Bell's*, 13 Nov 1825. Brailsford, *Bareknuckles*, p. 73.
146 *Bell's*, 15 Feb 1829. Brailsford, *Bareknuckles*, p. 119.
147 *Bell's*, 1 March 1829.
148 Vamplew, *Turf*, pp. 88–9.
149 *Bell's*, 14 Sept 1834. *BWM*, 16 Oct 1819.
150 *Annals*, Feb 1824, 145; March 1824, 187; April 1824, 301; May 1824, 355. *Bell's*, 9 Nov 1828.
151 *Bell's*, 15 July 1849.
152 Ford, *Cricket*, p. 22.
153 *Bell's*, 5 May 1839.
154 *Bell's*, 2 Nov 1828.
155 *Bell's*, 19 Oct 1845.
156 *Bell's*, 16 July 1848.
157 *Annals*, Sept 1822, 172; Sept 1823, 204. *BWM*, 31 March 1816, 13 Oct 1816. *SM*, May 1820, 80.
158 Ford, *Cricket*, p. 105.
159 Eastwood, *Governing Rural England*, p. 13.
160 *Bell's*, 18 Jan 1824.
161 *Bell's*, 6 Jan 1839.
162 *Bell's*, 1 Feb 1846.

163 *Annals*, Jan 1825, 38.
164 See Emsley, *Crime and Society*, pp. 29–31. The dramatic increase in the amount of crime was noted in the Court of Common Council; *Bell's*, 7 Feb 1836.
165 *Bell's*, 1 April 1849.
166 *Bell's*, 17 Jan 1841, 17 July 1842.
167 *WD*, 28 May 1820.
168 *WMC*, 11 Oct 1828.
169 *Bell's*, 24 Dec 1848.
170 *Bell's*, 5 Dec 1847.
171 *Bell's*, 18 June 1848.
172 *Bell's*, 13 July 1845.
173 Buckley, *Pre-Victorian Cricket*, p. 156.
174 *Bell's*, 11 Nov 1849.
175 Miles, *Pugilistica*, ii, pp. 17, 125.
176 *Annals*, Nov 1824, 306–307. *Bell's*, 24 Dec 1843.
177 *Bell's*, 11 June 1843.
178 *Bell's*, 17 Jan 1847.
179 *Bell's*, 4 Aug 1844.
180 *SM*, June 1828, 252.
181 Brailsford, *Sport, Time*, p. 64.
182 *Bell's*, 21 Aug 1831.
183 *Bell's*, 18 Dec 1842.
184 *SM*, Jan 1820, 251–2.
185 *BWM*, 9 Sept 1821.
186 *WD*, 30 March 1817.
187 *SM*, June 1831, 1324.
188 *Bell's*, 4 July 1841.
189 *Bell's*, 14 Jan 1849.
190 *Bell's*, 15 Dec 1844.
191 *Bell's*, 28 Sept 1845.
192 *Bell's*, 3 Aug 1828.
193 *Bell's*, 21 March 1847.
194 *Bell's*, 25 Jan 1829.
195 K. Chesney (1970) *The Victorian Underworld*, London: Temple Smith, pp. 268–76.
196 *Bell's*, 26 April 1846, 26 May 1850.
197 *Bell's*, 5 Sept 1830, 24 Dec 1848.
198 *M&S*, 6 July 1844.
199 *Bell's*, 2 Jan 1842. P.M. Young (1968) *History of British Football*, London: Stanley Paul, p. 67 states that 'In 1845 Eton instituted the office of referee'. In fact, the above example proves that they were being used in football games outside of the public schools before this.
200 Buckley, *Pre-Victorian Cricket*, p. 211.
201 *Bell's*, 11 July 1841.
202 *Bell's*, 11 March 1832.
203 *Bell's*, 26 Nov 1843.
204 C. Wright (1977) 'Before Tom Brown: education and the sporting ethos in the early nineteenth century', *Journal of Educational Administration and History*, 9:1, 9.
205 *Annals*, Sept 1824, 188.
206 *Bell's*, 19 May 1833, 11 Nov 1849.

207 *Bell's*, 16 April 1848.
208 *Bell's*, 14 Sept 1834. *SM*, July 1845, 13–14.
209 Vamplew, *Turf*, p. 91.
210 *Bell's*, 3 July 1842, 14 Jan 1849.
211 *Bell's*, 16 May 1830.
212 *Bell's*, 20 Dec 1829.
213 *Bell's*, 15 Sept 1833.
214 *Bell's*, 14 Feb 1836.
215 *Bell's*, 25 Aug 1839.
216 *Bell's*, 8 July 1838.
217 *Annals*, March 1826, 178. *Bell's*, 15 May 1831, 8 July 1832, 19 Aug 1832, 19 May 1833, 21 July 1839, 17 Dec 1843. W. Hazlitt (1824) 'The Fight', *The New Monthly Magazine*, 4, 104.
218 *Bell's*, 1 July 1849.
219 Harrison, *Drink*, pp. 39, 41.
220 *Bell's*, 27 Dec 1829, 2 April 1837, 3 June 1849. *SM*, Feb 1838, 303.
221 *Bell's*, 26 May 1844.
222 *Annals*, Sept 1822, 216. *BWM*, 26 Oct 1817.
223 Blaine, *Encyclopaedia*, pp. v, 130.
224 *Bell's*, 13 Feb 1848.
225 V. Dowling (1868) *Fistiana 1700–1852*, London (*Bell's Life*), pp. 120–51.
226 *NSM*, Jan 1840, 93–102. *Sporting Review*, July/Dec 1840, 299.
227 *SM*, Dec 1819, 129–30.
228 *Bell's*, 15 June 1845.
229 *Bell's*, 24 May 1846. *SM*, March 1846, 175.
230 *SM*, Sept 1835, 363–5.
231 *Annals*, Dec 1822, 386–7. *SM*, June 1827, 180.
232 *Bell's*, 2 March 1834, 31 Aug 1834. *JJC*, Sports, Box 9.
233 *Annals*, April 1825, 203. *Bell's*, 6 Aug 1848.
234 *Bell's*, 10 Jan 1836. *WMC*, 13 Oct 1827, 20 Oct 1827, 10 Nov 1827.
235 *BWM*, 25 March 1821.
236 *Bell's*, 19 Jan 1823, 16 Sept 1827.
237 *Bell's*, 21 July 1850.
238 *SM*, Jan 1837, 213.
239 *Bell's*, 3 March 1850.
240 *SM*, Jan 1817, 154; Feb 1817, 226–8, 269–71; Feb 1828, 242–3; Sept 1834, 375.
241 Craven (1839) *Walker's Manly Exercises*, London: Orr and Co. D. Walker (1840) *Defence Exercises*, London: Orr and Co.
242 *Bell's*, 13 Aug 1843.
243 W.L. Collins (1866) 'Our amusements', *Blackwoods*, c. 706. H. Ellington (1887) 'Athletes of past and present', *Nineteenth Century and After*, 21, 517–29.
244 *Bell's*, 13 Jan 1850.
245 Bovill, *English Country Life*, p. 207. Hutchinson, *Heythrop*, pp. 29, 30, 44.
246 *Annals*, Dec 1823, 390.
247 *Bell's*, 23 Dec 1827. *SM*, May 1832, 14.
248 *Bell's*, 28 Oct 1849. *SM*, Nov 1820, 63–4; June 1840, 239.
249 *Bell's*, 5 June 1831.
250 *Annals*, Feb 1828, 114.
251 *Bell's*, 29 April 1838.

252 *Bell's*, 22 Oct 1848. N. Wigglesworth (1992) *The Social History of English Rowing*, London: Frank Cass, p. 85.

253 *SM*, Aug 1833, 290.

254 *Bell's*, 1 July 1832.

255 *Bell's*, 30 July 1837.

256 *The New Statistical Account of Scotland* (1845), viii, p. 124.

257 *Bell's*, 23 Dec 1849. *SM*, July 1837, 240–41.

258 *Bell's*, 8 July 1849. G. Buckley (1954) *Historical Gleanings*, Manuscript, p 2. Contra Sandiford, 'Victorian cricket technique', 272, 283.

259 *New Statistical Account*, ix, 472.

260 *Bell's*, 16 Jan 1848.

261 *Annals*, Aug 1827, 96.

262 An insight into the growth of fraud can be gleaned from the Manchester area. Throughout the whole of Lancashire there was only one attempt at fraud in sports other than horse racing between 1793 and 1815. The first fraud in the Manchester area in a sport other than horse racing occurred in 1824. Between 1793 and 1823 there was just one fraud in the Lancashire/Manchester area in 227 events (0.44%). Between 1824 and 1850 there were 115 frauds in 3,063 events (3.75%) – a ninefold increase. Observers knew that this was a substantial underestimate: *Bell's*, 7 March 1841, 15 January 1843, 23 April 1843, 14 May 1843, 20 August 1843, 5 October 1845, 14 December 1845, 22 March 1846, 2 December 1849. By the end of the 1830s it was clear that corruption in horse racing in the Manchester region had become very sophisticated: *Bell's*, 7 October 1838, 18 November 1838.

263 See this volume, pp. 130–36.

264 *Bell's*, 7 Feb 1830.

265 *Bell's*, 7 June 1846, 22 Sept 1850.

266 *Bell's*, 3 Nov 1850, 29 Dec 1850.

267 *Bell's*, 25 Nov 1849, 3 Feb 1850, 2 June 1850.

268 B. Trescatheric (1983) *Sport and Leisure in Victorian Barrow*, Barrow: Hougenai, p. 5.

269 H. Abell (1898) 'Is cricket degenerating?', *National Review*, 31. A. Lyttleton (1899) 'Cricket reform', *National Review*, 34.

270 C. Alcock (1873) *The Football Annual*, London.

Chapter 7

Big Crowds, Big Money:
Mass Entertainment Comes to Britain

At the outset [leisure] was perceived to pose a real threat. It was an economic problem, for its quantity and irregularity for the mass of the people were counterposed to the work ideals of the industrialists ... and it was a political, social and moral problem for its practice, and the ideology bound up with that practice, could be threatening, disorderly and immoral. Its legitimacy for the people was denied: only 'the leisured' had leisure. By the end of our period, however, its legitimacy for all could be accepted.[1]

Cunningham's description of the widespread unease aroused by leisure between 1780 and 1880, hardly accords with the evidence that was set forth in Chapters 4 and 5, which demonstrated that the impact of official society, as embodied by Parliament and the local administration, on sporting activity, was far less negative than many scholars assume. This chapter illustrates the extent to which a leisure culture, based upon organized sporting activity, expanded between 1793 and 1850. This occurred despite the significant problems that were apparent in its supervision, particularly the corruption that manifested itself in particular areas and activities.

As we established in Chapter 2, the volume of both activity and expenditure in organized sport expanded, generally, between 1793 and 1850. This chapter details the growth both in competitive sport and the facilities designed to accommodate the crowds that it attracted. It also examines the social composition of both promoters and spectators. Cumulatively, it reveals a thriving world of activity, seemingly poised to blossom into a national industry.

As before, the chapter consists of two halves, based upon chronology, 1793 to 1815 and 1816 to 1850.

1793–1815

This first half is divided into three parts, beginning with a consideration of the competitive sporting culture, then moving on to a profile of the crowd, before finally considering the spectating opportunities available to the population.

Competitive Sport

From 1793 to 1815 British sport experienced a substantial growth in terms of both the volume of events and the amount of money spent on them. The sums expended in the latter period of the war exceeded prewar totals, as can be inferred from the only comparative data that we possess, the comprehensive record of the stakes of the most financially developed sport, horse-racing meetings, that are available in *The Racing Calendar*. The highest prewar figure, for 1790 was 96,865 guineas (1821/5), and was surpassed in real terms by every year after 1804.[2]

Between 1793 and 1815 we can trace a total of 3,100,202 guineas (1821/5) staked on 6,736 sporting events. A precise figure is given for the stakes in 4,677 cases, and words such as 'big' appear for a further 117 events. No stakes are listed for 1,942 events. As we saw earlier in the study the overall expenditure on sporting stakes increased by almost 900,000 g. in the later part, as compared to the earlier part of the French wars. This is surprising because during the latter period the amount of disposable income extracted by the government in the form of taxation increased steadily. Thus, the percentage of available wealth utilized for organized sport experienced a growth at a time when one would have expected the contrary to have been the case, due to the increase in taxation. In 1812 the amount staked on organized sport peaked, at 237,235 g. (1821/5), and even when it collapsed in 1815, the total, 178,906 g. (1821/5), was still bigger than any figure previous to 1809. On average, 134,791 g. (1821/5), were annually devoted to the stakes of sporting events. The reasons for this growth can be easily discerned. Essentially they stemmed from the fact that in the latter half of the eighteenth century the British economy enjoyed a pronounced expansion, generating enormous wealth. Additionally, the continental blockade initiated by France in 1806 limited British contact with Europe, probably encouraging many of the wealthy, who had previously undertaken 'The Grand Tour', to limit themselves to internal tourism within Britain, thus stimulating the growth of local facilities.[3] One of the major beneficiaries of this was probably home-based sport. The most obvious manifestation of this was the growth in the expenditure on stakes. However, as we shall shortly see, these were often surpassed by ancillary betting on all sports.[4]

The English were obsessed with gambling, enormous sums being betted on matters of chance, such as a wager between two wealthy men as to whose father would be the first to die.[5] The principal form of gambling was cards, which provided a crucial focus for genteel social life.[6] Card playing occurred at two major locations, private 'routs', in the dining rooms of female gamesters, and West End clubs.[7] The latter were centres of fraud, being effectively above the law.[8]

An examination of our sources reveals that sport was a very popular form of gambling, occurring even in the most genteel of sports, archery.[9] Horse-race meetings were the major recipient of speculation, with huge wins, £100,000 by Gully and £20,000 by Lord Derby, and losses, £18,000 by Mellish and £7,000 by Fletcher, being recorded.[10] The sums betted on horse racing increased dramatically, a commentator complaining in 1802 that 'a sweepstake of one or two hundred each, were some years considered stakes of great magnitude, but in the present year such betting is abandoned as too trifling'. He added that it was now common for one thousand guineas to be wagered.[11] Cumulatively, this could result in huge amounts of money being betted, such as £200,000 on the Flint–Thornton race.[12] Other sports were similar.[13] Occasionally individuals made bets of over a thousand pounds on pugilism and it was estimated that at least £50,000 was pending on the Cribb–Molineaux fight of 1811.[14] While such sums were not equalled elsewhere, many thousands of pounds were wagered on all sports, even on a race between two mail-coaches that occurred one Sunday.[15]

Assessing the relationship between the amount of money staked and that betted is impossible, for it is clear that there was often no relation between the two. On many occasions the stakes were far exceeded by the sums wagered. A prize-fight at Newton in 1802 was typical: the stakes were 50 guineas, the amount betted by the crowd, £2,000.[16] Evidence suggests that, cumulatively, the amounts wagered surpassed the agreed stakes, but there is no way of determining this. However, statements from a variety of journalists concerning a number of sports, including, most crucially, horse racing, establish that the amount of side bets were increasing throughout the latter period by comparison with the earlier. There is also one indicator which does support the idea that the amount betted on sporting events surpassed the agreed stakes, the fact that there were many examples of attempts to practise fraud at betting. It is to this that we must now turn.

Fraud occurred in a variety of ways. At the most elementary level, interested supporters would intervene at an event, endeavouring to trip up or injure competitors.[17] A second trick involved deception. Pedestrians were known to faint just before a race, or to lose an event when the stakes were low so as to lure opponents into increasing their betting.[18] The most common ruse was to conceal identity. Athletes and pugilists would pretend to be local country folk, jockeys would swap colours and one horse would be passed off as another.[19] Doping was also prevalent, especially in horse racing. In 1811:

> a true bill of indictment was found against Daniel Dawson charging him with poisoning the race-horses at Newmarket ... suspicion is first said to have attached to him from his backing against the injured horses and advising others with whom he stood in bets to do the same.[20]

However, such tricks were far less insidious than two other forms of corruption. The first was to bribe opponents to deliberately lose. This occurred in several sports, but especially at horse racing. The second was still more devious, depending as it did on a deliberate decision by a competitor or owner that he would lose, having betted extensively against himself via his confederates.[21] There are many examples of this in horse racing, a particularly blatant one occurring at Egham races where the favourite 'lost with far more difficulty than it took to win'.[22] One can certainly find examples in other sports during the period but not extensively so.

Corruption in betting was not invented in the Napoleonic era, though it is clear that during this period the connection between organized sporting activity and professional criminals became increasingly overt. Fraudulent horse racing had a long pedigree and one of the most infamous episodes occurred in 1791 when the Prince of Wales's horse, 'Escape', suffered a surprise defeat. Throughout the whole period the Jockey Club endeavoured to try and regulate the sport but its authority was limited and their legislation was usually a belated response to a very severe outbreak of criminal activity, such as the spate of poisonings in 1811.[23] Judging by the works of Bee, Deale and a parliamentary inquiry of 1844, *The Report From The Select Committee On Gaming*, the commercial expertise in fraud that had been perfected at horse racing long before the French wars, came to be increasingly applied to other sporting fields in the years after 1815.[24] In this sense, perhaps, sport during the French wars, with the very important exception of horse racing, was comparatively honest compared with the decades that followed.

Having shown that organized sport was a significant financial sector, involving as it did, immense side-betting, we must now consider its promoters.

The promotion of organized sport incorporated all classes and motives, ranging from enthusiast through to the hard-headed businessman. Interested parties often gravitated to London, especially certain West End clubs, Tattersall's Rooms and sporting pubs, such as that conducted by the ex-boxer, Richmond.[25] Sporting pubs were probably crucial because many top bookmakers, even extremely wealthy ones like O'Kelly, were not admitted to exclusive clubs, and such venues provided areas in which different ranks within the social hierarchy, possessing money and sporting expertise, could meet and organize matches.[26] This is supported by two betting lists for pugilism that have survived, which show that wagering was a very socially widespread activity, including aristocrats and greengrocers.[27] While we know comparatively little about bookmakers, it is clear that their emergence was crucial for the development of competitive sport. Their progress had been remarkably fast. Originally, they had occupied informal sites near the winning post at race-meetings, but soon migrated to special areas of the grandstand.[28] Judging by the gambling in London clubs, it seems likely that the very major bookmakers were involved there. As to the wider public, although some historians believe that betting lists only appeared in London's pubs, shops and warehouses after 1815, evidence suggests that long before then the middle and lower ranks were able to place bets in a myriad of pubs and sporting houses that permeated London.[29] The results of events were awaited eagerly at these places and such was the commercial value of this information, for it was common for bets to be taken after an event had been held, that immense efforts were made to be first with the news.[30] This, inevitably, led to attempts to interfere with communications, such as the shooting down of carrier pigeons.[31]

The backers and promoters of competitive sport spanned the whole social spectrum. Aristocrats provided large sums in a range of sports.[32] They were extremely jealous of their social position and while they were arranging articles for a prize-fight, determining the conditions, stakes and such like, forbade even the wealthiest tradesmen to enter the room.[33] Aristocratic patronage suffered seriously early in the period with the withdrawal of the Prince of Wales and Lord Barrymore, each of whom spent too lavishly on sport.[34] The connection of the aristocracy with sports, especially horse racing, invited severe criticism. Just below the aristocracy were a whole range of socially influential patrons. Two of these, Colonel Mellish MP and Colonel Thornton, were good athletes and knew a great deal about sport.[35] However, such knowledge did not prevent them both going through large fortunes and finishing up in comparative poverty. By contrast, professional bookmakers, notably Ogden, Captain O'Kelly and Mr Tattersall, started with very little and used sport to amass considerable wealth.[36] A number of other patrons, such as Major Durand, Mr Fletcher and Mr Fletcher Read, were largely distinguished for the ease with which they were parted from their immense inheritance. Still, no matter how many rich men were brought to the edge of bankruptcy by sport, there appears to have been no shortage of wealthy sponsors, stakes of hundreds and even thousands of pounds being easily raised.

Sometimes stakes were subscribed by consortiums, especially in pedestrianism. There, we find groups of friends, such as those belonging to the Foley hunt, or Oxford undergraduates, banding together to raise £2,000 to stake on an athlete.[37] Certain wealthy individuals, such as a potato merchant, also acted as backers.[38] Patriotism was the driving motive for various MPs to sponsor sailing and shooting competitions and William Cobbett, singlestick.[39]

Captain Barclay's objective was more commercially orientated, providing heavy financial backing for athletes that he regarded as having good prospects.[40] Similar motives appear to have influenced wealthy military gentlemen, though these were sometimes related to regimental loyalty.[41] Generally, events with smaller prize money were financed by publicans and other entrepreneurs, such as a silver cup provided for a cricket match by the proprietor of a theatre.[42] The general public was often approached for funding and many events, especially prize-fights, depended on such provision.[43] This form of subscription became very common in rowing as the period wore on and was utilized in various London districts to provide prizes for their local watermen to race for. On occasions, employers would back promising workers.[44] Sometimes an individual might act as his own backer, especially if he were wealthy, such as Barclay or Cribb, or most notable of all, Colonel Mellish, who staked £20,000 of his own money on himself.[45] One boxer, Medley, even supplied the whole of his 200 guinea stakes.[46] Additionally, there is considerable evidence of members of the lower orders acting as their own backers, in sports such as rat-fighting and bowling.[47]

As the finance that was focused upon sport increased, a large number of competitors possessing substantial expertise began to appear, and their activities received considerable attention in the press. This medium created and fostered an attractive image for sport, generating a new level of excitement. During the war three sporting events occurred which excited intense interest. To a certain extent, all three were novelties and owed their impact to the fervour that the press had helped to generate. The first, the horse race between Mrs Thornton and Mr Flint (1804), was portrayed as a battle of the sexes. The second, Captain Barclay's match (1809), man against the physical limits of endurance, and finally the Cribb–Molineaux fight (1811), a major racial war. Such events excited the nation and helped to transform sport's status. While a sporting infrastructure had existed before the war, the growth in the number of competitions, particularly the more spectacular, seized mass attention and transformed the spectating potential of sport.

The second part of the study focuses upon two issues; the development of a sector based upon the provision of facilities designed to cater for the crowds that were attracted by competitive sport, and a social profile of the spectators.

Spectators

By 1793 the commercial organization of sport had become well established and in the years that followed, especially after the imposition of the continental blockade, commentators took great pride in the extent of commercially organized sport, regarding it as demonstrating the economy's resilience. *The Manchester Mercury* reported that Gully 'is now at Norwich; and on Saturday evening last, he entertained the enlightened of that neighbourhood with a sparring-match, at which near 200 amateurs were present; the admission being only 5s each!!! – How are we ruined?'[48]

Entrepreneurial skills marketed sport in five discernible ways. The simplest type of event offered prizes in order to attract competitors, restricting entry to those who bought a meal – a common ploy by publicans who staged competitions in cricket, cock-fighting and pigeon-shooting.[49] The next sort of event aimed at drawing spectators to an area and selling them refreshments. Publicans were usually prominent among the sponsors, promoting many regattas and pedestrian matches.[50] The scale of their activity could vary considerably. At one extreme was the Epping Stag hunt, one of the major events in the London area; at the other were the rat-races held in small pubs.[51] Certain events, notably the Cotswold Games and the coursing meeting at Louth, were very lucrative for the local traders but largely promoted by groups that had little, or no, commercial interest.[52] A third, and rather rare commercial event, offered a very expensive prize and made a profit by charging competitors an entrance fee.[53] The fourth type of event was perhaps the commonest, making its money by charging spectators admission. Many 'cruel sports' derived their income this way. In Birmingham a bull-bait cost just a penny to watch, while at a London venue a variety of animals were baited five nights a week, for sixpence admission.[54] Some prize-fights and sparring displays could cost as little as three pence and sixpence.[55] Many sports, such as fencing, coursing and billiards, appear to have catered for a reasonably prosperous audience, charging half a crown entry.[56] It cost three shillings and sixpence to watch the rowing at Vauxhall, but the ticket also granted access to the gardens and the many entertainments that were held there.[57] Profits made on events were substantial in relation to the cost of living; a cock-fight made £12 at a time when a supply of basic foodstuffs such as a quartern loaf, a sack of potatoes and a pound of butter and beef could be had for a total of two shillings and nine pence.[58] Displays by prize-fighters were even more lucrative, yielding anything between £40 and £100. A fifth type of event endeavoured to use sport to draw crowds to additional entertainments. This was especially the case with both Vauxhall and Ranelagh gardens, as well as many holiday resorts.[59] Often, however, it is clear that it was a combination of attractions, both sporting and other entertainments, which drew crowds. A notable example of this were the various fairs that seemed to revitalize during the war.[60] Above everything, horse-race meetings were the magnets that drew the surrounding population. These events were strongly linked to local holidays and were times when both strangers and local country people would descend upon a town.[61] They created an intense social programme, including both race balls and the theatre. Many groups, including the town council, assisted in their promotion, though innkeepers, who often performed additional supervisory functions as well, were the most prominent.[62] An indication of the boost given to trade can be gleaned from the fact that in a single night in 1805 Preston's theatre took £150, at a time when the nation's principal theatre, Drury Lane, had never attained daily receipts of over £100.[63] Often, race week coincided with the meeting of the local Assizes, thus permitting the available entertainment to be further enlivened by the occasional hanging.

Horse racing was the best commercially developed sport. A number of courses, such as Pontefract, Chichester and Manchester, built grandstands and these were obviously perceived as worthwhile investments.[64] An indication of how attractive they were can be gleaned from the fact that the Bibury club, who ran the most exclusive meeting in Britain, built one, and were reaping profits of £150 by 1799.[65] Investors also did well – in 1810 those at the Fulwood course were reaping 10 per cent dividends at a time when government bonds were only paying 4.5 per cent.[66] Most race meetings were the centre for all types of attractions, with surrounding booths offering everything from gambling, alcohol, prize-fighters and circus attractions.[67] Such provision was a big business and at Ascot in 1793 the rents from the booths earned the course owners almost one thousand guineas. It cost an average of four guineas to hire a booth, a sum which a journalist assessed as providing 'ample proof what an incredible multitude must be assembled daily on such spots to reimburse the adventurers for their expenditure'.[68]

While other major sports were rarely as organized, they also gleaned good profits. It is clear that they went out of their way to offer an attractive programme, usually including several different sports. For instance, prize-fights would often be accompanied by backsword, bull-baiting, bear-baiting and dog-fighting.[69] At holiday times a mixture of sports would be conducted. Throughout the period there were also novelty events such as hawking, a fight between a dog and a monkey, a fight between a dog and a man, and a race between a steam engine and a horse.[70] Their aim was to attract both betting and crowds.

Mark Harrison defined a crowd as 'a large group of people in sufficient proximity to influence each other's behaviour'. Although sport received little attention in his work, which was concerned, primarily, with politics, he established that during the early nineteenth century many recreational events attracted large crowds.[71] Such findings are considerably amplified by a detailed study of the sporting culture of the period. Although we rarely have reliable information on crowd size for the 6,736 events that occurred throughout the period, it is evident from the sources that almost every sport attracted substantial numbers of spectators. Generally, such gatherings were described by phrases not numbers. In the following analysis the statements concerning horse-race meetings (that is a total of 2,111 events) have been entirely ignored because it is rarely clear whether they referred to a particular day or the whole schedule (which often lasted for three or more days). Thus, the total number of events that we are dealing with is 4,625.

During the period, 143 events were described by words that indicated the presence of significant numbers. The most minor terms of description used was that of 'crowded' or 'numerous', and these occurred on four occasions. At the other end of the range were the phrases 'biggest ever', used three times, and 'immense', also used three times. The most popular phrase was 'big' (97 times), and then 'huge' (29 times). Additionally, on 81 other occasions, terms relating to figures were given. The smallest size recorded is 150, mentioned just once, and the largest, 20,000, a claim made on three occasions. The most common description was the term 'thousands', used 17 times, followed by the number 10,000, used on 11 occasions. The attention received by the various sports was by no means uniform. The size of the crowd watching pugilism was noted 69 times, while many other sports were rarely ever mentioned. Cumulatively, if one discounts horse-race meetings, mention was made in our sources of the crowd size in 224 out of 4,625 events, which is over 4 per cent.[72] Given the very imprecise nature of our data it is impossible to realistically estimate the total volume of crowd size throughout the period, but if we restrict our attention to those figures and phrases which clearly indicate that we are dealing in terms of thousands of people (including phrases such as 'big' but excluding 'large') we have 167 sporting events that were not horse-race meetings. Each year there was an average of 201 events that were not horse-race meetings. As the above evidence indicates, in an average year slightly over eight of these would draw a crowd that were numbered in thousands. While this figure, amounting to under 5 per cent, may seem small, it must be remembered that it is very incomplete and excludes horse-race meetings, which were far and away the most popular sport of the period.[73] A better idea of the popularity of sport can probably be gleaned from pugilism, the activity for which our sources provide the most copious information. Out of the 485 prize-fights that were recorded, 57 events had crowds of over a thousand people, about 11 per cent. The effect of such a sport on an area could be dramatic, drawing many of the surrounding population away from their work.[74] It could also attract mass influxes of visitors. On one occasion this was so great that the local population, who were ignorant of the impending prize-fight, believed that the French had just landed and stimulated a flood of refugees.[75] While we can only gain a very small insight into the size of the crowds drawn to sporting events, even this very attenuated picture suggests that it was capable of generating large gatherings every year.

Our sources shed considerable light on the social composition of the spectators. In only two sports, archery and tennis, do they appear to have been predominantly from the upper and middle ranks. Similar exclusive distinctions were occasionally apparent at horse-race meetings, such as at Epsom, where the first day of the meeting was set aside for the social elite.[76] Generally, events were socially mixed, as at the Windsor Bachelors' annual bull-bait which drew 'a great concourse of various descriptions of persons'.[77] Entrance to horse-race meetings had always been free, but after 1740 there was an increased attendance of major meetings by the lower orders, which led to a desire by the socially elite to segregate themselves, prompting courses to create grandstands.[78] On occasions, as at the Artillery Cricket Ground in 1744, and a major billiard match in 1804, increased entrance charges were deliberately introduced in order to restrict the size of the crowd.[79] This appears to have been rare, but the general trend throughout the period was for the increasing commercial exploitation of sport, which inevitably limited the contact between groups of different economic means, though this did not prevent the attendance of pit men from Newcastle at the city's expensive cockpit.[80] However, finance was not the sole criterion for social differentiation at sport. England during the Napoleonic wars was a society of ranks, in which everyone had a particular place. This became especially apparent at certain sporting events, particularly horse-race meetings, which tended to attract representatives from every strata.[81]

Spectators for most sports incorporated all classes, though there appears to have been little social mixing. A sailing match on the Thames in 1800 typifies the situation. There was a huge, predominantly lower-class crowd watching from the banks while the social elite, including the Turkish ambassador, followed the race from a barge.[82] However, in certain sports the social ranks came into closer contact. Although prize-fighting was a legally dubious activity, on ten occasions it attracted significant attendance by aristocrats. This peaked at the Sam–Belcher fight of 1807 where 'it would be no exaggeration to say, that to mention the names of the gentry present, would be to enumerate about one-fifth of the court calendar'.[83] Reports of both prize-fights and bull-baits often portray close, in certain cases even intimate, contact between the social ranks, as if class distinctions were submerged by the excitement of sport.[84] Unquestionably, some members of the wealthy elite displayed a catholic appetite for entertainment, the obituary of one noting that:

Almost from his infancy he was an attendant upon all the fairs, boxing matches, races and diversions of every kind round London, from the ring made by first rate amateurs of the fancy down to the weekly badger baiting in Black Boy-alley. He was no less a constant attendant upon the execution of criminals before Newgate, &c. and was generally so well acquainted with their history, that he might well have been applied to as a kind of Old Bailey Chronicle.[85]

By contrast, the social structure at horse-race meetings effectively precluded such interactions. The royalty at Ascot 'mingled affably', but with the top end of society, not the lower orders.[86] Judging by the 1720s there were pronounced differences in the behaviour of members of the upper class at sporting events. Cock-fighting was a very raucous sport, but the pit at Whitehall was far more sedate than its rival because it catered for a 'more select', though equally privileged, audience.[87]

The vast majority of spectators at an event were local members of the lower orders, although both their ability and desire to attend varied regionally, depending upon their work patterns. It is clear, however, that it was common for spectators to walk some six miles to watch a cricket match, and this was even used by the government as an indicator of the distance that it was regarded as acceptable for members of the militia to travel.[88] The presence of lower-class spectators, in fairly large numbers, substantiates Vamplew's claim that they had sufficient leisure time, though the lack of detailed information concerning their expenditure makes it far more difficult to assess his contention that they lacked spending power.[89] The most prominent factor affecting attendance of events was communications, which could prevent even the keenest supporters travelling. This occurred in both 1805 and 1807, where the distance from London prevented the attendance at a prize-fight of large numbers of spectators.[90] Londoners, it appears, were renowned for their attendance of prize-fights, a fact which suggests that they had considerable access to available leisure. This is consistent with a discovery in an earlier chapter which demonstrated the comparative independence of the region's sporting culture from annual, holiday events. In many senses these Londoners, who travelled long distances to watch prize-fights, were the very first hard core sports fans. They were the product of an age in which organized competitive sport had grown into a significant commercial force.

As we have seen, the best available evidence demonstrates that there was a great expansion in both the amount of competitive sporting activity and the finance expended upon it. In turn, the interest which this attracted stimulated a vigorous commercial sector, satisfying the public's desire for spectacle. Unquestionably, leisure – especially sport – was beginning to attain the status of a commercial industry, with an increasingly socially diverse group of promoters. It is now time to consider the impact that such developments had upon the leisure opportunities of the general population, the subject of the third part of our study.

Opportunities for Leisure

Theoretically, we can divide up sporting events into two broad categories according to their promoters' aims – traditional and commercial. 'Traditional' signifies those promotions in which the sole aim was to please the spectator, without an anticipated financial benefit. By contrast, the principal aim of 'commercial' promotions was the attainment of profit. It has been contended that up to 1750 the gentry, through a mixture of self-interest and paternalism, supported plebeian culture. However, the relationship between the ranks that had existed in pre-industrial society was eroded by the growth of the commercial economy. This led the gentry to cease sponsoring and supporting popular culture, withdrawing their patronage of 'traditional' events, with the result that there was a serious decline in the number of activities that were staged without the aim of profit.[91] From this, it is argued that the sporting opportunities available to the lower orders suffered a drastic decline. There are fundamental problems with this contention. First, lack of reliable data for the period before 1750 renders any comparisons between that and a later period doubtful, especially as a great many of the events that were classified as the embodiment of entertainment created by the disinterested patronage of the gentry, were of very recent creation, as the example of 'rustic sports' demonstrates. Rustic sports incorporated a number of athletic activities containing a strong element of humour, such as climbing up a greasy pole. They were alleged to have occurred on particular holidays for hundreds of years, due to the patronage of the local gentry, who shared in the fun. However, few of such events had a long history, and the sports themselves were no older than the eighteenth century.[92] In the period after 1750 they were promoted by both the gentry and entrepreneurs, principally, it appears for financial motives. The gentry were more likely to exhibit an interest in the social benefits of activities, perceiving the provision of rustic sports for their tenantry as a way of cultivating both the physical and moral virtues of 'old England', and thus giving an added legitimacy, and antiquity to their rule. Some commentators regarded such events in explicitly political terms, urging that 'we wish the youth of nobility to grow up proud of the love of their tenantry' and regarded such provisions as helping to expose 'the captivating fallacy of revolutionary doctrines'.[93] Predominantly, however, even during the Napoleonic wars, there is little indication of disinterested altruism. Despite the deprivation suffered by much of the population, very little of the money expended on sport was devoted to charity, though most sports occasionally contributed donations, to widows, children and prisoners of war.[94] Similarly, certain competitive events – such as ploughing matches, sheep-shearing, stock-breeding and horticulture – were promoted for practical, patriotic, reasons.[95] They were rarely profitable for their promoters and with the conflict's end were curtailed.[96] Other sports, such as races for cart horses and fishing boats, were both practical and, one suspects, profitable: they continued to be promoted in the postwar period.[97]

This is the basic point, and the second serious flaw in the argument contending that the leisure opportunities for the general population were declining. The growth in financially expensive competitive sport did much to expand the scope of sporting events and the sponsorship of these often included both the gentry and entrepreneurs. The infusion of greater finance meant that events expanded in size and sophistication, with new entertainments being created and older ones enjoying development. The scope of such promotions varied and they can be gradated according to the amount, variety and complexity of the sports which they contained, and most importantly of all the costs involved in financing them. The gentry's main contribution to some events, such as the annual battles between villages in Yorkshire was to simply refrain from interfering. [98] Often, however, the fostering of amusements required a more creative input and a number of championships occurred, in football, singlestick and wrestling, organized by gentry sponsorship.[99] The most expensive types of activities promoted by the gentry were such events as horse races and regattas, which an aristocrat might sponsor during local holidays.[100] Clearly, some of the more organized 'traditional' events, such as horse-race meetings, regattas and such like, presented substantial financial opportunities, possessing the potential to become 'commercial' sports in their own right. The distinction between 'traditional' and 'commercial' events was principally related to size: small events sponsored by the gentry tended to be acts of patronage, while the larger ones often had a commercial dimension. This is sometimes apparent in the prize lists. In smaller events rewards were principally food and clothes; while the larger events would offer large money prizes, such as 50 guineas.[101]

Throughout the period an increasing fusion appears to take place between 'traditional' and 'commercial' sport, typified by the growing sophistication found in festival events. Traditional entertainment, sponsored by acts of gentry patronage, persisted, but in many events their scope expanded, embracing elements of the entrepreneurial sector, effectively becoming commercial ventures. In essence, a third type of event was added to 'traditional' and 'commercial', one which blended the two, involving acts of patronage but also offering the sponsor the possibility of financial gain. While these three categories had been present before 1793, the growth in competitive sport inevitably led to the expansion of both the more commercially orientated branches. In view of this, even if there were any decline in the amount of 'traditional' sport, a contention lacking evidence, the increase in the volume of 'commercial' sport, much of which – as was shown in an earlier section – was accessible to the working-class spectator, would have been fully compensated for.

We can see that during the French wars there was a significant increase in the expenditure on competitive sport, sponsored by a wide range of patrons. Large, socially mixed, crowds were drawn to many of these events, and at certain venues facilities were organized to exploit this. As yet, however, this process was patchy, many events occurring in which there was little commercial organization.

1816–50

In this second part of the chapter we first examine the finance involved in competitive sport, then we consider the facilities that were developed to exploit the interest created by organized sporting events; and finally we examine sporting activity that was not promoted principally for commercial reasons.

Competitive Sport

Stakes and betting　As we saw earlier, the evidence shows that the volume of sporting events and the total amount expended on stakes, though subject to pronounced fluctuations, experienced a large increase between 1816 and 1850.[102] Also, to a limited extent, British competitors journeyed abroad, notably to win big prizes in an American foot race in 1844.[103] An idea of the money staked on individual events can be gleaned from Table 7.1. In most instances, it was not uncommon for sums similar to the largest recorded stakes in each particular sport to be deployed. The most notable exceptions to this were hopping, which was very much a one-off, sheep-shearing and tennis.

The increasing sums involved in sport, and the machinery necessary to organize them, were assembled in a range of locations where matches would be made and stakes held, including public venues such as race-booths and sporting houses, as well as exclusive clubs like Searle's and Crockford's.[104] Such places were also the focus of betting. The techniques of bookmaking had become increasingly sophisticated, and by the 1840s, speculations such as 'sweepstakes', which had much in common with lotteries, were very popular with the working class.[105] Betting was one of a range of services available at many pubs, which included entertainment and tuition in various sports. It was also possible to gamble at most sports' grounds, or the pubs attached to them. One in Manchester was described as follows:

> [A]ll was busy activity: the proceedings on the interior reminded us of the transactions of a banking establishment, such as the dispatching of the circulating medium, the deposits being duly acknowledged by the officials appointed for the occasion.[106]

With the proprietor charging sixpence in every pound for administering betting transactions, this was a very lucrative operation.[107] Certain race-meetings, for instance Doncaster, owed much of their success to the excellence of their betting facilities. Not all venues were so well regulated – the IOUs in one London pub were simply 'pencilled in' and were as valueless as 'blotting paper'.[108] The focus for betting was London's Tattersall's Rooms, a venue where social distinctions melted in the pursuit for profit.[109] The rooms' proprietor supervised betting, by posting defaulters' names on blackboards and pronouncing decisions on disputed events, such as cancelling all bets in the Ward–Abbot fight when it was discovered to be a fix.[110] The presence of large sums of money meant that pickpockets were an eternal menace there.[111]

Table 7.1   Largest stakes on single sporting events, 1816–50

Sport	Amount	Year
Archery	100 g.	1834
Badger-baiting	£50	1825
Billiards	£1,000	1834
Bowling	£100	1830
Cock-fighting	£500	1833
Cricket	1,000 g.	1827
Dog-fighting	£100	1841
Foot racing	1,000 g.	1825
Golf	£500	1831
Hopping	£650	1827
Horse feat	600 g.	1819
Horse race	2,000 g.	1818
Nurr and spell	£100	1828
Pedestrianism	1,000 g.	1828
Pigeon-shooting	1,000 g.	1846
Pugilism	£500	1840
Quoits	£100	1844
Rackets	£100	1838
Ratting	£100	1841
Rowing	500 g.	1829
Sack-racing	£50	1828
Sailing	£500	1842
Sheep-shearing	100 g.	1822
Single-stick	100 g.	1830
Skating	100 g.	1821
Steeplechasing	1,000 g.	1829
Swimming	50 g.	1821
Tennis	100 g.	1816
Wrestling	£110	1826

While London was the most important centre for gambling, throughout the entire period there was an immense regional diversity in both the sports betted on and the odds offered.[112] 'Odds' often varied dramatically, the favourite in one region sometimes being the outsider elsewhere. To an extent the intelligence disseminated nationally by the sporting press diluted this, but this medium was itself vulnerable to misinformation, often stemming from interested parties.[113] Access to information was crucial, particularly the results of events, which, for much of the period were transmitted via horseback and pigeons.[114] Efforts were made to ensure the early supply of such data and on occasions this was used corruptly, bets being taken on events by those already in possession of the result.[115]

In the early postwar years, the amount betted on horse-racing declined, while that on pugilism increased.[116] The latter culminated with the 'million-pound fight' between Randall and Turner in 1818.[117] Horse racing rapidly recovered, and by 1828 the major races each attracted £600,000 in betting.[118] There was heavy betting on almost every sport, though much of this tended to be concentrated at the venues where the event was held, such as £35,000 on a cricket match between Manchester and All England, or the £2,500 regularly betted on individual foot races at Belle Vue.[119] Such concentrations of finance reflected an expanding sophistication in various provincial centres. For instance, from the late 1820s Manchester was able to mount large-scale events on a regular basis. Accompanying this growth in the complexity and size of betting facilities at provincial centres was an increasingly comprehensive communications network, embodied by the introduction of the telegraph to certain sports' grounds. Thus, while the provinces were becoming increasingly able to organize their own sporting culture, expansions in communications meant that finance was becoming more fluid between areas. The infrastructure catering for those that wished to bet was immense, and incorporated every class, hence the working class would sometimes pawn their clothes in order to back a favourite.[120] Betting was clearly a very significant part of the attraction which sport had for the working man. Often, crowds would stake everything on their local heroes. Thus, in 1838, when the Londoner, Mountjoy, beat the Yorkshireman, Drinkwater, a commentator chastised the winner's supporters: 'the Londoners again lost the opportunity of netting large sums, for want of perfect confidence in their man, for the Yorkshiremen shook their purses at them in the most provoking manner'. [121]

The increase in the amount of money involved in sport led to a dramatic expansion of corruption.[122] Whereas during the Napoleonic wars horse-race meetings had been the only activity in which this was a major problem, from the 1820s most sports were afflicted by criminal machinations.[123] Attempts to subvert sporting events fell into four categories. First, interested parties would buy the cooperation of a competitor. The most overt case of this occurred in 1832, when a consortium used a front man to buy the horse Ludlow in order to ensure that it did not win a race in which they had backed heavily against it.[124] Similarly, athletes were often bribed, the boxer Hickman being paid £1,800 to lose in 1822, and it was almost unknown for 'square' contests to occur in any sport in particular districts.[125] Second, the competitor would be subject to interference. Both athletes and animals were often the victims of doping, though it was also known for boxers to be arrested via the machinations of either their opponents or sometimes even their own backers.[126] Third, stakeholders were intimidated or attacked: 'some of the Durham roughs being so lawless as to enter the house of the stakeholder and after securing the door attacked him in the most brutal manner'.[127] Fourth, most drastically of all, the referee would be intimidated into awarding victory contrary to the rules. As the period wore on this became very common, removing even the veil of 'fair play' from sporting contests. Its occurrence in the Caunt–Bendigo fight of 1845 prompted Spring, the highly respected former champion boxer, to refuse to pay his bets on the loser, thus making defaulting morally legitimate in the eyes of many.[128]

Promoters   In the early postwar years there was an immense amount of betting involved in pugilism and this led to a great deal of corruption ('crossing'), alienating many patrons.[129] The response of Carter's Cumberland backers was typical:

> The Cumberland fancy have had a meeting and after reading the account of the battle between Spring and Carter in the London papers, and judging from other sources of information, were unanimously of the opinion that Carter made a cross of the battle. They are therefore one as to the resolution of the withdrawing all support from him in future.[130]

On a broader canvas *Bell's* noted that 'the Corinthians, we have repeatedly had occasion to observe, have ceased to grant either the light of their countenances or the aid of their purse towards the encouragement of the ring'.[131] Thus, by 1832 boxers were struggling to raise stakes of £20.[132] Likewise, in rowing, *Bell's* stated that '[we] allude to the scarcity of watermen's rowing matches ... the fact is the watermen, or at least a portion of them, owe their loss of the extensive patronage they received to their own conduct'.[133]

The withdrawal of upper- and middle-class organizers meant that the commercial element in many sports became more overt.[134] The increased onus on the attainment of profit magnified the opportunities for corruption. Whereas up to the 1820s the social elite, though arranging events to suit themselves, had at least displayed some concern for those they backed, occasionally halting a fight in order to save their representative from unnecessary punishment, the backers that replaced them showed no such scruples.[135] On a number of occasions losing boxers were abandoned injured on the battlefield.[136] More sinisterly still, backers whose fraudulent intentions were frustrated by their fighter's refusal to deliberately lose, sometimes informed the authorities of the intended pugilistic encounter and thus got the pugilist arrested for breach of the peace.[137] While aristocratic patrons had often insisted that there were no admission charges to watch pugilism, thus rejecting very large sums, the 'speculators' who predominated in the 1840s extracted every possible penny.[138] Also, they often refused to honour debts.[139] A judge described boxers as being 'merely the tools of publicans and others, who made use of them for a mercenary object'.[140] In a letter on 'the regeneration of the ring', the former champion boxer, Spring, wrote: 'the business of match-making has fallen into the hands of publicans and others, who back men not for the sake of sport itself, but for the sake of personal advantage of their own house, or the sums which they may risk on the issue of the battle'.[141]

By then, aristocrats had long since withdrawn from the sponsorship of boxing. In fact, from at least 1824 they were reluctant to even be seen at prize-fights.[142] They did, however, continue financing other sports, and a social profile of the sponsorship of sporting activity between 1816 and 1850 broadly resembles that of the previous era. Nonetheless, the balance had clearly shifted, with smaller, more socially insignificant groups, playing a far more important role.[143]

Local commercial factors appear to have determined many decisions, such as the transferring of finance from horse racing to cricket in the Brighton area in 1837.[144] Sponsorship often came from local firms, who valued the advertising and the opportunity to service the needs of spectators.[145]

Publicans were active everywhere. They would provide cups for foot races, rowing, swimming and such like, as well as organizing dog-fights, bull-baits and a myriad of other entertainments.[146] Inns formed the headquarters for many sporting bodies, notably cricket clubs, and in country towns such as Banbury, much of the provision of entertainment was dependent upon publicans, a fact typical of the country as a whole.[147] The owners of sports' grounds engaged in like promotions, providing cups for cricket and foot racing.[148] Sportsmen themselves were not slow to recognize the opportunities that the creation of spectacle offered, cricketers such as Clarke assembling teams of experts with which to tour the country.[149] Some made fortunes from their animals, a racing dog securing winnings of over £100.[150] Most profitable of all were horses. While it was expensive to keep and enter them, a successful mount, such as Cyprian, could secure £3,140 from three races.[151] Additionally, horses could be bred for sale.[152] Many sportsmen supplied their own stakes, though Neal's capacity to raise £300 for his fight in 1831 was unusual.[153] More common was the runner Ben Hart, scraping together everything he had, £27, in 1840.[154] Tradesmen often sponsored competitive sport as a commercial speculation, and businessmen like Beardsworth specialized in providing stakes.[155] Professional backers, such as the important Manchester men who travelled down to a major London foot race in 1849, had emerged by the end of the period.[156]

Not everything was so calculating. Often backers contributed small sums for essentially sentimental reasons, boxers deriving a great deal of their finance from groups belonging to the same ethnic or trade background as themselves.[157] Public schoolboys tended to adopt particular watermen, providing their stakes for races against those championing a rival institution.[158] Both pugilistic and rowing clubs in particular areas sponsored favoured competitors, usually from a mixture of sentiment and commercial acumen.[159] Such a combination had long manifested itself in the involvement of wealthy and aristocratic sponsors. These were typified by Mellish, the MP who devoted his fortune to sport, and Captain Barclay, an aristocrat who acted as both backer and trainer for the athletes in his charge.[160]

Many of the promoters and competitors were stimulated by a desire for glory, the quest to become, or promote, a champion, rather than money, as was made clear in a sailing event: 'in all these cases the stake is a matter of far less importance than the credit and character of the boat'.[161] From 1817 the sporting press often identified competitors as being the best in England at their particular sport. However, the establishment of systematic championships in most activities was slow in coming, though one was created for rowing in 1831.[162] This, despite the fact that ideas concerning the correct organization of one in coursing, for example, appeared as early as 1826.[163] Despite the lack of an organized national championship, local pride often stimulated the promotion of big events, notably the rowing races that occurred in Newcastle during the 1840s.[164] While the factors motivating such events were not overtly commercial, the interest they aroused transformed them into big financial concerns. Sometimes the involvement was less partisan, the annual promotion of both the Cotswold and Tyneside Games stemming from a love of spectacle.[165]

By 1831 millions of pounds were involved in horse racing and in 1842 'Ringwood' observed that it was simply a commercial business.[166] Much the same could be said for many other sports, for, as we have seen, the stakes that they involved were often considerable. This, coupled with the attention provided by the sporting press, ensured that competitors established national reputations and events such as the race in 1844 between Sherwood and Robinson, the two best 'hundred yard' runners, was eagerly awaited, attracting big crowds.[167] Certain novelty events – female pugilism, a fight between a dog and a monkey – drew many spectators.[168] Similarly, the occurrence of a sport rarely known in an area, such as a pedestrian match from 1816 in Oxfordshire, or a steeplechase at Oxford in 1842, attracted thousands.[169] The hosting of certain big events, for instance the Spring–Langan fight of 1824 at Chichester, transformed the interest in sport throughout that whole area.[170]

The expansion of competitive sport, and the attention devoted to it, magnified the commercial possibilities of the opportunities offered for the creation and promotion of an industry designed to service the spectator. This represents the next part of our study and consists of three components: a consideration of the various ways profit could be obtained, an assessment of the techniques involved in improving commercial exploitation, and a social profile of the crowd.

Commercial Sporting Facilities

Ways of generating profit   The profits from sporting activity essentially stemmed from three categories: gate money, refreshments and ancillary expenditure.

While, as we have seen, gate money had long been important during the French wars, as late as the 1820s, facilities for staging large events were sometimes poorly built.[171] The Spring–Langan prize-fight drew 30,000 people, paying 10 shillings each, and was conducted in a ramshackle structure.[172] By comparison with the French wars, there was a much greater attention focused upon gate money. Originally, sports such as pedestrianism and cricket were held in many of the commercial gardens, such as Ranelagh, Sydney, Cremorne, Hulme and Belle Vue.[173] However, from the 1830s an increasing number of grounds devoted to sport began to appear, such as Hyde Park in Sheffield, Jackson's, Hippodrome, Stadium and Cremorne, all in London, and Belle Vue and Hulme in Manchester; the last three developing from the gardens.[174] Both Hulme and Belle Vue were extraordinarily successful, the latter establishing itself as the top venue in the country by the 1840s.[175] While most of the grounds specialised in particular sports, the range of activities they each offered was substantial, collectively embracing everything.[176] They also provided additional services, such as the sale of sporting animals, training in various sports, and articles detailing rules for particular events.[177] Other specialist venues, such as race courses and cricket grounds, presented foot racing and pigeon-shooting.[178] Many publicans began to create specialized running tracks, the earnings from which soon came to dominate their business.[179] Much of the incentive for such a development stemmed from actions by the police against road-running.[180] Some indication of the scope of such developments can be gained from the capacity of the sports' ground that was attached to the Brecknock Arms pub in London – it could hold 7,000 spectators.[181]

Although on occasions established venues, such as Copenhagen House, paid for the right to stage major events, many of the facilities were the creations of speculative consortiums, such as 'The American Arena' in Manchester, or the various swimming baths that appeared throughout the country.[182] Additionally, companies would build facilities for race grounds, such as Epsom, and speculators rent the space from them, often using them for non-sporting events.[183] Race-tracks like Goodwood made vast sums from hiring amusement booths. Illegal and semi-legal sports could also do well. Dog-fighting venues drew thousands of spectators, nationally, throughout the period.[184] The popularity of ratting blossomed everywhere towards the end of the 1840s, 'pits' permeating many regions, their owners providing a range of services.[185] Their success was due to good management. By contrast, internal disputes meant that after 1831 pugilism lacked a central venue in London, thus depriving itself of the revenue and organization vital to the prosperity of an illegal sport. Prior to this, large profits had been obtained from sparring exhibitions.

While gate money had always been significant in certain sports, by 1842 it was central to every activity. Naturally, to a certain extent, it simply reflected public fads, by the end of the period dog-racing enjoyed national prominence, while in the 1820s it had been trotting.[186] Receipts could be substantial, as shown in Table 7.2. The supply of this revenue depended upon employing trustworthy staff, often policemen, who would prevent gate-crashing, a common problem in the 1820s that sometimes deprived entrepreneurs of their anticipated profit.[187] Additionally, criminal elements, such as costermongers, would often intrude, preventing the legitimate authorities from selling tickets and retailing their own instead.[188] The hiring of venues presented further expense. At first, sparring exhibitions did very well; it costing just eight guineas to hire London's Fives Court.[189] However, profits dwindled when a rival venue appeared and towards the end of the period most of the gate money for such displays went in overheads.[190]

Table 7.2   Receipts from sporting events

Sport	Sum	Year
Cricket	£200	1827
Foot racing	£102	1848
Horse racing	1,000 g.	1827
Pugilism	200 g.	1822
Wrestling	£99	1849

The finance involved in presenting sports events varied considerably. Clarke charged £100 for setting up a cricket match, some cock-fights cost as little as five pounds.[191] Competitors would often insist on a share of the gate money. This was often so lucrative in prize-fights that a boxer would sell his right to name the venue for sums of £50 or more.[192] Many proprietors, especially at foot racing, were 'miserly', though important athletes insisted on a three-way split.[193] A detailed account from 1848 reveals that the proprietor made two pounds six shillings clear profit from takings of £12.[194] The aim was to maximize gate money, foot races sometimes being cancelled if the assembled crowd was regarded as insufficient.[195] Conversely, admission charges would be doubled for major events in cricket and foot racing.[196]

Refreshments, typically alcohol and food, represented a significant portion of the revenue accrued by most sports' grounds. Even quite minor cricket grounds sold wine and one of the major problems afflicting the Hippodrome Race Track was its lack of an alcohol licence.[197] However, comparatively speaking, refreshments were of far more significance to sporting pubs.[198]

Generally, sport was presented as one of a number of attractions at pubs, such as the mixture of songs, comedy and boxing held at the Garrick Head.[199] Boxers were often publicans and therefore sold tickets to sparring exhibitions or hosted the displays at which the stakes for prize-fights were presented.[200] Additionally, they would offer particular events, notably pedestrian displays or 'bag foxes' to entice customers, or simply provide recreational facilities, such as rackets.[201] Prizes would sometimes be offered for particular events, for instance bowls and pigeon-shooting, the entrance money for which would include refreshments and meals.[202]

Ancillaries can be divided into four categories: transport, servicing, equipment and tourism. Transport was a significant part of the expense involved in sporting activity. For example, it was estimated that the crowd watching the Randall–Martin prize-fight in 1821 paid some £12,000 to reach the venue.[203] By the 1840s, ferrys, canals, trains and steamers were all employed; though the last two were of more significance.[204] Although steamers, in 1817, were the first to be used to carry spectators, trains had more long-term impact, being utilized for a wider range of sports.[205] The problem with steamers was that it was easy to charter rivals and undercut prices.[206] Consequently, facilities were improved, one boat to a prize-fight offering 'an excellent brass band on board, and jigs, polkas, and quadrilles'.[207] This led to bigger overheads and though it was often worthwhile for entrepreneurs to pay boxers for the right to provide a steamer, profits of £150 sometimes being gained, on occasions ventures were 'anything but profitable'.[208] One unscrupulous entrepreneur, having marooned his passengers on an island 'taking advantage of the trap in which the visitors were caught he doubled the toll'.[209] Trains had wider geographical accessibility and by the 1840s most sporting events advertised their rail connections, organizing intersecting coaches.[210] From the start profits had been good, a company selling £375 worth of sixpenny tickets to watch Manchester races in 1838, and by 1845 over a thousand pounds was expended visiting Tyne Regatta.[211]

The services involved in established seasonal recreations, such as sailing, shooting and fox-hunting, brought great employment to many areas. A well groomed fox-hunting pack was reckoned to cost £3,000 a year, and in Surrey alone the packs pumped £16,000 into the local economy in 1832.[212] This tended to enrich almost everyone in an area. At Brighton, for instance, local labourers charged visitors half a crown to witness the kill at a hare-hunt.[213] The most dramatic change occurred at Lutterworth. Whereas earlier farmers had sabotaged the hunts and 'sent their men out at night, previous to the intended "meeting" to drive the foxes from covert', [214] such hostility ended and the town began to provide good signposts and lighting, the inhabitants sharing in the prosperity of the commerce resulting from fox-hunting. By contrast, the excessive exactions at Melton Mowbray had severely reduced the number of packs based there.[215] Sailing was a big employer in particular areas, notably Edinburgh and Cowes.[216] The influx of those wishing to hire shooting grounds was a great boon in the north. Despite attempts to control prices and weed out plots that were of little sporting value, the owners' profits increased steadily, with ignorant visitors continually being leased worthless land.[217]

Sporting equipment was produced for two main groups: spectators and participants. The most elementary for the spectator were the varieties of ephemera, including pictures and busts, that were produced. Race goers were offered 'portable meals'.[218] Also, they could be kitted out with clothes, an advert declaring

ASCOT RACES. Who would appear and intermingle with Royalty without a GOOD HAT.[219]

Participants were catered for by special shops that sold the latest sporting equipment, including 'the fishing gear employed by champions', stopwatches and cricket bats.[220] Of more importance was another form of sporting equipment, namely, animals. As a business, the supply of animals expanded in importance, with entrepreneurs such as Redfern supplying most of Lancashire's pigeons.[221]

Similarly, the popularity of ratting meant that supplying rats was 'a good profession', boys in Glasgow earning ten shillings a week from it.[222] Much of the traffic in deers, dogs, cubs, pheasants and such like was illegal, the animals having been stolen and the resulting profits being destined for the underworld.[223]

The term tourism describes the trade enjoyed throughout an area by servicing the wants of spectators that had been drawn there by sporting events. These can be broadly divided into three types: deliberate initiatives, annual events and occasional events.

Deliberate initiatives commenced in the 1820s, when many places, such as North Fleet, Herne Bay, Lytham, Sherbourne and Fleetwood, began to offer sport as a way to attract visitors.[224] Activities varied considerably, including archery, bowls, steeplechasing, regattas and pigeon-shooting.[225] Particular venues, notably Brighton, promoted themselves as sporting playgrounds, in a desire to attract London excursionists.[226] Similarly, Ashton commercialized established customs such as 'the Black Lad', which was transformed from an effigy into an armour-clad man riding about, in order to discourage the local population from journeying away by railway on wakes days.[227] Not everywhere was so organized; Gravesend's potential tourists were put off by the lack of a police force in the evening, which meant that yobs ran wild.[228] At Southend refreshments were bad and expensive.[229]

Another sport that areas were beginning to use to attract visitors was stag-hunting. The sport that had once been exclusively for the monarch had been reduced to a ludicrous form of pageantry during the French wars, and the royal pack continued to decline, due mainly to poaching and household economies.[230] Yet the sport itself grew, becoming an established commercial spectacle in two separate ways due to the intervention of the steam engine. First, stag-hunting became integrated into spectacular events, such as steeplechases and performances of Handel's *Messiah*, attracting a large, socially diverse, audience, many of whom were brought by trains. Second, railway connections, notably the Great Western, enabled the creation of stag-hunting packs that were filled with commuters.[231] The once regal sport was now conducted according to the railway timetable.

A more established form of entertainment were major annual events, such as Henley Regatta, the Kingston Shrove-football, top cricket matches at Canterbury or various horse-race meetings.[232] Their presence allowed tradesmen to regularly overcharge spectators and gave birth to a substantial entertainment culture of theatres, gambling houses, small booths and hawkers.[233] These offered a range of attractions, including various sideshows.[234] Given the fact that spectators tended to save their money for such holidays, earnings from such facilities could be substantial and there were many complaints that the right to rent booths and other venues was artificially restricted to local residents.[235] It is clear that at Henley exploitation occurred, *Bell's* stating that 'we have received several letters complaining of the imposition practised on the visitors by some of the inn-keepers and others ... one room demanded five shilling entry ... for a niggardly cold collation ... coach drivers charged ten shillings each for a distance of nine miles'.[236] Major annual sporting events were vital in areas such as Epsom, where the government's proposed ban on gambling booths was opposed because 'hundreds of persons must be reduced to a state of utter destitution'.[237]

Local authorities tended to do well from such ventures. For instance, the race meeting at Doncaster yielded a regular profit of over £2,000, thus persuading both the council and judiciary to swallow their moral scruples and shield gamblers from the law.[238] While the municipal reforms of 1835 made it illegal for the council to offer public money as prizes in the races, the influx of an increased number of middle-class tradesmen onto the town councils, whose business interests were served by the annual race meetings, ensured their continued promotion.[239] However, many of those whose businesses benefited considerably from such events, for instance local railways, contributed little towards their sponsorship.[240] In fact, at Epsom, the exactions of the sites owner, the local MP, Briscoe, were such that many of his constituents threatened to depose him at the next election.[241] Generally, as the period wore on, both the amount of rural meetings and the significance of the involvement of the local community declined, especially when the taxes due on farmers' horses entered in 'hack' races was substantially increased, thus effectively extinguishing their participation.[242]

The value to an area of large occasional events had been long recognised; the Neat–Hickman fight of 1822 bringing some £10,000 to the Berkshire region.[243] Hotels often benefited, every single one in Oxford being 'packed' for the steeplechase in 1840.[244]

Techniques of commercial exploitation As the period wore on the commercial exploitation of sport became steadily more accomplished, increasing the amounts generated by gate money, the sale of refreshments and various ancillary services. While it would be mistaken to suggest that examples of this do not appear before 1830, the main improvement occurred in the later period. These developments can be broadly detailed as follows.

Far more attention was paid to selecting the week of events, so as to avoid clashing with rival fixtures, a problem that had persistently afflicted Shrewsbury races.[245] Efforts were also made to utilise communications, especially railways, the want of which meant that Egham races, in contrast to that at Epsom, declined rapidly.[246] The correct pricing of admission charges was also vital, as the fate of the Hippodrome, a venue that alienated its potential audience by overcharging, demonstrated.[247] At venues such as Belle Vue, both the course itself, and spectating facilities, were improved, with previously poor grandstands being completely overhauled.[248] Likewise, officials were employed to keep the course clear, a particular necessity at pigeon-shooting venues throughout the country where 'outscouts', illegal interlopers who insisted on taking pot-shots at the birds, endangered lives.[249]

At both foot races and regattas, efforts were taken to ensure that competitors were easily distinguished.[250] Henley's rowing competitors were instructed 'that all the crews shall provide themselves with small colours or flags, the same to be nine inches long and seven inches wide and attached to a brass spindling'.[251] Similarly, various lighting effects illuminated protagonists, heightening the spectacle.[252] An advert for the boxing displays that were held regularly at a pub in London is typical:

> the boxers will wear white flannel drawers, ring shoes, their respective colours around their waists, and set to in a regular roped ring ... the whole arrangement being intended to convey an ideal picture of a real prize contest.[253]

The rules of sports such as cricket and the programmes of horse races were changed in order to increase the public's enjoyment by speeding them up. Wrestling went still further, one of the competitors 'danced a highland fandango in regular costume'. A spectacle that prompted 'a female in the pit [who] was so delighted with the extraordinary ability of the Black, that she rose from her seat and exclaimed "Here's sixpence my lad" '.[254] At Epsom a band was introduced to 'diminish the tedium between races', the reporter conceding that 'attempts must be made to prevent racing becoming unfashionable like the theatre'.[255] Providing entertainment was a presiding concern, and a variety of sports were often conducted at a particular event. Horse races, for example, often being accompanied by rowing, athletics and rustic sports.[256] Occasionally, as with ratting in the 1820s, a new sport was invented. The result was amazing; although the event did not start until eight, people started queuing at four.[257] Various novelties were also introduced, archery displays were given by American Indians, cricket matches were played between cripples, eliciting 'roars of laughter'.[258]

In order to ensure the entry of quality competitors, a number of venues offered good prizes.[259] This was a necessity at singlestick, where competitors were reluctant to risk injury unless there was a good potential reward.[260] The case was slightly different at horse racing. There, entry costs were often high and the lack of rewards for second place meant that at many tracks, for instance Lewes – where Lord Egremont's horses dominated – there was little incentive for outsiders to compete.[261] Additionally, the cups offered as prizes were worth far less than their purported value.[262] Above everything, however, corruption was rife, and many provincial steeplechases were fixed.[263]

Between 1830 and 1850 the management of many big annual sporting events, particularly horse races, became increasingly professional.[264] In many senses this was inevitable because the departure of the local gentry to spend the season in London removed key supporters from many provincial events.[265] While, predominantly, the commercial opportunities presented by sport expanded, many speculators lost money, the Thames Regatta of 1843 being a particularly extensive example of this.[266] Some small-time promoters spent periods imprisoned for debt.[267] Collectively, commercial sport prospered. The only exception to this was boxing, where the failure of pugilists to cooperate with one another rendered it impossible to maintain a lucrative London venue.[268]

Spectators   When one turns to consider the social composition of spectators, it is clear that the bulk of most crowds were from the working class.

Generally, royalty did not display an interest in sport during the period, though they were sometimes present at major race-meetings, William IV being attacked at Ascot in 1832.[269] Aside from horse racing, which attracted a following from every social layer, the nobility's attendance of sporting events diverged into two extreme camps. On the one hand were the various 'cruel sports', where they interacted with semi-criminal elements characterized as 'the fancy', alternatively, they had access to genteel activities such as fencing and tennis.[270]

Although our sources rarely mention either the size of the crowd drawn to an event, or the admission charged, their descriptions often indicate that large paying audiences, numbering thousands, were present. Tables 7.3 and 7.4 provide some insight into this. Table 7.3 details the number of events between 1840 and 1850, excluding horse-race meetings, in which crowd sizes exceeding a thousand were reported by the press. Table 7.4 compiles the largest crowd and cheapest admission charge specifically given for a sport between 1816 and 1850. As with Table 7.3, such information is simply an indicator of the organized sporting activity that was occurring, for although it is often clear from the reports given by our sources that large crowds were drawn to sporting events, rarely did they include detailed estimates of crowd size.

The profits attainable from servicing a mass audience in sporting entertainment meant that social exclusivity was increasingly undermined. With the exception of Newmarket, where the Jockey Club endeavoured to limit the access of the lower orders to the races, sporting venues everywhere became far less exclusive.[271] By

Table 7.3   Crowds exceeding 1,000, 1840–50

Year	Number of events
1840	33
1841	41
1842	36
1843	29
1844	48
1845	43
1846	48
1847	50
1848	54
1849	60
1850	48
Total	**490**

Table 7.4   Largest crowd and cheapest admission charge for several sports, 1816–50

Sport	Number	Year	Cost	Year
Badger-bait	–	–	6d	1822
Cock-fight	–	–	1s	1838
Camping	7,000	1822	–	–
Coursing	4,500	1823	–	–
Cricket	20,000	1833	1s	1848
Dog-fight	1,000	1829	5s	1827
Fencing	–	–	2s	1822
Fives	–	–	2s 6d	1819
Foot race	20,000	1846	3d	1839
Horse race	80,000	1823	6d	1850
Lion bait	–	–	11s	1825
Pedestrianism	10,000	1823	6d	1818
Pigeon-shoot	5,000	1825	6d	1842
Pony race	4,000	1837	6d	1840
Pugilism	50,000	1822	6d	1831
Rabbit hunt	3,000	1847	–	–
Rackets	1,000	1833	–	–
Ratting	2,000	1822	6d	1848
Rowing	100,000	1832	1s	1843
Sailing	20,000	1824	–	–
Singlestick	6,000	1817	6d	1837
Skating	7,500	1823	–	–
Stag-hunt	4,500	1833	–	–
Steeplechase	20,000	1840	–	–
Swimming	4,000	1841	–	–
Trotting	–	–	6d	1848
Wrestling	20,000	1822	6d	1816

the middle of the 1830s Manchester Races had become 'more popular and less fashionable', a phenomenon manifesting itself at Bibury, once the most exclusive race-meeting in Britain, from 1846, whence they began admitting spectators by the trainload.[272] Of course, this simply magnified the desire to exhibit one's social position in additional ways. The most comical were the battles for primacy between the vehicles belonging to the various layers of society as they left the race-track: 'the usual crush took place amongst the vehicles at the close of the day: in the struggle which invariably takes place for precedence in leaving the park two or three were discarded in consequence'. A day or so later the battle was less fierce but 'a few wrecks of vehicles were again left upon the field'.[273] Efforts were continually made to segregate spectators, by either social criteria, as at Heaton Races, or cost, providing first and second class travel on the steamers and trains that were chartered for prize-fights. Such efforts usually failed and an additional ingredient, 'the rough', was increasingly apparent, particularly at working-class sports such as pugilism and foot racing, where violence was common, sometimes from off-duty soldiers.[274] Generally, the police were comparatively impotent, especially against the well organized depredations of criminal gangs.[275] The latter could wreak havoc, *Jackson's* reported that at Oxford races 'the light fingered gentry were very active each day on the course, and made a fine harvest; indeed the number of robberies committed is almost incredible'.[276]

As we observed earlier, there is no reason for believing that lack of free time had a significant impact on the attendance of sporting crowds.[277] Of altogether more significance, judging by our sources, was money. On a number of occasions we are specifically told that local economic troubles severely restricted attendance, especially of the middle-class spectator.[278] However, numerically, they were of secondary importance. Throughout the period, especially in large urban areas, our sources make clear that the bulk of spectators at the very large crowds attracted to sporting events were from the working class. This presence was to end the participation of the higher ranks and was crystallized by the once elite horse-race meeting at Heaton where:

> Earl Wilton rode the mare in the first heat; but the crowd being so dense, and the course so difficult to keep well, His Lordship narrowly escaped riding over a man in the first race, and consequently declined riding any more that day.[279]

Non-commercial Sport

Storch identifies three factors – the decline in the patronage of the gentry, greater official intervention, and the growth of commercial leisure – as explaining the decline of traditional entertainment between 1800 and 1850.[280] Others go further, maintaining that because there was little commercial leisure that was accessible to the lower orders before 1850, the decline in traditional entertainment meant that there was effectively a 'vacuum' in terms of the recreational opportunities of the bulk of the population.[281]

As we have seen, commercial leisure accessible to the lower orders was prominent throughout the French wars, a trend that continued in the years after Waterloo. In 1838, Howitt claimed that wakes lacked the variety of earlier times.[282] Yet this seems doubtful, because traditional recreations were changing, interacting with new, commercial forces, which tended to expand opportunities. This is characterized by a 'harvest home' from Sussex in 1823 which was described as offering 'pleasant merry sports, which has the prospect of profit attached'.[283] In

1846 'every village, almost without exception, in the northern counties, manages to have one great day throughout the year – a day devoted to amusement and recreation'.[284]

Non-commercial sports fall broadly into four categories. The most disinterested were acts of charity, involving either financial donations or the provision of employment. There were a number of examples of this, typified by a cricket team donating ten shillings each to their unemployed opponents in 1819.[285] Dying trades, such as watermen, were often assisted by events, such as the Thames Regatta, which provided them with work.[286]

A second category of events were promoted entirely for the love of the resulting sport rather than anticipated commercial rewards. This was one of the motivations for Oxbridge dons to sponsor matches at cricket and rowing between the servants of their respective universities. Additionally, however, as an Oxford fellow revealed during a homily he gave at the match banquet, the events were intended to display the gratitude which they felt towards their servants because 'it is the will of providence that there should be different classes of society but the strength of society depended on the connection of one link with another'.[287] Sports such as wrestling and cricket often disapproved of commercial involvement, thus it was common for spectators to be granted free admission.[288] Cups were subscribed to 'foster the science' and expensive matches organized.[289] Even quite small cricket teams, such as a newly founded Todmorden side, took considerable expense and trouble, having their pitch drained and levelled, for no commercial gain.[290] On at least one occasion, that of Manchester Cricket Club, the incentive for the creation and development of a new ground was unrelated to commercial aims. Rather, it stemmed from the troubles that they were having with the landlord of their existing ground.[291]

A large number of sponsors subscribed to events for political and commercial reasons, regarding them as a good way of projecting themselves.[292] At Woolwich, 'as a consequence of the rivalry between the Old Woolwich and the Watermens Steamboat companies, two regattas have taken place'.[293] Journalists were on the look-out for such events. Upon discovering that a Tory MP was sponsoring a regatta, *Bell's*, a Liberal paper, declared 'there is more to this than meets the eye in these proceedings; but out of evil comes good ... however sinister the object'.[294] Political interests were particularly apparent in the promotion of local race meetings, the maintenance of such sponsorship often being dependent upon the continuance of an area's support for the local powerholder.[295] Local aristocrats and MPs tended to support or neglect race-meetings as part of their management of local political and social affairs.[296] The defeat of an MP could lead to a drastic decline in its sporting activity, as occurred at Preston when Lord Derby's relative was rejected.[297] Groups would also use sports to accomplish particular social agendas. Thus, the local gentry at Warrington took over and expanded the local regatta but were careful to ensure that the events were segregated socially, thus terminating what they regarded as an undesirable practice, the mixing of the classes.[298]

The promotion of a large number of events that were held during holidays involved a mixture of disinterested patronage and commercial acumen, with many of the middle and upper classes acting as sponsors.[299] A number of events, such as races for 'Peter Boats', were both practical and commercial.[300] Throughout the period there was a tendency to expand the commercial scope of such entertainments, with events such as horse racing, which presented considerable commercial opportunities, replacing minor attractions embodied by rustic sports. In 1838 this occurred throughout Lancashire.[301] Many regarded horse-race meetings as having profound political and social benefits, especially in 1833, when some feared revolution. *Jackson's* spoke in praise of Oxford races, declaring 'it matters not whether it be a ball, an archery meeting, or a race, so long as persons of all parties are assembled, and enjoyment is the order of the day'.[302]

Commentators often presented the aristocratic provision of horse races and such-like as an act of disinterested, social, patronage. One described Goodwood thus:

> there, the husbandman is destined to reap the reward of his labour, watched over and fostered by an Aristocracy who know that all sorts and conditions of men were formed to take a part in the social harmony; that the humblest are links without which the chains of society would fall asunder.[303]

While the chief aim of the Goodwood meeting was to entertain the local tenantry, significant efforts were made to ensure profits, with over £700 being taken in admission money every year. Not only that, although such gate money was justified as being necessary to cover debts incurred by improvements that had been made to the course, there was no assurance that these charges would cease when the costs had been cleared.[304] By contrast, Lord Wilton refused to charge admission to Heaton Races, an event which embodied disinterested patronage.[305]

Conclusions

Long before the Napoleonic war, a reasonably sophisticated sporting infrastructure existed, incorporating a range of events, including both the traditional and commercial. These two sectors, involving the seemingly contradictory impulses of patronage and profit, had often interacted and overlapped, but the tremendous commercial forces that were unleashed during the war accelerated this. This stemmed from a robust economy and was amplified by the probable growth of internal tourism resulting from the continental blockade. Sport appears to have been a major beneficiary of this, receiving ever larger sums of money. In fact, the commercial element became increasingly prominent, intruding even into genteel activities, such as archery, where events were held for financial prizes, and the exclusive recreation of stag-hunting, there being an increasing onus on deer parks becoming profitable concerns.[306] It seems likely that many other classes took a lead from the wealthy in the sponsorship of sport, the promotion of which incorporated a wide range of the social structure. Consequently, the financial component grew in sophistication, transforming many of the established patterns of activity. The effect was particularly felt in the amount of money staked on events and the facilities that were developed to accommodate spectators. Many of these ingredients had already begun to manifest themselves long before 1793 and England's enforced isolation for over twenty years ensured that these developments achieved an important stage in their fruition.

This growth accelerated between 1816 and 1850, driven by the expansion in both events and expenditure on sport. Geographically, the horizons had also expanded, as had the social diversity of promoters. The culture became more sophisticated, with entrepreneurs deploying substantial financial expertise, and creating increasingly large-scale events on a regular basis. Generally, this was conducted as a far more efficient business by comparison with the French wars, increasing numbers of events levying admission charges. By 1850, almost all of the 40,000 crowd at Manchester's race meeting paid admission money, the lowest cost being one shilling.[307] The crowds that were drawn to the newly emerging facilities were predominantly working class. Cumulatively, it led to the significant expansion of both the amount of sporting activity accessible to the general population and the profits realizable from sport.

By the end of the 1840s there was a substantial commercial sporting culture, that was almost as sophisticated as its successors of forty or so years later. It was the onset of the 'amateur' ideal that was to impede this progress. The upper and middle classes, far from promoting and fostering commercial sport, came to oppose it bitterly. This is the subject of the next chapter.

Notes

1 Cunningham, *Industrial Revolution*, p. 198.
2 We may also note that while the stakes involved in horse racing increased substantially in the latter half of the eighteenth century, they were still far smaller than the figure for 1790. Borsay, *Urban Renaissance*, p. 216.
3 E. Moir (1964) *The Discovery of Britain: The English Tourist 1540–1840*, London: Routledge.
4 *SM*, Aug 1814, 195–6.
5 *SM*, Jan 1793, 240, July 1794, 225–6.
6 *SM*, March 1793, 367; Oct 1798, 38; Dec 1804, 146–7; April 1805, 54.
7 *SM*, Jan 1794, 189; March 1794, 320.
8 Deale, *Life in the West*, i, 179–80.
9 *SM*, Feb 1794, 239; Aug 1812, 236.
10 *BWM*, 20 July 1806. *MM*, 27 June 1815. *SM*, April 1803, 55. *Times*, 9 June 1794.
11 *BWM*, 20 April 1800. *SM*, June 1802, 164; Aug 1804, 271.
12 *WD*, 2 Sept 1804.
13 *Bell's*, 9 Sept 1838. *SM*, May 1793, 124; Jan 1794, 225–6; Oct 1811, 3–4.
14 *BWM*, 4 Aug 1811. *SM*, July 1800, 185; Feb 1808, 266.

15 *BWM*, 21 Aug 1808.
16 *BWM*, 5 Sept 1802. *SM*, Nov 1798, 104; July 1800, 185; Sept 1808, 285–7.
17 *BWM*, 6 Dec 1801.
18 *SM*, Sept 1808, 286–7; March 1811, 307; Oct 1813, 33.
19 *SM*, April 1794, 45–6; July 1802, 220–21.
20 *BWM*, 18 Aug 1811.
21 Egan, *Boxiana*, i, p. 162. *SM*, Nov 1793, 108; Dec 1793, 153; Dec 1808, 109.
22 *SM*, Nov 1793, 106.
23 *BWM*, 20 Aug 1815. *MM*, 10 Sept 1811. *SM*, May 1811, 97.
24 Bee's revelations appeared in the *Annals of Sporting and Fancy Gazette* throughout that periodical's life. Deale issued a number of exposés of corruption in sport, the most famous being *Life in the West*.
25 *SM*, April 1795, 3–5.
26 *SM*, Sept 1793, 332.
27 *SM*, July 1800, 185; Dec 1800, 98.
28 Chinn, *Better Betting*, pp. 7, 41.
29 *BWM*, 6 Oct 1805. Contra Chinn, *Better Betting*, p. 68.
30 *BWM*, 8 Dec 1805.
31 *SM*, Jan 1811, 166.
32 *SM*, March 1793, 369; Aug 1800, 230.
33 *Bell's*, 3 Jan 1830.
34 *SM*, April 1793, 50.
35 Brander, *Soho for the Colonel*, pp. 211–14. *SM*, Dec 1808, 108–110.
36 *BWM*, 15 July 1810. *SM*, April 1795, 3.
37 *SM*, Sept 1804, 315; April 1813, 24–5.
38 *SM*, Oct 1813, 3–5.
39 Dyck, *William Cobbett*, pp. 21, 234. *SM*, Aug 1807, 210.
40 *SM*, May 1812, 131–2.
41 *WD*, 29 Jan 1804.
42 Buckley, *Pre-Victorian Cricket*, p. 171. *SM*, July 1808, 195.
43 *Times*, 30 Nov 1800.
44 *SM*, May 1812, 90–91.
45 *BWM*, 11 May 1806, 10 May 1807.
46 Miles, *Pugilistica*, i, p. 201.
47 *BWM*, 13 Oct 1805. *SM*, March 1810, 311.
48 *MM*, 8 Dec 1807.
49 *Jackson's*, 23 Feb 1793, 26 Oct 1802, 19 May 1804. Malcolmson, *Popular Recreations*, p. 71.
50 Wigglesworth, *Rowing*, p. 35.
51 *WD*, 8 April 1804.
52 *Jackson's*, 30 April 1803. *SM*, Nov 1814, 51.
53 *Times*, 5 Sept 1801.
54 Reid, 'Beasts and brutes', p. 134. *SM*, April 1805, 19–20.
55 *SM*, Jan 1808, 208.
56 *Jackson's*, 23 April 1796. *SM*, Feb 1798, 260.
57 *Times*, 28 July 1808.
58 *BWM*, 30 Jan 1803.
59 *SM*, Sept 1804, 285.
60 *SM*, Aug 1810, 244.

61   *Jackson's*, 21 July 1798.
62   Borsay, *Urban Renaissance*, pp. 214, 219, 338, 341–2, 347.
63   *BWM*, 23 July 1805. *WD*, 23 Jan 1803.
64   *BWM*, 22 Sept 1805. *SM*, July 1802, 225. *WMC*, 15 May 1813.
65   *SM*, May 1799, 61. *VCH Oxfordshire*, ii, 364.
66   *Fulwood Racecourse Minute Books 1790–1829* (LCRO: DDX 103/4). B. Mitchell (1988) *British Historical Statistics*, Cambridge: Cambridge University Press, p. 678.
67   *BWM*, 25 Dec 1814. *SM*, June 1795, 167; July 1809, 196; Aug 1809, 278–9. *WMC*, 28 May 1814.
68   *SM*, May 1793, 102.
69   *SM*, July 1799, 176; Oct 1801, 45; May 1803, 110–11.
70   *SM*, Dec 1796, 157; May 1799, 102. *Times*, 8 July 1808.
71   Harrison, *Crowds*, pp. 120, 134.
72   For a discussion of sources used see this volume, pp. 9–10.
73   See for example: *BWM*, 25 Sept 1803, 16 Sept 1804. *SM*, June 1805, 165–6.
74   *SM*, Oct 1807, 29.
75   *SM*, April 1803, 20.
76   *BWM*, 29 May 1814.
77   *SM*, Dec 1806, 160.
78   Borsay, *Urban Renaissance*, p. 305.
79   Ibid., p. 303. *SM*, Oct 1804, 44.
80   Holt, *Sport and the British*, p. 17.
81   *SM*, Dec 1812, 128.
82   *BWM*, 13 July 1800.
83   *SM*, July 1807, 193–5.
84   *SM*, Dec 1806, 160.
85   *SM*, March 1821, 283.
86   *SM*, June 1794, 129.
87   Van Muyden, *A foreign view of England*, p. 281.
88   Ford, *Cricket*, p. 127.
89   Vamplew, 'Sport of kings', 307–308.
90   *BWM*, 9 June 1805, 2 Aug 1807.
91   See this volume, pp. 7–8.
92   *SM*, Dec 1802, 132; Aug 1810, 211. The Cotswold Games could trace a long antiquity, though in his article, E. Gosse (1878) 'Captain Dover's Cotswold Games', *Cornhill Magazine*, 37, 720, dismisses their eighteenth-century manifestation as the 'vulgarised' creation of publicans.
93   *SM*, Nov 1805, 84.
94   *BWM*, 27 Feb 1803. *SM*, March 1793, 370; April 1795, 53; Aug 1795, 260.
95   *BWM*, 3 Dec 1797. *SM*, July 1796, 274; Dec 1798, 158–60.
96   *Jackson's*, 13 May 1814, 2 Oct 1814.
97   *SM*, June 1798, 165; Aug 1812, 237.
98   *WD*, 3 July 1803.
99   B. Barton (1874) *History of the Borough of Bury and Neighbourhood*, Bury: Wardleworth, p. 41. *Jackson's*, 14 Sept 1793. *SM*, May 1811, 99.
100 *SM*, July 1808, 188; Aug 1808, 243–4; March 1811, 99. *Times*, 30 Nov 1808.
101 *SM*, July 1795, 223; Aug 1802, 282. *Times*, 30 Nov 1808.
102 See this volume, pp. 21–3.
103 *Bell's*, 17 Nov 1844.

104   J. Badcock (1828) *Living Picture of London*, London: T. Hughes, pp. 237–9, 243–4. *Bell's*, 18 April 1827, 2 Jan 1831, 12 July 1835, 4 Nov 1838, 25 April 1841, 15 Feb 1846, 8 March 1846. Deale, *Life in the West*, i, pp. 84–5. *WD*, 1 Feb 1818.

105   *Bell's*, 7 May 1848. Chinn, *Better Betting*, p. 51. Clapson, *Popular Gambling*, pp. 23, 90. *NSM*, March 1834, 292–6.

106   *Bell's*, 16 May 1847.

107   *Bell's*, 23 Feb 1845.

108   *Bell's*, 16 July 1848.

109   Egan, *Book of Sports*, p. 179.

110   *Annals*, Dec 1822, 399. *Bell's*, 27 Aug 1837. Egan, *Book of Sports*, pp. 181–4.

111   *Annals*, July 1824, 63.

112   *Bell's*, 12 April 1829. *WD*, 14 Dec 1817.

113   *Annals*, May 1822, 328; Aug 1822, 111; Aug 1827, 102.

114   *BWM*, 2 Jan 1820. *WMC*, 4 Oct 1834.

115   *Bell's*, 28 Nov 1824, 12 April 1829. *WMC*, 4 Oct 1834.

116   *SM*, Sept 1817, 292; Dec 1821, 104. *WD*, 8 June 1817.

117   *Bell's*, 16 March 1828.

118   Badcock, *Living Picture*, p. 255. *Bell's*, 26 Sept 1830.

119   *Bell's*, 5 Sept 1847, 3 Sept 1848. *SM*, Aug 1829, 306.

120   *Bell's*, 30 Sept 1838. *WMC*, 5 May 1832.

121   *Bell's*, 4 Sept 1838.

122   Badcock, *Living Picture*, pp. 244, 254, 258. Deale, *Life in the West*, i, p. lx; ii, pp. 15–34, 43, 53–5. Ford, *Cricket*, p. 21.

123   *Bell's*, 18 Nov 1829, 14 Oct 1838. Deale, *Life in the West*, i, p. 260. *Gaming* (1844), 927. Wade, *Black Book*, p. 106.

124   *Bell's*, 16 Sept 1832, 23 Sept 1832, 30 Sept 1832, 21 Oct 1832.

125   *Annals*, July 1822, 43. *Bell's*, 28 June 1829, 13 Nov 1842, 30 Aug 1843. There were occasional exceptions: *Bell's*, 30 July 1843, 13 Aug 1843.

126   *Bell's*, 28 March 1830, 22 March 1840.

127   *Bell's*, 5 Oct 1845.

128   *Bell's*, 19 Oct 1845.

129   *Bell's*, 25 Sept 1825, 8 Jan 1826. *SM*, May 1819, 94–5. *WD*, 10 Aug 1817.

130   *SM*, May 1819, 94–5.

131   *Bell's*, 6 June 1824.

132   *Bell's*, 23 Dec 1832.

133   *Bell's*, 27 Aug 1837, 17 Sept 1837, 22 Nov 1840, 29 Aug 1841.

134   Brailsford, *Sport, Time*, p. 64.

135   *Bell's*, 17 April 1831. Brailsford, *Sport, Time*, pp. 45, 63. *SM*, Sept 1820, 269–70, 292. Aristocrats were also guilty of letting their fighters down, see Brailsford, *Bareknuckles*, p. 29.

136   *Bell's*, 30 April 1837.

137   *Bell's*, 31 May 1840, 28 Oct 1849.

138   *Bell's*, 14 April 1844, 21 April 1844, 19 May 1844. *WD*, 2 Dec 1821, 16 Dec 1821.

139   *Bell's*, 18 March 1832, 20 May 1832, 8 Nov 1835, 1 Nov 1840. *SM*, Dec 1835, 203.

140   *Bell's*, 6 Oct 1850.

141   *Bell's*, 14 April 1844.

142   *Bell's*, 28 Nov 1824.

143   *Bell's*, 9 May 1830, 3 Nov 1850. *WD*, 25 July 1819.

144   *SM*, March 1837, 414.

145   *Bell's*, 15 Sept 1822. Wigglesworth, *Rowing*, p. 37.
146   *Bell's*, 21 June 1829, 15 July 1832, 22 March 1846, 19 July 1846. *M&S*, 1 July 1843. Reid, 'Beasts and brutes', pp. 14, 25. *WMC*, 12 June 1830.
147   Buckley, *Pre-Victorian Cricket*, p. 78. Harrison and Trinder, *Banbury*, p 52.
148   *Bell's*, 21 May 1848, 28 Jan 1849.
149   C. Boyle (1884) 'The game of cricket', *QR*, 158, 477. Cunningham, *Industrial Revolution*, p. 114. K. Sandiford (1983b), 'Amateurs and professionals in Victorian county cricket', *Albion*, 15:1, 33. W. Vamplew (1985), 'Not playing the game: unionism and British professional sport 1870–1914', *IJHS*, 2:3, 236. The idea that Clarke's touring team transformed local cricket, in regard to Manchester at least, is incorrect – see Harvey, Leisure, p. 9.
150   *Annals*, Sept 1825, 184. *Bell's*, 14 Jan 1849. *NSM*, Aug 1834, 35.
151   *Bell's*, 6 July 1834, 17 July 1836. Vamplew, *Turf*, p. 174.
152   *SM*, March 1841, 421–3; May 1841, 31–2; July 1841, 158–61.
153   *Bell's*, 20 March 1831, 15 May 1831. *BWM*, 11 April 1819.
154   *M&S*, 19 Dec 1840.
155   Egan, *Book of Sports*, pp. 117–19.
156   *Bell's*, 5 Aug 1849.
157   *Annals*, Nov 1827, 267–8. *Bell's*, 23 Aug 1829, 22 May 1831. Miles, *Pugilistica*, iii, 81.
158   *Bell's*, 22 May 1831.
159   *Bell's*, 4 Sept 1831, 10 May 1835. *BWM*, 21 Dec 1817. *WD*, 27 Dec 1818.
160   *SM*, Aug 1816, 243–4; Oct 1817, 10–17; Dec 1817, 105–107.
161   *Annals*, Aug 1823, 131. *Bell's*, 6 June 1824, 5 July 1840.
162   Wigglesworth, *Rowing*, pp. 60, 68.
163   *SM*, July 1826, 194–6.
164   *Bell's*, 30 Nov 1845. Halladay, *Rowing*, p. 18.
165   *SM*, July 1830, 253. *New Statistical Account of Scotland*, ii, p. 15.
166   *SM*, Sept 1831, 361; March 1842, 373–6.
167   *Bell's*, 6 Oct 1844.
168   *Bell's*, 10 Oct 1824, 17 Aug 1831. *WD*, 27 Aug 1820, 17 June 1821.
169   *Bell's*, 13 March 1842. *BWM*, 24 March 1816.
170   *Annals*, July 1824, 60.
171   *Annals*, Oct 1822, 258.
172   Miles, *Pugilistica*, ii, p. 25.
173   *Annals*, Jan 1825, 54. *Bell's*, 20 June 1824, 30 May 1830, 16 June 1833.
174   *Bell's*, 17 July 1831, 2 Sept 1832, 28 Aug 1836, 23 Oct 1836, 23 June 1839, 30 June 1850.
175   *Bell's*, 1 July 1832, 9 Jan 1848.
176   *Bell's*, 22 May 1836.
177   *Bell's*, 20 Sept 1840, 2 April 1848, 22 July 1849.
178   *Bell's*, 10 Nov 1839, 15 Feb 1846.
179   *Bell's*, 3 Jan, 7 Feb, 14 March, 11 April, 2 May, 23 May, 11 July, 5 Dec 1847.
180   *Bell's*, 14 April 1850, 5 May 1850.
181   *Bell's*, 22 May 1842.
182   *Bell's*, 15 June 1834, 28 Jan 1849, 18 March 1849, 23 Sept 1849.
183   *Bell's*, 16 Feb 1845, 30 May 1847. *SM*, Jan 1829, 241; Feb 1829, 367. Vamplew, *Turf*, p. 21n.
184   *Bell's*, 19 March 1837, 21 Nov 1841.

185 *Bell's*, 15 Dec 1850.
186 *Annals*, Aug 1825, 121. *Bell's*, 27 Oct 1850.
187 *Annals*, June 1828, 41–3. *Bell's*, 31 Oct 1824, 11 April 1847.
188 *Bell's*, 19 July 1840. *WD*, 23 March 1817.
189 *Annals*, Feb 1822, 115.
190 *Annals*, Feb 1822, 116–17. *Bell's*, 17 Nov 1839.
191 *Bell's*, 24 Feb 1828, 22 Aug 1841, 1 June 1845, 24 June 1849.
192 *Bell's*, 29 March 1829.
193 *Bell's*, 9 March 1845, 2 April 1848, 25 Feb 1849.
194 *Bell's*, 9 Jan 1848.
195 *Bell's*, 17 March 1844.
196 *Bell's*, 30 July 1848, 24 Sept 1848, 28 Oct 1849.
197 *Bell's*, 29 Oct 1837. *M&S*, 20 July 1844.
198 *Bell's*, 15 March 1835, 6 Sept 1835, 16 Feb 1840, 23 Feb 1840.
199 *Bell's*, 5 Feb 1837, 28 March 1841, 9 May 1841, 22 Sept 1844, 30 Jan 1848. Walton and Poole, 'Lancashire Wakes', pp. 105–106.
200 *Annals*, Jan 1822, 53; Sept 1823, 183–4. *Bell's*, 5 Oct 1828.
201 *Bell's*, 5 May 1839. *WMC*, 17 Feb 1827, 2 Aug 1828.
202 *Bell's*, 20 Sept 1840, 15 March 1846, 8 Oct 1848.
203 *BWM*, 16 Sept 1821.
204 *Bell's*, 16 Oct 1842. *M&S*, 5 Dec 1840.
205 *WD*, 11 May 1817.
206 *Bell's*, 30 May 1847, 28 May 1848. Brailsford, *Sport, Time*, pp. 90–91, discusses the relative advantages of steamers and trains for pugilism.
207 *Bell's*, 27 Sept 1846.
208 *Bell's*, 23 July 1843, 12 May 1844, 1 Sept 1844.
209 *Bell's*, 16 Oct 1842.
210 *Bell's*, 11 Feb 1849.
211 *Bell's*, 30 Nov 1845. *WMC*, 16 June 1838.
212 *Bell's*, 25 Nov 1832. *SM*, Nov 1837, 97.
213 *SM*, March 1833, 383.
214 *Bell's*, 8 Jan 1843.
215 *Bell's*, 29 Jan 1843, 28 Jan 1849.
216 *Bell's*, 21 June 1829, 22 April 1832. *SM*, April 1829, 403; Aug 1835, 308; Nov 1835, 39.
217 *Bell's*, 25 Nov 1849.
218 *Bell's*, 5 June 1831, 18 April 1847, 15 April 1849, 29 April 1849.
219 *Bell's*, 29 May 1831.
220 *Bell's*, 4 Sept 1831, 2 Feb 1840, 8 Dec 1850.
221 *Bell's*, 30 July 1848, 29 Oct 1848, 10 Dec 1848.
222 *Annals*, Nov 1822, 340. *Bell's*, 2 Jan 1848, 31 March 1850. Chesney, *Victorian Underworld*, pp. 293–300.
223 *Bell's*, 21 Oct 1832, 28 Oct 1832, 5 June 1836. Bovill, *Nimrod and Surtees*, pp. 45–52.
224 *Bell's*, 13 April 1834, 15 Aug 1841, 6 May 1849. Egan, *Book of Sports*, pp. 364–6.
225 *Bell's*, 16 Sept 1827, 3 Jan 1841.
226 *Bell's*, 27 March 1825.
227 *M.Ex*, 30 March 1850.
228 *Bell's*, 15 Oct 1837.
229 *WD*, 30 Sept 1821.

230 *Annals*, Dec 1823, 409.
231 *Bell's*, 24 March 1839, 17 Aug 1845, 8 Nov 1846.
232 *Bell's*, 23 June 1839. J. Thorne (1876), *Handbook for the Environs of London*, London, p. 401.
233 *Bell's*, 9 Sept 1827, 23 June 1839, 24 July 1842. *Exchange Herald*, 19 June 1821. *JJC*, Sports, Box 12. *SM*, Sept 1836, 383. *WD*, 17 Aug 1817. *WMC*, 10 May 1828.
234 *Bell's*, 25 March 1838. *NSM*, July 1834, 155. *WD*, 6 April 1817.
235 *Bell's*, 8 Jan 1832, 25 April 1837, 18 April 1841. *Jackson's*, 15 May 1830. *Gaming*, pp. vii–viii, 1220.
236 *Bell's*, 23 June 1839.
237 PRO HO 45 05696.
238 *Bell's*, 18 Sept 1836, 11 Dec 1836. Brailsford, *Sport, Time*, p. 58. *Gaming*, p. 1039.
239 A. Eadie (1990), The Structure and Organization of English Horse Racing (c. 1830–1860), Oxford D.Phil., p. 300. Thompson, 'The town and city' in *CSH*, i, p. 69.
240 *Bell's*, 14 Aug 1836, 21 May 1837, 22 Dec 1850.
241 *Bell's*, 18 Feb 1838, 9 May 1841. *SM*, Nov 1834, 20–21; May 1835, 45.
242 *Bell's*, 29 April 1849, 30 Dec 1849.
243 *Annals*, Jan 1822, 54.
244 *Bell's*, 6 March 1836, 13 March 1840.
245 *Bell's*, 14 April 1833. *SM*, July 1843, 9–10.
246 *Bell's*, 29 Aug 1841. *M.Ex*, 29 Aug 1849. *Gaming*, p. 1396.
247 *Bell's*, 9 May 1841.
248 *Bell's*, 5 Sept 1830, 4 June 1843, 25 March 1849.
249 *Bell's*, 10 June 1838, 18 Jan 1846, 13 Dec 1846, 9 May 1847, 9 Jan 1848.
250 *Bell's*, 8 July 1832.
251 *Bell's*, 11 May 1845.
252 *Annals*, Feb 1822, 116. *Bell's*, 25 May 1828.
253 *Bell's*, 13 Feb 1842.
254 *Bell's*, 23 May 1830, 3 Jan 1836, 27 March 1836, 3 April 1836, 17 May 1840, 8 May 1842, 13 April 1845, 18 May 1845.
255 *Bell's*, 30 Aug 1830.
256 *Bell's*, 5 Aug 1827, 10 Dec 1843. *M&S*, 5 Oct 1844, 30 May 1846.
257 *Bell's*, 29 Dec 1822.
258 *Bell's*, 3 Jan 1836, 10 March 1844, 20 July 1845.
259 *Bell's*, 5 July 1840, 23 May 1841.
260 *Bell's*, 6 June 1830.
261 *Annals*, Nov 1823, 314–15. *Bell's*, 6 July 1834, 28 June 1835. *WD*, 6 Aug 1820.
262 *Bell's*, 2 Sept 1832.
263 *Bell's*, 31 March 1850.
264 *Bell's*, 18 Sept 1831, 2 Oct 1831, 13 Nov 1831, 20 Nov 1831, 1 Sept 1833, 11 Nov 1849. *SM*, Nov 1835, 23–5.
265 *Bell's*, 19 Oct 1845.
266 *Bell's*, 15 Sept 1839, 9 July 1843, 23 June 1844.
267 *Bell's*, 21 Dec 1828, 27 Aug 1843.
268 *Bell's*, 30 Dec 1827, 27 Feb 1831, 21 Aug 1831, 16 Oct 1831, 12 June 1836, 22 Dec 1839, 10 Dec 1843, 17 Dec 1843, 24 Dec 1843, 4 Feb 1844, 18 Feb 1844.
269 *Bell's*, 5 June 1831, 24 June 1832.
270 *Bell's*, 22 Jan 1826, 19 June 1836. *NSM*, Aug 1839, 136.
271 Walvin, *Leisure and Society*, p. 24.

272 *Bell's*, 21 June 1846. *WMC*, 13 June 1835, 28 May 1836.

273 *WMC*, 1 Oct 1831.

274 *Bell's*, 30 April 1843, 21 July 1844, 2 Dec 1849. Birley, *Sport*, p. 177. Buckley, *Pre-Victorian Cricket*, pp. 155–6.

275 *Bell's*, 29 Aug 1824, 11 Dec 1842.

276 *Jackson's*, 21 Aug 1824.

277 Contra Vamplew, *Pay up*, pp. 281–2.

278 *Bell's*, 14 April 1833, 31 Jan 1847, 3 Oct 1847, 31 Oct 1847, 26 March 1848.

279 *SM*, Nov 1836, 243.

280 Storch, 'Persistence and change in nineteenth century popular culture', pp. 7, 13.

281 Harrison, *Drink*, p. 331. Malcolmson, *Popular Recreations*, pp. 89, 170–71.

282 Howitt, *Rural Life*, ii, 271.

283 *Annals*, Oct 1823, 272.

284 *Bell's*, 15 Nov 1846.

285 *Bell's*, 13 Oct 1844. Buckley, *Pre-Victorian Cricket*, p. 109.

286 *Annals*, Oct 1823, 279. *Bell's*, 31 Aug 1823, 25 April 1830, 7 Oct 1832. Halladay, *Rowing*, pp. 9–10.

287 *Jackson's*, 3 Aug 1850.

288 *Bell's*, 11 March, 18 March, 25 March, 16 Sept 1849. Boyle, 'The game of cricket', 478. Litt, *Wrestliana*, p. 29. *M&S*, 13 May 1848.

289 *Bell's*, 27 Feb 1825, 2 March 1845, 10 Aug 1845, 26 Aug 1849, 5 May 1850, 22 Sept 1850. *BWM*, 6 Sept 1818.

290 *M.Ex*, 27 March 1850, 24 July 1850.

291 *M&S*, 1 April 1848, 13 May 1848.

292 *Bell's*, 9 Oct 1836.

293 *Bell's*, 21 Aug 1842.

294 *Bell's*, 10 Sept 1837.

295 *Bell's*, 2 Oct 1831.

296 *Annals*, Oct 1824, 208–209; July 1825, 41. *SM*, May 1834, 21; Dec 1834, 151.

297 *Bell's*, 12 Aug 1832. *SM*, Dec 1834, 151.

298 Wigglesworth, *Rowing*, pp. 125–7.

299 Poole, 'Oldham Wakes', p. 79.

300 *Bell's*, 3 Aug 1845, 17 Aug 1845.

301 *WMC*, 21 July 1838.

302 *Jackson's*, 24 Aug 1833.

303 *SM*, Sept 1835, 370.

304 *Gaming*, pp. 1193–221.

305 *Bell's*, 22 Oct 1837. In earlier days the principal tradesmen of the area were the major sponsors of Heaton Races; 4 Oct 1829.

306 *SM*, Jan 1794, 239; Feb 1803, 271; Aug 1812, 236.

307 *M.Ex*, 18 May 1850.

Chapter 8

Better Than Working for a Living: Professional Sportsmen … and Women

Blackthorn gentelmen cricket playeres wishes to play a seval geam of cricket on Wison Monday the north sid – A gainst the est sid for aney soum that agred on at Miting Wickets to be Pitesh at 10 Clock.[1]

As the above challenge for a cricket match illustrates, between 1793 and 1850 there was substantial active participation in commercial sport by all social ranks, though little interaction occurred between them. The extent of the involvement of particular elements varied drastically, in terms of its range – certain ethnic groups being largely restricted to particular sports, and volume – women making little comparative impact. Yet beyond this, sport offered significant commercial opportunities to a wide group of people, presenting the possibility of lucrative careers. However, towards the end of the first half of the nineteenth century, a shift in social attitudes led to the deprecation of the financial element in sport, and the consequent limitation of the role and status of 'professionals' in a number of fields. This occurred at a time when commercial sport was expanding rapidly and had the effect of artificially restricting the degree of contact between different social groups.

This chapter examines these developments by comparing the culture existing during the French wars with that of the succeeding period, 1816 to 1850. The first half examines the effect which sport had on the various component groups that made up Britain during the French wars. It begins with an analysis of the factors segregating participation in sport, and is followed by a consideration of the involvement in sport of peripheral groups within British society. The third part considers the opportunities available to skilled competitors, professionals, to utilize their ability to obtain financial and social advancement.

1793–1815

The Segregation of Sport

The terms amateur and professional   During the French wars the terms 'amateur' and 'professional' were of far less importance than in the period after 1830. Additionally, so far as they were defined, their meanings were completely different from ours. The term 'amateur' was not even mentioned by Samuel Johnson, and during the French wars was synonymous with 'gentleman' and, though difficult to define, referred to social rank, rather than sporting ability.[2] In the 1720s the term gentleman was given to any well dressed person wearing a sword.[3] By the Napoleonic war the definition had come to depend far more upon the notion of 'honour', which was a 'moral feeling, unspotted, undeformed, without which no gentleman can exist'.[4] The constituent elements of 'honour' were rooted in character and defied rational analysis. Far from precluding an individual from competing in sport for money, it was almost unknown for an 'amateur' to do otherwise. Some, notably Lord Beauclerk, acquired considerable wealth this way, accumulating £700 a year from cricket.

Samuel Johnson defined 'professional' as 'relating to a particular calling or profession', and 'profession' as 'calling; vocation, known employment'. He described a 'professor' as 'one who publickly practises or teaches an art'. During the French wars the words 'professional', 'professor' and 'professed' were used interchangeably, and referred to those possessing a level of expertise.[5] It was unrelated to whether an individual taught a sport, some 'teachers' were never referred to as 'professors' and certain 'professors' did not teach.[6] Also, certain athletes, such as Wood and Wilding, who utilized their talent to win money, were never referred to as 'professors'.[7] The term was certainly not restricted to anyone earning their living exclusively from sport, as a report of a boxing match from 1808 makes clear: 'a carpenter of the name of Josephs, and Groves, a sawyer. The combatants were both professionals from Somersetshire.'[8] Nor was it related to social class, for it was sometimes applied to aristocrats such as Captain Barclay, a 'professor of athletics'.[9] The terms 'amateur' and 'professional' were not mutually exclusive and contemporaries would have seen no contradiction in referring to skilled upper-class sportsmen, such as Barclay or Beauclerk as 'professional' 'amateurs'.

'Amateurs' rarely ever played against those who were not ranked as gentlemen, for the different social orders would hardly mix on terms of such intimacy.[10] Thus, gentlemen only rode their own horses at courses such as Bibury, where, until 1814, ordinary jockeys were forbidden.[11] The conditions at Bibury were not uncommon, and reflected the fact that British sport was segregated along social lines. Yet this was not the only basis of distinction. In fact, as we shall see in the coming section, segregation also occurred along economic and geographic lines.[12]

Factors segregating sport British sporting events were often restricted to particular social groups or occupations from certain areas.[13] For instance, even at the very beginning of our period, players were excluded from cricket matches because they had not lived in an area for sufficient time. Events open to anyone, even from the same social class, were quite rare. One of the few events which did endeavour to attract societies nationally was held at Blackheath in 1793 and related to archery, a genteel sport.[14] Usually, entry to events, even to members of other societies, was restricted, if only because of the different rules used. Clubs were the major sporting institutions, often possessing their own distinctive uniforms and with rules based on 'the ancient usage of custom'.[15] They were often very restrictive bodies, sometimes limited to former members of the same school. Public school models were occasionally applied to the creation of clubs: Oxford's Bullingdon Cricket Club was based on that of Winchester public school.[16] The club appears to have been the chief sporting unit throughout the social spectrum. Generally, as with the eight coursing clubs that existed throughout the period, membership was subject to a ballot, but this did not necessarily mean that the cost of entry was expensive.[17] For instance, at cricket, membership costs could vary from one shilling to two pounds a year, depending upon the club.[18] While the social composition of a club tended to be uniform, some access was possible. From 1800 the Marylebone Cricket Club admitted gentlemen as well as aristocrats.[19] Similarly, a shooting club organized by Lord Beauclerk and a number of other aristocrats, included many people without titles.[20]

The rules of events often prevented members of the lower orders competing against their social betters: rowing races stipulating that 'only those rowing for pleasure may enter'.[21] In 1803 it was determined by a court that a farmer was eligible for a gentleman's horse race because no one could prove that he did not fulfil the criteria 'of having a good education, liberal manners, moral good conduct and independence of status'.[22] Generally, there was little interaction between the various social ranks at sport, who mingled rather than mixed.[23] This substantiates, to some extent, Peter Burke's contention that by 1800 the upper class had separated themselves from popular culture.[24] However, the various classes seem to have possessed a shared love and pride in sport.[25] To an extent, the war did have a unifying effect on British society.[26] It is, however, probably exaggerated to claim, as Boyle did, that Britain avoided revolution because of the more intimate relationship between the classes, embodied by aristocrats playing cricket with their servants.[27] While, by virtue of the number of players required, it was inevitable that cricket-mad aristocrats, such as Lord Beauclerk, had to include their servants in matches, it is unlikely that this represented a significant relationship.[28] Beauclerk was one of the few aristocrats who did play, and was renowned for his bad temper and lack of sportsmanship. Such facts suggest the paradoxical conclusion that Britain was able to avoid revolution because the general population did not have much informal contact with aristocrats of his type.[29] It would also be erroneous to portray cricket as a game that necessarily promoted social acquiescence; the radical Tom Paine was present at a dinner held by the Hambledon Cricket Club.[30]

Sports rarely broke down strictly according to class lines. The different social orders played the same sports, but separately. However, archery, coursing and tennis seem to have been games for society's upper groups, while backsword, pugilism and wrestling were the preserve of working-class competitors. In cock-fighting, cricket and sailing, a member of the social elite would work closely with experts from the lower orders. It is clear that this relationship did not always conform to the accepted patterns of deference; the cock-feeder Bromley, for instance, was often criticized for haughtily ignoring his patron's advice.[31] Aside from this, except for those occasions when the elite themselves were involved in competitive sports, their principal role was to sponsor skilled members of the lower orders, who were 'hand picked'.[32]

Yet this in itself was very significant. The extent of both the participation of the lower orders in organized sport, and the admiration that their ability excited among the upper ranks, mirrored their social significance by comparison with their foreign counterparts. The relationship between the various ranks in Britain tended to be less deferential and this manifested itself in two quite pronounced ways. First, on a number of occasions arguments between gentlemen and their social inferiors were resolved by pugilism, much to the astonishment of visiting foreigners.[33] Thus, in a very fundamental sense, there was equality between the various social ranks, though given the fact that many of the lower orders were poorly fed, there were clear limits to this.[34] Second, while generally the various orders adopted the recreations and dress of those above them, a certain amount of influence was exerted in the opposite direction.[35] The most visible symbol of this were the various coach driving clubs whose young, aristocratic members, delighted in being mistaken for working men. The various social classes appear to have adhered to a similar culture and value system, which placed an intense emphasis on honour and individual worth. Despite lacking political power, the lower orders regarded themselves as having the 'rights' of a free people, and thus a stake in society, and this may well have defused political tensions.[36] In terms of sport this was reflected both in the widespread nature of participation in 'popular recreations', and the use of such skills to earn money, a fact which distinguished them from societies elsewhere.[37]

The social composition of participants A close study of the details given concerning the names of every competitor in seven major sports (though excluding the two most popular ones in terms of the number of events – namely, horse-race meetings and cricket – because the information was too limited) conducted throughout the period, reveals 2,125 people. Of these, it is possible to identify the occupations of 783 competitors, that is, 37 per cent. This sample breaks down into 208 occupational groups, incorporating every possible sector, including those in retail, craftsmen and service (see Table 8.1). It is likely that certain categories, such as labourer, were heavily underrepresented, because their occupations were not regarded as worthy of note. By contrast, more socially significant competitors, or those whose occupation was unusual, were far more likely to have them mentioned. Despite this, only 29 competitors belonged to the social elite, bearing titles such as esquire, honourable, Lord, Sir, and their opponents were usually from a similar social position. However, certain members of the elite, notably Colonel Thornton, Mr Mellish and Lord Beauclerk, were not only very keen practitioners, but also expert. The war's influence is apparent from Table 8.2, in which military

Table 8.1 Distribution of occupations among seven key sports, 1793–1815

	Number of individuals	Different occupations
Pugilism	365	127
Pedestrianism	143	72
Foot racing	98	57
Horse races	70	26
Horse feats	66	30
Athletics	21	10
Rowing	21	07
Total	**784**	**208**

Table 8.2 Most popular occupations for sportsmen, 1793–1815

Occupation	Numbers Counted
Military	118
Butchers	48
Farmer	39
Coachman	30
Shoemaker	26
Waterman	18
Publican	17
Tailor	13
Gentleman	12
Baker	11
Weaver	11
Carpenter	10

personnel formed by far the commonest designation, though this incorporated a range of ranks.

There was considerable variety in the amount and range of the occupations of persons practising organized sports. For instance, despite the gruelling reputation of prize-fighting, participants included many skilled workers. This was probably due to the pervasive belief that pugilism was an acceptable way of resolving conflict but the incentive of financial reward probably exerted an influence. Judging by the names of cricket teams, they were created according to geographical location rather than their members' occupation.[38] Anecdotal evidence indicates that most horses at race meetings were ridden by either their owners or owners' grooms.

During the French wars sport was divided into various compartments, embodied by clubs, whose members tended to mix exclusively together. Yet outside of this there was a substantial culture, in which a variety of groups participated, the bulk of whom were from the lower orders.

Peripheral Groups

Nationality   Both the groups which may be described as most alien to Britain – 'negroes' and Jews – were restricted to a very narrow field of sport, pugilism. The Jewish community was larger and more well established than that of the 'negroes' and some of its members were very supportive, being willing to supply promising Jewish boxers with stakes.[39] By contrast, the black groupings had a very fragmented structure and young, hopeful, pugilists had to rely on the assistance of established black fighters and sympathetic white patrons. There seems to have been little spirit of mutual assistance, as on at least one occasion one 'negro' fighter had another imprisoned for debt.[40] Jewish fighters could look to the example of Mendoza, a former champion of Britain, for inspiration, whereas the black community lacked a figure of remotely that stature. Jews also suffered far less prejudice, as is amply demonstrated by the different experiences of top Jewish boxers, such as Mendoza and Dutch Sam, and their 'negro' counterparts, Molineaux and Richmond. Both Mendoza and Molineaux had fights for the championship of Britain but whereas the Jew received fair play, Molineaux was cheated of victory: 'from the antipathy to a black being the champion of England'.[41] Jewish fighters were treated with respect by both their own and the wider community. Negroes had no such shelter and even someone such as Richmond, who ran a profitable sparring school and pub, had to endure daily insults.[42] His experiences were, however, nothing compared with the abuse which Molineaux suffered in the press and the physical assaults he received, such as having bricks thrown at him in Glasgow.[43] Yet, there was another side to the experience of 'negro' fighters. Unlike the Jews, 'negroes', or 'men of colour', exerted an hypnotic fascination on English society and when Molineaux first visited Brighton people 'flocked' to see him and he was invited to many of the best houses. It was success, the very real possibility that he would become champion of England, that turned people against him.[44] However, for a brief period of time Molineaux was able to enjoy the high life by earning and spending big sums of money. The lack of a community in which to take refuge inevitably meant that 'negro' fighters led a very precarious existence but boxing did at least offer a way of asserting some self-respect and earning a living, which is perhaps why so many 'negroes' pursued it.[45] Given the fact that until 1834 blacks held as slaves in Britain were not emancipated, the careers and success of 'negro' boxers border on the extraordinary.[46]

There was a very sharp difference in the way other members of the British Isles responded to sport. The English press showed little interest in Wales, portraying it as a place in which harsh religious feeling had largely wiped out the indigenous sporting culture.[47] Despite the fact that the London-based Highland Society seem to have been quite dormant, Scotland received more attention, efforts being made to explain the rules of golf and curling.[48] The foremost sportsman of the period, Captain Barclay, was a Scot, though like many of his countrymen, who appear, generally, to have happily seized the opportunities that were offered by the union with England, he did not stress his culture.[49] By contrast, the London-based Irish community used sport as a way of espousing a fierce nationalism, with boxers such as Dogherty declaring 'Ireland forever'.[50] Irish sport in the metropolis had more variety than every other non-English group put together. However, all of its sports were fiercely violent, consisting of pugilism, hurling, cudgels, bludgeons and such like.[51] Substantial elements of the London-based community identified with its sporting heroes, and hundreds followed the funeral of the pugilist, Powers.[52]

Age and sex   Children were rarely either seen or heard in the sporting press throughout the war. On two occasions they competed in organized sporting events but generally were only mentioned when their games went drastically wrong and resulted in serious injury or death.[53] Yet a good deal was written about the role of sport in educating children and manly sports formed a significant component in the shared gentry experience at public schools.[54] Letters indicate that education was often regarded in nationalistic terms, its aim seeming to be the creation of an army of fit, determined patriots. Certain sports and toys were particularly encouraged because they fostered military values.[55] The aim of such training was not simply physical. Sport, it was felt, could assist the development of a good moral character.[56] Also, by allowing boys to manage their own affairs and settle disputes among themselves by boxing, a tough independence could be cultivated.[57] This was regarded as the crucial difference between the British and the French, in that 'the upper class on the continent interfere with every pleasure of the lower orders which they please to decree dangerous or improper'.[58] French schoolmasters were similar, producing cowed, inadequate boys. By contrast, British boys, like their adults, made their own decisions.[59]

While British boys might have been encouraged to assert and display their independence, despite the long war conducted by land and sea, there is little indication from contemporary sources that this had any impact on the behaviour of women. Although some of the genteel did become more active in public life, and a few working-class women disguised themselves as men in order to enlist, the war's impact, generally, appears to have been slight.[60] The most strident expression of feminine independence occurred on the sporting field, with the exploits of Mrs Thornton, rather than in political demonstrations or at the theatre. As we shall see, her behaviour unsettled many, such triumphs appearing to subvert the whole social order.

To a considerable degree the debate on women's sport was an issue of social class. With the exception of wrestling, where the rules specifically excluded women competitors, lower-class women indulged in almost every sport.[61] Many of these had a commercial aspect to them. Throughout the period women can occasionally be found competing in foot races and pedestrian matches for sums of up to £10.[62] More widespread were the various 'smock races' that were part of almost every rustic festival. Matches had also long been occurring between village cricket teams that were made up entirely of women. In 1811 noblemen arranged a match between two teams of women, representing Hampshire and Surrey, for 500 guineas a side.[63] Since the 1720s entertainments in London theatres had included displays by 'Gladiators', 'scantily clothed' women fighting one another with wooden staves.[64] During the Napoleonic period this martial spirit continued to manifest itself among women and there were at least 18 female prize-fights.[65] These often drew large crowds and on occasions even very formidable men, coal heavers and watermen, lost fights to these women for money. Also, significant figures, notably Jackson and Mendoza, acted as seconds in these fights.[66] Yet some contests were purely personal. England was a society in which strength and courage were highly respected and it was not uncommon for men to fight over women and women over men, in well organized rings that went some way to preventing complete savagery. Such public resolutions of conflict were far from harmless rituals and were typical of a robust society in which certain women pursued distinctively male roles, such as taking part in heavy drinking matches and pursuing the physically arduous job of coach driving. More generally, lower-class women within society were often very tough and assertive, such qualities culminating in the disciplined way they organized their own riots against the price of bread.[67]

While commentators sometimes complained about the behaviour of women, particularly the blood lust they displayed at prize-fights, and urged that they be educated and improved, such appeals were on behalf of the lower orders as a whole, rather than women in particular. The real debate on the role of women in sport related to the behaviour of those above the lower orders. The sporting conduct that was regarded as acceptable within the lives of such women appears to have been compartmentalized depending upon whether they were in the country or the town. In rural society some ladies belonging to the gentry did indulge in certain field sports, even becoming accomplished at hunting and shooting.[68] While such behaviour should not be overestimated, it was not only accepted, but highly approved of, for a single lady who owned an estate to take her tenants hunting on occasions. Life in town, especially in society, seems to have been far more confined. Women were restricted to certain fashionable sports such as ass-racing, leap frog and skating. Their experience of more vigorous activities was restricted to spectating.[69] The competitive energies of these ladies were expended on cards, where large sums were often lost at the private parties that were named 'routs'. On such occasions passions that were rarely given an opportunity for public expression were ventilated and fights between 'genteel' ladies occurred over money. Inevitably, there were also fights between such women over men.[70]

Such behaviour was, however, an occasional aberration from the accepted genteel norm, quite different from the challenge presented by the 'modern amazons', who sought to promote a far more independent woman. They took their lead from Mary Wollstonecraft's book in which she had called for the equality of the sexes. Increasingly, women's clothes were criticized for being erotic, as they became ever more revealing.[71] Plays, such as *The Rage*, appeared in London, in which the heroine 'instead of being feminine and tender was full of boldness and just like a man'.[72] This outlook found its most intense expression in sport. While some sporting societies were mixed it was rare for the sexes to actively participate. Archery, one of the few sports in which such interactions took place, never permitted men and women to compete against one another. Generally, archery events were just another social function in which the sexes could meet and marry. In fact, at several societies, the ladies did not even compete together for prizes; instead these were drawn for by lottery.[73] The Duke of Dorset, who was regarded as having extraordinarily liberal views, encouraged women to pursue every type of sport but forbade them to ever compete against men.[74] In 1796, a Miss Barlow won 100 guineas by driving her curricle and pair from Romford to Whitechapel within a stipulated period of time.[75] Such an exploit was unusual but nothing in comparison with the deeds of Mrs Thornton.

At York, in August 1804, Mrs Thornton conducted a horse race against Mr Flint for 1,000 guineas. The match had received extensive notice in the press for two or so weeks previously, and was watched by a crowd that was variously described as numbering between 40,000 and 100,000.[76] On the eve, and just after the match, press coverage reached saturation point. The reaction of the public varied. Some were outraged that a woman should behave so boldly and make such a public exhibition of herself. Others, considered it praiseworthy and admired Colonel Thornton for permitting his wife to behave in this manner.[77] Predominantly, the coverage was prurient, especially concerning her alleged French background. Much was also made of her clothes, which were described in enormous detail, especially the way she rode side-saddle in buckskin breeches. A number of coarse jokes and rhymes that were current at the time were reprinted.[78] A few people, however, recognized that the contest had transformed sport and that rules would have to be created to regulate contests between the sexes. One, was very direct, declaring; 'if women cast off sensibility they must compete as men'. He wished to get rid of the side-saddle and advocated 'a simple contrivance ... could remove all objection to a lady's sitting astride; as to the circumstances of pregnancy, I do not see much difficulty there, since an allowance of weight might be easily settled, in proportion to the advanced period or bulk'.[79] Mrs Thornton herself, who had been leading in the race but lost because she fell from her horse, made a number of suggestions concerning the future regulation of such matches. She criticized Flint for the ungentlemanly way he had behaved, especially in riding past her without bothering to check that she was uninjured after her fall.[80]

The public response to the York match was incredible. The demand for pictures of the event was so great that they were mass produced. Theatres throughout the land, from Sadlers Wells to Bartholomew Fair, staged plays based around it.[81] The race can be fairly described as the first great national sporting event, and the mere suspicion that the 'Yorkshire folly', as Mrs Thornton was known, might make an appearance, was enough to boost attendance everywhere. In the following year Mrs Thornton won a race against the famous jockey, Buckle, but soon gave up the sport and turned against Colonel Thornton, berating him publicly. She had, in fact, never been his wife, but rather a servant on his estate.[82] In one light, the whole of her career could simply be seen as an act of manipulation by him in order to gain publicity. Yet, for a short period of time she enjoyed tremendous fame, or infamy, and to this day remains the only woman to have beaten a top class jockey in a horse race. With her retirement, sport for upper-class women effectively ended for the duration of the war, though persisting among the lower ranks.

As we can see, the various peripheral groups within Britain enjoyed considerable access to the sporting culture, though it is clear that in the case of blacks and women, part of their appeal seems to have been 'freak'.

Sport and Social Mobility

The situation before 1793   Long before the Napoleonic war a number of people had obtained their employment principally for their sporting skills. Footmen were often chosen for their speed at running or talent at boxing, while good cricketers were employed as estate workers and jockeys as grooms.[83] While in certain sports, such as fox-hunting, even very crucial employees like the whipper-in, continued to be treated as liveried servants, gradually the status of both jockeys and boxers improved. However, this must not be overstressed – as late as 1790 top jockeys were still being treated as playthings by their aristocratic patrons, who organized a prize-fight between two of them.[84] Yet the general tendency was, especially in big money sports, for the status of skilled sportsmen to improve. This was facilitated by the establishment of boxing as a significant spectator sport, enabling pugilists such as Broughton and Mendoza to present regular exhibitions. Such potential was not found in every sport, as the impoverished death of the great athlete, Foster Powell, demonstrated. Despite winning many extraordinary races he had made almost nothing out of his sporting exploits and was forced to sustain himself on his earnings as a clerk. By contrast, as *The Sporting Magazine* acidly observed, many others had literally made hundreds of pounds by betting on him, without rewarding him at all.[85]

Earning a living from sport during the French wars   There were seven principal ways in which a sportsman could utilize his talent to earn money. The first of these was patronage. As we saw earlier, sportsmen were often taken on into a great man's retinue as servants, and this practice continued, as with the boxer Richmond who was employed by Lord Camelford. This position could provide a certain social status and was regarded as being especially useful to black fighters, who could obtain some shield against the considerable prejudice which they confronted. Yet, predominantly, its effect was harmful. First, a number of patrons, typified by Lord Camelford, were simply bullies who deliberately created trouble, thus entangling their retinue in stupid disputes. Far more seriously, many prize-fighters lacked sufficient character to avoid being corrupted by such intimacy with the rich and powerful. Often, they would ape aristocratic vices and squander large sums of money. As success at pugilism was invariably short lived, boxers soon lost their aristocratic friends and patrons, often finishing up with almost nothing. This characterized what was, essentially, a one-sided relationship. Patrons arranged fights to fit in with their social calendars and occasionally left injured fighters unattended while they watched other bouts.[86] Yet they could be generous, even rewarding brave, though unsuccessful, displays.[87] However, by comparison with the past, aristocratic patronage seems to have been declining, replaced by a more diverse range of sponsors, the general public. Increased press attention meant that it was possible for sportsmen to be catapulted to fame, as occurred with Wilson, an itinerant bookseller, who had recently been imprisoned for debt, whose courageous stamina captured the public's attention.[88] The result was that a number of separate subscriptions were started on his behalf, one of which obtained £100 in two hours. His success spawned imitators, notably Eaton, a failed baker who invested such money as he had in an attempt to gain public support by a great sporting feat.[89] Yet sustained press attention was not a necessity. Foot racers, such as Ellerby and 'The Pieman', simply made a good impression on the crowd, and were rewarded by collections, the latter's reaching almost twenty guineas, which was about six months' wages for an agricultural labourer.[90] More commonly, it was boxers, both winners and losers, who received such recognition for their bravery.[91] The wider public could also behave generously, as with the silver cup that was subscribed for Tom Cribb when he became the boxing champion of England.[92] On one occasion, a man who had won £6,000 by betting on a prize-fighter conferred a pension of £100 a year on its victor, 'The Tinman', out of gratitude.[93]

Betting was the second way sportsmen could earn money. While competitors would occasionally bet on themselves – Cribb winning £400 by backing himself to beat Molineaux at boxing – with the exception of billiards, where betting was a player's chief means of reward, it was rare.[94] Betting by sportsmen tended to occur on other activities, such as horse racing, probably reflecting a degree of 'inside' knowledge. Another, though rather more obscure area, related to the practice of fraud, and involved sportsmen deliberately losing. This occurred in a number of sports, especially at horse-race meetings, with the offender either receiving payment for losing or using confederates to bet on his defeat.

Tuition was a third way for sportsmen to earn money. This principally occurred at boxing, though it can be found in other sports, notably foot racing, horse racing and cricket. Many tutors were itinerant, and able to earn reasonable livings, boxers charging five shillings a lesson.[95] Some did especially well, notably the top pugilists who toured areas of France during periods of peace.[96] There were also a number of established venues, particularly sparring schools attached to pubs in London, and jockey-training centres at Newmarket.[97]

A fourth way for sportsmen to earn money was through stakes. Prizes for events were sometimes substantial, victory in the annual Hampshire single-stick event was worth about a year's wages to a local labourer.[98] The amount of the stakes which a successful competitor was able to keep for himself depended heavily on the means he had used to raise the money. Usually, the backers took the lion's share, though by the end of the period this had changed dramatically in boxing. By then, the pugilist, Scroggins complained when he received the whole of the winnings of the £50-a-side fight, claiming that he should have been permitted to keep the bulk of the money which his patron had subscribed as well. *The Sporting Magazine* chided him for his greed, saying 'in former times, first rate men were glad to receive five or ten guineas as a conqueror'.[99]

Display was a fifth way for sportsmen to make money. Contemporaries in the press were quite clear about the reasons for this change in pugilism; an alternative mode of earning a living had appeared, namely the sporting display.[100] Long before the war spectators had been charged entrance fees to watch prize-fights, and other more theatrical displays, such as fencing by D'Eon and blindfold chess by Philidor.[101] However, during the war the provision of spectacle expanded, with pubs hiring athletes to perform intensive feats in order to attract customers.[102] Race meetings invariably had booths in which pugilistic displays occurred, spectators being charged five shillings. While sport and drama had always been closely linked, gatherings in sports as diverse as archery and pugilism including songs and acting, after 1793 the fusion attained a new intensity.[103] Theatres would put on plays based around sporting events, including competitors such as Wilson, who was paid 50 guineas to appear for five nights performing extracts from his sporting challenge.[104] While all sports benefitted from this, pugilism experienced the principal growth. Exhibitions took place in theatres, sometimes between acts of a drama, and were invariably well lit and choreographed.[105] These fights were bloodless, and often watched by the wealthy, including genteel ladies.[106] While it cost £18 to hire the theatre, the five shilling tickets regularly yielded takings of over £100, resulting in substantial profits.[107] Given the fact that certain areas, such as Norwich, where Gully performed for six consecutive weeks, had enormous appetites for these events, a pugilist with an established reputation could easily earn £50 to £100 every month.[108] To put such sums in perspective, it must be borne in mind that both miners and skilled textile workers would be lucky to earn £70 in one year. The very top fighters were even able to give such exhibitions in front of the aristocracy at the private homes of socially influential patrons.[109] As early as 1808 the press realized this, and noted ruefully that this discouraged top boxers from risking themselves in fights.[110] The feeling by the end of the period was that boxers earned far too much and that the sport had become a business unrelated to promoting the national courage. Media attention meant that many pugilists became household names and this even resulted in tours by impersonators who endeavoured to pass themselves off as famous boxers, 'The Game Chicken' being a particular sufferer.[111]

A sixth way of earning money was to provide a service. For example, sportsmen such as Buckle, Gibbon and Bromley, were often used to train animals, both for competitive events (for example, greyhounds and cocks), or theatrical performances (such as horses and bulls).[112] Both jockeys and cricketers were hired to compete in events, receiving an extra fee if they won. Pugilists utilized their physiques to generate additional income, being hired as bully-boys by theatre managers to curb those protesting about increased prices, and stage-coach firms to assault the drivers of their rivals.[113] More peacefully, Gregson earned money by posing as a statue for artists.[114]

Finally, a seventh way to earn money was through books and pictures. These major potential sources of revenue remained largely untapped by sportsmen. Most of the works that did appear were the product of sports writers rather than practitioners, the exceptions being books published by Chiffney (horse racing), Mendoza (boxing), Osbaldeston (shooting) and Philidor (chess). Likewise, 'sportsmen' such as Mrs Thornton and Captain Fairmen, gained nothing from the pictures and prints that were produced of them.[115]

Careers   Throughout the Napoleonic war members of the lower orders such as Gregson, Eaton and Wilson, consciously elected to try and earn their living from sport. The aim of Wilson was to acquire sufficient money from one major sporting achievement to enable him to set himself up in business.[116] This was not a particularly unusual ambition and a number of sportsmen professed a similar aim, some even accomplishing it – usually to become publicans, an occupation that provided Gregson with a much better income than prize-fighting.[117] During this period sportsmen appear to have had far greater and more varied opportunities for earning money from their particular talent, a fact assisted greatly by the attention provided by a sporting media. Inevitably, this changed their status with their patrons, as was shown in the case of the boxer Scroggins.

Successful sportsmen were able to display considerable independence, especially by comparison with the very servile position of even the most senior employees of a fox-hunting pack. There, it was acknowledged that only the most deferential obtained promotion and even then duties consisted of many very menial tasks.[118] By contrast, top sportsmen were often very wealthy and able to mix with many of the social elite. Two of them, Jackson and Gully, obtained significant social positions, the latter even becoming an MP. His fortune was acquired in a variety of ways, including the purchase of a race horse.[119] Yet, for the vast majority, lack of experience in dealing with money meant that the very large sums that they acquired slipped through their fingers. Molineaux earned considerable amounts of money on his boxing tours but arrived back with nothing. Within two years he was imprisoned for debt, a fate that had earlier afflicted another champion boxer,

Mendoza.[120] Mr Andrews, the top billiard player, won hundreds of pounds from the game but lost it all gambling at cards.[121] The saddest case of all was that of the boxer Hooper, nicknamed 'The Tinman'. As earlier noted, in 1795 a grateful backer conferred an annuity of £100 a year on him: four years later he starved to death in the workhouse.[122] Such a drastic change of fortune was typical of the whole sporting world in which very large, comparatively astronomical, sums of money changed hands rapidly. A man's fortunes could oscillate violently and for those who lacked a clear business head and a considerable degree of luck the consequences could be bankruptcy. This held as much for the rich, often aristocratic, promoters of sport as it did for the humbly born sportsmen. Many of the wealthy promoters went through several fortunes and though they never starved to death in workhouses, left but a fraction of what they had inherited. By contrast with the penurious ends of many top boxers, hunt servants tended to die reasonably well cared for.

1816–50

The second half of this chapter consists of three parts: the segregation of sport, peripheral groups and careers in sport.

The Segregation of Sport

Clubs   Voluntary associations had been pervasive in British society, especially since the 1780s, and displayed considerable variety, including religious, educational and recreational.[123] The bulk of these were for the middle and upper classes, though the lower orders often created similar institutions. Sport was similar, with the club representing the most fundamental structure, possessing a membership that was essentially socially homogeneous. At the summit were those clubs restricted to the upper ranks. Bodies such as the Jockey Club were highly exclusive and able to manipulate their power to exclude others, notably, in 1830, Gully, from a mixture of social snobbery and a fear of the mounts at his disposal.[124] The social elite had a considerable number of archery clubs, and this sport was regarded as being particularly beneficial, because it fostered interaction between the prestigious, thus preventing 'peculiarities' from developing.[125] It would be mistaken to imagine that this social homogeneity ensured the absence of conflict. During the 1830s sailing clubs became embroiled in politics, and many potential members were 'blackballed for party reasons'.[126] Yet in most societies, especially those for sailing and archery, members were far keener on exhibiting themselves in uniforms, often of an inappropriate rank, than in conducting feud.[127] The social boundaries of the membership of most clubs was slight. A London pigeon-shooting club that was created in 1846 was typical, being purely for nobles and gentlemen.[128] Similarly, cricket clubs, such as Henfield and I Zingari, catered purely for leisured gentlemen.[129] Often the intake was extremely restrictive. For instance, many of the rowing clubs for gentleman-amateurs that were based in London, such as Leander, were exclusively for old boys from particular public schools and universities.[130]

Slightly beneath these elite institutions in rank were the various middle-class clubs that were present in cricket, pigeon-shooting, sailing, coursing and bowling. Some, such as Rochdale Cricket Club and Cheetham Hill Bowling Club, were comparatively socially accessible, and in response to an influx of members tightened their rules and increased membership fees. Rochdale CC illustrates the social latitude existing at certain clubs. Although they were an essentially middle-class organization, in 1833 they acted as patrons for an itinerant entertainer, behaviour scarcely conforming to accepted notions of 'respectability'.[131] Yet the vast bulk of clubs were socially segregated, a rare exception being the North of England Coursing Club, where the balloting was strict, but a prospective member's social status unimportant.[132]

By comparison with the earlier era, there were far more clubs from the lower orders, and as the period wore on, these increased, especially in cricket, a game that prospered among the working class. There were a wide variety of these, including mill workers, tradesmen, cabinet-makers, and even chimney sweeps, who played with brooms.[133] Though less dramatic, archery clubs enjoyed a growth in some areas, especially as cheap facilities became available in the increasing number of public and private parks.[134] Many rowing clubs were pub based and with a predominantly working-class membership.[135] The sporting activities of the lower orders were also regulated by social restrictions. Thus, London watermen refused to row in the same boat as their Oxford counterparts, to whom they felt superior, and the lower-working-class in Lancaster were excluded from many of the area's sports.[136]

Limitations on access   Restrictions on access to sporting clubs and events were pervasive and usually consisted of two types. Primarily, competitors had to belong to a particular geographic region. Second, they had to stem from a certain social rank. This remained largely the case despite the expansion of improved communications.[137] Many events at regattas and race-meetings were specifically for groups from particular areas.[138] Similarly, at cricket there were many disputes over the eligibility of particular players, especially whether professionals could represent county teams.[139] The sport where this was most prominent was wrestling, especially the Cumberland and Westmorland variety. Despite the fact that societies practising this form of wrestling were created nationally, entry was still restricted to those stemming from the two counties. In fact, disputes often occurred between the respective members from Cumberland and Westmorland, especially over the relative distribution of funds. More seriously, the quality of competitors was seriously weakened by the local imposition of a variety of arbitrary additional rules that were designed to limit access, sometimes targeted at specific individuals.[140] Generally, sporting events open to anyone seem to have been rare, notable exceptions being wrestling at Newcastle in 1841, and the Manchester and Salford Regatta of 1849, where many races were open to non-members.[141] More typical was Lancaster's Regatta, from which outsiders were often disqualified for either nebulous or non-existent reasons.[142]

Yet despite the socially impervious nature of clubs and events, a substantial amount of sporting activity embraced a range of different classes.[143] Throughout the period many top cricketers were from the middle class and above, including 20 out of the 40 best bowlers in 1850.[144] Gentlemen and aristocrats, such as Lords Fitzroy and Winchlesea, regularly competed with their social inferiors, and military teams were sometimes made up of a mixture of ranks.[145] Certain well bred sportsmen, notably Osbaldeston, were effectively professional athletes, devoting their talents to a range of activities.[146] Commentators were unanimous in declaring that such sporting interactions were harmful to the quality of the sport practised by the socially elite, especially the use of professional trainers at rowing, and bowlers at cricket. The latter practice meant that most 'gentlemen' were very weak bowlers.[147] The intrusion of gentleman-jockeys was a disaster for the previously socially select course at Heaton.[148] Similarly, the lack of a balloted club for pigeon-shooting undermined the sport, the intervention of outscouts, who, though not competitors, would take pot-shots at birds, reducing events to anarchy.[149]

The changing meaning of 'amateur'   Holt's contention that 'The term "professional" came into use in the 1850s and "amateur" in the 1880s' is mistaken.[150] While, as we have seen, 'amateur' and 'professional' were not mutually exclusive terms during the French wars, by 1830 this had changed, an article on rowing distinguishing amateurs from 'professors (for in the parlance of 1830 rowing for gain is considered as one of the professions – consequently a "waterman" is now held to be a professor)'.[151] By 1832, as Egan made clear, 'professional' had derogatory connotations.[152] As the first half of the nineteenth century progressed this feeling intensified. It appears to have been fostered by two separate attitudes. In the first place, as one competitor complained, a large portion of the population 'censoriously considers ... being engaged on a rowing match a sort of sin – as stamping him with the discredit of being a sporting character, and as taking him away improperly from his professional occupation. In cricket it is notorious that feigned names are constantly used'.[153]

In essence, participation in sport was often considered to be improper. Additionally, the upper and middle class were demanding more social segregation in recreation, in order to exclude the lower orders. This attitude fed through into sport, encouraging upper- and middle-class competitors to restrict their contact with the lower classes. Further justification for this was provided by the deleterious effect that professionals were perceived as having on sport. As we have seen, many in the upper ranks considered that the tuition that professionals provided harmed rather than improved their play. More seriously still, professionals were intimately associated with the corruption that was so prevalent in sport. Consequently, there was a pervasive feeling within upper- and middle-class sporting circles that there was a need for quarantine from the influence of professionals.[154]

The definition of 'professional' changed substantially from 1830. Whereas, as we have seen, during the French wars 'professional' simply referred to the level of expertise, from 1830 it stemmed basically from two factors: the social position of the individual, and earning money from sport. Accompanying this, was a redefinition of 'amateur'. During the French wars this had simply referred to the social rank of those classified as 'gentlemen', but after 1830 an additional criterion, the participation in sport for money, was included. More profoundly, 'amateur' and 'professional' were defined oppositionally. Thus, whereas previously, the two concepts had been mutually compatible, they became mutually exclusive.

The response of particular sports towards professionalism varied substantially. Although cricket was a game in which social distinctions were rigidly enforced, separate clubs existing for both 'gentlemen' and 'tradesmen', matches did occur between the different social orders, with the teams dining together afterwards. A notable exception to this was Oxford University, who, having played a match against the local residents, 'ordered a tent for the citizens to dine in by themselves, which they indignantly refused to do'.[155] Cricket accommodated professionals within its socially well-defined parameters by treating them as servants.[156] The use of professionals was widespread, one captain stating that there was 'scarcely a gentleman's match anywhere in which domestics are not included'.[157] Social distinctions within sailing were easy to make, bodies such as the Thames Yacht Club excluding all working boats, thus ensuring that fishing vessels were disqualified from races stipulating 'gentlemen' competitors.[158]

Whereas sailing had few disputes over eligibility, the other aquatics sport, rowing, was persistently enmired in such troubles. To an extent this was a surprise, as races involving both lower-class protagonists, watermen, and upper-class gentlemen, essentially overt amateur versus professional competitions, were common in the 1830s, occurring as late as 1843 in Oxford.[159] Similarly, professionals had often been engaged by many rowing clubs, and were used as trainers by public schools, the universities and such like.[160] The organization of the sport varied widely, according to both region and event.[161] Both clubs and races within regattas were often restricted to particular social groups, the criteria were complex and varied between regions. In 1846 *Bell's* stated:

> on the London river many of the most distinguished amateur clubs are engaged in trade, but of course, this does not include journeymen or mechanics, whose crews are generally called 'landsmen', to distinguish them from gentlemen amateurs and professional watermen.[162]

Two significant changes occurred in 1839. First, the written rules of the Henley Regatta imposed rigorous social criteria concerning the eligibility of competitors, excluding all those who were not from either the universities, public schools or officers.[163] Second, the concept of a 'respectable' individual deploying his physical or intellectual prowess for money, invited intense disapproval, as the following letter made clear:

> An English gentleman may stake his money on his yacht or his race-horse or any game in which chance is involved; and in such cases the stake may be necessary to excite an interest in the event, but will he habitually prostitute his own powers of body and mind for 'lucre' in public matches.[164]

The rules of the Oxford–Cambridge race of 1839 incorporated both concepts, eliminating the use of watermen as coxes, and the employment of stakes. As previously noted, races at many regattas had long been socially segregated, but the increasingly exacting nature of the new criteria caused many disputes, such as that at Lancaster in 1846, over the eligibility of competitors.[165] In fact, its application at certain major regattas, notably the Thames, meant that there were large social groups for whom there were no events.[166] Thus, the Thames Regatta instituted a Tradesmens Challenge Plate 'for that numerous respectable body, who may not be of the grade of gentlemen-amateurs, and are still removed from the status that would entitle them to be classed as landsmen'.[167] Yet such effects were marginal by comparison with the polarization caused by the redefinition of amateurism, whereby 'a man who rows against a waterman for a purse of money is ipso facto disqualified from contending in any amateur race'.[168] All those rowing for money were regarded as professionals and therefore excluded from all future amateur events.[169] Thus, whereas previously everyone had raced for money, competitors such as Bone, who wished to compete in separate races at the same event, one for money, the other for a cup, were forced to use assumed names or face exclusion from amateur contests.[170]

The creation and adoption of such an ethic represented a radical departure in rowing. Wigglesworth suggests that it was a product of two developments. First, many middle-class students left public schools imbued with the notion of the 'immutability of rank and social status', and thus excluded watermen. Second, this 'amateur ethic' was a response to 'the growth of an overtly professional class of oarsman'.[171] While this has a certain plausibility, for the decline in their trade increased the watermen's dependence upon competitive rowing, the most likely targets of such a rule were not the watermen, who rarely rowed against upper- and middle-class competitors, but semi-professionals. The impetus for this may well have stemmed from a far more commercially advanced sport, horse racing, to which we now turn.

As with many regattas, it was common for horse-race meetings to have a number of events in which entry was restricted to particular social categories, such as tradesmen, members of a fox-hunting club and suchlike. A substantial number of events, sometimes whole meetings, were restricted to jockeys who were 'gentlemen'. However, the sacrifices required to achieve a riding weight of eight and a half stone meant that few gentlemen were eligible jockeys.[172] Thus, though owners did occasionally ride their horses at events, many hired 'gentleman-jockeys' to ride on their behalf, especially after 1835 when Heaton, the last of the socially exclusive meetings, permitted them to be used.[173] The social qualifications of many gentleman-jockeys were extremely dubious, for they often assumed false titles.[174] This led to a variety of attempts to ensure the genuineness of their claims because it was felt that authentic gentlemen were demeaned by contact with such frauds.[175] Arriving at acceptable criteria was difficult; at the Croxton Park meeting of 1840 'even publicans and rough riders were allowed to enact the part of gentleman-jockeys'. In 1841 the course overcompensated for this, excluding many competitors.[176] Generally, throughout the country a mixture of social and ethical notions were employed. One definition demanded that gentleman-jockeys be either officers or those belonging to a recognized club in which membership involved balloting.[177] Alternatively, a gentleman competitor was 'one who has at no time received pay as a rider or remuneration, and who is not carrying on any business'.[178] Similar notions were advanced for steeplechasing, though there it was conceded that qualifications were more lax, and that the very provision of weight advantages for gentlemen encouraged fraud.[179]

By 1845 the cumulative effect of the endless disputes concerning gentleman-jockeys led one expert to declare:

> let us have gentlemen; let us have yeomen, plebeians, or the middle-classes: let us have jockeys, and servants; but let the line of demarcation between the grades not be done in faint lines, but in a good, honest, broad, black one. The higher grades would not then be compelled to treat the lower with an unbecoming hauteur from a fear of a too near approximation; nor the lower grades be perpetually struggling to attain that unattainable title 'gentleman'. By each adhering to his proper station, each would receive the proper respect due to that station.

If not, he thought it better to simply base events upon the weight of the horse.[180] This, it was felt, would end the opportunities for corruption. Given that at least part of the justification for having gentlemen riders was the notion that they would be 'impervious to fraud', the radical segregation advanced in many sports during the 1840s, separating 'amateurs' from those competing for money prizes, had a certain rationale.[181] Thus, although stakes, sometimes very substantial ones, had been used in many sports, including the boat race of 1829, their removal was widespread, involving working-class cricket teams as well.[182]

The most obvious explanation for the emergence of such bitter opposition to financial stakes was the impetus exerted by evangelical religious feeling, which peaked around this time.[183] Additionally, those in the middling ranks were beginning to define themselves differently in terms of the values they espoused, in response to the inroads of particular elements of the lower orders. This suggests the emergence of a more class-based society, in which whole groups belonging to a particular economic and social milieu adopted distinctive moral attitudes and behaviour. This accords, somewhat, with the work of Joyce, who maintained that the emergence of the English working class was a gradual process, becoming salient after 1860. Joyce regards class as being determined by a number of ingredients, which include both leisure and work.[184] The changing, and indeed hardening, of the definition of 'professional', could reflect a wider transformation within society, involving the gradual replacement of 'ranks' by 'class', and an attempt to impose new boundaries. During the French wars there appears to have been a far more relaxed attitude towards the social hierarchy, society consisting of a series of discrete, though unambiguous, ranks. The following description of the crowd at Egham Races is typical:

> The company was numerous, and consisted of Nobility and Gentry, the first class; of gentry of the second class; of Gentlemen farmers, a third; the sons and daughters of industry, viz middling tradesmen, inn-keepers and publicans, a fourth class; and fifth of servants and others in the humbler walks of life. NB The highest order of inn-keepers should be classed with the gentlemen farmers (three).[185]

By the 1830s, despite the club remaining the fundamental unit in British sport, the increase in the amount of activity resulted in wider social interaction. This blurred many of the distinctions in rank, promoting a new defensiveness concerning social position and a need to define this more aggressively. It may well be that the transformation in the meaning of the term 'amateur' from simply being a 'gentleman', to someone who does not compete for financial reward, reflected this.

Peripheral Groups

Nationality   Between 1816 and 1850 the sporting activity of blacks and Jews was centred upon pugilism, though 'men of colour', acting as publicans, sometimes organized dog-fights. Entertainment provision seems to have been the chief sector of black activity, as typified by the boxer Sutton, who also worked as a singer and dancer.[186] Boxing offered blacks a way of gaining respect, the fighter Robinson being praised for his sportsmanship.[187] Yet courage did not guarantee acceptance: despite losing after a brave display the badly injured Kendricks was unable to hire a coach home because he was black.[188]

The period witnessed an increasing tendency among the smaller nations within Britain to regard sport as a manifestation of their unique cultural identity, typified by a movement to revive the ancient Welsh games, that included both sport and bardism.[189] Naturally, given the invention of Highland tradition that was to culminate with the Celtic Society acting as George IV's bodyguard when he visited Edinburgh in 1822, it was the London-based Scots that were the keenest exponents of this, with various Highland clubs organizing events, to which those without kilts were excluded.[190] The Inverness Games were for the elite of Scottish society and mixed Ossian's poems with 'traditional' sport.[191] More authentically, golf and shinty clubs were established by Scots in England.[192]

By contrast with this, the Irish, despite their far richer cultural tradition, gained attention solely for pugilism, a sport they used as a way of displaying national identity. This became most salient at the funerals of major figures, such as the boxer Donnelly, which was attended by 80,000 people.[193] Fighters such as Langan, though based in Manchester, emphasized their Irishness, attracting backers who 'put down a good portion of the stakes "for the honour of ould Ireland" '.[194] More sinisterly, prize-fights that pitted Irishmen against either Welsh or English boxers stirred up violent passions, reports stating that one in Ireland had to be prevented because the authorities were convinced that if the Englishman were to win he would be killed by the mob.[195] Such animosity manifested itself among Irish-Americans, who persecuted the English fighter, Burke, preventing him from earning a living in America.[196]

Age and sex The sporting activity of those English people who were not adult males varied considerably, depending upon their social class, with working-class women enjoying far more activity than their middle-class counterparts, and the reverse for children. As a category, the elderly was largely non-existent, aside from a brief craze for pedestrian displays by those of both sexes in 1822.

Between 1816 and 1850 working-class women enjoyed a variety of sporting activity, including rowing races at seventeen venues, three foot races, sixteen pedestrian matches, at least four prize-fights, a curling match and eight cricket fixtures.[197] Additionally, some women organized dog-fights, and in certain areas they were able to pursue archery, in either pubs or parks.[198] Yet it would be mistaken to imagine that such activity was regarded as acceptable, for its principal appeal was salacious; even the comparatively liberal condemning women rowers as 'oars' and refusing to notice female pugilism.[199] However, some women did command respect, the deeds of the promethean rower, Mary Drake – nicknamed 'Scotch Moggy' – being recorded with great gusto. When she and Johnson lost a 'mixed doubles' race she attributed:

> her opponents' victory to the laziness of Johnson, and seizing one of the oars, aimed a blow at his head, but fortunately missed him. She then went to work at him with her fists, to the great amusement of the bystanders, till he begged for mercy. With some difficulty he was rescued from her herculean grip.[200]

The experience of middle-class women of such events was restricted to spectating, for their chief modes of exercise were gymnastics, archery, shooting and fox-hunting. The first two sports were generally regarded as 'healthy' ways of displaying the female figure.[201] Many women were accomplished archers, and in Shropshire 'the ladies were more admired for their skill in archery than the gentlemen'.[202] By 1850 county matches were occurring with teams incorporating both sexes.[203] As Brailsford observed, from the 1850s women's sport suffered a decline, the middle-class female ideal precluding such activity.[204] Yet the same period witnessed the emergence of greater female involvement in fox-hunting.[205]

Although receiving far more encouragement than women, sport among boys was barely organized. While a number of commentators espoused the virtuous examples presented by pugilism and athletics, such formal training as was offered, for instance the military exercises organized by Clius, was focused upon the sons of officers.[206] Junior sports for the lower orders were rarely organized, though occasional events occurred, notably in swimming.[207] Age restrictions were placed upon most events, and were enforced by regular consultation of the parish register.[208]

Many middle-class parents chose a practical education for their children, and emphasized leisure activities that facilitated this.[209] Yet some did attend public schools in which a more prominent role was given to sport. This rarely seems to have been due to a conscious volition of the tutors, though in many senses the tough environment espoused by 'muscular christians' in the period after 1850, was present long before this, due, largely, to adult indifference to the suffering of boys.[210] Many writers praised the virtues of allowing boys to regulate their own affairs by boxing, urging that it produced tough, 'manly' characters.[211] Fagging caused many scandals, notably that at Westminster in 1828, but was vigorously defended.[212] By contrast, masters displayed little interest in sport, and the notion that Thomas Arnold formulated an educational philosophy in which games inculculated moral virtues, has been thoroughly discredited.[213] Headmasters such as Butler, considered sport to be of some recreational value, adhering to a generally agreed notion that such activities could assist the task of keeping the boys within bounds, thus preventing them from causing mischief in the surrounding community.[214] The chief supporters of sport were parents, and the few organized events that did occur tended to be initiated by old boys.[215] It would be many years before certain activities, for example cricket at Eton, were organized adequately.[216] In the years before 1850 public school sport was largely informal, rarely interacting with either other public schools or outsiders.[217]

By comparison with the French wars there was far more use of sport by different nationalities within Britain to express their identity. However, with the notable exception of the Irish, such displays occurred within the confines of Britain, there being little anti-English sentiment. Women enjoyed far more activity than their descendants would do for many generations. It is surprising to note how little influence was exerted by the public schools, and the boys educated in them. While historians were to claim that they would effectively create modern sport, it is clear that in the first half of the nineteenth century at least, they were almost without external effect. The people who were vital to the creation and development of sport in the period between 1816 and 1850 were the professionals, the individuals to whom we next turn.

Careers

Getting noticed   In order to obtain commercial rewards from sport it was necessary to attract public attention by either a gimmick or a significant achievement. Although eccentricities, such as Lloyd's impersonations of a semaphore telegraph, gained temporary attention, real adulation, received by the rower Clasper, who was the subject of music-hall songs, came from expertise.[218] However, despite improvements in communications, there were very few sporting celebrities, perhaps only the boxers Cribb and Spring, and the American runner, Jackson.[219]

Dependence upon sport   Careers in sport consisted of four categories, namely: a temporary measure; seasonal; semi-professional; and professional.

In the 'temporary measure' category, unemployment and debt was the motivation for a number of pugilists, athletes (M'Mullen) and cricketers (Adams) pursuing sport for a living. Adams, for instance, was 'an Inn-keeper who found himself out of business'.[220] Often, individuals would use sport as a way of obtaining money and connections in order to establish themselves in business, as with Stone (single-stick) and Sutton (boxing). Sutton tried to use boxing to establish himself as a singer and dancer but this life undermined his marriage, eventually persuading him to try and earn a living as a wine merchant.[221] The decline of trades such as watermen led to their practitioners pursuing sport. This was ironic because the techniques involved in being a waterman tended to detract from an individual's capacity to race competitively.[222]

In the 'seasonal' category, professional cricketers were engaged for two or three summer months, the rest of the year being spent following another trade in which they were skilled, such as publican, hairdresser and tailor.[223] On occasions, as with Sampson, who was 'regularly engaged' by Durham, the player would abandon cricket because 'his business as a publican pressed heavily'.[224] Essentially, sportsmen were flexible, boxers such as Pixton working as brick-makers during the summer, when that trade was more profitable than pugilism.[225] Wrestlers also had established jobs for most of the year but during the season would tour the country competing for prizes, a successful athlete earning over £2 a week.[226]

By far the most common sporting career was that of the semi-professional (our third category), though the extent of their dependence upon sport varied significantly, and can be gradated into five groups. The least dependent upon sport were those such as Cann, who rarely played for money, or publicans like Boardman, whose sporting activity was essentially subsidiary to his business.[227] Just below this were many sporting publicans, typically the runner Hart, who used sport as a way of supplementing their income while they became established, but having done so virtually abandoned it because it was comparatively unprofitable.[228] The third group used sport as an ancillary, their main business consisting of commercial premises. These varied; the publican, Pixton, trained boxers, while Kendricks occasionally fought, though derived his more regular income from running a brothel.[229] There was a substantial difference between this group and the next sector, the members of which were largely dependent upon their sport, though pursuing a range of additional occupations. There were many of such people, the occasional occupations of the runner, Coates, including undertaking and acting.[230] The embodiment of semi-professionalism was Townsend. He ran some 500 pedestrian matches in his career but also worked as a waiter in sporting pubs and as a gaslighter.[231] The most dependent of all, were those whose occupation was principally their sport. Many cricketers were employed primarily as bowlers, though they had additional functions, acting as groundsman and valet.[232] Often, they would sell equipment. Some boxers and runners were based in pubs, and though they had jobs there, were principally employed for their sporting prowess.[233] The runner, Metcalf, was continually changing his occupation, and was effectively dependent upon sport. He, like the boxer Sharp, a higler (a seller of goods derived from poachers), was a semi-criminal.[234]

To a considerable extent the career of the semi-professional sportsman was a continuum, in which a single individual could encompass every gradation throughout his life. The example of the cricketer, Girling, is instructive. He was a hatter, who was hired by two Manchester-based clubs in 1845 to act as groundsman and bowler. By the following year he was earning additional money by selling cricket equipment from the Manchester Club's ground. Gradually he expanded his stock to include hats and became sufficiently independent to give up bowling. For a year or so, he continued working as the Club's groundsman, while he built up his hatting business. By 1849 he had entirely renounced cricket, and was selling hats from premises in the high street.[235]

The most obvious indications of professionalism were: an individual's willingness to migrate to compete in events, as with the Manchester runners Tallick and Greenhalgh, who journeyed to America;[236] to advertise for work, as a number of jockeys and cricketers did;[237] and to work through a career structure, an avenue open to fortunate jockeys.[238]

While sport was rarely an individual's sole means of livelihood over a long period, many had long careers, notably the pedestrian, Eaton, 1815 to 1846.[239] Our case study of Manchester provides a detailed insight into the extent of careers in three sports, namely foot racing, horse racing and pugilism. Some foot racers, notably Hart (15 years), Howarth (11 years) and Smith (11 years) had long careers, and as Table 8.3(a) shows, almost fifty runners were active for five or more years. Similarly, although data for jockeys active in Lancashire only commences in 1823, Lye (24 years), Templeman (24 years) and Whitehouse (19 years) were very active. Also, 49 jockeys had careers of five or more years (Table 8.3(b)). Due to the fact that Manchester-based fighters were often dormant for long periods – Davis, for instance, had eight fights between 1815 and 1836 – their careers are better assessed by their number of fights rather than the span of years. Jones had nineteen fights (1831–39), Massey eleven (1842–47), and ten fights for both Hall (1840–45) and Pixton (1827–39). Eleven boxers had five or more fights (Table 8.3(c)).

Table 8.3 Career length for four sports in Manchester, 1816–50

	(a) Foot racing			*(b) Horse racing*	
Years	Number	Percentage	Years	Number	Percentage
7	16	2.4	7	27	10.1
6	7	0.8	6	12	4.5
5	26	3.3	5	10	3.7
4	31	3.9	4	8	3.0
3	55	7.0	3	11	4.1
2	131	15.8	2	14	5.2
1	513	65.8	1	183	69.0
Total	779	100	Total	265	100

	(c) Pugilism			*(d) Cumulative*	
Years	Number	Percentage	Years	Number	Percentage
7	8	7.8	7	51	4.45
6	1	0.9	6	20	1.74
5	2	1.9	5	38	3.31
4	7	6.8	4	46	4.00
3	7	6.8	3	73	6.36
2	17	16.6	2	162	14.13
1	60	58.8	1	756	65.90
Total	102	100	Total	1146	100

Cumulatively, more than eleven hundred people in the Manchester area participated in the three organized sports, over one hundred of whom had careers lasting five or more years (Table 8.3(d)). These facts suggest that a substantial group of competitors were professionals/semi-professionals.

Earning a living from sport, 1816–50   There were several ways in which sportsmen could utilize their skills to earn a living, and these can, essentially, be accommodated into four categories: patronage; competitive sport; spectacle; and services.

Regarding the first category, patronage, in the early years after Waterloo patrons were of far less importance in most sports.[240] The improved marketing of skills provided sportsmen with more independence. However, by the 1840s costs had accelerated, especially in boxing, and greater emphasis was given to gate money. Sport had become far more of a business and many of those promoting it were not generous, extracting as much as they could in return for as little as possible. Thus, the patronage of generous, or at least honest, backers became important, if one was to avoid the fate of boxers such as Bostock, who won £25 and received just seven pounds and ten shillings.[241]

Generally, patronage declined, resulting in an expansion of efforts to establish formal, inclusive, charity funds, that were not dependent upon the largesse of an individual. There was a variety of such initiatives. In sports such as pugilism, resources were created for specific individual causes, such as subscriptions for a dead fighter's family or for the legal costs of a boxer in court.[242] More widespread acts of patronage were targeted at watermen, especially by steam boat companies, 'the directors consciously showing great anxiety to give [work to] those who have served their apprenticeship to the river, and whose avocation has been seriously injured since the introduction of steamers on the Thames'.[243] Efforts to supplement their income involved the provision of events in which they could be employed, such as those involving the Coronation Fleet and the Thames Regatta, as well as more overtly charitable donations, the creation of alms houses.[244] A contrary mode of approach was initiated in horse racing, when, in 1838, an insurance scheme designed to support contributing jockeys of 'unblemished character' and their families, was developed.[245] The idea spread and was eventually promoted by Lord Bentinck in 1846.[246] A similar scheme emerged in cricket, initially designed to assist retired players, but eventually focused upon all contributing members.[247] Disputes led to its demise in 1849.[248] Although still incipient, such schemes promised a greater independence for sportsmen. The only activity that rejected it was fox-hunting, where the old patterns of patronage were regarded as ensuring the care of hunt servants.[249]

Regarding the second category, competition was fundamental to sporting activity. The fame of every sportsman, no matter how much of a showman, stemmed ultimately from competitive achievement. Some pursued more than one sport, though aside from the multi-talented Osbaldeston, and some pugilists, this was rare.[250] Earnings from competition consisted of five elements: prizes, stakes, side-betting, gate money and collections. Large prizes were rarely in money, except in America, where the Manchester runner, Barlow, won $300.[251] The attainment of the title of 'champion' in boxing allowed the holder to possess valuable belts and cups, as well as dictating the size of the stakes involved in future 'championship bouts'.[252] These varied dramatically. During his tenure Carter insisted that they be small: Ward, as holder, demanded huge sums.[253]

As was shown previously, the amount staked and betted on events was often substantial, though obviously it was not always the competitor who reaped the bulk of the rewards, it being common for others to subscribe the sums. Some, such as the boxers Neal and Gaynor, provided their own stakes, thus becoming 'more independent'.[254] Despite this, the increased overheads in competitive sport ate into winnings and less public rewards, especially side-bets, grew in importance. In one sport, pedestrianism, this had always been vital, it being common for an athlete to accomplish a number of goals within an overall event for side-bets, such as travelling a certain distance within a stipulated period of time. Generally, their relative significance increased.[255] Thus, the runner Marlow received £600 for winning a race that had a £15 stake.[256] Inevitably, such covert transactions leant themselves to fraud.

Gate money had always been important, the venue of a prize-fight in 1817 being moved in order to ensure its supply, and by the 1840s immense sums were made.[257] Often, proprietors, instead of dividing the receipts fairly with the competitors, were greedy, 'thus making fraud inevitable'.[258] An important addition to competitors' finances during the French wars was the collection from the crowd after the event. This was usually performed by 'gentlemen' sportsmen, such as Barclay or Jackson, especially the latter.[259] Shortly after Waterloo this fell into decline, thus depriving deserving losers of rewards and therefore rendering corruption more likely.

Between 1816 and 1850 the marketing of sport as a commercial spectacle (our third category) intensified. As we have seen, such promotions were common during the French wars, and the structure of many of these persisted unchanged, notably the use of sporting animals at the theatre, or the presentation of prize-wherrys during performances of the play *The Waterman*.[260] However, it became increasingly common for sportsmen, especially established boxers – or those impersonating them – to tour the country, sparring in various theatres and pubs, and this improved presentational techniques.[261] Pugilistic displays became increasingly theatrical, often including scenes from dramas such as Egan's *Life in London*, a play which deliberately portrayed sport as spectacle.[262] Other, more minor figures, like the boxer Pixton, and cricketer, Girling, gradually accrued money and established a business.[263]

Not everyone was so fortunate. Mendoza and Scroggins died in wretched poverty. Many former boxers ended their years struggling to keep the ring clear or performing menial tasks in pubs, where they were 'stared at'.[264] To avoid such a fate, young boxers like M'Grath emigrated.[265] Bankruptcy afflicted many, including foot racers, jockeys, boxers and cricketers.[266] The last category included the greatest player of the day, Mynn, who at his peak was being paid £5 a match.[267] Sport was a very precarious career. An indication of this can be gleaned from the volatile life of the boxer, Massey. Despite winning £405 in stakes, he was variously robbed and rewarded by his backers, declared bankrupt, and then able to set up in business as a publican a few months later.[268] Unquestionably, a sportsman's relations with his backers was vital. Some, notably the cricketer, Hawkins, and the boxer, Baldwin, were destroyed by close contact with the rich, from whom they contracted expensive habits that were to destroy them financially when their careers floundered.[269] The proportion of winnings extracted by backers renders it difficult to assess the earnings of sportsmen. For instance, both the rowers Clasper and Coombes, won over £2,000 in their careers, but were never wealthy men, though they did attain financial security.[270] The same was true for the boxer, Perkins, who won £205. The runner, Hart, won £215 in his career but was virtually 'penniless'.[271] He used the fame and spotless reputation as a runner to promote his long-time publican business, actually obtaining a potentially lucrative licence to sell spirits.[272] Such an approach was an effective way to use sport.

Conclusions

During the French wars there was extensive participation in commercial sport by a wide range of groups in British society, especially the lower orders, ethnic minorities and women. While there was very little interaction between the various ranks, the most fundamental structure in sporting activity, the club, specifically excluding contact with outsiders, those competing in commercial sport faced few social restrictions. Consequently, sport was an area in which people from poor backgrounds could gain access to significant wealth. Evidence indicates that between 1793 and 1815 over two thousand individuals supplemented their income with earnings from competitive events. Of these, a hundred or so (at least 43 pugilists alone), were effectively what we would regard as professionals, depending almost entirely upon competitive sport for their livelihood.[273]

Between 1816 and 1850 the range of available commercial openings for professionals increased, reflecting the expansion of organized sport. During this period, in Manchester, for instance, a study of three major sports reveals that there were more than eleven hundred competitors, one hundred of whom appear to have been professionals. While it is true that we do not possess sources of remotely the same comprehensiveness for Manchester's sporting activity during the French wars, there is no hint of such enormous activity in the earlier period.

Although clubs remained largely segregated, on social and geographic lines, the increased number and range of events meant that far more interaction occurred. This was probably part of a general convergence throughout society, but from the 1840s it had a dramatic effect on sport. Whereas previously, most sporting events were held for stakes, the financial element came to be disapproved of, and stringent efforts were made to segregate 'amateurs', that is 'gentlemen', from those that competed for money, the 'professionals'. Hence, professionals were increasingly excluded from events, though the responses of the various sports differed. Thus, while the commercial expansion of sport was eroding the social distinctions that had always been present, the effect of this new attitude, which claimed moral justification, was to fossilise the existing structure and prevent contact.

It is interesting to observe that although this attitude was to later become closely linked with the role of the public schools, it long preceded their involvement. Such notions were to have a very stultifying effect on commercial sport. Not only did it remove many administrators, financiers and competitors from commercial sport, but these influential people actually opposed its existence.[274] An elaborate ideology of 'amateurism' was constructed, revolving around the correct moral conduct of participants in sport. Holt stated that the 'middle-class amateur ... had greater pretensions to being "civilized" ... claimed to put less of a price on victory than the working-class for whom victory was all important'.[275] He contrasted this with the working-class who 'imbued sport with a masculine value system of their own which differed markedly from the Christian ideal'.[276] It need hardly be said that a substantial amount of the adherence to the ideology of 'fair play' was purely rhetorical, there being an abundance of examples of poor sportsmanship by those belonging to public schools.[277] The comments of a wicket-keeper who had played in the major public school cricket matches for 28 years are instructive. Of batsmen, he stated that 'he knows well enough when he is out, and when he has been caught out an honourable man would accept the situation and not try to escape by an umpire's mistake. I am bound to say, though, that I have only known one batsman decline to profit from such a mistake'.[278] Yet despite this, the ideology of amateurism, a manichean division created by fusing morality and social class, effectively excluded professionals for some thirty years. Of course, even in the heyday of 'amateurism', the 1860s, exceptionally talented individuals such as W.G. Grace, who made a fortune from cricket, were not classed as 'professionals' because they had alternative, 'respectable', occupations.[279] But Grace was rare. More typical was 'athletics', the constituent sports of which were the same as 'pedestrianism', except that the latter was for 'professionals', 'athletics' being strictly 'amateur'.[280] As need hardly be said, today such polarizations have almost evaporated in every sport in Britain.

Notes

1 *Jackson's*, 13 June 1829.
2 W. Burn (1964) *The Age of Equipoise*, London: Allen and Unwin, p. 257. Cunningham, *Industrial Revolution*, p. 135. W. Woodgate (1888) *Boating*, London: Longman, p. 209.
3 Van Muyden, *Foreign View Of England*, p. 212.
4 Napea, *Letters from London*, pp. 241–2.
5 *BWM*, 29 Nov 1807. *SM*, Jan 1804, 172; Oct 1807, 8; Jan 1808, 208; Sept 1809, 291; Nov 1812, 85.
6 *SM*, April 1808, 45; July 1808, 193.
7 *BWM*, 26 April 1807, 2 Aug 1807, 11 Oct 1807.
8 *SM*, Sept 1808, 287.
9 *BWM*, 11 Oct 1807.
10 While watermen did act as coxes, there is little evidence of them 'rowing' with gentlemen during this period, contra Wigglesworth, *Rowing*, pp. 66, 186.
11 *SM*, May 1846, 316–18.
12 *SM*, Oct 1805, 47.
13 *SM*, Aug 1801, 268; June 1808, 147; Aug 1811, 233; Nov 1811, 89.
14 *SM*, April 1793, 59.
15 *Cheetham Hill Bowling Club Minutes Book* 1812 (in MRL). *SM*, May 1798, 73.
16 T. Chandler (1991) 'Games at Oxbridge and the Public Schools, 1830–1880: the diffusion of an innovation', *IJHS*, 8:2, 175.
17 Blaine, *Encyclopaedia*, pp. 586–8.
18 G. Buckley (1956) *More Historical Gleanings*, Manuscript, p. 55. Ford, *Cricket*, p. 47.
19 Ford, *Cricket*, p. 76.
20 *SM*, Nov 1809, 56.
21 *SM*, June 1807, 107.

22 *SM*, Aug 1803, 267.
23 Ford, *Prize-fighting*, pp. 149–50.
24 Burke, *Popular Culture*, p. 270.
25 *BWM*, 3 June 1804, 15 Sept 1811. Cottrell, 'Devil on two sticks', p. 266. *SM*, Oct 1803, 43; Feb 1809, 239–40; April 1811, 37; June 1814, 138; July 1814, 179.
26 While initially, in 1793, the nation was divided in its attitudes towards the war, by 1804 Britain was united against France. Emsley, *British Society and the French Wars*, pp. 19, 115–16.
27 Boyle, 'Game of cricket', 463.
28 B. Darwin (1935) *John Gully and his Time*, London: Cassell & Co., p. 217.
29 Bowen, *History of Cricket*, pp. 81–2.
30 F. Ashley-Cooper (1924) *The Hambledon Cricket Chronicle 1772–1796*, London, p. 97.
31 *SM*, Feb 1800, 262.
32 *SM*, Feb 1799, 298; Sept 1799, 4; Oct 1805, 47. *Times*, 7 Nov 1807.
33 Bovill, *Nimrod and Surtees*, p. 9. Napea, *Letters from London*, pp. 77–9. *SM*, Oct 1795, 163; Nov 1796, 92; Feb 1801, 240–41; July 1801, 194. Van Muyden, *Foreign View of England*, p. 181.
34 R. Porter (1982) *English Society in the Eighteenth Century*, London: Croom Helm, p. 29.
35 *SM*, Feb 1807, 238–41.
36 Thompson, *Making of English Working Class*, pp. 78–88.
37 R. Holt (1981) *Sport and Society in Modern France*, London: Macmillan, pp. 6, 7, 105. *SM*, Nov 1792, 69–71; Jan 1793, 194–7, 220–21; July 1795, 201; Oct 1797, 36; Oct 1798, 44–5; Sept 1799, 302–305; March 1803, 329–30; Aug 1808, 240.
38 Ford, *Cricket*, p. 109. *SM*, July 1800, 195; July 1811, 188.
39 Egan, *Boxiana*, i, p. 322.
40 *SM*, April 1813, 24–5.
41 *SM*, March 1811, 285.
42 *Bell's*, 3 Jan 1830. Egan, *Boxiana*, i, p. 448.
43 *BWM*, 5 June 1813. *SM*, Nov 1811, 90–91.
44 *BWM*, 21 April 1811, 29 Sept 1811.
45 Mahone, a black boxer born in Britain, was also a musician. *SM*, March 1811, 306.
46 F. Shyllon (1974), *Black Slaves in Britain*, Oxford: Oxford University Press, p. 230.
47 *SM*, June 1805, 156; July 1811, 190.
48 *SM*, June 1804, 253–4; May 1812, 51–4; Dec 1813, 143–4.
49 Colley, *Britons*, pp. 119, 123, 129, 140–41. J. Grainger (1986) *Patriotisms: Britain 1900–1939*, London: Macmillan, pp. 50–51.
50 *SM*, May 1813, 66.
51 *SM*, Nov 1792, 101; Feb 1797, 283; Aug 1809, 229; Aug 1812, 275; Sept 1812, 283; Aug 1813, 196; Sept 1814, 276.
52 *SM*, June 1813, 143.
53 *BWM*, 19 Oct 1806, 12 June 1808. *SM*, March 1804, 315; Nov 1807, 44.
54 Colley, *Britons*, pp. 167, 170.
55 *SM*, May 1802, 77; Oct 1808, 40; Aug 1809, 228; July 1810, 183–4.
56 *SM*, Jan 1811, 141–2.
57 *SM*, Nov 1808, 65.
58 *SM*, Feb 1809, 240.
59 *SM*, Feb 1809, 239–40.

60 *BWD*, 17 July 1803. Colley, *Britons*, p. 250. *SM*, July 1795, 221; Nov 1795, 106; Nov 1799, 65–6; May 1804, 107.

61 *BWM*, 12 Sept 1802, 16 Jan 1813. *SM*, July 1793, 245; July 1804, 210.

62 *BWM*, 3 July 1808. *MM*, 8 Nov 1808. *SM*, June 1794, 175; April 1795, 55; Aug 1795, 280; April 1799, 25–6; Aug 1799, 244–5; June 1802, 169; Sept 1806, 289; May 1811, 99; Aug 1811, 238; June 1815, 137.

63 *BWM*, 6 Oct 1811. *JJC*, Sports Box 4. *SM*, June 1796, 168. *Times*, 20 June 1793.

64 Van Muyden, *A Foreign View of England*, p. 277.

65 *BWM*, 18 Aug 1805, 21 June 1807, 13 Sept 1807. *SM*, Aug 1793, 316; June 1794, 175; Feb 1796, 276–7; Sept 1799, 321; Aug 1800, 234–5; Nov 1803, 96; May 1804, 107; Aug 1804, 272; June 1807, 150; July 1807, 200; Oct 1807, 42; Aug 1809, 244; Dec 1811, 139.

66 *SM*, Oct 1793, 50; Oct 1799, 46; Aug 1800, 235; May 1804, 171; Aug 1807, 209; June 1808, 145; July 1813, 195.

67 *BWM*, 22 May 1796. *SM*, June 1803, 168; Oct 1814, 60.

68 *SM*, June 1794, 154–5; Oct 1796, 6, 28; Dec 1796, 152–4; April 1799, 8; Oct 1799, 47; April 1803, 32–4, June 1803, 133–7; Dec 1803, 159; Oct 1804, 42; Jan 1813, 171; Oct 1815, 34. *Times*, 7 April 1795, 22 March 1799.

69 *SM*, Jan 1794, 199; Oct 1800, 33; Sept 1803, 321–3; Sept 1808, 288.

70 Van Muyden, *Foreign View of England*, p. 180. *SM*, Jan 1794, 189; Feb 1794, 289; June 1796, 145–6; Aug 1800, 234–5; Nov 1803, 96; May 1804, 107; Aug 1804, 278.

71 *SM*, Oct 1794, 41; Feb 1802, 247–8.

72 *SM*, Jan 1795, 208.

73 *SM*, Sept 1793, 368; July 1794, 282; Sept 1794, 294; Sept 1804, 282.

74 *SM*, April 1803, 13–14.

75 *SM*, March 1796, 238.

76 *Jackson's*, 1 Sept 1804. *SM*, Jan 1805, 170–71; Feb 1806, 223–4; March 1806, 298. *Times*, 24 Aug 1804, 11 Sept 1804.

77 *SM*, Sept 1804, 281–2; March 1806, 296–8.

78 *BWM*, 19 Aug 1804. *SM*, Sept 1804, 319–20. *WD*, 26 Aug 1804, 2 Sept 1804.

79 *SM*, Sept 1804, 281–2.

80 *BWM*, 16 Sept 1804. *Jackson's*, 24 Aug 1805. *SM*, Sept 1804, 284. *WD*, 16 Sept 1804.

81 *SM*, Sept 1804, 281–3; Oct 1804, 319–20. *Times*, 30 Aug 1804, 1 Sept 1804.

82 Brander, *Soho for the Colonel*, pp. 212–13. *SM*, Oct 1840, 451. The colonel gave her a yearly pension of £25.

83 Ford, *Cricket*, pp. 53–4. Strutt, *Sports and Pastimes*, p. 66. Vamplew, *Turf*, pp. 146, 149.

84 *The World*, 5 Jan 1790. Ridiculed in *SM*, Feb 1818, 226.

85 *SM*, April 1793, 48.

86 *SM*, Oct 1803, 6–7; Sept 1805, 294–5.

87 *SM*, Aug 1803, 231.

88 *MM*, 17 Oct 1815. Richardson, *Local Historian's*, iii, p. 124.

89 *SM*, Dec 1815, 138–9.

90 *SM*, Aug 1794, 283; June 1813, 139–40.

91 *BWM*, 6 Nov 1808. *SM*, Dec 1805, 129; June 1813, 142.

92 *SM*, Dec 1811, 118–20.

93 *SM*, Aug 1795, 279.

94 *SM*, Oct 1811, 20.

95 *BWM*, 16 Dec 1804. 22 Nov 1807. Ford, *Cricket*, p. 95. *SM*, March 1795, 331; April 1805, 45; Oct 1805, 46; Jan 1807, 205; Oct 1807, 8; Jan 1808, 208; July 1808, 193; Sept 1808, 287; Dec 1808, 141; Sept 1809, 291. *WD*, 8 July 1804.

96 *BWM*, 23 May 1802. *SM*, July 1814, 181.

97 *Bell's*, 3 Jan 1830. Egan, *Boxiana*, ii, 234–5.

98 Dyck, *William Cobbett*, p. 21.

99 *SM*, July 1815, 184–5.

100 *SM*, April 1808, 33; June 1812, 131; June 1813, 143.

101 *Jackson's*, 23 April 1796. *SM*, March 1797, 314–15. *The World*, 8 May 1789. The memoirs of 'Chevalier D'Eon' are 'purely apocryphal', *Once a Week*, 5 (1861), 585–8.

102 *BWM*, 17 Sept 1815.

103 Egan, *Boxiana*, i, pp. 471–82. *SM*, Feb 1793, 310; April 1793, 63; Sept 1794, 294; Nov 1798, 104.

104 *MM*, 17 Oct 1815.

105 *SM*, Feb 1808, 266.

106 *SM*, Oct 1802, 17; May 1810, 79.

107 *SM*, May 1812, 91; July 1815, 185–6.

108 *BWM*, 20 Dec 1807.

109 *SM*, Oct 1814, 42; Aug 1815, 236.

110 *SM*, April 1808, 33–4.

111 *SM*, June 1806, 146; Jan 1809, 203.

112 Egan, *Boxiana*, i, pp. 433, 438–9. *SM*, June 1805, 117. Taplin, *Sporting Dictionary*, i, p. 137.

113 *BWM*, 15 Oct 1809. *SM*, Jan 1813, 171.

114 Darwin, *Gully*, p. 33.

115 *SM*, Sept 1804, 282; Feb 1808, 265.

116 He evidently failed in this. Richardson, *Local Historian's*, iii, pp. 235–6.

117 Egan, *Boxiana*, i, 356. *SM*, April 1809, 44; Sept 1815, 246; Nov 1815, 91–2.

118 *SM*, Oct 1802, 4.

119 Darwin, *Gully*, p. 72.

120 *SM*, Oct 1811, 24. *WD*, 14 Oct 1804.

121 *SM*, June 1806, 142–3.

122 *SM*, April 1799, 8.

123 R. Morris, 'Clubs, societies and associations', in Thompson, *CSH*, iii, pp. 396–405, 411–12.

124 Vamplew, *Turf*, pp. 83–4.

125 *Annals*, Oct 1822, 228.

126 *SM*, July 1833, 233–4.

127 *Bell's*, 13 Feb 1831. *JJC*, Sports, Box 1.

128 *Bell's*, 22 Feb 1846.

129 *Bell's*, 13 Oct 1850. J. Lowerson and J. Myerscough (1977), *Time to Spare in Victorian England*, London: Harvester, p. 125. K. Sandiford (1982a) 'Cricket and the Victorians: A Historiographical Essay', *Historical Reflections*, 9:3, 431.

130 *Bell's*, 10 June 1832. Wigglesworth, *Rowing*, pp. 61, 122.

131 *Bell's*, 6 Jan 1828, 25 May 1828, 13 Oct 1850. G. Buckley (1956) *More Historical Gleanings*, Manuscript, p. 56. *Cheetham Hill Bowling Club Minutes Book*, 1821. J. Gilchrist (1910) *The Lancaster Cricket Club 1841–1909*, Lancaster, pp. 4–6. *WMC*, 9 Nov 1833, 21 March 1835.

132 H. Cox (1899) *Coursing And Falconry*, London: Longman, p. 196.

133 *Annals*, Oct 1827, 224. *Bell's*, 2 Sept 1827, 23 Sept 1827, 28 Oct 1838, 31 July 1842. Buckley, *Pre-Victorian Cricket*, p. 158. *SM*, Aug 1816, 244. Brooke Smith, *Growth And Development of Popular Entertainment*, p. 149.

134 *WMC*, 11 May 1839.

135 *Bell's*, 12 April 1840. J. Corbett (1907) *The River Irwell*, Manchester: Chetham, p. 101. Wigglesworth, *Rowing*, pp. 67, 160.

136 Speak, 'Social stratification', p. 60.

137 *Bell's*, 10 Jan 1841.

138 Vamplew, *Turf*, p. 25.

139 *Bell's*, 13 Oct 1839, 3 July 1842, 5 Sept 1847, 24 Oct 1847. *SM*, Nov 1846, 308.

140 *Bell's*, 24 Feb 1828, 21 May 1837, 11 Feb 1838, 11 April 1841, 26 May 1850.

141 *Bell's*, 24 Jan 1841, 29 July 1849.

142 *Bell's*, 19 Sept 1847.

143 *Annals*, Jan 1822, 66; Feb 1822, 135; May 1822, 346; June 1822, 421; July 1822, 59; Nov 1822, 327–8. *Bell's*, 28 Feb 1841. *SM*, March 1822, 302.

144 *Bell's*, 29 Oct 1848, 27 Oct 1850, 3 Nov 1850.

145 *Bell's*, 13 Sept 1840. Buckley, *Pre-Victorian Cricket*, p. 79. *WMC*, 27 July 1839.

146 *Bell's*, 4 Dec 1831.

147 *Bell's*, 15 June 1845. *SM*, March 1846, 175.

148 *SM*, May 1846, 316–17.

149 *Bell's*, 12 Nov 1843.

150 R. Holt, *Sport and the British*, p. 103.

151 *SM*, June 1831, 131.

152 Egan, *Book of Sports*, p. 370 n.

153 *Bell's*, 8 Aug 1841, 2 March 1845. Contra Shearman, *Athletics and Football*, p. 40.

154 *Bell's*, 3 Sept 1843.

155 *Bell's*, 3 Aug 1828, 8 May 1836, 17 June 1838.

156 Sandiford, 'Cricket and Victorian Society', 33.

157 *Bell's*, 6 Sept 1829.

158 *Bell's*, 22 Aug 1824, 5 April 1835, 3 May 1840.

159 *Bell's*, 2 Aug 1829, 20 June 1830, 11 July 1830, 26 Nov 1843.

160 Wigglesworth, *Rowing*, p. 63.

161 Ibid., 122.

162 *Bell's*, 12 July 1835, 11 Oct 1846.

163 *Bell's*, 19 May 1839. Halladay, *Rowing*, p. 45.

164 *Bell's*, 29 Sept 1839, 6 Oct 1839, 13 Oct 1839, 20 Oct 1839.

165 *Bell's*, 12 June 1842, 13 Aug 1843, 11 Oct 1846, 1 Nov 1846, 15 Nov 1846. Speak, 'Social stratification', pp. 49–50.

166 *Bell's*, 5 July 1846, 3 June 1849. Wigglesworth, *Rowing*, pp. 66, 76, 127–9.

167 *Bell's*, 11 May 1845.

168 *Bell's*, 21 July 1850.

169 *Bell's*, 4 Aug 1836, 30 June 1850.

170 *Bell's*, 9 Aug 1840, 21 June 1850. Halladay, *Rowing*, pp. 30, 47.

171 Wigglesworth, *Rowing*, pp. 54, 187.

172 *SM*, Feb 1838, 291. Vamplew, *Turf*, p. 161.

173 *SM*, Nov 1835, 2; May 1846, 316–17. *WD*, 19 Oct 1817.

174 *Bell's*, 27 May 1838.

175 *SM*, May 1839, 432.

176 *SM*, May 1841, 25.
177 *SM*, March 1838, 346; Sept 1839, 376.
178 *Bell's*, 28 June 1840, 9 Aug 1840. *SM*, Feb 1838, 292.
179 *Bell's*, 29 Jan 1837, 3 Jan 1847, 10 Jan 1847, 21 Feb 1847, 26 Nov 1848, 28 July 1850. *SM*, March 1837, 395.
180 *SM*, April 1845, 224–5.
181 *Bell's*, 3 March 1833. *SM*, Nov 1831, 33.
182 *Bell's*, 11 May 1845, 4 Oct 1846. Brailsford, *Sport, Time*, p. 115. Halladay, *Rowing*, p. 43. Wigglesworth, *Rowing*, pp. 45–6, 122.
183 Quinlan, *Victorian Prelude*, p. 103.
184 P. Joyce (1991) *Visions of the People*, Cambridge: Cambridge University Press, pp. 9, 11, 329.
185 *SM*, Dec 1812, 128.
186 *Bell's*, 28 July 1844.
187 *SM*, March 1816, 277.
188 *SM*, Jan 1822, 271.
189 *SM*, Dec 1833, 111. See also P. Morgan (1883) 'From a death to a view: the hunt for the Welsh past in the romantic period', in E. Hobsbawm and T. Ranger (eds) *The Invention of Tradition*, Cambridge: Cambridge University Press, pp. 54–92.
190 *Annals*, July 1822, 51. *Blackwoods*, xii (1822), 354–5. H. Trevor-Roper (1983) 'The Highland tradition in Scotland', in Hobsbawm and Ranger, *Invention of Tradition*, pp. 21–3, 26, 29–30.
191 *BWM*, 2 Sept 1821. *SM*, Oct 1821, 41–2.
192 *Annals*, Aug 1824, 72. *Bell's*, 23 May 1841. *SM*, Aug 1817, 243.
193 *WD*, 13 March 1820.
194 *Annals*, June 1824, 39. *Bell's*, 5 Oct 1823. *Exchange Herald*, 2 April 1824.
195 *Annals*, March 1826, 182. *SM*, Oct 1818, 120.
196 *Bell's*, 9 July 1825, 8 Oct 1825, 1 Jan 1837.
197 By contrast, there were only two events by Scottish women during this period; see N. Tranter (1994) 'Women and sport in nineteenth century Scotland', in G. Jarvie and G. Walker (eds), *Scottish Sport in the Making of the Nation: Ninety Minute Patriots*, Leicester: Leicester University Press, pp. 27–9.
198 Aspin, *Lancashire*, p. 102. Brailsford, *Sport, Time*, p. 137. *M&S*, 12 Sept 1846.
199 *Bell's*, 25 Aug 1833, 1 Sept 1833, 8 Oct 1843.
200 *Bell's*, 12 Sept 1830.
201 *NSM*, May 1831, 31.
202 *SM*, Aug 1821, 242–3.
203 *Annals*, Sept 1827, 108. *Bell's*, 15 Sept 1850.
204 Brailsford, *Sport, Time*, pp. 131–7. See also the essays by J. Hargreaves, K. McCrone in Mangan and Park, '*Fair Sex*'.
205 Bovill, *Nimrod and Surtees*, pp. 91–2.
206 *Annals*, June 1823, 420–21.
207 *Annals*, March 1827, 164. *Bell's*, 20 Aug 1837, 13 May 1838, 12 July 1840.
208 *Bell's*, 23 Feb 1834, 27 April 1834, 29 Aug 1847.
209 L. Davidoff (1990), 'The family in Britain', in Thompson, *CSH*, ii, p. 79. *WR*, xxxvii (1842), 109–110.
210 J. Mangan (1982) 'Social Darwinism and English upper class education', in *Proceedings of the British Society of Sport History*, Liverpool: Liverpool University Press, p. 11. Wright, 'Before Tom Brown', 14.

211 *Bell's*, 27 April 1834. *Eton College Magazine* (1834), 217.

212 P. Thompson (1829) 'The system of fagging', *WR*, 10, 244–8.

213 J. Honey (1977) *Tom Brown's Universe*, London: Millington, pp. 1–2. E. Mack (1938), *Public Schools and British Opinion 1780–1860*, London: Methuen, p. 337.

214 T. Chandler (1984) Origins of Athletic Games in the English Public School 1800–1880, Ph.D. Stanford, p. 48. *SM*, Nov 1829, 14. M. Tozer (1981) 'From muscular Christianity to "esprit de corps": games in the Victorian public schools of England', *Stadion*, 7:1, 118.

215 *Bell's*, 6 Nov 1842, 8 Nov 1846. T. Chandler (1988) 'Emergent athleticism: games in the English Public Schools 1800–1860', *IJHS*, 5:3, 325. Chandler, *Origins*, p.76. Mack, *British Opinion*, p. 223. Shearman, *Athletics and Football*, pp. 42, 47.

216 R. Lyttleton (1894) 'Eton cricket', *National Review*, 23, 425–6, 432.

217 Honey, *Tom Brown's*, pp. 239–40. Except for Westminster and Winchester, the archives of public schools lack information on sport previous to 1850.

218 *Annals*, Nov 1823, 352; March 1824, 213. *Bell's*, 4 April 1830, 13 Feb 1842. *BWD*, 6 May 1821. Egan, *Book of Sports*, p. 402n. Halladay, *Rowing*, p. 19.

219 *Bell's*, 20 July 1823, 1 Nov 1846.

220 *Bell's*, 16 March 1823, 8 June 1823, 5 Sept 1847.

221 *Bell's*, 5 March 1843, 28 July 1844.

222 *Bell's*, 22 Aug 1824, 21 Sept 1828, 23 April 1843, 21 May 1843.

223 *Bell's*, 21 May 1848. W. Mandle (1972) 'The professional cricketer in England in the nineteenth century', *Labour History*, 23, 45. *SM*, Jan 1839, 223; July 1845, 13; Oct 1846, 285; Nov 1846, 309.

224 *Bell's*, 13 July 1845.

225 *Bell's*, 1 Sept 1839.

226 *Annals*, Aug 1822, 119.

227 *Bell's*, 28 Sept 1834, 21 Jan 1849.

228 *Bell's*, 2 Jan 1831. Buckley, *More Gleanings*, p. 93.

229 *Bell's*, 18 Aug 1822, 7 March 1841.

230 *Bell's*, 8 Feb 1829.

231 *Bell's*, 30 Nov 1834, 14 May 1837.

232 *Bell's*, 7 May 1848.

233 *Bell's*, 16 Aug 1840, 27 April 1845.

234 *Bell's*, 26 Dec 1824, 10 Feb 1828, 21 Dec 1828, 18 Sept 1831.

235 *M&S*, 5 April 1845, 29 Aug 1846, 15 April 1848. *M.Ex*, 24 Feb 1849.

236 *Annals*, March 1827, 160. *Bell's*, 29 May 1836, 25 Aug 1844, 17 Nov 1844, 29 Dec 1844.

237 *Bell's*, 10 April 1842, 18 April 1847, 22 Aug 1847. *M&S*, 13 June 1846.

238 *Bell's*, 9 Feb 1845. *SM*, Sept 1831, 362, 364.

239 *Bell's*, 2 Aug 1846. *SM*, Jan 1816, 173–4; Dec 1816, 131–3.

240 Though it must be noted that at least one contemporary journalist thought differently. *WD*, 23 Aug 1818.

241 *Bell's*, 11 Sept 1831, 2 April 1848, 2 July 1848, 20 Aug 1848.

242 *Bell's*, 27 June 1830, 26 July 1840.

243 *Bell's*, 11 Sept 1842.

244 *Annals*, Oct 1823, 279. *Bell's*, 27 April 1830, 17 May 1840, 20 Aug 1843, 24 Dec 1848.

245 *Bell's*, 14 Feb 1841. *SM*, Feb 1838, 301–302.

246 *Bell's*, 7 June 1846.

247 *Bell's*, 3 May 1840, 10 May 1840, 25 April 1841, 5 Sept 1841, 17 May 1846. Vamplew, 'Not playing the game', 242–3.

248 *Bell's*, 29 Oct 1848, 3 Dec 1848, 6 May 1849.

249 *SM*, June 1822, 134; July 1822, 203.

250 *BWM*, 6 Sept 1818.

251 *Bell's*, 17 Nov 1844.

252 *Bell's*, 19 June 1831, 17 July 1831.

253 *WD*, 22 Nov 1818.

254 *Bell's*, 20 March 1831, 8 May 1831.

255 *SM*, June 1818, 148–9.

256 *Bell's*, 19 Sept 1830.

257 Egan, *Boxiana*, ii, pp. 413–14.

258 *Bell's*, 13 Oct 1844, 7 Jan 1849, 4 March 1849.

259 *SM*, Oct 1816, 23. *WD*, 19 Sept 1817, 10 May 1818, 30 Jan 1820.

260 *Bell's*, 15 Sept 1822.

261 *Annals*, Feb 1824, 97. *Bell's*, 4 April 1824. *SM*, Dec 1816, 148. *WD*, 23 April 1820.

262 *Bell's*, 28 Nov 1841.

263 *Bell's*, 1 Sept 1839, 10 Nov 1844. *M&S*, 24 Feb 1849.

264 *Annals*, May 1823, 339. *Bell's*, 22 June 1823, 8 May 1836, 11 Sept 1836, 6 Nov 1836. *SM*, Jan 1837, 275.

265 *Bell's*, 25 June 1848.

266 *Annals*, Feb 1823, 86–7.

267 *Annals*, Jan 1826, 59. *Bell's*, 30 Aug 1840. Mandle, 'Professional cricketer', 6. *SM*, Jan 1826, 166–7; Sept 1831, 363.

268 *Bell's*, 1 Nov 1840, 7 Jan 1844, 18 June 1848, 13 Aug 1848.

269 *Bell's*, 14 Aug 1831. *SM*, Oct 1846, 285.

270 Wigglesworth, *Rowing*, pp. 90–91.

271 *Bell's*, 5 Sept 1841, 19 Sept 1841.

272 *Bell's*, 6 Oct 1844.

273 Miles, *Pugilistica*, see vols 1 and 2.

274 A sense of the odium felt for the financial element in sport can be seen in Boyle, 'Game of cricket', 467–8, 478. M. Ensor (1898), 'The football madness', *Contemporary Review*, Nov, 757.

275 Holt, *Sport and the British*, p. 174.

276 Ibid., p. 173.

277 See for example, C. Andrews (1983) 'Patricians v Plebeians, 1883 cup final', *History Today*, 24. S. Gore (1894) 'Harrow Cricket', *National Review*, 23, 681. Honey, *Tom Brown's*, p. 215. Mangan, 'Social Darwinism and English upper class education', p. 11.

278 N. Lyttleton (1895) 'Some Eton and Harrow matches, 1858–1864', *National Review*, 25, 700.

279 Boyle, 'Game of cricket', 482.

280 Brailsford, *Sport, Time*, pp. 108, 110.

Epilogue

As we have seen, throughout the first half of the nineteenth century there had been a steady growth of an organized sporting culture, which had attained an increasing commercial sophistication. However, between 1851 and 1870 the culture fragmented. The increase in the amount of events and finance involved in sport outgrew the culture's capacity to supervise itself, leading to widespread corruption. This sullied the image of sport and eroded the unity that the culture had enjoyed. One consequence of this was a rejection of the commercial element in sport, crystallized by the changing meaning of 'amateur'. Previously, this had simply indicated social rank, and did not preclude playing for financial stakes. However, 'amateur' came to mean sport in which the commercial element was absent. This transformation of attitude culminated in 'amateur' sport segregating itself from the commercial sporting culture, thus depriving the latter of significant levels of expertise – administrative, legal, financial and competitive. It was this which impeded the evolution of the commercial sporting culture that had developed in the first half of the nineteenth century. Gradually, particularly in the years between 1870 and 1880, the culture reintegrated itself, with the socially influential 'amateur' element participating, both as competitors and administrators, in commercial sport. This modified the commercial culture, removing its more corrupt elements and transforming sport into a substantial nationally based leisure industry.

Appendix

Sources

A number of scholars contend that we have comparatively little material concerning the sporting activity of both the pre-industrial and early-industrial periods and that this probably leads us to significantly underestimate it.[1] This seems plausible when one considers the severe lack of archival sources from later in the period for two areas in which one would expect copious information, cricket clubs and sport in public schools.[2] Malcolmson maintained that 'in contrast to most historical studies ... no primary sources are conspicuously of central importance'. Thus, he adopted a catholic attitude towards sources, his 'research net' being 'widely cast'.[3] Yet this assumption is erroneous. While Malcolmson used National and County Records and local histories, he effectively ignored the most vital sources of all, namely the many periodicals and newspapers that specialized in recording sporting activity. Consequently, he was unaware of the plethora of sporting activity occurring throughout the period: a fact that substantially undermines the conclusions which his sources led him to; that there was a serious decline in sport and recreation between 1750 and 1850.

The current study is based upon a systematic examination of the various newspapers and periodicals that dealt with sport throughout this period. In addition, it utilizes other contemporary documents, such as local newspapers, periodical articles, autobiographies, novels, Parliamentary Papers, and various material pertaining to local and national government. One of the key advantages of the sporting newspaper *Bell's* is that it produced, verbatim, letters and reports from its readers. Additionally, *Bell's* policy of publishing letters critical of the information found in its columns provides a check upon its reliability. Like the *Sporting Magazine*, it admitted when its information was mistaken.[4] *Bell's* also provides us with an insight into the way the protagonists viewed themselves. In this sense, the information resembles that acquired by the anthropologist, for it is based upon an empathetic understanding of the culture. This forms the perfect counterweight to many of the official documents which were compiled by informers and outsiders. Attention has been devoted to the compilation of quantified data, by collecting references to sport throughout Britain in all the major sources during the French wars, and references relating to activity in Oxfordshire and Manchester in the principal sporting works between 1816 and 1850. The methodology here used is set out in Chapter 2.

The source material for this study can be broadly classified under four headings: private papers and collections; the press; official documents; and contemporary books.

Private Papers and Collections

This category consists of contemporary records, often in manuscript, by relevant institutions and individuals. Many of these are held in local libraries and collections.[5] With the exception of Rugby, who refused to help, every major public school that was active during this period responded to the author's requests for information. However, only Westminster and Winchester contain archives relevant to this period. Other supervisory bodies, such as the MCC, Jockey Club and FA, also provided assistance.

Essentially, these sources contain two types of information: minutiae, and details of private meetings. Among the minutiae are detailed membership lists, accounts books and suchlike, enabling the construction of a very detailed picture of the organization. Some records relate to internal meetings conducted by the club, and reveal the process by which rules were selected and amended. Collectively these two sorts of information provide a detailed internal account of the organization. Such data can often help to put the organization's role in perspective. For instance, given the paucity of internal records relating to sport in public school archives it is clear that the public schools have less obvious orientation towards sport than has generally been supposed.

The Press

Newspapers formed a very important component of the study, with both a large number and a wide variety being occasionally consulted. Extensive runs were examined of the following. National: *Bell's Life In London*, *Times*, *Weekly Dispatch*, *Weekly Messenger*. Local: *Exchange Herald*, *Manchester Examiner and Times*, *Manchester Herald*, *Manchester Mercury*, *Manchester and Salford Advertiser*, *Wheeler's Manchester Chronicle*, *Jackson's Oxford Journal*.

A second element of the press were sporting periodicals, large numbers of which were considered. Complete runs of the following were examined: *The Annals Of Sporting and Fancy Gazette*, *New Sporting Magazine*, *Racing Calendar*, *Sporting Kalendar*, *Sporting Magazine*. Various articles relating to sport often appeared in non-specialist journals. Fortunately, excellent collective indexes are available for these.[6]

Basically the press provided two types of material, information and opinion. Until the 1830s their general approach to these areas was uniform, though there were variations in the comprehensiveness of coverage. From the 1830s this uniformity collapsed, with various newspapers and periodicals mounting fierce attacks on particular activities, and ultimately ceasing to define them as sport, a subject that is discussed in Chapter 3.

By virtue of being public, and often subject to reply – though not always in the same organ – there are substantial advantages to the information contained in the press as compared to private sources, the latter's information not being subject to general challenge. On the other hand, the coverage of the press was only as good as the information they were provided with. Thus, for example, were it not for the existence of the archives of Sheffield Football Club, we would know nothing about their formation in 1857, for it was never mentioned in the contemporary press.

The richest source by far was *Bell's*, because it dealt with every sport far more comprehensively than its rivals. Additionally, its columns were often made up of letters from the protagonists themselves, which, especially after the introduction of the penny post in 1840, meant that they provided an excellent insight into the sporting culture of the lower orders. Given this, Holt's claim that it was local, rather than national newspapers, that provided the better insight into popular, especially working-class, culture, during the nineteenth century, appears doubtful.[7] The chief technical difficulty with newspapers is their lack of a useful index.

Official Documents

Material relevant to the regulation of sport appears in both local and national archives. This study was fortunate in utilizing the excellent index by Canon Oldfield relating to materials for Oxfordshire. National material was located in the Home Office series in the Public Record Office, as well as relevant editions of Parliamentary Papers, *Hansard* and its predecessors.

Official sources contain three different types of information: private letters from the public, private letters from officials, and evidence presented publicly. While this offers a range of opinion, in practice it was often of comparatively limited objective value. The aim of memorials from the public was to accomplish a particular goal, a fact which lent itself to exaggeration.[8] Similar accusations could be levelled against the appeals of officials for increased help.[9] Government select committees were often made up of like-minded individuals, and this ensured that much of the evidence that was presented supported views which the various members had long subscribed to, thus diluting its value, a subject that is dealt with in Chapter 5.[10]

Contemporary Books

A substantial number of texts, including novels, dealing with sport, appeared during the nineteenth century, many previous to 1850. Their use to historians varies considerably. Certain novels, notably those by Deale and Surtees, were the work of experienced sportsmen, and of considerable value. More commonly, sporting scenes were episodes in stories and often of limited interest to the historian. Additionally, judging by pugilism, a large number of chap-books were produced relating to sport.[11] Unfortunately these do not appear in the relevant collections held by the Bodleian and British Museum libraries.

Notes

1 Walton and Walvin, *Leisure in Britain*, pp. 3–4.
2 K. Sandiford (1982b), 'English cricket crowds', *IJHS*, 9:3, 5.
3 Malcolmson, *Popular Recreations*, p. 3.
4 See, for example, *Bell's*, 12 May 1822, 13 April 1828, 22 Nov 1835, 27 May 1849. *SM*, Sept 1816, 288; June 1818, 152. After 1823 *Bell's* ceased to provide even the most rudimentary index, thus rendering it a difficult source to use. R. Bowen recognized its value and observed that it was 'a largely unquarried source': *Cricket*, p. 89.
5 For a helpful guide see various works in R.W. Cox (1994) *History of Sport: A Guide to the Literature and Sources of Information*, Cheshire: Frodsham.
6 While the various periodicals and newspapers were essentially based in England, their coverage of Scottish material was extensive.
7 R. Holt (1990) *Sport and the Working Class in Britain*, Manchester: Manchester University Press, p. 2.
8 See this volume, p. 173.
9 In 1848 the government rejected requests from the mayor for military assistance against the street football at Derby because they believed, correctly, that he was exaggerating the problem; HO, 45, 1800.
10 See this volume, pp. 89–91.
11 There is an excellent bibliography for pugilism in, Brailsford, *Bareknuckles*, pp. 164–5.

Bibliography

Manuscript Sources

Bodleian Library, Oxford:
(1) John Johnson Collection
Collection of Chap-books
Sports (Boxes 1–16) and Large Folders (1–2)
(2) Harding Collection
Harding Murder Sheets II–III B 9 (262–83)
(3) *Police Reports (Proctors Records)* (1829–31, 1835–37, 1844)

British Library:
Windham Papers Addit MS 37931

Football Association (London):
FA Minute Books, 1863–74

Jockey Club (London):
Jockey Club Minute Books, 1836–71

Lancashire County Record Office (Preston):
Correspondence concerning sporting rights on the Grassyard Hall Estate,
    1790–1824. (DDGa 30/9)
Fulwood Racecourse Minute Books, 1790–1829 (DDX 103/4)
Haslingden, Crubden Coursing Company Rules, 1841 (DDX 118, 146, 5–12)
Letter prohibiting quoits on the Black Swans premises, 1840 (DDPr 130/21)
Orders of JP's to constables and overseers concerning playing at leaping, football
    and quoits on the Sabbath, 1727–1851 (DDNw 9/12)
Order of Suppression of games on Sundays, Fulwood, Preston 1801 (PR 2021)
Preston Union Hunt Subscription List, 1770 (DDX, 146)

Lancaster Reference Library:
Lancaster Rowing Club Minute Books, 1844–49

Manchester Chess Club Library:
Bryn, A. (1948) *A History Of Chess in Lancashire* (Unpublished, dated 1948)

Bryn, A. (1953) *A History Of The Manchester Chess Club* (Unpublished, dated 1953)

Manchester Reference Library:
Cheetham Hill Bowling Club Minute Books, 1812–32 (MS/797/9/M1)
Didsbury Archers and Hunters Accounts Book, 1792–93 (M62/1/2)
Didsbury Bowling Green, 1793–96 (M62/1/2)
Knutsford Races Ticket Sales, 1838 (C6/2)
The Mersey Archers (C 17/3/90/1)

Marylebone Cricket Club Library (Lords Cricket Ground, London):
Buckley, G.B. (1940) *The Scores of Cricket Matches* (Unpublished, 1940)
Buckley, G.B. (1942) *Cricket Notices* (Unpublished, 1942)
Buckley, G.B. (1954) *Historical Gleanings* (Unpublished, 1954)
Buckley, G.B. (1956) *More Historical Gleanings* (Unpublished, 1956)
Buckley, G.B. (1957) *An Index of Minor Matches in Cricket Scores and Biographies* (Unpublished, 1957)

Oxfordshire County Record Office:
Oxfordshire Quarter Sessions Rolls, 1687–1830
Prize-fighting: 'Pitched battle at Botley 1828' MOR LX/4

Public Record Office:
HO 41
HO 45
HO 52

Sheffield City Archives. 52 Shoreham Street, Sheffield, S1 4SP:
Football Club Records (FCR 1–5, 10–11)

Westminster School (London):
Town Boy Ledger, 1815–62

Printed Sources

Primary sources

Government Papers:
Bibliotheca Lindesiana. Handlist of Proclamations issued by royal and other constitutional authorities (London, 1893–1901)
A Bill to prevent bear baiting and other cruel practices, 4 March 1825

Act to prevent the malicious wounding and wanton cruelty to animals, 9 June 1809 (651)

An Act for the more effectual prevention of cruelty to animals, 19 July 1848

Bill for preventing the practice of bull-baiting and bull-running (1801–2 (70) I. 251)

Bill to alter applications of penalties for offenses against Highway Laws (1818)

Bill to consolidate and amend the several laws relating to cruel and improper treatment of Animals etc (1835, II (93). 27 March). Amended by Committee 5 June 1835 (107). Amended on recommitment 11 Aug 1835 (123)

Bills to amend Acts for the preservation of Public Highways as rules to notices of appeals against diverting public highways (1814–15)

Bills to amend Acts for preservation of Highways in England by authorising appointment of special surveyors (1816)

Bills to consolidate and amend laws relating to highways in England (1830–31) (1831)

Bill to consolidate and amend several laws relating to the cruel and improper treatment of animals and mischiefs arising from the driving of cattle, and to make other provisions in regard hereto, 18 April 1832

Bill to prevent cruel and improper treatment of cattle, 6 May 1825

Children's Employment Commission on Mines (PP 1842)

Hansard Parliamentary Debates:
xxix (1835) 14 July
cvi (1849) 13 June
Cruelty to Animals Prevention Bill, 9 May 1849
Report from the Select Committee on Gaming (PP vi, 1844)
Report of the Select Committee on Newspaper Stamps (PP. xvii (1) 1851, (558))
Report of the Select Committee on Public Walks and Places of Exercise (1833)
Statutes at Large From the 9th year of King George II to the 25th year of King George II

Newspapers and periodicals:
The Annals of the Sporting and Fancy Gazette (1822–28)
An Historical List of All Horse-Matches Run (1729, 1749)
Bell's Life in London (1822–50)
Bell's Weekly Dispatch (1796–1830)
Bell's Weekly Messenger (1796–1822)
Cobbett's Annual Register (1802)
Derby and Chesterfield Reporter (1845)
The Derby Mercury (1846)
The Exchange Herald (Manchester) (1820–26)
The Era (1838–50)
The Illustrated London News (1843, 1850)

Jackson's Oxford Journal (1793–1850)
Manchester and Salford Advertiser (1840–48)
Manchester Examiner and Times (1848–50)
Manchester Herald (1820–24)
The Manchester Mercury and Harrop's General Advertiser (1793–1811, 1815–19)
The Meteor (Rugby) (1876, 1880)
The New Rugbean (1860–61)
New Sporting Magazine (1831–45)
News of the World (1843, 1845)
Northern Star (1846)
Notes And Queries (1880–81, 1885, 1891, 1900, 1904, 1909, 1931). The periodical
has an excellent index.
Penny Magazine (1833, 1839)
Pierce Egan's Life in London (1824)
Poor Man's Guardian (1831–32)
The Racing Calendar (1793–1850)
Reynold's Weekly Newspaper (1850)
The Sporting Kalendar (1751–57)
The Sporting Magazine (1792–1850)
Sporting Review (1840)
Sportsman and Veterinary Journal (1835–37)
Sunday Times (1830, 1840)
Surrey Comet (1868)
Thacker's Courser's Annual (1842–50)
The Times (1793–1816, 1825, 1835, 1845, 1850)
Tom Spring's Life in London (1840–42). The paper was nothing to do with the
boxer Tom Spring.
The Weekly Dispatch (1801–04, 1814, 1817–22)
Wheeler's Manchester Chronicle (1812–14, 1826–39)
The World (1787–91)

Books:
Alcock, C. (1873) *The Football Annual*, London.
Alcock, C. (1874) *Football: Our Winter Game*, London: Field.
Alison, A. (1832) *Principles of the Common Law of Scotland*, Edinburgh: Cadell.
'An Amateur' (1852) *The Aquatic Oracle*, London: Simpkin, Marshall and Co.
Andrews, C.B. (1934) *The Torrington Diaries*, London: Methuen.
Andrews, W. (1891) *Old Church Lore*, Hull: Andrews and Co.
An Answer to Three Scurrilous Pamphlets Entitled The Jockey Club (1792) London.
Animadversions On A Late Publication Entitled The Jockey Club (1792) London.
'An Old Colleger' (1892) *Eton of Old*, London: Griffith.
Arbuthnot, A. (1910) *Memories of Rugby and India*, London: Allen and Unwin.
Arnold, T.D. (1851) *The 1st Day of the 6th Match*, Rugby.

Badcock, J. (1823) *Slang: A Dictionary*, London: T. Hughes.

Badcock, J. (1828) *A Living Picture of London*, London: T. Hughes.

Barton, B. (1874) *History of the Borough of Bury and Neighbourhood*, Bury: Wardleworth.

Bee, J. (alias J. Badcock) (1824) *Boxiana*, iv, London.

Bibliotheca Lindesiana, viii, *Handlist of Proclamations Issued By Royal and Other Constitutional Authorities*, London, 1893–1901.

Blaine, D. (1840) *An Encyclopaedia of Rural Sports*, London: Longman.

Borrow, G. (1851) *Lavengro*, i, London: John Murray.

Bourne, F. (1887) *English Newspapers*, ii, London: Chatto and Windus.

Brand, J. (1810) *Observations on Popular Antiquities*, Newcastle: J. Johnson.

Burn, R. (1869) *Justice of the Peace*, London: H. Miller.

Carlyle, T. (1843) *Past and Present*, London: Chapman Hall.

Chambers, R. (1888) *Book of Days*, Edinburgh: Chambers.

Cobbett, W. (1819) *The Parliamentary History of England From the Earliest Period to the Year 1803*, xxv, 1800–1802, London: Longman.

The Cock-fighter: A True History (1795).

Cox, H. (1899) *Coursing and Falconry*, London: Longman.

Craven (1839) *Walker's Many Exercises*, London: Orr and Co.

Deale (1828) *Life in the West; Or, The Curtain Drawn, by a Flat Enlightened*, London: Saunders and Otley.

Diary of Jacob Bee of Durham (1910) Surttees Soc, vol. 118.

Disraeli, B. (1844) *Coningsby*, London: Allen and Co.

Dowling, V. (1868) *Fistiana 1700–1852*, London.

Egan, P. (1812) *Boxiana*, i–iii, London: Smeeton.

Egan, P. (1832) *Pierce Egan's Book of Sports*, London.

Engels, F. (1844) *The Condition of the Working Class in England*, 1958 edition, London: Blackwell.

The Female Jockey Club (1792), London.

Fishwick, H. (1874) *The History of the Parish of Kirkham in the County of Lancaster*, Lancaster: Cheetham Soc.

Fishwick, H. (1889) *History of the Parish of Rochdale in the County of Lancaster*, Rochdale: Cheetham Soc.

Frost, T. (1874) *Old Showmen*, London.

Gaskell, Mrs (1847) *Mary Barton*, London.

Gaskell, Mrs (1857) *The Life Of Charlotte Bronte*, London.

Godfrey, Capt J. (1747) *A Treatise on the Useful Science of Self Defence*, London.

Hone, W. (1827a) *The Table Book*, London.

Hone, W. (1827b) *The Everyday Book*, London.

Hone, W. (1832) *The Year Book*, London.

Howitt, W. (1838) *Rural Life of England*, London.

Howitt, W. (1850) *The Country Year Book*, New York.

Iota (1858) *The Boat Racing Calendar 1835–1852*, London.

Jackson, N.L. (1899) *Association Football*, London: George Newnes.

Lawley, F. (1892) *Index of Engravings of the Sporting Magazine 1792–1870*, London.

Lawrence, A.J. (1881) *Rugby School Register 1675–1849*, London: J.S. Crossley.

Lawrence, A.J. (1897) *The Origins of Rugby Football*, Rugby: J.S. Crossley.

Lillywhite, A. (1863) *Cricket Scores and Biographies*, London: Longman. (This was actually written by A. Haygarth.)

Litt, W. (1823) *Wrestliana*, Whitehaven: R. Gibson.

Malthus, T. (1798) *First Essay on Population*, London.

Memoirs of the Life and Exploits of George Wilson, The Celebrated Pedestrian, Who walked 750 Miles in 15 Days, London.

The Minor Jockey Club, or, A Sketch of the Manners of the Greeks (1792) Bath: Farnham.

Moritz, C. (1797) *Travels Chiefly on Foot, Through Several Parts of England in 1782*, London.

Morley, H. (1859) *Memories of Bartholomew Fair*, London.

Napea, O. (1816) *Letters From London: Observations of a Russian During a Residence in England*, London: Hughes. (This was actually written by J. Badcock.)

New Statistical Account of Scotland (1845).

'Old Rugbaen' (1848) *Recollections of Rugby*, London. (This was actually written by C.H. Newmarch; see *Notes And Queries* (Jan/June 1909) 355.)

Parkyns, T. (1727) *The Inn-Play or Cornish-hugg Wrestling*, London.

Pigott, C. (1792a) *The Jockey Club; or a Sketch of the Manners of the Age* (parts 1,2,3), London.

Pigott, C. (1792b) *The Female Jockey Club*, London: D.L. Eaton.

Pigott, C. (1793) *Persecution: The Case of Charles Pigott Contained in the Defence He had Prepared*, London: D.L. Eaton.

Pigott, C. (1794) *The Whig Club, or a Sketch of the Manners of the Age*, London.

Pindar, P. (Pseud) (1815) *The Bench in an Uproar!! or Chop-Fallen Magistrate*, London.

Richardson, M. (1841–46) *Local Historian's Table Book*, London.

Shearman, M. (1889) *Athletics and Football*, London: Longman.

Sketchley, W. (1814) *The Cocker*, London.

Statistical Account of Scotland (1973), East Ardsley.

Statutes at Large: vi. From the 9th year of King George II to the 25th year of King George II, London.

Stokes, F. (ed.) (1765) *The Bletchley Diary of Reverent William Cole*, London: Constable and Co., 1931 edition.

Stonehenge (1856) *Manual of British Sports*, London: Routledge and Co.

Strutt, J. (1801) *The Sports and Pastimes of the People of England*, London: William Reeves.

Taplin, W. (1803) *Sporting Dictionary*, London.

Thacker's Courser's Annual Remembrancer and Stud Book 1850–1851, London.

Thom, W. (1813) *Pedestrianism*, Aberdeen.

Thorne, J. (1876) *Handbook for the Environs of London*, London.

Van Muyden (ed.) (1902) *A Foreign View of England in the Reign of George I and George II: The Letters of Monsieur César De Saussure to his Family*, London: John Murray.

Wade, J. (1835) *The Black Book, Or Corruption Unmasked*, London: Effingham Wilton.

Walker, D. (1836) *Exercises For Ladies; Cultivated to Improve and Preserve Beauty*, London.

Walker, D. (1840) *Defence Exercises*, London: Orr and Co.

The Whig Club, or a Sketch of the Manners of the Age (1794) London.

Whyte, J. (1840) *History of the British Turf*, London.

Wilson, G. (1815) *Sketch of the Life of George Wilson the Black heath Pedestrian: Who Undertook to Walk 1,000 Miles in 20 Days, Written by Himself*, London.

Wilson, J.M. (1869) *Imperial Gazetteer of England and Wales*, Edinburgh.

Woodgate, W. (1888) *Boating*, London: Longman.

Articles:

Abell, H. (1898) 'Is cricket degenerating?', *National Review*, 31.

A.G.G. (1867) 'A big side at Rugby', *London Society*, 12.

Alcock, C. (1890) 'Association football', *English Illustrated Magazine*, 8.

'A football match' (1890) *All the Year Round*, 66 (Jan/June 1890).

'Are we an athletic people?' (1897), *New Review*, 16.

Boyle, C. (1884) 'The game of cricket', *QR*, 158.

Boyle, C. (1889) 'Gambling', *QR*, 168.

C(artwright), J.D. (1864) 'Football at Rugby, Eton and Harrow', *London Society*, 5.

Chambers Information for the People, 84 (1842), 544.

'Chevalier D'Eon' (1861) *Once a Week*, 5.

Collins, W. Lucas (1861) 'School and college life: its romance and reality', *Blackwoods*, 89.

Collins, W. Lucas (1866) 'Our amusements', *Blackwoods*, 100.

'Cricket, as it was and is' (1863) *Once a Week*, 8.

'Cricket legislation' (1864) *London Society*, 6.

'Doncaster: its spirits and saturnalia' (1846) *Bentley's Miscellany*, 20.

Doxey, J. (1868) 'Wirksworth football play', *The Reliquary*, 9.

Dutt, M. (1899) 'The last camping match', *Badminton Magazine*, 9.

Ellington, H. (1887) 'Athletes of past and present', *Nineteenth Century and After*, 21.

Ensor, M. (1898) 'The football madness', *Contemporary Review*.

'English gaming houses' (1829) *WR*, 11.

Eton College Magazine (1832), 7.

'Football' (1864) *Chambers Journal.*

Ford, T. (1857) 'Tom Brown's schooldays', *Quarterly Review*, 102.

'Games' (1864) *Chambers Journal.*

Gore, S. (1894) 'Harrow cricket', *National Review*, 23.

Gosse, E. (1878) 'Captain Dover's Cotswolds Games', *Cornhill Magazine*, 37.

Graham, R. (1899) 'The early history of the F.A.', *Badminton Magazine of Sports and Pastimes*, 8.

Hazlitt, W. (1822) 'The fight', *The New Monthly Magazine*, 4.

Hutchinson, H. (1893) 'Evolution of games at ball', *Blackwoods*, 153.

Jesse, E. (1854) 'History of cricket', *Bentley's Miscellany*, 36.

Kebbel, T. (1886) 'The English love of sport', *Fortnightly Review*, 39.

Lyttleton, A. (1899) 'Cricket reform', *National Review*, 34.

Lyttleton, N.G. (1895) 'Some Eton and Harrow matches 1858–1864', *National Review*, 25.

Lyttleton, R.H. (1894) 'Eton cricket', *National Review*, 23.

Macgregor, R. (1878) 'Old football gossip', *Belgravia*, 34.

Macgregor, R. (1880) 'Cricketana', *Belgravia*, 42.

Maxwell, H. (1892) 'Games', *Blackwoods*, 152.

North, C. (1826) 'Gymnastics', *Blackwoods*, 21.

'On fighting: By a young gentleman of the fancy' (1820) *London Magazine*, i.

Paget, J. (1883) 'Recreation', *Nineteenth Century*, 14.

'Popular customs and superstitions in Herefordshire' (1822) *Gentleman's Magazine*, 92.

'Professionals in English sport' (1888) *Saturday Review*, 14 April.

Pycroft, J. (1876) 'Fifty years a cricketer', *London Society*, 30.

'Reminiscences of a cricketer' (1865) *London Society*, 8.

'Review of Tom Brown's Schooldays' (1857) *Saturday Review*, 3 Oct.

Smith, S. (1808) 'On the Society for the Suppression of Vice', *Edinburgh Review*, 13.

Stephens, F. (1858) 'Review of Tom Brown's Schooldays', *Edinburgh Review*, 107.

Thompson, P. (1829) 'The system of fagging', *WR*, 10.

'Trial of Fraser v Berkeley and another, Dec 3 1836' (1837) *Fraser's Magazine*, 15.

'The wall game' (1883) *Saturday Review*, 56, 1 Dec.

Secondary Sources

Books:

Altick, R. (1957) *The English Common Reader*, Chicago: University of Chicago Press.

Anderson, M. (1990) 'Social implications of demographic change', in F.M.L. Thompson (ed.) *The Cambridge Social History of Britain 1750–1950*, ii, Cambridge: Cambridge University Press.

Armstrong, W.A. (1990) 'The Countryside', in F.M.L. Thompson (ed.) *The Cambridge Social History of Britain 1750–1950*, i, Cambridge: Cambridge University Press.

Ashley-Cooper, F. (1924) *The Hambledon Cricket Chronicle 1772–1796*, London: Herbert Jenkins.

Aspin, C. (1969) *Lancashire: The First Industrial Society*, Preston: Helmshaw.

Bailey, P. (1978) *Leisure and Class in Victorian England*, London: Routledge.

Bale, J. (1982) *Sport and Place*, London: Hurst.

Best, G. (1971) *Mid-Victorian Britain 1851–1875*, London: Weidenfeld.

Birley, D. (1988) 'Bonoparte and the Squire: chauvinism, virility and sport in the period of the French wars', in J. Mangan (ed.) *Pleasure, Profit and Proselytism: British Culture and Sport at Home and Abroad 1700–1914*, London: Frank Cass.

Birley, D. (1993) *Sport and the Making of Britain*, Manchester: Manchester University Press.

Black, J. (1985) *The British and the Grand Tour*, London: Stroud.

Black, J. (1987) *The English Press in the Eighteenth Century*, London: Croom Helm.

Borsay, P. (1989) *The English Urban Renaissance*, Oxford: Clarendon.

Bovill, E. (1959) *The England of Nimrod and Surtees 1815–1854*, Oxford: Oxford University Press.

Bovill, E. (1962) *English Country Life 1780–1830*, Oxford: Oxford University Press.

Bowen, R. (1970) *Cricket: A History of its Growth and Development Throughout the World*, London: Eyre and Spottiswoode.

Brailsford, D. (1988) *Bareknuckles*, Cambridge: Lutterworth.

Brailsford, D. (1991) *Sport, Time and Society: The British at Play*, London: Routledge.

Brailsford, D. (1999) *A Taste for Diversions: Sport in Georgian England*, Cambridge: Lutterworth.

Brander, M. (1961) *Soho for the Colonel*, London: Geoffrey Bles.

Briggs, A. (1972) *Victorian People 1851–1867*, Chicago: Chicago University Press.

Buckley, G.B. (1935) *Fresh Light on Eighteenth Century Cricket*, Birmingham: Cotterell and Co.

Buckley, G.B. (1937) *Fresh Light on Pre-Victorian Cricket 1709–1837*, Birmingham: Cotterell and Co.

Burke, P. (1978) *Popular Culture in Early Modern Europe*, London: Temple Smith.

Burn, W. (1964) *The Age of Equipoise*, London: Allen and Unwin.

Carr, R. (1976) *English Fox-hunting*, London: Weidenfeld.

Cashman, R. and McKernan, M. (eds) (1979) *Sport in History*, Queensland: New South Wales Press.

Cashman, R. and McKernan, M. (eds) (1980) *Sport, Money, Morality and the Media*, Queensland: New South Wales Press.

Cattin, J. (1900) *The Real Football*, London.

Chesney, K. (1970) *The Victorian Underworld*, London: Temple Smith.

Chinn, C. (1991) *Better Betting with a Decent Feller*, London: Harvester Wheatsheaf.

Clapham, J. (1934) 'Work and wages', in G.M. Young (ed.) *Early Victorian England*, i, Oxford: Oxford University Press.

Clapham, J. and Clapham, M. (1934) 'Life in the new towns', in G.M. Young (ed.) *Early Victorian England*, i, Oxford: Oxford University Press.

Clapson, M. (1992) *Popular Gambling and English Society 1823–1961*, Manchester: Manchester University Press.

Clarke, J. and Critcher, C. (1985) *The Devil Makes Work*, Chicago: University of Chicago Press.

Colley, L. (1992) *Britons: Forging the Nation 1707–1837*, London: New Haven.

Corbett, J. (1907) *The River Irwell*, Manchester: Chetham.

Corfield, P. (1982) *The Impact of English Towns 1700–1800*, Oxford: Oxford University Press.

Cottrell, S. (1989) 'The devil on two sticks: Francophobia in 1803', in R. Samuel (ed.) *Patriotism: The Making and Unmaking of British National Identity*, i, London: Routledge.

Cox, R.W. (ed.) (1994) *History of Sport: A Guide to the Literature and Sources of Information*, Cheshire: Frodsham.

Cranfield, G. (1978) *The Press and Society*, London: Longman.

Cunningham, H. (1980a) *Leisure in the Industrial Revolution 1780–1880*, London: Croom Helm.

Cunningham, H. (1980b) 'Leisure and culture', in F.M.L. Thompson (ed.) *The Cambridge Social and Economic History of Britain 1750–1950*, ii, Cambridge: Cambridge University Press.

Cunningham, H. (1987) 'The Metropolitan fairs: a case study in the social control of leisure', in A. Donajgrodzki (ed.) *Social Control in Nineteenth Century Britain*, London: Croom Helm.

Cunningham, H. (1989) 'The language of patriotism', in R. Samuel (ed.) *Patriotism: The Making and Unmaking of British National Identity*, i, London: Routledge.

Dale, T. (1901) *The Eighth Duke of Beaufort and the Badminton Hunt*, London: Constable and Co.

Darkwell, C. (1983) *Studies in the Social History of Sport*, London.

Darwin, B. (1934) 'Sport', in G.M. Young (ed.) *Early Victorian England*, i, Oxford: Oxford University Press.

Darwin, B. (1935) *John Gully and his Time*, London: Cassell and Co.

Daunton, M. (1990) 'Housing', in F.M.L. Thompson (ed.) *The Cambridge Social History of Britain 1750–1950*, ii, Cambridge: Cambridge University Press.

Davidoff, L. (1990) 'The family in Britain', in F.M.L. Thompson (ed.) *The Cambridge Social History of Britain 1750–1950*, ii, Cambridge: Cambridge University Press.

Delves, B. (1981) 'Popular recreation and social conflict in Derby 1800–1850', in E. Yeo and S. Yeo (eds) *Popular Culture and Class Conflict 1790–1914*, London: Harvester.

De Waal, A. (1964) *The Discovery of Britain: The English Tourist 1540–1840*, London: Routledge.

Donajdrozki, A. (1977a) 'Social police and the bureaucratic elite: a vision order in an age of reform', in A. Donajdrozki (ed.) *Social Control in Nineteenth Century Britain*, London: Croom Helm.

Donajdrozki, A. (ed.) (1977b) *Social Control in Nineteenth Century Britain*, London: Croom Helm.

Dunning, E. and Sheard, K. (1979) *Barbarians, Gentlemen and Players*, London: Martin Robertson.

Dyck, I. (1992) *William Cobbett and Rural Popular Culture*, Cambridge: Cambridge University Press.

Eastwood, D. (1994) *Governing Rural England*, Oxford: Oxford University Press.

Emsley, C. (1979) *British Society and the French Wars 1793–1815*, London: Macmillan.

Emsley, C. (1987) *Crime and Society in England 1750–1900*, London: Longman.

Fabian, A. and Green, G. (1960) *Association Football*, i, London: Caxton.

Fletcher, S. (1987) 'The making and breaking of a female tradition: women's physical education in England 1880–1980', in J. Mangan and R. Park (eds) *From 'Fair Sex' to Feminism*, London: Frank Cass.

Ford, J. (1971) *Prize-fighting*, Newton Abbot: David and Charles.

Ford, J. (1972) *Cricket: A Social History 1700–1835*, Newton Abbot: David and Charles.

Ford, J. (1988) *Ackermann*, London: Ackermann.

Garside, P. (1990) 'London and the Home Counties', in F.M.L. Thompson (ed.) *The Cambridge Social History of Britain 1750–1950*, i, Cambridge: Cambridge University Press.

Gash, N. (1983) *Robert Surtees and Early Victorian Society*, Oxford: Clarendon.

Gibson, A. and Pickford, W. (1906) *Association Football and the Men Who Made It*, London: Caxton.

Gilchrist, J. (1910) *The Lancaster Cricket Club 1841–1909*, Lancaster.

Girouard, M. (1981) *The Return to Camelot: Chivalry and the English Gentleman*, London: New Haven.

Golby, J. and Purdue, A. (1984) *The Civilization of the Crowd: Popular Culture in England 1750–1900*, London: Batsford.

Grafton, C. and Taylor, P. (1991) *Government and the Economics of Sport*, London: Macmillan.

Grainger, J. (1986) *Patriotisms: Britain 1900–1939*, London: Macmillan.

Gray, D.J. (1982) 'Early Victorian Scandalous Journalism: Renton Nicholson's *The Town 1837–1842*', in J. Shattock and M. Wolff (eds) *The Victorian Periodical Press: Samplings and Soundings*, Leicester: Leicester University Press.

Halladay, E. (1990) *Rowing in England: A Social History*, Manchester: Manchester University Press.

Hammond, J. and Hammond, B. (1930) *The Age of the Chartists 1832–1854*, London: Longman.

Hargreaves, J. (1987) 'Victorian familism and the formative years of female sport', in J. Mangan and R. Park (eds) *From 'Fair Sex' to Feminism*, London: Frank Cass.

Harrison, B. (1971) *Drink and the Victorians*, London; Faber and Faber.

Harrison, B. and Trinder, B. (1969) *Drink and Sobriety in an Early Victorian Country Town: Banbury 1830–1860*, London: EHR.

Harrison, J.F.C. (1971) *The Early Victorians 1832–1851*, London: Weidenfeld.

Harrison, M. (1988) *Crowds and History: Mass Phenomena in English Towns, 1790–1835*, Cambridge: Cambridge University Press.

Harvie, C. (1989) 'Scott and the image of Scotland', in R. Samuel (ed.) *Patriotism: The Making and Unmaking of British National Identity*, ii, London: Routledge.

Hellmuth, F. (ed.) (1990) *The Transformation of Political Culture*, Oxford: Oxford University Press.

Hine, R. (1929) *The History of Hitchin*, London: Allen and Unwin.

Hobsbawm, E. and Ranger, T. (eds) (1968) *The Invention of Tradition*, Cambridge: Cambridge University Press.

Hollis, P. (1970) *The Pauper Press*, Oxford: Oxford University Press.

Holt, R. (1981) *Sport and Society in Modern France*, London: Macmillan.

Holt, R. (1989) *Sport and the British: A Modern History*, Oxford: Clarendon.

Holt, R. (1990) *Sport and the Working Class in Britain*, Manchester: Manchester University Press.

Honey, J. (1977) *Tom Brown's Universe*, London: Millington.

Howell, D. and Barber, C. (1990) 'Wales', in F.M.L. Thompson (ed.) *The Cambridge Social History of Britain*, i, Cambridge: Cambridge University Press.

Howkins, A. (1981) 'The taming of Whitsun: the changing face of a nineteenth century rural holiday', in E. Yeo and S. Yeo (eds) *Popular Culture and Class Conflict 1790–1914*, London: Harvester.

HPT (1924) *Old Time Cricket*, Nottingham.

Hutchinson, G. (1934) *The Heythrop Hunt*, London: John Murray.

Innes, J. (1990) 'Politics and morals', in F. Hellmuth (ed.) *The Transformation of Political Culture*, Oxford: Oxford University Press.

Jackson, N. (1932) *Sporting Days and Sporting Ways*, London: Hurst and Blackett.

Jarvie, G. and Walker, G. (eds) (1994) *Scottish Sport in the Making of the Nation: Ninety Minute Patriots*, Leicester: Leicester University Press.

Johnson, R. (1977) 'Educating the educators: "Experts" and the state 1833–1839', in A. Donajgrodzki (ed.) *Social Control in Nineteenth Century Britain*, London: Croom Helm.

Joyce, P. (1990) 'Work', in F.M.L. Thompson (ed.), *The Cambridge Social History of Britain 1750–1950*, ii, Cambridge: Cambridge University Press.

Joyce, P. (1991) *Visions of the People*, Cambridge: Cambridge University Press.

Judd, M. (1983) 'Popular culture and the London fairs', in J. Walton and J. Walvin (eds) *Leisure in Britain*, Manchester: Manchester University Press.

Kiernan, V. (1988) *The Duel in European History*, Oxford: Oxford University Press.

Koss, S. (1981) *The Rise and Fall of the Political Press in Britain*, London: Hamilton.

Langford, P. (1989) *A Polite and Commercial People: England 1727–1783*, Oxford: Oxford University Press.

L(eigh), R. A(usten) (1902) *Upon St Andrews Day 1841–1901*, Eton.

Longrigg, R. (1977) *The English Squire and his Sport*, London: Joseph.

Lowerson, J. (1982) 'English middle class sports', in *Aspects of the Social History of Sport: Proceedings of the British Society of Sport History*, Liverpool: Liverpool University Press.

Lowerson, J. and Myerscough, J. (1977) *Time to Spare in Victorian England*, London: Harvester.

Lyte, H.C. Maxwell (1911) *A History of Eton College*, London: Eton.

Mack, E. (1938) *Public Schools and British Opinion 1780–1860*, London: Methuen.

Magoun, F. (1938) *History of Football*, Bochum-Langendreer.

Maguire, J. (1986) 'Conceptual and methodological confusion in the analysis of nineteenth century leisure – the case for Historical Sociology', in J. Mangan and R. Small (eds) *Sport, Culture, Society*, Glasgow.

Malcolmson, R. (1973) *Popular Recreations in English Society 1700–1850*, Cambridge: Cambridge University Press.

Malcolmson, R. (1981) *Life and Labour in England 1700–1780*, London: Hutchinsons.

Mangan, J. (1981) *Athleticism in the Victorian and Edwardian Public School*, Cambridge: Cambridge University Press.

Mangan, J. (1982) 'Social Darwinism and English upper class education', in *Aspects of the Social History of Sport: Proceedings of British Society of Sport History*, Liverpool: Liverpool University Press.

Mangan, J. (ed.) (1988) *Pleasure, Profit and Proselytism: British Culture and Sport at Home and Abroad 1700–1914*, London: Frank Cass.

Mangan, J. and Park, R. (eds) (1987) *From 'Fair sex' to Feminism*, London: Frank Cass.

Mangan, J. and Small, R. (eds) (1986) *Sport, Culture, Society*, Glasgow.

Marples, M. (1954) *A History of Football*, London: Secker and Warburg.

Mason, A. (1980) *Association Football and English Society 1863–1915*, London: Harvester.

Mason, A. (1988) *Sport in Britain*, London: Faber and Faber.

Mason, A. (1994) 'Sport', in J. Dan Vann and R.T. Van Ardsel (eds) *Victorian Periodicals and Victorian Society*, Toronto: Modern Languages Assn.

McCalman, I. (1988) *Radical Underworld*, Cambridge: Cambridge University Press.

McCrone, K. (1987) 'Play up! Play up! and play the game: sport at the late Victorian girls' public school', in J. Mangan and R. Park (eds) *From 'Fair sex' to Feminism*, London: Frank Cass.

McIntosh, P. (1982) 'The history of sport and other disciplines', in *Aspects of the Social History of Nineteenth Century Sport: Proceedings of the British Society of Sport History*, Liverpool: Liverpool University Press.

McKendrick, N., Brewer, J. and Plumb, J.H. (1982) *The Birth of a Consumer Society: The Commercialization of Eighteenth Century England*, London: Hutchinson.

Metcalfe, A. (1990) 'Potshare bowling in the mining communities of East Northumberland 1800–1914', in R. Holt (ed.), *Sport and the Working Class in Britain*, Manchester: Manchester University Press.

Miles, H.D. (1906) *Pugilistica*, Edinburgh: Weldon and Co.

Mitchell, B. (1988) *British Historical Statistics*, Cambridge: Cambridge University Press.

Mitchison, R. (1990) 'Scotland', in F.M.L. Thompson (ed.) *The Cambridge Social History of Britain*, i, Cambridge: Cambridge University Press.

Moir, E. (1964) *The Discovery of Britain: The English Tourist 1540–1840*, London: Routledge.

Morgan, P. (1983) 'From a death to a view: the hunt for the Welsh past in the romantic period', in E. Hobsbawm and T. Ranger (eds) *The Invention of Tradition*, Cambridge: Cambridge University Press.

Morris, R. (1990) 'Clubs, societies and associations', in F.M.L. Thompson (ed.) *The Cambridge Social History of Britain*, iii, Cambridge: Cambridge University Press.

Morrison, S. (1932) *The English Newspaper*, Cambridge: Cambridge University Press.

Morsley, C. (1979) *News from the English Countryside*, London: Harrap.

Mort, F. (1987) *Dangerous Sexualities: Medico-Moral Politics in England since 1830*, London: Routledge.

Munsche, P. (1981) *Gentlemen and Poachers: The English Game Laws 1671–1831*, Cambridge: Cambridge University Press.

Murray, D. (1927) *Memories of the Old College of Glasgow*, Glasgow.

Neuberg, V. (1971) *Popular Education in Eighteenth Century England*, London: Fontana.

Newman, G. (1987) *The Rise of English Nationalism: A Cultural History 1740–1830*, London: Weidenfeld.

O'Brien, P. (1993) 'Political preconditions for the industrial revolution', in P. O'Brien and R. Quinault (eds) *The Industrial Revolution and British Society*, Cambridge: Cambridge University Press.

O'Brien, P. and Quinault, R. (eds) (1993) *The Industrial Revolution and British Society*, Cambridge: Cambridge University Press.

Oddy, D. (1990) 'Food, drink and nutrition', in F.M.L. Thompson (ed.) *The Cambridge Social History of Britain 1750–1950*, ii, Cambridge: Cambridge University Press.

Oldham, J.B. (1952) *A History of Shrewsbury School*, Oxford: Wilding and Son.

Park, R. (1987) 'Sport, gender and society – a transatlantic Victorian perspective', in J. Mangan and R. Park (eds) *From 'Fair Sex' to Feminism*, London: Frank Cass.

Perkin, H. (1969) *The Origins of Modern English Society*, London: Routledge.

Phillips, R. (1925) *The Story of Scottish Rugby*, Edinburgh: Foulis.

Phillips, S. Kendall (1980) 'Primitive Methodist confrontation with popular sports', in R. Cashman and M. McKernan (eds) *Sport, Money, Morality and the Media*, Queensland: New South Wales.

Poole, R. (1983) 'Oldham wakes', in J. Walton and J. Walvin (eds) *Leisure in Britain*, Manchester: Manchester University Press.

Poole, R. and Walton, J. (1982) 'The Lancashire wakes in the nineteenth century', in R. Storch (ed.) *Popular Culture and Custom in Nineteenth Century England*, Manchester: Manchester University Press.

Porter, R. (1982) *English Society in the Eighteenth Century*, London: Croom Helm.

Quinlan, M. (1941) *Victorian Prelude: A History of English Manners 1700–1830*, New York.

Redfern, A. (1983) 'Crewe: leisure in a railway town', in J. Walton and J. Walvin (eds) *Leisure in Britain*, Manchester: Manchester University Press.

Redford, A. (1940) *History of Local Government in Manchester*, London: Longman.

Reid, D.A. (1982) 'Interpreting the festival calendar: wakes and fairs as carnivals', in R. Storch (ed.) *Popular Culture and Custom in Nineteenth Century England*, London: Croom Helm.

Reid, D.A. (1990) 'Beasts and brutes: popular blood sports', in R. Holt (ed.) *Sport and the Working Class in Britain*, Manchester: Manchester University Press.

Reid, J.C. (1971) *Bucks and Bruisers: Pierce Egan and Regency England*, London: Routledge.

Rogers, P. (1974) *The Augustan Vision*, London: Weidenfeld.

Rowe, D.J. (1990) 'North East', in F.M.L. Thompson (ed.), *The Cambridge Social History of England*, i, Cambridge: Cambridge University Press.

Rule, J. (1982) 'Methodism, popular beliefs and village culture in Cornwall 1800–1850', in R. Storch (ed.) *Popular Culture and Custom in Nineteenth Century England*, London: Croom Helm.

Sambrook, J. (1986) *The Eighteenth Century: The Intellectual and Cultural Context of English Literature 1700–1789*, London: Longman.

Samuel, R. (ed.) (1989) *Patriotism: The Making and Unmaking of British National Identity*, London: Routledge.

Shattock, J. and Wolff, M. (eds) (1982) *The Victorian Periodical Press: Samplings and Soundings*, Leicester: Leicester University Press.

Shearman, M. (ed.) (1904) *Football*, London: Oakley and Co.

Shyllon, F. (1974) *Black Slaves in Britain*, Oxford: Oxford University Press.

Smith, S. (1980) *The Other Nation*, Oxford: Oxford University Press.

Solly, G. (1933) *The Rugby School Register*, Rugby: George Over.

Speak, M. (1988) 'Social stratification and participation in sport', in J. Mangan (ed.) *Pleasure, Profit and Proselytism: British Culture and Sport at Home and Abroad 1700–1914*, London: Frank Cass.

Speck, W.A. (1983) *Society and Literature in England 1700–1760*, London: Macmillan.

Spufford, M. (1981) *Small Books and Pleasant Histories*, London: Methuen.

Stevenson, J. (1977a) 'Social control and the prevention of riots in England 1789–1829', in A. Donajgrodzki (ed.) *Social Control in Nineteenth Century Britain*, London: Croom Helm.

Stevenson, J. (1977b) 'The Queen Caroline Affair', in J. Stevenson (ed.) *London in the Age of Reform*, Oxford: Oxford University Press.

Stevenson, J. (ed.) (1977c) *London in the Age of Reform*, Oxford: Blackwell.

Stevenson, J. (1993) 'Social aspects of the Industrial Revolution', in P. O'Brien and R. Quinault (eds) *The Industrial Revolution and British Society*, Cambridge: Cambridge University Press.

Storch, R. (1977) 'The problem of working-class leisure: some roots of middle-class moral reform in the industrial north; 1825–1850', in A. Donajgrodzki (ed.) *Social Control in Nineteenth Century Britain*, London: Croom Helm.

Storch, R. (1980) ' "Please to remember the 5th of November": conflict, solidarity and public order in southern England 1815–1900', in R. Storch (ed.) *Popular Culture and Custom in Nineteenth Century England*, London: Croom Helm.

Storch, R. (1982a) 'Persistence and change in nineteenth century popular culture', in R. Storch (ed.) *Popular Culture and Custom in Nineteenth Century England*, London: Croom Helm.

Storch, R. (ed.) (1982b) *Popular Culture and Custom in Nineteenth Century England*, London: Croom Helm.

Surel, J. (1989) 'John Bull', in R. Samuel (ed.) *Patriotism: The Making and Unmaking of British National Identity*, iii, London: Routledge.

Thomas, K. (1983) *Man and the Natural World*, London: Allen Lane.

Thompson, D. (1971) *The Early Chartists*, London: Routledge.

Thompson, E.P. (1970) *The Making of the English Working Class*, London: Victor Gollancz.

Thompson, E.P. (1991) *Customs in Common*, London: Merlin.

Thompson, F.M.L. (1963) *English Landed Society in the Nineteenth Century*, London: Routledge.

Thompson, F.M.L. (ed.) (1990a) *The Cambridge Social History of Britain 1750–1950*, Cambridge: Cambridge University Press.

Thompson, F.M.L. (1990b) 'The town and the city', in F.M.L. Thompson (ed.), *The Cambridge Social History of Britain 1750–1950*, Cambridge: Cambridge University Press.

Tischler, S. (1981) *Footballers and Businessmen: The Origins of Professional Football in England*, London: Holmes and Meier.

Tranter, N. (1990) 'Organised sport and the working class of central Scotland, 1820–1900: the regulated sport of quoiting', in R. Holt (ed.) *Sport and the Working Class in Britain*, Manchester: Manchester University Press.

Tranter, N. (1994) 'Women and sport in nineteenth century Scotland', in G. Jarvie and G. Walker (eds) *Scottish Sport in the Making of the Nation: Ninety Minute Patriots*, Leicester: Leicester University Press.

Trescatheric, B. (1983) *Sport and Leisure in Victorian Barrow*, Barrow: Hougenai.

Trevor-Roper, H. (1983) 'The Highland tradition in Scotland', in E. Hobsbawm and T. Ranger (eds) *The Invention of Tradition*, Cambridge: Cambridge University Press.

Vamplew, W. (1976) *The Turf: A Social and Economic History of Horse Racing*, London: Allen Lane.

Vamplew, W. (1979) 'The sport of kings and commoners: the commercialisation of British horse racing in the nineteenth century', in R. Cashman and M. McKernan (eds) *Sport in History*, Queensland: New South Wales Press.

Vamplew, W. (1980) 'Playing for pay: the earnings of professional sportsmen in England 1870–1914', in R. Cashman and M. McKernan (eds) *Sport, Money, Morality and the Media*, Queensland: New South Wales Press.

Vamplew, W. (1988a) *Pay up and Play the Game: Professional Sport In Britain 1875–1914*, Cambridge: Cambridge University Press.

Vamplew, W. (1988b) 'Sport and industrialisation: an economic interpretation of the changes in popular sport in nineteenth century England', in J. Mangan (ed.) *Pleasure, Profit and Proselytism: British Culture and Sport at Home and Abroad 1700–1914*, London: Frank Cass.

Vann, J. Dann and Ardsel, R.T. Van (1978) *Victorian Periodicals: A Guide to Researchers*, New York: Heffer and Sons.

Vann, J. Dan and Ardsel, R.T. Van (1994) *Victorian Periodicals and Victorian Society*, Toronto: University of Toronto Press.

Vincent, D. (1981) *Bread, Knowledge and Freedom: A Study of Nineteenth Century Working Class Autobiography*, London: Methuen.

Vincent, D. (1982) 'The decline of the oral tradition in popular culture', in R. Storch (ed.) *Culture and Custom in Nineteenth Century England*, London: Croom Helm.

Vincent, D. (1989) *Literacy and Popular Culture: England 1750–1914*, Cambridge: Cambridge University Press.

Walton, J. (1990) 'North West', in F.M.L. Thompson (ed.), *The Cambridge Social History of Britain 1750–1950*, i, Cambridge: Cambridge University Press.

Walton, J. and Poole, R. (1982) 'The Lancashire Wakes in the nineteenth century', in R. Storch (ed.) *Culture and Custom in Nineteenth Century England*, London: Croom Helm.

Walton, J. and Walvin, J. (1983) *Leisure in Britain*, Manchester: Manchester University Press.

Walvin, J. (1975) *The People's Game*, London: Allen Lane.

Walvin, J. (1978) *Leisure and Society 1830–1950*, London: Longman.

Welcome, J. (1982) *The Sporting World of Surtees*, Oxford: Oxford University Press.

White, R. (1963) *Life in Regency England*, London: Putnam.

Wiener, J. (1978) 'Circulation and the stamp tax', in J. Dan Vann and R.T. Van Ardsel (eds) *Victorian Periodicals: A Guide to Researchers*, New York: Heffer and Sons.

Wigglesworth, N. (1992) *The Social History of English Rowing*, London: Frank Cass.

Williams, R. (1992) *The Long Revolution*, London: Longman.

Wright, A.R. (1940) *British Calendar Customs in England*, London: William Glasher.

Wright, J. (ed.) (1902) *The English Dialect Dictionary*, London: Henry Frowde.

Wrigley, E. (ed.) (1972) *Nineteenth Century Society*, Cambridge: Cambridge University Press.

Wrigley, E. and Schofield, R. (1981) *The Population History of England 1541–1871*, Cambridge: Cambridge University Press.

Yeo, E. and Yeo, S. (1981) *Popular Culture and Class Conflict*, London: Harvester.

Young, G.M. (ed.) (1934a) *Early Victorian England*, Oxford: Oxford University Press.

Young, G.M. (1934b) 'Portrait of an age', in G.M. Young (ed.) *Early Victorian England*, ii, Oxford: Oxford University Press.

Young, P.M. (1962) *Football in Sheffield*, London: Stanley Paul.

Young, P.M. (1968) *A History Of British Football*, London: Stanley Paul.

Articles:

Anderson, R. (1987) 'Sport in the Scottish universities', *IJHS*, 4:2.

Andrews, C. (1983) 'Patricians v Plebeians, 1883 cup final', *History Today*, 24.

Arnold, T. (1902) 'A talk with J.J. Bentley', *Windsor Magazine*, 15 (Dec 1901/May 1902)

Aspinall, A. (1948) 'Statistical accounts of the London newspaper in the eighteenth century', *English Historical Review*, 80 (April).

Bailey, P. (1977) 'A mingled mass of perfectly legitimate pleasures: the Victorian middle-class and the problem of leisure', *Victorian Studies*, 21.

Baker, W. (1979) 'The making of a working class football culture in Victorian England', *JSH*, 13:2.

Bale, J. (1981) 'Cricket in pre-Victorian England and Wales', *Area*, 13:2.

Botham, F. and Hunt, E. (1987) 'Wages in the Industrial Revolution', *EcHR*, 40, 2nd Ser.

Brailsford, D. (1982) 'Sporting days in eighteenth century England', *IJHS*, 9:3.

Brailsford, D. (1984) 'Religion and sport in eighteenth century England', *IJHS*, 1:2.

Chandler, T. (1988) 'Emergent athleticism: games in the English Public Schools 1800–1860', *IJHS*, 5:3.

Chandler, T. (1991) 'Games at Oxbridge and the Public Schools, 1830–1880: the diffusion of an innovation', *IJHS*, 8:2.

Crafts, N. (1983) 'British economic growth, 1700–1831: A review of the evidence', *EcHR*, 36:2.

Devon and Cornwall Notes and Queries, 10 (1918–19), 113–14.

Eastwood, D. (1994) 'Men, morals and the machinery of Parliamentary legislation, 1790–1840', *Parliamentary History*, 13:2.

Ford, W. (1903) 'The waste of time at cricket', *National Review*, 41 (Aug).

Harrison, B. (1967) 'Religion and recreation in nineteenth century England', *Past and Present*, 38.

Harrison, B. (1973) 'Animals and the state in nineteenth century England', *English Historical Review*, 88.

Harvey, A. (1999) 'Uncovering football's missing link: the real story of the evolution of modern football', *European Sports History Review*, 1.

Hopkins, E. (1982) 'Working hours and conditions during the Industrial Revolution: A reappraisal', *EcHR*, 35:1.

Kellet, M. (1994) 'The power of princely patronage: pigeon shooting in Victorian Britain', *IJHS*, 11:1.

Lindert, P. and Williamson, J. (1983) 'English workers living standards during the Industrial Revolution: A new look', *EcHR*, 36:1. (This was replied to by M. Flinn (1984), *EcHR*, 37:1, accompanied by a rejoinder from Lindert and Williamson.)

Lowerson, J. (1984) 'Sport and the Victorian Sunday: the beginnings of middle-class apostasy', *IJHS*, 1:2.

Maguire, J. (1986) 'Images of manliness and competing ways of living in late Victorian and Edwardian Britain', *IJHS*, 3:3.

Malcolmson, R. (1984) 'Sport in society: A historical perspective', *IJHS*, 1:1.

Mandle, W. (1972) 'The professional cricketer in England in the nineteenth century', *Labour History*, 23.

Mandle, W. (1973) 'Games people played – cricket and football in England and Victoria in the late nineteenth century', *Historical Studies*, 15.

Mandle, W. (1981) 'W.G. Grace as a Victorian hero', *Historical Studies*, 19.

Mason, A. (1988) 'Football and the historians', *IJHS*, 5:1.

Reid, D. (1988) 'Folk football, the aristocracy and cultural change: A critique of Dunning and Sheard', *IJHS*, 5:2.

Reid, D.A. (1976) 'The decline of Saint Monday 1766–1876', *Past and Present*, 71.

Roberts, M. (1983) 'The Society For The Suppression of Vice and its early critics 1802–1812', *Historical Journal*, 26.

'Rugby football in the sixties', *Cornhill Magazine* (Nov 1922).

Russell, D. (1988) 'Sporadic and curious: the emergence of rugby and soccer zones in Yorkshire and Lancashire 1860–1914', *IJHS*, 5:2.

Sandiford, K. (1982a) 'Cricket and the Victorians: A historiographical essay', *Historical Reflections*, 9:3.

Sandiford, K. (1982b) 'English cricket crowds', *IJHS*, 9:3.

Sandiford, K. (1983a) 'Cricket and Victorian society', *JSH*, 17:2.

Sandiford, K. (1983b) 'Amateurs and professionals in Victorian county cricket', *Albion*, 15:1.

Sandiford, K. (1984) 'Victorian cricket technique and industrial technology', *IJHS*, 1:3.

Sandiford, K. and Vamplew, W. (1986) 'The peculiar economics of English cricket before 1914', *IJHS*, 3:3.

Schofield, R. (1973) 'Dimensions of illiteracy in England 1750–1850', *Explorations in Economic History*, 10.

Sparrow, W. (1931) 'The origin of racing journalism', *Chambers Journal*, 7th Series, 21.

Stone, L. (1969) 'Literacy and education in England 1640–1900', *Past and Present*, 22.

Storch, R. (1975) 'A plague of blue locusts', *JSH*, 20.

Storch, R. (1976) 'The policeman as domestic missionary: urban discipline and popular culture in northern England 1850–1880', *JSH*, 9:4.

Sturdee, R. (1903) 'The ethics of football', *WR*, 159.

Tranter, N. (1987a) 'Popular sports and the industrial revolution in Scotland: the evidence of the Statistical Accounts', *IJHS*, 4:1.

Tranter, N. (1987b) 'The social and occupational structure of sport in central Scotland during the nineteenth century', *IJHS*, 4:3.

Tozer, M. (1981) 'From muscular Christianity to "esprit de corps": games and the Victorian public schools of England', *Stadion*, 7:1.

Vamplew, W. (1985) 'Not playing the game: unionism and British professional sport 1870–1914', *IJHS*, 2:3.

Watson, G. (1920) 'Shrove-tide football', *Border Magazine*, 25 (Feb).

Wright, C. (1977) 'Before Tom Brown: education and the sporting ethos in the early nineteenth century', *Journal of Educational Administration and History*, 9:1.

Unpublished theses:

Allan, K. (1947) Recreations and Amusements of the Industrial Working Class in the second Quarter of the Nineteenth Century, With Special reference to Lancashire. University of Manchester MA, Diss.

Chandler, T. (1984) Origins of Athletic Games in the English Public School 1800–1880. Stanford University, Ph.D.

Eadie, A. (1990) The Structure and Organisation of Horse Racing (c. 1830–1860). The Development of a National Sport. Oxford University, D.Phil.

Eastwood, D. (1985) Governing Rural England: Authority and Social Order in Oxfordshire 1780–1840. Oxford University, D.Phil.

Harvey, A. (1990) Leisure in the Bleak Age. Birkbeck College, London University, MA, Diss.

Smith, M.B. (1970) The Growth and Development of Popular Entertainments and Pastimes in Lancashire Cotton Towns 1830–1870. Lancaster University, M.Litt.

Index

admission charges 166, 170
Aiken 120
amateur 126, 180, 189–90, 204–7, 216–17, 225
America 163
American Arena 169
animal 10, 124, 138
Annals of the Sporting and Fancy Gazette, The 228
 sales of 46
annual sport 15, 17–18, 25–26
aquatics 10, 16, 19–20, 29 n. 41
archery 6, 16, 96, 117, 159, 164, 174
art 37–38, 40
Ascot 157, 175
athletics 10

Badcock, J. (aka Bee, Napea) 53, 154
Bailey, P. 3
Bale, J. 19
Banbury 25, 167
Barclay, Capt. A. 89, 122, 130, 141, 155, 167, 190
Barclay match 121, 156
Barrymore, Lord 38, 155
Beardsworth 53, 129, 167
Beauclerk, Lord 190–91
Bee (see Badcock, J.)
Beer Act 90
Belle Vue 25, 165, 168, 173
Bell's Life in London 19–20, 45–51, 100, 131, 133–5, 166, 172–3, 178, 205, 227–9
 sales 46, 48
 supervision of sport 50–52
Bell's Weekly Messenger 9, 40, 43, 47, 75, 228
 sales 40
Bendigo 48
Berkely, Grantley 87–8, 103

betting 153–4, 199 (see also gambling)
Bibury club 119, 157, 176, 190
billiards 156, 159, 199
biography 38–9, 53
Blaine D. 54, 88, 137
bookmakers 154, 164
books 51, 125, 129, 151
Bowen, R. 19–20
bowling 155, 203
Boyle, C. 191
Brailsford, D. 45–8
Brecknock Arms 167
Bromley 39, 192, 201
Broughton 118, 198
Buckle 198
Buckley, G. 10, 19
bull-baiting 35, 38, 43, 47, 63, 65, 69–71, 73, 87, 94, 97, 103–4, 116, 156–7, 159, 167
Burke, P. 191
Burn, W. 217

Camelford, Lord 39, 198–9
careers 201–2, 211–15
Carlyle, T. 83, 105
Caunt–Bendigo fight 99, 133, 166
chap-books 32, 41
Chiffney 40
children 195, 210
Clarke, J. 167, 170
clergy 68, 130
clubs 191, 202–3
Coates 212
Cobbett, W. 79 n. 75, 87, 155
cockfighting 16, 40, 47, 49, 55, 68–9, 87, 93, 94, 97–8, 117, 124, 156–7, 159–60, 191–2
codes (rules) 36, 99–100, 116–20, 124–30, 139–40, 165–6
commercial sport (see sport, commercial)

communications 45, 166
  telegraph 165
competitive sport (see sport, competitive)
contracts 116
Copenhagen house 169
corruption 31, 42, 135–6, 163–6, 174, 181
  n. 24, 214–15, 225 (see also crime,
  fraud)
Cotswold Games 156, 168, 182 n. 92
coursing 16, 19, 20, 103, 117, 125, 127–8,
  131, 156, 168, 191, 203
courts 75–77
Cremorne gardens 168–9
Cribb, T. 39, 54, 75, 155, 199
Cribb–Molineaux 153, 156
cricket 3, 16, 77 n. 4, 84–5, 88, 120, 126,
  127, 130–31, 135–6, 138, 144 n. 42,
  156, 159, 165, 167, 170, 172, 174,
  178, 191, 193, 196, 203–4, 207
crime 73, 95–7, 118, 147 n. 164, 154, 169,
  177 (see also corruption)
Crockford's gaming house 163
crowds 156–60, 175–8
cruel sport (see sport, cruel)
Cumberland Society 117
Cumberland and Westmoreland 126–8, 138
Cunningham, H. 2, 151
curling 36

Dawson 153
Deale 154, 229
deer parks 179
Derby 104
Derby, Lord 38, 124, 152
diet 123, 136
dog fight 49, 97–8, 102, 157, 167, 169
dog racing 167, 169
dog v monkey 158, 168
Doncaster 163, 173
Dowling V. 34, 48–51
duelling 35, 73–4, 80, 88, 95, 105
Durand 155
Dutch Sam 136

Eaton 40, 199, 201, 212
economy 4
education 84–85
Egan, P. 37, 43, 45–7, 53–4, 123, 204
elderly competitors 209

Elias, N. 3
Elwes 39
enclosures 2, 7–8, 76
English Chronicle, The 34
Epsom 159, 169, 173–4
equipment 171–2
Era, The 47–8, 50
evangelicals 32, 63–4, 68, 83, 85
Exchange Herald 228

Factory Act, 1847 90
Fairman, Captain 122
fairs 74, 157
female pugilism 47, 168, 196
fencing 156
finance 152–3
Fives court 169
Fletcher 152, 155
Fletcher Read 155
Flint, Mr 38, 153, 197
foot races 10, 16, 99, 102, 131, 133, 135,
  165, 167, 170, 212
football 17, 72, 97–8, 115–16, 134–5, 142,
  143 n. 8, 162, 172
fox hunting 45, 49, 52, 67, 72, 76–84,
  87–8, 92, 99, 103, 124, 171, 196–8
fraud 149 n. 262, 153–4 (see also
  corruption)
French Revolution 70

gambling 152–3, 163–5, 173 (see also
  betting)
Game Laws 34–6, 65–7, 101
Gaming
  Select Committee on 89–90, 137, 154
gate money 169–70, 179–80 (see also
  admission charges)
Gayer, A. xii
gentlemen 76, 130–32, 140–41, 190–91,
  202, 204–7
Gentleman's Magazine 32
gentry 2, 64, 161–2
geographical distribution 21–4
George IV 47, 95, 208
Gilpin 38
Girling, W. 212
Godfrey, J. 32
Golby, J. 3, 87
Goodwood 169, 179

Grand Duke Nicholas 43
Great Exhibition 142
Gregson 201
Gully 105, 152, 156, 201–2

Halladay, E. 19
handicapped 142
hanging 157
hare-hunt 171
Harrison, B. 87
Harrison, M. 17, 158, 182
Hart, B.167
health 137–8 (see also diet)
Henley Regatta 125, 131, 172, 205
Hippodrome 169, 173
history (see sport, history)
holidays 15–17, 25
Holt, R. 2, 115, 119
horse feats 10, 16–17, 47, 68
horse racing 3, 10, 13, 15–17, 23, 72, 80 n.
    103, 92, 97, 99, 120–21, 135, 142,
    153–4, 157–60, 170, 174, 180 n. 2,
    193, 199, 206, 212
Howitt, W. 54, 103, 177
Hulme gardens 168
hurling 94
Hyde park (Sheffield) 169

income tax 152
industrialisation 2, 83
Irish 195, 209

Jackson 54, 121, 130, 196
Jackson's Oxford Journal 9, 117–18, 119,
    128–9, 132, 228
Jackson's stadium 169
Jews 194, 208
Jockey Club 10, 34, 49, 68–9, 88, 95, 100,
    117–19, 128–9, 133, 154, 175, 202
jockeys 153, 198
Johnson, S. 1, 190

Kendricks 211
Kent 44, 55
King's Royal Stag Hounds 69

labour aristocracy 83–4
labour discipline 8, 24 (see also work)

Lancashire 12, 20, 23–26, 98, 104, 125,
    178, 212
Lancaster Regatta 51
legislation 2, 24, 34, 65–66, 102
leisure 160–62 (see also labour discipline,
    work)
    limitations on access 203
Lilywhite, A. 49
literacy 32, 42
living standards 8
local courts 99–100
local government 93–99, 173
local supervision of sport (see sport, local
    supervision)
London Chess Club 117
lower orders 64–5, 69
Lutterworth 171

Malcolmson, R. 2, 65, 227
Manchester 15, 20, 21, 24–26, 89, 157,
    165, 171, 176, 178
Manchester and Salford Advertiser 47, 49,
    228
Manchester Examiner and Times 228
Manchester Mercury 9, 37, 44, 156
Marylebone Cricket Club (MCC) 117–19,
    127–9
Medley 155
Mellish, Mr 132, 155, 167
Melton Mowbray 171
Mendoza 196, 198
Meynell, H. 124
military 70–73
    use of sport 91–93
militia 72
Mills 53
Mitchell, B. xii
Molineaux, W. 37, 39, 75
moral assessment of recreation (see
    recreation, moral assessment)
Moreland 38
Morning Chronicle, The 48
Morning Post, The 45

Napea (see Badcock, J.)
navy 91–2
negroes 199, 201
New Pugilistic Club 129
News of the World 48

Newspaper Stamps, Select Committee on 52
New Sporting Magazine 46, 228
  turnover 51
'Nimrod' 45, 55
non-commercial sport (see sport, non-commercial)

Ogden 155
O'Kelly 39, 154–5
Old Hats Pigeon Shooting Club 119
oral rules 125 (see also codes)
organized sport (see sport, organized)
Osbaldeston, W. 41
Oxfordshire (Oxford) 20, 22–26, 73, 97–8, 155, 168, 173, 177
Oxford–Cambridge rowing rules 206

Paine, T. 191
Parkyns, T. 118
Parliament 63, 65, 71–2, 90, 100–101, 124
  and sport 83–91
patronage 162, 213–14,
pedestrianism 3, 10, 19, 20, 29 n. 41, 36, 40, 44, 131–3, 135, 153, 168
penny post 42, 229
Perkin H. 104
pigeon shooting 19, 68, 87, 119, 125, 131, 135, 156, 204
Pigott, C. 34
Pixton, S. 211
playing space 8, 102
Plumb, J. 9
poaching 66–7
police 93–4, 97, 104–5, 169, 172
politics 32–3, 94, 178, 202
Poor Man's Guardian, The 46
population xii, 26
press 31–60, 125
  readers' letters 45
prices xii
Prince of Wales 154–5
prize money 174
professionals 189–90, 204–5, 210–17
promoters 154–5, 166–8
public schools 223–8
Public Walks Committee 89
publicans 2, 166–7

pugilism 16–17, 19–20, 35, 40, 46, 73–4, 84–5, 87 n. 3, 93–99, 102, 104, 118, 120, 125, 131–2, 135–6, 153, 155–60, 165–6, 169–71, 174, 183 n. 135, 191–3, 198–200, 212
  Fair play club 129, 133
  Pugilistic Club 118, 121, 188
Purdue A. 3, 87

Qui Tam 89–90

Racing Calendar 9–10, 23, 32, 228
railways 84, 90, 171–3 (see also communications)
Ranelagh 157, 168
rat races 156
rational recreation 2
ratting 97, 115, 129, 169, 172
recreation
  moral assessment 67–71
referees 10, 50, 96, 116, 120–22, 130–36, 139–40, 165–6
refreshments 156, 170
regattas 156, 162
respectable 2
Richmond 23, 123, 154, 198
Ringwood 198
Rostow, E. xii
rowing 19, 75, 94, 119, 120, 125, 132, 135–6, 155, 157, 166–8, 173–4, 178, 203–4, 206
royal family 92, 175
Royal Staghounds 35, 172
RSPCA 86–8, 102
rustic sports 161

sabbatarianism 84
sailing 117, 135–6, 139, 155, 159, 167, 171, 191
Sampson 211
Scotland 195, 208
segregation of sport (see sport, segregation)
Sheridan, T. 64–70
shooting 16–17, 29 n. 41, 66–67, 72, 87, 105, 155, 171
single stick 155, 162, 174
skill 10, 16
Skittles Association 117
Smith, Sidney 70–71

social composition 159–60, 192–4
social mobility 198
social segregation 178, 190–92, 216–17
Society for the Encouragement of Vice 103
Society for the Suppression of Vice 34–6, 68–9
sport (defined) 1, 33, 42, 47, 52, 54–5, 87
  commercial 4, 102–3, 161, 166, 168–77, 225
  competitive 152–6, 163–8
  cruel 2, 34–8, 47, 64, 86, 87, 103, 116
  earning a living from 198–201, 215
  history 39, 54
  local supervision 72–77
  moral change 100–105
  non-commercial 177–9
  opinions on 34
  organized 10, 116
  sales of reading matter 40–41, 46, 48
  science 122–4, 136–9
  segregation 202–208
  weekly 15, 17–18, 25–6
sporting activity, volume of 8–13, 18–23
sporting calendar 13–17, 24–27, 173
sporting events, traditional 116, 161–2
Sporting Kalendar, The 32, 228
Sporting Magazine 9, 33–42, 44–52, 54, 68–9, 74, 198, 227–8
  sales 40, 45
sporting press
  before 1815 31–41
  after 1815 41–55
sports grounds 168–9, 173
Spring, Tom 133, 166
Spring–Langan 168
Stadium 169
stag hunting 156, 172
stakeholders 99–100
stakes 163–6
steam engine *v* horse 158
steamers 170–71
steeplechase 36, 49, 87, 92, 168, 174
Storch R. 177
strength 17
Sunday Times, The 48
Surtees R. 53, 229
Sutton 211
swimming 167
Sydney gardens 168

Tattersall 154–5, 163
temperance movement 84, 86
tennis 159, 163
Thames Regatta 174, 206
theatre 42, 157, 197–8, 200
Thornton, Col. 38, 124, 155, 198
Thornton, Mrs. 40, 153, 195, 197–8, 201
Thornton *v* Flint 156
time 102, 144 n. 61
Times, The 9, 34, 38, 43–5, 48, 228
'tin man' 199, 202
Tom Brown's Schooldays 55
Topham 31
tourism 172, 179
Town, The 47
Tozer, R. 223
training 122–3, 137
transport 170–71
trotting 19, 20, 169
tuition 199–200
Tyne Regatta 171
Tyneside games 168

urban development 7–8

vacuum 7–8, 65
Vamplew W. 160
Vauxhall 157
vegetarianism 144 n. 50
veterinary college 72, 91, 124
veterinary science 40

Wales 195
Walvin J. 115
Weekly Dispatch, The 9, 43, 45–6, 228
  sales 46
weekly sport (see sport, weekly)
Wellington 95–6
Wheeble 32, 34
Wheeler's Manchester Chronicle 228
Wigglesworth N. 206
Wilson, George 34, 38, 75, 199–201
Windham 32, 69–71, 79 n. 80
women in sport 137, 195–6, 209–10 (see also female pugilism)
Wood 121
work 93 (see also leisure)
World, The 3, 31

wrestling 19, 94, 125–6, 135, 162, 170, 174, 178, 191, 203–4

Young England 54, 85–6